The Billy the Kid Reader

Billy the Kid, ca. 1880. The only authenticated likeness, a ferrotype that reverses the actual image. Author's Collection.

The Billy the Kid Reader

Edited by Frederick Nolan

UNIVERSITY OF OKLAHOMA PRESS : NORMAN

Also by Frederick Nolan

The Life and Death of John Henry Tunstall (Albuquerque, 1965)
The Lincoln County War: A Documentary History (Norman, Okla., 1992)
Lorenz Hart: A Poet on Broadway (New York, 1994)
Bad Blood: The Life and Times of the Horrell Brothers (Stillwater, Okla., 1994)
Portraits of the Old West (London, 1997)
The West of Billy the Kid (Norman, Okla., 1998)
The Sound of Their Music: The Story of Rodgers & Hammerstein (rev. ed.,
    New York, 2002)
The Wild West: History, Myth and the Making of America (London, 2003)
Tascosa, Its Life and Gaudy Times (Lubbock, Tex., 2007)

Acknowledgments for previously published selections appear on pages
367–69.

Library of Congress Cataloging-in-Publication Data

The Billy the Kid reader / edited by Frederick Nolan.
    p.   cm.
  Includes bibliographical references and index.
  ISBN-13: 978-0-8061-3849-7 (hardcover : alk. paper).
  1. Billy, the Kid. 2. Billy, the Kid—In literature. 3. Outlaws—Southwest, New—
Biography. 4. Frontier and pioneer life—Southwest, New. 5. Southwest, New—
Biography. 6. Legends—Southwest, New. 7. Outlaws—Southwest, New—His-
toriography. 8. Frontier and pioneer life—Southwest, New—Historiography.
9. Southwest, New—Historiography. I. Nolan, Frederick W., 1931–
  F786.B54B55   2007
  364.15'52092—dc22
  [B]

                                                                2007002325

The paper in this book meets the guidelines for permanence and durability of
the Committee on Production Guidelines for Book Longevity of the Council on
Library Resources, Inc. ∞

1 2 3 4 5 6 7 8 9 10

For Morgan and Joyce Nelson, with love.

Contents

Illustrations

Preface

> The history of the race, and each individual's experience, are thick
> with evidence that the truth is not hard to kill and a lie well told is
> immortal.
>
> Mark Twain

No famous figure of the American West has more successfully and more
tantalizingly resisted definitive understanding than Billy the Kid. Despite
the publication since his death in 1881 of hundreds of books, numerous
movies, and countless words of journalism about him, the truths of his real
life and his real self remain stubbornly elusive. In seeking a key to that
enigma, it seemed to me that a selection of the most seminal, the most
influential of those writings—from the first dime novel, which appeared
within two weeks of his death, to the present day; from the birth of the
legend to the beginnings of the truth—might provide it, in the process
not only constituting a fully rounded and satisfyingly different overview,
but also enhancing and clarifying the reader's comprehension of the
Kid's life, personality, and legend, no matter whether that reader was
coming to the story for the first time or the thousandth.

Those many books, those countless words of journalism, an enormous
historical grab-bag ranging in style and content from "trash," through
"bad, but good," "good, but neglected," and finally to "excellent, but
little known and/or from difficult to impossible to find," presented a
formidable editorial challenge. Choosing between, say, Emerson Hough's
"The Fight of Buckshot Roberts" (a perfect example of an author who
knew better preferring legend to fact) and Almer Blazer's more prosaic
but infinitely more real account of the same event, or deciding whether
to exclude the over-familiar *Authentic Life* by Pat Garrett in favor of
Charlie Siringo's unashamed rip-off, was never going to be easy, and so it
proved throughout.

The selection of excerpts and articles that follows represents in almost equal parts the two distinct and different periods of Billy the Kid studies. The first of these, made up largely of the works of writers characterized by Richard Maxwell Brown as "the popularizers," lasted from 1881 until almost halfway through the twentieth century. During those seventy years, the story remained largely mired in the legend propagated by the inventions and inaccuracies contributed to *The Authentic Life of Billy the Kid* by Pat Garrett's amanuensis "Ash" Upson, in turn elaborated upon by such writers as Charles Siringo, Emerson Hough, and, most notable of all, Walter Noble Burns, romanticizing the Kid's life and exaggerating the importance of his part in the events in which he was involved. Burns's success not only promoted the Kid to an entry in the *Dictionary of American Biography* but also triggered another small avalanche of "me, too" books, some of them written by or for people who had known the Kid or who had been participants in the Lincoln County troubles; more often than not they were as unreliable as the romantic nonsense that had inspired them.

To be fair, there were some who took a harder line, as in 1937, when Jack Thorp set out to debunk the myth of the Kid's killings in an article for the Federal Writers Project (later expanded into the chapter from *Pardner of the Wind* that is featured in this anthology). It gathered pace in Burton Rascoe's 1941 biography of Belle Starr, which offered the observation (albeit based upon Noah Rose's horrendously retouched version of the original ferrotype) that if the only known photograph of Billy was anything to go by, he had been "a nondescript, adenoidal, weasel-eyed, narrow-chested, stoop-shouldered, repulsive-looking creature with all the outward appearance of a cretin"—a far cry indeed from Burns's "little cyclone of deadliness whirling furiously, purposelessly, vainly, between two eternities."

There were a few other honorable contributions to the truer story, notable among them William A. Keleher's *The Fabulous Frontier* in 1945 and Irving McKee's biography of Lew Wallace two years later, but it was not until the middle of the century, hard on the heels of the appearance and discrediting of "Brushy Bill" Roberts—and perhaps even to some degree prompted by it—that a new generation of "grassroots" researchers ("logical, indefatigable, at horrific dollarage per gram," as Eugene Cunningham so neatly put it) appeared on the scene and began the long-overdue task of turning legend into history. The watershed came in 1952 with the publication of "New Light on the Legend of Billy the Kid" by Robert N. Mullin and Philip J. Rasch. From that point forward, dedicated historians such as Maurice Garland Fulton, Keleher, Mullin, and the phenomenal Rasch collectively rewrote the Kid's story, in the process revolutionizing the way the subject was researched and presented.

In 1954, the first Billy the Kid bibliography—listing 437 books, magazine articles, movies, and even gramophone records, nearly all of them created in the pre-watershed years—was compiled and published by Jeff C. Dykes. Only a few years later, nearly everything listed in it was rendered a relic, first by the publication of Frazier Hunt's *The Tragic Days of Billy the Kid* (based largely on the work and research of Fulton and Mullin), then in 1957 by William A. Keleher's *Violence in Lincoln County*, and after that by a blizzard of articles by Phil Rasch that were harbingers of an extraordinary body of work destined to continue for another quarter of a century.

The historical revelations embodied in these and later publications not only laid the foundation for present-day scholarship, but cumulatively they have brought about a complete reassessment of our perceptions of Billy the Kid. Knowing more about who he was and what the world he lived in was like, we are able now to better understand some of the life choices the Kid made and the reasons he may have had for making them. Perhaps in the not too distant future the day will come when the professional historians join up with the grassroots researchers and put the whole story into its proper historical context.

Whether or not that happens, however, we are a long way yet from a definitive biography of Billy the Kid. More than a century and a quarter after his death, we still do not know for sure where he was born, the name of his father, or the location in which he spent his childhood. Even what we think we actually do know is not necessarily so. Many accepted versions of events in the Kid's life are still taken as read in spite of the fact that they are little more than unchallenged tradition; there are an almost limitless number of questions yet to be asked, let alone answered.

Take, for only one instance, the deaths of Robert Olinger and James Bell on that April day in 1881 when the Kid escaped from his makeshift jail in Lincoln. It is a *sine qua non* that the Kid killed both of the deputies guarding him, but—and it's a big "but," because there isn't a scintilla of hard evidence to support the proposition—what if the accepted account of events is totally untrue? Remember, Pat Garrett had gone to White Oaks, ostensibly to buy lumber for the Kid's gallows, leaving two trusted deputies to guard the prisoner. No sooner was he gone than they concurred in a fatal error of judgment when, leaving Bell in charge of the Kid, Bob Olinger took all the "Tularosa ditch war" parole prisoners across to the Wortley for supper. In his absence, there was (as far as we know) no one in that big old rambling building except the Kid and Bell. Which means, since no one has ever mentioned padlocked doors or other security measures, that just about anyone, or for that matter several people—the Kid had a lot of friends in Lincoln—could very easily have slipped into the courthouse and given the Kid a weapon, or even shot Bell to set Billy free.

If—and of course it's as big an "if" as the "but" that preceded it—the possibility exists that someone could have done any or all of that (and exist it most certainly does), then by definition all the theories about how the Kid escaped (the gun hidden in the privy, or Billy bashing Bell over the head with his handcuffs) need to be rigorously reexamined. Once the process begins, similar questions can, and must, be asked about almost all the events in the Kid's brief and bloody life—and even his death. I would dearly like to hope that this book will encourage someone, somewhere, to begin asking them.

A NOTE ON NAMES AND SPELLINGS

Not a few of the writers whose works appear in this collection (and/or their publishers) were misinformed, careless, or cavalier about the spelling of proper names and places. Therefore, to avoid peppering every page with bracketed interpolations and the irritatingly journalistic [*sic*], the text of each selection—mistakes, misprints, misspellings, inconsistencies, and all—has, with only occasional exceptions, been reproduced exactly as it appeared at the time of its original publication.

Acknowledgments

The author gratefully acknowledges the assistance he received in compiling this anthology from Cheryl Adams, Library of Congress, Washington, D.C.; Lilian H. Bidal, Albuquerque, New Mexico; Dr. Don Carleton, Center for American History, University of Texas at Austin; Carol Christiansen, Random House, New York; Bonnie B. Coles, Library of Congress, Washington, D.C.; Dr. Bruce Dinges, Arizona Historical Society, Tucson; Harold L. Edwards, Bakersfield, California; Craig Fouts, San Diego, California; Kevin Galvin, English Westerners Society, Kingston-upon-Thames, England; Scott Gipson, Caxton Printers, Caldwell, Idaho; Terri Grant, El Paso Public Library, El Paso, Texas; Marjorie Jackson, Ann Arbor, Michigan; Peter Jackson, Plymouth, Michigan; Averil J. Kadis, Enoch Pratt Free Library, Baltimore, Maryland; Sandi Keeton, University of New Mexico Press, Albuquerque; Robert G. McCubbin, Santa Fe, New Mexico; Dennis Northcott, Missouri Historical Society; St. Louis; Elliott Oring, Long Beach, California; Colin Quigley, University of California, Los Angeles; Jim Rogers, *Frontier Times Magazine*, Mountain Grove, Missouri; Joseph G. Rosa, Ruislip, England; Ann Schultis, Parkville, Missouri; Russ Taylor, Brigham Young University, Provo, Utah; John Vallier, University of California, Los Angeles; Crystal Vining, Scott, Louisiana; Mary Wachs, Museum of New Mexico Press, Albuquerque; Shan Watkins, Colorado State University, Fort Collins; Susan Wentroth, Oklahoma Historical Society, Oklahoma City; and Professor Tanya Zanish-Belcher, Iowa State University, Ames.

PART ONE

The Legend

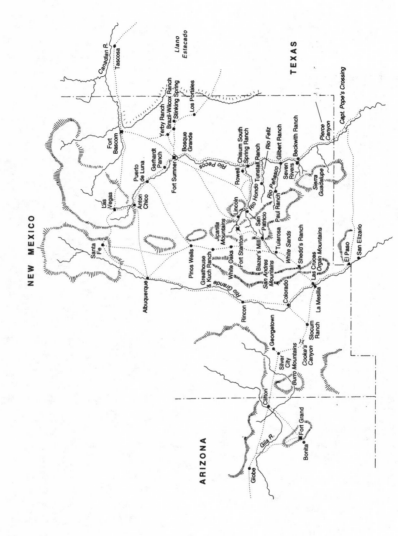

Billy the Kid's West, 1873–1881. From Frederick Nolan, *The West of Billy the Kid* (Norman: University of Oklahoma Press, 1998).

The True Life of Billy the Kid

Don Jenardo

The endearing curiosity that follows is, as far as can be ascertained, the very first complete narrative of the life of Billy the Kid. It was on thousands of newsstands within six weeks of the Kid's death on July 14, 1881, antedating by six or seven months the better-known, but scarcely more accurate, *Authentic Life of Billy the Kid,* ghostwritten for Pat Garrett by Ash Upson, which did not see the light of day until April 1882. The story itself was probably based on the many newspaper stories that appeared after the Kid was killed and two short pieces that had appeared in the *National Police Gazette,* many of whose authors (like Don Jenardo, soaking up their information from newspaper reports of the Kid's death) claimed that Billy's real last name was McCarthy and that he had been born in New York. The killing of William Morton and Frank Baker, the assassination of Sheriff William Brady, and the pardon by Governor Lew Wallace are all included; John Chisum, Lawrence G. Murphy and James J. Dolan, Alexander McSween (as McSwain), and Tom O'Folliard (O'Fallaher) put in appearances, but with little connection to the facts (for instance, in the finale, betrayed by a man named Riaz, the Kid is killed by a *rifle* bullet fired by Pat Garrett on *August* 14, 1881).

No. 451 in Frank Tousey's "Five Cent Wide-Awake Library," this "true life" was not, as claimed by the publisher, written by Mexican author Illion Constellano; rather, it was the work of John Woodruff Lewis, a well-known and prolific dime-novelist, and it had—much like its subject—a short, sensational life. Two years after its appearance, the postmaster general of the United States launched a cleanup of the dime-novel industry by threatening to withhold second-class mailing privileges from publishers who glorified bandits and outlaws. Tousey responded by substituting stories that did not "tend to incite murder" for sixty-six of his outlaw series, one of which was Jenardo's *The True Life of Billy the Kid.* Although thousands of copies were printed and sold, only three appear to have survived; at last report, two were in private collections, and the third was in the

Library of Congress. A rather fragile sixteen-page photo-offset reproduction with commentary and notes by J. C. Dykes, published in an edition of 1,000 copies in 1956, has also now become scarce.

CHAPTER I. EARLY HISTORY: THE FIRST MURDER

The West has always been prolific in criminals. Scarce is one noted character swept away from earth, ere another comes to take his place. A land that is stranger to civilization, and where the strong arm of the law seldom reaches its victim, where might is right, can not do otherwise than breed hosts of such characters, as those whose biography we have set out to write.

Billy the Kid's true name was William McCarthy. He was born in the State of New York (some have located his birthplace as the City of New York, but this is doubtless a mistake) in year A. D. 1859 or 1860.

When Billy was a very small boy, his father emigrated to the Territory of New Mexico, and settled his family in Silver City, Grant County. There were but three children in the family, two sons and a daughter. Billy was the youngest of the three. He has a sister and a brother still living in the Territory. The brother, whose name is John McCarthy, is a miner, and regarded by all who know him as an honest, fair-dealing man. His sister has married a respectable miner, and in fact Billy seems to be the only black sheep in the entire flock.

His father was poor, and the entire family were compelled to "put their shoulders to the wheel," to assist in making a living. Billy was young and exceedingly small for his age, so it was very difficult to find anything for him to do. He had a passion for horses, and soon became one of the best riders in all the country. He readily found employment in assisting the herders, or cow boys as they are called, in herding cattle.

It was the cow boys who gave the lad the euphonious cognomen of Billy the Kid. Billy was a delicate looking child, with a thin pale face, slender frame, light blue eyes, and fair hair. He was the last person one would take to be a desperado.

His voice was soft and effeminate, his hands, though exposed to wind and weather, always seemed soft as a woman's. He readily became a favorite of the rough cow boys, and there is no doubt but what it was his earlier associations with them that led him to seek the mad lawless career that finally brought him to ruin and death.

Don Jenardo's *True Life of Billy the Kid*. Author's Collection.

The rough men frequently furnished the lad with liquor. They thought it fine sport to see the "Kid on a high." Billy's father died when the boy was thirteen years of age, and his mother married a man named Henry Antrim. Shortly after her marriage she moved to Georgetown, New Mexico, where she still resides.

The lad never lived with his step-father, merely spending a few weeks there when out of employment.

One day, when fifteen years of age, he found himself out of employment and money. As he was "loafing" about Silver City, he met an acquaintance named Tom O'Fallaher, from Texas, who was in the same condition.

"What shall we do?" asked the Kid. "Dun no," answered Tom, who, though of Irish descent, had none of the brogue about him. "Are ye flat broke?"

"Not a dust," answered the Kid.

"We might strike a job," said Tom.

"Yes, but I want to make it faster than that," the Kid replied.

"How?"

"Hold still, Tom, and I'll tell ye."

"Go on, then."

"Joe Taylor, who keeps the store here, has lots o' dust. He keeps it in the drawer in his store. *Quien sabe.*"

"You bet, Billy, I'll go yer halvers."

The compact was made, and as thoroughly understood as if they had spent weeks in concocting the plan.

Consequently that night, provided with tools, the young burglars entered the door of the store by cutting the lock out, and had just pried open the money drawer, when Joe Taylor, who slept in the rear room, was aroused by the noise.

Seeing the youthful burglars, he made a swoop upon them, and seized the Kid by the throat. O'Fallaher made his escape. A complaint was at once preferred against Billy, and he lodged in jail.

He was very small for his age, and soon won the sympathy of the jailer's wife, and, more especially of his daughter, the beautiful, dark-eyed Nettie.

She visited the little fellow in his confinement, and as she noticed his pale cheeks growing paler day by day it was no wonder that her heart went out toward the criminal.

"Are you lonely here, Billy?" she asked one day, as she brought his dinner to his cell.

"I am," he responded, in a tone very sad and feeble.

"Would you like me to visit you oftener?"

"I would," he answered, "but, Nettie, there is something I prefer even to your sweet presence. Something I must have or die."

"What?" she asked.

"Liberty. Confinement in the dungeon is slowly wearing my life away. I cannot endure it much longer, and if you would not see me taken away from here dead, then provide some way whereby I can escape living."

Nettie shed tears; she told her mother what the poor little prisoner had said, and they wept together over his sad fate.

"Something must be done for him, mother," said Nettie. "He mustn't be left to languish and die there alone in that horrible cell."

The mother studied the matter over, and then agreed with her daughter to aid the prisoner to escape. Many other women than Mrs. Jones have made the same blunder. A too tender heart has often given many criminals their liberty, and turned them out to prey upon society.

A plan was arranged, and put into execution, by which Billy, who being very slender, crawled out at the jail chimney.

Nettie and her mother furnished him with clothes, and, after kissing his fair rescuer, and promising to ever give her the warmest corner in his heart, he left Silver City.

The night was intensely dark, but the Kid was a stranger to fear.

He made his way to Arizona, where he engaged as herder, on the ranche of a Mr. Mason.

Here he labored for two years in a quiet and unassuming manner. When he was about seventeen years of age the fickle-minded youth, forgetting Nettie, placed his affections on a Mexican senorita named Quiseta.

Whether the attachment of the youth was an ardent, honest one, or merely a passing fancy, is not exactly known.

The character of the senorita has been questioned, and yet we are inclined to believe that, if understood, Senorita Quiseta was no more than the common, dashing belle of the present day.

Lacking in culture, she made it up with her beauty and excellent voice.

Billy was desperately in love with her, and perhaps, had his affections been returned, he might have settled down to a quiet life and made a good citizen.

But a young miner named Frank Douglass, with broader shoulders, higher brow, and finer form, won the Mexican beauty's heart.

Douglass and Senorita Quiseta were betrothed, and the day of their wedding fixed. A Mexican Catholic priest was asked to officiate at the services, and Billy the Kid, who professed to be a friend of Frank Douglass, invited to be present.

On the very day before the wedding was to take place, the Kid invited Frank to take a hunt on the prairie for deer. They crossed a narrow chain of hills and mountains on their horses, and had shot a buck and were returning.

On the way back they were compelled to cross a small rivulet.

"Is not that clear water, Frank?" asked the Kid.

"It is," was Frank's reply.

"Would you not like to drink of it?"

"I would, for I am thirsty." Handing the rein to Billy, the young man dismounted and stooped down over the spring to drink.

With a devilish grin on his face, the Kid drew his pistol and aimed it directly at the head of the kneeling man.

"Crack!" went the pistol, and young Douglass fell forward on his face, shot through the brain.

Billy the Kid had committed his first murder, but not unobserved.

The beautiful senorita, not a hundred yards away, had witnessed the dastardly act, and with a piercing scream she ran down to the brook, and threw herself on the prostrate body.

Billy fled, and was pursued by an armed body of men, but succeeded in making his escape into New Mexico.

CHAPTER II. THE LINCOLN COUNTY WAR

Just at the time of the first atrocious murder committed by Billy the Kid, the Lincoln County War, in the Territory of New Mexico, broke out, and for a while raged with uncontrollable fury.

The war originated among the leading herdsmen, and was disgraceful and ferocious in the extreme. It originated in the determination of old John Chisum, the great cattle king, and his partner, Alexander McSwain, to establish a monopoly in the cattle-grazing business. They drove eighty thousand head of cattle into the Pecos Valley.

The herds of the smaller ranchers were swept away by the rolling avalanche of hoofs and horns.

Ranches or herds of a few hundred head would be swept on with the invincible tide, and it was useless to attempt to reclaim them.

In vain the smaller herdsmen complained to Chisum and McSwain that they were being robbed; in vain they sought by fair means to regain their animals.

The law could not reach them, and but one result must follow. Collisions were the result between the rancheros, and not unfrequently bloody.

At last all the smaller herdsmen, in order to meet the coming tidal wave, joined their fortunes with the firm of Murphy, Dolan & Co.

Both sides enlisted all the men they could, and preparations were made for a severe struggle.

One evening, as the little army of Chisum & McSwain was encamped on the banks of a creek, a small being, more boy than man, was seen to advance toward the camp.

The cow boys and rancheros looked on him with not a little curiosity. He was mounted on a black mustang, a powerful animal for both speed and endurance. He was not over five feet and two inches in height, had a rather sallow complexion, caused doubtless by exposure to the weather.

Had a belt about his waist which supported a pair of silver-mounted revolvers, and a long two-edged knife. Holsters were at his saddle bow which contained two more pistols, and he carried in his hand a short repeating rifle. There was a strap attached to the rifle by which he could support it on his back when he desired.

"Who is that strange-lookin' cuss?" said a cow boy, as the horseman continued to advance in a fearless manner.

"Hold up there," said a youthful desperado, springing from his seat on the grass, and shading his eyes with his hands. "I know him."

"Who is he, Tom?"

"Billy the Kid, who was put in jail in Silver City two years ago, and broke out."

"What's he a doin' here?" growled the first speaker.

"Dun'no," answered Tom. "But I'll bet we kin get him on our side. I know Billy, an' he is just the chap that old Chisum wants."

He left the others and ran out on the plain toward the horseman. Seeing him coming, Billy drew rein and prepared for the meeting, be it hostile or friendly.

"Helloa, Billy, how are ye?" cried Tom.

The Kid was astonished at meeting on his return no other person than his friend and former associate, Tom O'Fallaher.

"Hey, Tom, old pard, glad to see ye," cried the Kid, spurring his mustang, and galloping alongside his friend.

He sprang from his saddle, and the meeting of these young desperadoes was affecting.

"Where have ye been, Billy?" asked Tom.

"Over in Arizona."

"What doin'?"

"As a ranchero."

"When did ye leave?"

"Two days ago."

"Got into a little fuss, eh?"

"Yes, had a row with a chap about a Mexican girl."

"You came out ahead, did ye?"

"You bet I did, with a gang o' about two hundred devils after me," laughed the reckless Kid.

"Well, Billy, I'm glad ye come."

"Why, Tom, some new game up?"

"Yes, we're hevin' a reg'lar war here, an' old Chislum is payin' the highest price for good marksmen."

"I'll jest suit him then, an' he'll suit me," said the Kid.

"If anybody should come after ye, Billy, ye'll be perfectly safe here."

"Well, I don't know but what I'd as soon kill them as is after me as not, but if old Chisum hez money to pay fur blood, he couldn't strike a better chap than me."

"Well, Billy, he'll do it."

"I've got a taste, Tom, an' I like it. I loved a girl, another fellow got ahead of me, an' I shot him down and left. I'm in for more o' the same kind o' work."

"Then let's go back an' hunt up old John."

Old John was found, and Billy the Kid was employed as one of the herdsmen of Chisum and McSwain, which was only another name for murderer and cattle-thief.

The next day they moved the immense herd upon the higher grounds. As they advanced, two hundred armed men were seen guarding a large drove of cattle upon an elevation about three miles distant.

"Them fellers have some of our cattle over there," said old John Chisum as be rode along in front of his cow boys.

"Let's take 'em then," cried Tom.

"That is jest what I want you to do," said old John.

With a wild shout, Billy the Kid, and his no less dauntless partner, galloped away over the plain, making a circuit and coming in on the left wing of the herdsmen. The spot was unguarded and the cracks of their long whips stampeded and put to the run about one hundred head of cattle.

The herders discovered them, and came sweeping down on the young cattle thieves. Dashing into the midst of the fleeing animals, Billy and Tom threw themselves flat on their horses back to back, and with their repeating rifles opened fire on the herders.

Even old John was astonished at such a daring feat, and horsemanship.

"Crack, crack, crack!" rang out their rifles with remarkable rapidity, and the pursuing herdsman began to fall.

"Crack, crack, crack, crack!" rang out a score of rifles from the pursuers; their bullets flew over the young horsemen and killed or wounded the cattle.

The volley only tended to increase the speed of the flying animals, and drive them from the real owners to the cattle thieves.

The result of the daring act was three of Murphy, Dolan & Co's. men unhorsed, and one hundred head of cattle stolen.

The pursuers paused, and seeing that nothing but an actual engagement would recover the lost property, began a consultation of war.

The forces were equally matched, and old John ordered his men to be ready to defend their property from the ravages of the marauders.

"Ye did well, youngster," he said, to Billy the Kid, grasping him by the hand. "You and your pardner are worth your weight in gold. Now we are goin' to hev a battle with them thieves, I want you to preserve yer good reputation."

A fight on the plains among the cow-boys is always bloody. The cow-boy is a strange specimen of the genus homo. Part civilian, part soldier, and in many cases thief:

He is a crack shot with the rifle, and an expert horseman. Some are honest, and seek by this wild exciting life to make an honest living, yet many are given to plunder.

The temptation to swoop down on an unprotected ranche and drive off the fat herds is great.

The men who had just suffered by the daring act of the Kid and his "pard," were exasperated beyond endurance.

Not only were they enraged at the loss of their stock, but their pride was piqued at being outwitted, and run into by a pair of kids, as they term boys. A fight was inevitable.

Old John was not loath for an engagement. He spoke a few words of encouragement to his men, though that was scarcely necessary, and then the line was formed.

Not much military skill was used or required by either. It was simply to form two lines and sweep down like an avalanche on each other.

Billy the Kid rode by the side of his employer. With a wild shout old John Chisum's herders dashed forward upon Murphy, Dolan & Co.

The conflict is almost indescribable. It was a charge that had about it the fury of the whirlwind.

A crashing volley of rifle shots, falling men, plunging horses, cries of wounded and groans of dying.

The Kid's rifle cracked repeatedly, and through the floating clouds of smoke could be seen a herdsman fall at each shot.

His repeating-rifle empty, he grasped the rein in his teeth, and, with a pistol in each hand, dashed forward like a fiend incarnate.

"Crack, crack, crack!" rang out the pistol shots right and left among the foe, until he struck their line like an avalanche.

Murphy, Dolan & Co. could not withstand the onslaught, and their herders fled, leaving the plain strewn with their cattle in the hands of their enemy.

CHAPTER III. THE KID AS AN OFFICER

All through the Lincoln County war no man was more blood-thirsty or faithful to the cause of his employer than the youth Billy.

The war finally terminated, or at least there was a cessation of hostilities. Everything was favorable to the boasting cattle kings. They were permitted to keep the largest portion of the stolen property.

Instead of being brought to justice, old John Chisum became an influential man on the frontier, figuring even with high officers and politicians.

Through his influence Billy the Kid was appointed constable in February, 1879.

It was now to be hoped that the reckless youth would somewhat mend his way, and become a respected citizen.

He still, however, served his master with the same savage ferocity. Old John Chisum was jealous of other cattle dealers in the valley, and never lost a chance to harass and annoy them.

Thomas Catron, formerly of Lafayette county, Missouri, and Hon. Stephen B. Elkins, once a delegate in Congress, had large herds in the Pecos valley.

William Morton and Frank Baker were two honest herdsmen in their employ, and had always been faithful to the interests of their employers.

Chisum had employed every means known to a cunning man to steal these herders from Catron and Elkins, but without avail. They were not to be bought with gold, and resented all the advances of the old scoundrel with scorn.

Going before a magistrate he swore out a warrant against Morton and Baker, charging them with stealing cattle from his herds. The charge was false, but he had his plans for revenge.

The warrant was placed in the hands of Billy.

"You had better take a deputy with you," said the magistrate, when the warrant was put in Billy's hands.

"No," the youthful officer answered, "I will be equal to two such rascals as they."

"Here is McCluskey, he can go with you as well as not."

"I don't want him," said the Kid, with a strange smile on his face, "yet he can go if he will take the chances."

"That fellow is a perfect demon," said the magistrate to himself, as Billy went away with McCluskey; "I believe he loves to kill."

Billy and McCluskey mounted their horses and rode over to the cattle ranche of Catron and Elkin.

"Is William Morton and Frank Baker here?" he asked, of a cow boy near.

"There they stand," said the herder, pointing to two men not far away.

"Surrender! you are my prisoners!" he cried, drawing his revolver instead of his writ.

The men looked up, not a little alarmed, but seeing that it was the constable, one of them replied:

"We surrender, of course, to an officer of the law, but would like to know with what we are charged?"

"Stealing cattle," he answered, with an oath, holding his pistol in a threatening manner, at their heads.

"Put up your pistol, Billy," said McCluskey. "They surrender, they will go with you, without trouble."

"Shut up your mouth, McCluskey," growled the Kid. "I am constable not you." But for the time being he put his pistol in his belt.

The prisoners were made to walk in front of Billy and McClusky.

"Now if you make the least effort to escape, I will shoot you both down in the road."

"We shall make no effort to escape," replied William Morton. "We have committed no crime, and we shall not run from any."

"You lie you ——— scoundrel!" cried Billy, with an oath. "You stole cattle from John Chisum and Alec McSwain."

"No we never," Baker answered.

"You lie, you scoundrel," thundered the enraged boy, "and if you deny it again, I will shoot you dead in your tracks."

He snatched his Colt's revolver from his belt, and cocked it, waving it about in a threatening manner.

"Come, come, Billy," said McCluskey, "you must remember you are an officer of the law now. You should not allow your temper to get away with you. These men are your prisoners and you should treat them like men, not as brutes."

Billy flew into a rage and swore as only a cow-boy of long experience can, concluding with:

"I'll kill 'em yet, before I get 'em to the magistrate, ——— 'em!"

"No you won't, Billy, not while I am along."

"You! why you ——— cowardly whelp, I'll shoot you if you interfere in my affairs," the Kid replied.

The men walked slowly along, trembling every moment in fear of their lives. When near the ranche of John Chisum the constable said:

"This is near enough."

"What do you intend to do?" asked McCluskey.

"Shoot 'em down," was the Kid's reply.

"That will be murder."

"Murder thunder, that's Chisum's orders, and they must be obeyed," the lad replied.

"You shall not harm a hair of their heads, Billy," said McCluskey, with determination.

"I shan't, eh! Who'll hinder me?"

"I will."

"You, now, see here, Sam McCluskey, you have just said that enough. Open your mouth again for these cowardly coyotes, an' I'll drop you to the sod."

"I will, while I live, defend the helpless men."

Billy drew his pistol, and McCluskey grabbed for his, but the boy murderer was too quick for him.

The Kid's slender arm shot out, putting the pistol almost against the head of McCluskey.

"Bang!" went the pistol.

The deputy constable fell from his horse, and the animal dashed wildly away.

The prisoners, seeing that death was sure, took to their heels.

Taking deliberate aim at Morton he fired. The man fell screaming to the earth, with a broken spine.

Leaving him, the Kid put spurs to his horse and overtook Baker. With the rein in his teeth, and a pistol in each hand, he actually riddled him with bullets. He then returned and shot Morton through the head.

Dismounting, he dipped his finger in the blood, and made two cross marks on his writ; then, mounting his horse, rode to the office of the magistrate.

"Where are your prisoners?" asked the justice.

"I left 'em," replied the Kid, with the grin of a devil.

"You did not arrest them, eh? Well, what return do you make on the writ?"

"I have already made my mark on the writ, you can fill it out," he said, coolly, drawing forth the paper, and showing the two crosses made with the blood of his victims.

"Great God!" cried the justice, "you have killed them. Where is McCluskey?"

"Ah! I forgot to make one for him," replied the Kid, with a hideous leer.

"Murderer!" shrieked the magistrate, "get out of my presence!" and the frightened justice fled through the rear door of his office.

With the laugh of a demon, Billy the Kid went out to his horse, vaulted into the saddle, and rode away.

CHAPTER IV. THE SHERIFF'S FATE

The triple murder incensed the officers of the law, and a warrant was placed in the hands of Sheriff Brady and his deputy George Hindman.

After making the ghastly return to his writ, Billy the Kid rode directly to the ranch of old John Chisum.

The ranchman met him at the door, and asked him if he had succeeded.

"I have," was the reply.

"How?"

"They are both dead."

"Did you kill Morton and Baker?"

"I did, and more, too."

"Who?"

"I shot McCluskey."

"Heavens, boy! what did you do that for?"

"He was in the way, and the chance was too good to be lost," replied the desperado, with a cruel laugh.

"You young monster," said Chisum, in a tone which showed he was not altogether displeased, "you will have all the bloodhounds in the country on you."

"I will be ready for them," said the youthful daredevil.

Dismounting, he went into the ranch of his employer, and returned with his repeating rifle.

"If any man pursues me, just tell him to come on," said the Kid, mounting his horse and galloping away.

Scarce was he out of sight before the sheriff and his deputy came up to old Chisum.

"Have you seen Billy this morning?" the sheriff asked.

"He was here a few moments ago," replied the old sinner.

"Which way did he go?"

"I did not notice."

"Is there any one here who can tell us anything of his whereabouts now?"

"No, I am sure there is not."

"Well, Chisum," said the sheriff, evidently vexed at the unconcerned manner of the cattle king, "you had better be a little more interested in this matter, for I tell you plainly, you are suspicioned of concealing the Kid."

"Is he wanted?" asked Chisum, with assumed surprise.

"Of course he is, and you know it."

"What for?"

"Murder."

"Murder; who is murdered?"

"McCluskey, Baker, and Morton."

"There must be some mistake about it. He went to arrest Baker and Morton, and McCluskey was his deputy."

"But the devil murdered all three of them."

"Impossible."

"But true; their bodies have just been found near McSwain's ranch and brought in."

While Brady was conversing with old John, Hindman mingled with the herders, and soon gained all the information he wanted concerning the escaped outlaw.

Watching his opportunity, he beckoned the sheriff aside and said:

"I know where he is now."

"Where?"

"He went in the direction of McSwain's ranch, and we will doubtless find him there."

The two mounted their horses and galloped down the road after the Kid.

"I believe," said the sheriff, "that old John Chisum is aiding that little villain to escape."

"I know it," Hindman answered. "A cow-boy saw old John in conversation with Billy, and he held Billy's horse while the little demon went in and got his rifle. When Billy came out he gave him some advice, and the Kid rode away in this direction."

"The little demon then has his rifle?" said the sheriff; with some concern.

"He has," replied Hindman.

"Then we will have no easy task before us. We must keep a sharp lookout, for if he gets the drop on us, we are as good as dead men."

The men rode at a swift gallop until the ranch of McSwain was in sight.

McSwain's house was situated in the suburbs of the town of Lincoln. It was a costly edifice, built of hewn stone, the finest house in the country; was constructed so strong that it would make an excellent fort.

The buildings were surrounded by an adobe wall, about four feet high, surmounted by pickets of iron.

"Hold!" said Hindman, drawing rein, as they came in full view of the house.

"What is the matter?" asked the sheriff, following his example.

"I see the devil now!"

"Where?"

"Look right over that adobe wall that surrounds McSwain's house."

The officer did as directed and caught sight of a small head peeping over the wall. The small basilisk eyes gleamed like the orbs of a serpent. He had a brimless cap on his head, and was a poor object for a shot with a pistol at that range.

Notwithstanding the desperate character of the Kid, the officers evidently thought he would surrender to them and stand his trial, especially as the chances were good for his coming clear.

"Come out of there, Billy," cried the sheriff. No response came, and the boy watched his would be captors.

"I will advance on him, George, and do you keep a close watch on his movements. Have your revolver ready, and if he makes an effort to use his arms, shoot him down."

It was evident that the sheriff did not appreciate the desperate character with which he had to deal.

He left Hindman standing in the road, holding his horse by the bit, while he advanced to get nearer the Kid.

"Billy!" the sheriff shouted.

"Is that you, sheriff?" asked Billy.

"Yes, it is; come out of there!"

"What for?"

"I want to see you."

"Come in then."

"Come out."

"I'll not do it."

"Then I'll be compelled to make you."

"You had better go on, and let me alone."

"I shall not do it; you must come with me as my prisoner."

"A prisoner? What am I to be arrested for?"

"Murder."

"Murdering who?"

"Baker, Morton, and McCluskey."

"They were prisoners, and tried to escape."

"McCluskey was no prisoner."

"But he was trying to aid them in escaping, and I shot him down."

"Come out of there, Billy, and stand your trial like a man."

"I will not do it."

"Then you must take the consequences," said the sheriff, advancing his horse to the adobe wall.

The Kid made a movement, and the barrel of his rifle came above the wall.

Crack! went the pistol of Hindman; the ball whizzed within an inch of the boy's head.

Instantly his rifle was cocked and leveled at Brady. The sheriff saw his danger and tried to get his pistol off but the nimble hands of Billy were too quick for him.

The sharp report of a rifle rang out, and Sheriff Brady grasped at the air a moment, then clung to the saddle.

The horse whirled about with such a momentum that the body was thrown from the saddle, and fell limp and lifeless at the roadside.

"Now for you!" shouted the Kid, leaping upon the wall and leveling his rifle at Hindman.

The deputy sheriff saw his danger and wheeled his horse to fly.

Crack! went the rifle, sharp and keen.

"Oh, Lord!" cried the man who clung to the saddle for a few moments, while the horse plunged madly down the road; then the body, losing its balance, fell to the road.

Both sheriff and deputy had been shot through the body, and both were dead.

"What have you been doing, Billy?" asked a voice in the yard, near where the murderer stood.

Turning, he beheld Mrs. McSwain, the beautiful and accomplished wife of one of his old employers.

"I have just been teaching a couple of fellows not to interfere with me," the lad replied, with the same cold, wicked smile on his face.

"I thought they had already learned that," the lady replied.

"It seems that these fellows had not; however, they will never bother me again; I must go now."

Descending from the wall, he walked across the beautiful lawn, and, mounting his horse upon the opposite side of the adobe wall, rode away.

It was doubtless the intention of Billy to leave the country, at least to quit Lincoln County, but another mystic line in the web of fate changed his purpose.

He left the village behind him, and was riding carelessly along the road, when he came across his steadfast friend, Tom O'Fallaher.

"Helloa, Billy, which way now?" cried Tom.

"I can't say," the Kid answered. "I rather thought it was best to get away from here."

Graves of Sheriff William Brady and George Hindman, 1983. Hindman's marker was stolen and has never been recovered. Photograph by the author.

"Been having more trouble?"

"Yes."

"What?"

"There seemed to be a conflict of authority between Sheriff Brady and me. We come together and I left him."

"Good!" said Tom, with an air of satisfaction. "You killed him, and I'm glad of it, for he is a —— rascal, and has all along been in with Murphy, Dolan & Co. Where are you going?"

"To Texas, or anywhere to get out of here."

"No, no, don't think of that," said Tom. "Since the war is over so many of our fellows have been thrown out of employment, and we have organized a band of cow-boys. We want a captain, and you are the man."

In less than twenty-four hours Billy the Kid was in command of twenty of the worst desperadoes ever known in the territory of New Mexico.

They immediately began operations; robbing stagecoaches, stealing cattle, murdering, and plundering indiscriminately.

When the band was organized and began business, others joined until it swelled to a considerable force, commanded and controlled by Billy the Kid.

CHAPTER V. TURNER IN PURSUIT OF THE BANDITS

Marion Turner was deputy sheriff of Lincoln county, and on the 8th day of June, 1879, he had a warrant placed in his hands for the arrest of Billy the Kid. There were five indictments for murder against the young rascal. His victims were Morton, Baker, McCluskey, Brady and Hindman.

Knowing how useless and dangerous it was to attempt the capture of the Kid alone, and with an insufficient force, he organized a posse of thirty-five of the most experienced horsemen and riflemen in the entire country.

The posse selected were all fine-looking men, strong and wiry, men to whom fear was a stranger, and fatigue unknown.

Marion Turner was a young officer of manly bearing, brave and determined. He had engaged in the undertaking, and was determined that come what would, Billy the Kid should be put down.

When the Kid heard that Turner was after him, he said to his men:

"Boys, we will either have some hard fighting, or hard running to do before we are out of this. Turner is no common man."

His force consisted of sixty-three, and yet with that great odds in his favor, the Kid seemed to avoid an engagement.

The outlaws moved in a body up the Pecos Valley, followed by Turner and his posse.

On the evening of the 16th of June, one of the advance guard sighted two outlaws about three hundred yards away, riding very leisurely along.

He raised his rifle and fired, but his aim was inaccurate, and the men returning the shots without effect galloped on out of sight.

Turner hearing the report of rifles, galloped ahead of the main body of his men to learn the cause. On being informed what had occurred, he hurried up his main force. The portion of the country they were in was wild. The mountain ranges seemed to gradually approach each other until they evidently met a few miles further on, forming the Pecos pass or Canon.

The grass grew almost as tall as the back of a horse, and formed an excellent ambuscade, if the foe chose to make use of it.

The outlaws left a plain broad trail behind, which the frontiersmen found no difficulty in following.

The sun was nearly down when the man in advance fired on the two rear-guards of Billy the Kid, and night soon overtook both foe and officer's posse, not far apart.

The[y] had passed out of Lincoln into San Miguel county on the head waters of the Pecos.

The outlaws encamped on one side of the stream, and Turner's posse on the other. All night long they could see each other's camp fires, and the settlers could hear the shouts and ribald songs of the cow-boys.

At dawn the sheriff had his men ready. After swallowing a cold breakfast, they moved cautiously forward on the enemy.

They were compelled to advance through a thick wood a fourth of a mile up the stream, where they came to a ford.

This they found guarded by a dozen cow-boys. The crack of a few rifles rang out on the morning air, and Turner, knowing that everything depended on instantaneous action, ordered a charge.

With a wild yell the frontiersmen dashed down the banks, into the stream, pouring in a deadly fire that swept six of the outlaws into eternity. The others fled, and before the main camp of Billy the Kid could be aroused, Turner and posse with horses and equipments had crossed the river.

The deputy sheriff then made detour of the outlaw's camp, to take them in the rear.

They found the Kid on the alert and ready for battle.

Both forces adopted the old Indian method of fighting from behind trees; some on horseback, and some on foot.

The rapid discharge of. fire-arms rang out, and columns of smoke arose in air, to soar away among the tree tops.

The sun arose to look down upon a scene of carnage.

Billy the Kid, with his usual reckless daring, went hither and thither along his line urging his men on by word and act. His shrill voice, sharp and clear, could be heard above the roar of battle.

His unerring rifle cracked frequently, and seldom without results disastrous to his assailants.

Turner and his men hugged the trees and fought desperately. The cowboys were forced to fall back and recross the Pecos. Turner was close at their heels and commenced a running fight which lasted for three days.

The first day the cow-boys, under their youthful leader, stubbornly resisted every inch of ground.

But little progress was made, and at night the two forces worn out, encamped within sight of each other, not five miles from the ford where the battle commenced.

During the night, rumor spread among the men of the Kid, that Lieut. Col. Dudley, with two companies of colored troops, was advancing to reinforce Turner.

"Well, Billy, what had we better do?" asked Tom O'Fallaher, who had been raised to the responsible position of first lieutenant.

"Do? why we must get back to Lincoln as soon as we can," said the Kid.

"To Lincoln! why we fled from that place?"

"Well, if we did, we have more friends there than elsewhere. Chisum and McSwain will stay by us to the last."

"But we will be running right into the hands of the soldiers."

"We will find them run their hands into us, if we remain here."

"When will you retreat; to-night?"

"No, not before morning, the men are tired, and want sleep."

"That Turner is a devil," said Tom.

"He can't be hit with lead," said the Kid.

"Nonsense."

"It is true."

"Why do you think so?"

"I had a dozen fair shots at him to-day, and never touched him. The man my rifle cannot bring down is a witch or a devil."

"His men are all desperate fighters."

"I never struck a harder lot."

"They have driven us at every point to-day."

"We will recruit some men, when we get to Lincoln, and capture the town. Once inside we will fortify the place and bid defiance to everybody."

"Do you think we can count on Chisum and McSwain?" asked Tom.

"I am sure of it; they told me again and again that they would be willing to aid me in such emergencies as this."

The next morning the echoes of the woods awoke with sharp detonations, at early dawn. The firing was slower and more deliberate than the day before, but, the range being greater, was less effective.

Both bodies moved out of the timber into the level plain and kept moving all day, exchanging an occasional shot.

"I will give a reward of a thousand dollars to any man who will bring down Billy the Kid," said Turner, who had fired a number of times at the young desperado without effect.

"You might double that reward and have no fears of losing a cent of the reward," replied Reuben Miles, an old plainsman and hunter, "who could ever get a bead on that thin streak of a little devil, that flits from place to place so rapidly as not to be seen."

The daring acts of Billy on the three days' running fight would fill volumes. Not an hour passed that he did not recklessly expose his life. Sometimes riding at a hard gallop in front of the advancing posse, he would empty every shot of his repeating rifle at them, and escape unhurt amid a storm of balls.

On the evening of the third day, the outlaws, an hour ahead of their pursuers, entered Lincoln amid shouts and yells. McSwain opened his doors to them, and offered his beautiful dwelling as a fortification. The Kid was not slow to avail himself of it.

McSwain with twenty ranchmen even volunteered to assist in defending the outlaws.

CHAPTER VI. BATTLE AT McSWAIN'S HOUSE

McSwain's house was almost a fortification in itself, yet not a little time was spent in strengthening the adobe wall that surrounded it, and in arranging the furniture for the best possible defense.

McSwain's beautiful wife did all in her power to encourage the desperadoes. Her graceful form could be seen moving here and there, putting a bandage around a wounded arm, or a plaster on a cut. She was as brave as she was beautiful, and displayed an energy worthy of a better cause.

Tom O'Fallaher had taken a position on the roof to watch for the enemy.

"Here they come like devils," he cried to those below him.

"Inside all," shouted Billy, as the thunder of hoofs was heard coming down the street. "Now don't waste a shot. Take aim, and drop your man. Give 'em —l!"

The last command was accompanied by a rattling volley of fire-arms, that might well answer the demand of the chieftain.

Wild yells arose upon the air. Never had the little town of Lincoln witnessed such a scene.

"Crack; crack, crack!" rang the shots from the repeating-rifle of Billy the Kid, and his bullets made fearful havoc among the ranks of the assailants.

"Stand your ground, brave cow-boys!" he yelled, sharp and clear above the roar of battle, springing to the eastern side of the inclosure, where the enemy were endeavoring to make a breach in the wall.

With a revolver in each hand, he poured a constant stream of fire and leaden hail in the face of his foe, which withered their ranks so that they were compelled to retire.

"Hurrah! hurrah! my brave lads," shouted McSwain, fighting like a demon. "Strike hard, and strike home. Hurl back the fiends, sweep them from the face of the earth."

Leaping on the adobe wall, he emptied both barrels of his shot gun in the face of the officers' posse.

The storm of bullets and buck-shot was more than even the hardy herdsmen of Marion Turner could endure, and they fell back to a respectful distance, leaving several dead and wounded near the adobe wall.

Sheltering themselves behind houses, walls, fences, and boulders of stone, the assailants commenced a rifle practice on the inmates of the house.

On the second morning of the siege, Colonel Dudley, with two companies of soldiers, arrived on the scene, and at once opened fire on the outlaws.

"We have the infernal niggers on us now," said the Kid to Tom, as he observed the reinforcement.

"They will not fight, and we will be able to whip a thousand such vagabonds, in this house," replied Tom.

The outlaw had taken for his headquarters the parlor of Mrs. McSwain, a room that was elegantly furnished.

"Have courage," said Mrs. McSwain, entering the parlor; "do not despair, and I will give you some music to encourage you."

The troops opened a terrible fire on the house, the balls rattling like hail against the walls, and through the windows.

Mrs. McSwain opened the piano, and as coolly as though she was entertaining an evening party, seated herself before it.

Her jeweled fingers ran over the keys and sent forth soul-stirring notes.

High above the roar of battle, crash of bullets and cries of combatants, rose the sweet clear voice, in soul-stirring battle songs.

The sound of that beautiful voice and sweet-toned piano, in such cheering strains, seemed to make demons out of the outlaws.

"Fight lads, shoot them down!" shouts the youthful outlaw chief. "Let your battle-cry be, 'Billy the Kid, forever.'"

Yell upon yell arose, and still plainly could be heard the notes of the piano, and sweet voice of the singer.

The sheriff's posse and soldiers heard it.

"Turner," said Lieut.-Col. Dudley, "do you hear that?"

"What?"

"Is not that some one singing in the house?"

"It certainly is."

"And don't you hear a piano?"

"Can you make out what it means?"

"No, I cannot. Can you?"

"Only that some woman is singing in there to encourage the thieves, and her voice puts the devil in every man. It makes them worse than if they had taken gun-powder and brandy."

"It certainly does," said Turner.

Sweet and clear above the hum of battle rang the silvery voice, and accompaniment.

Turner listened for a few moments in amazement, and then said:

"I have it now."

"What, or who is?" asked Col. Dudley.

"McSwain's wife."

"The owner of the house?"

"Yes."

"Heavens, is she insane?"

"No; both she and her husband have always sided with Billy the Kid. He was long in the employ of Chisum and McSwain."

"Well, why is she singing and playing that piano on such an occasion as this?"

"To encourage the outlaws. There goes the Scottish war song."

High, sweet and clear, rose the famous old

War Song

"To horse—to horse! the standard flies
The bugles sound the call;
The Gallic navy stems the seas,
The voice of battle's on the breeze—
Arouse ye, one and all!

From high Dunedin's towers we come,
A band of brothers true;
Our casques the leopards spoils surround,
With Scotland's hardy thistle crowned;
We boast the red and blue.

Oh! had they marked the avenging call
Their brethren's murder gave,
Disunion ne'er their ranks had mown,
Nor patriot's valor, desperate grown,
Sought freedom in the grave.

Shall we, too, bend the stubborn head,
In freedom's temple born;
Dress our pale cheek in timid smile
To hail a master in our isle,
Or brook a victor's scorn.

Then farewell home! and farewell friends!
Adieu each tender tie!
Resolved we mingle in the tide,

Where charging squadrons furious ride,
To conquer, or to die.

To horse—to horse! the sabers gleam
High sounds our bugle call;
Combined by honor's sacred tie;
Our word is *Love* and Liberty!
March forward, one and all!"

Yell upon yell arose high above the battle din at the conclusion. Showers of bullets and buck-shot were poured into the advancing columns of soldiers.

The cow-boys seemed like madmen, and were perfectly reckless in their resistance.

"What woman or devil would dare sing during such a fight as this?" said Dudley.

"No woman but McSwain's wife," replied Turner. "They are Scotch descent, and the song is a favorite of hers."

"Turner, we must put an end to that music."

"How will you do it?" asked Turner.

"Get the direction of the infernal instrument, and shoot it to pieces," replied the colonel.

"But that would jeopardize the life of the woman."

"Cannot help that. The infernal instrument must be shattered. It is doing more devilment than a dozen rifles. It inspires the cowardly cow-boys to acts of devilment beyond description."

Twenty men with heavy rifles got the range of the piano from the sweet notes it sent forth, and began to fire into it.

The first ball that pierced the beautiful rose-wood frame did not disturb the fair singer. But another, another, and another crashing through it with such ruinous effect, induced even the brave Mrs. McSwain to abandon it. In a few minutes the key-board was shattered to pieces, and the beautiful instrument useless.

Night settled over the scene. The hope of the outlaws was well-nigh gone. The yard and house were filled with the dead and wounded.

In sullen, gloomy silence the doomed men awaited their fate.

When morning came, the assailants waited until the sun was well up before they renewed the contest. Then they advanced slowly upon the house, pouring in a steady fire all the while.

Turner determined that the struggle which had begun six days before, should end before the sun set.

At two o'clock in the afternoon, he had six men prepared with buckets of coal oil, and then dashed on the house with all his force.

A storm of bullets and buckshot met them, yet the oil was poured over the side of the house, veranda, and into the doors and windows.

Being almost instantaneously ignited, the house was in flames.

"We must cut our way out," cried the Kid, and with a shrill cry, he and his friend Tom led the way, followed by McSwain and the others.

A terrible hand-to-hand fight ensued. Pistol shot answered pistol shot at such close quarters, the muzzles passed.

McSwain was shot through the head, and fell dead in the arms of his wife.

In the break from the burning house the Kid's partner, Tom O'Fallaher, the small boy from Texas, noticed one of his friends fall.

Amid a perfect storm of ball and buckshot, he coolly returned and picked up his comrade. He was carrying him away when he discovered he was dead, then, dropping the body, he drew his pistol and knife, and fought like a demon by the side of the Kid, until the two had escaped to their horses. Vaulting in the saddles, they galloped away amid a storm of bullets.

In this last melee six soldiers and two of Turner's posse, with twelve of the Kid's cow-boys, were killed. Never was a fight longer or bloodier, considering the numbers engaged.

CHAPTER VII. GOVERNOR WALLACE'S PARDON

Marion Turner and Col. Dudley made no effort to pursue the Kid and the remnant of his band that had escaped. Six days hard fighting was to much for even men of iron.

Their men were exhausted, many of them wounded, horses worn out, and in fact they felt willing, for the time being, to let the Kid alone.

Billy and Tom galloped out of the town about four miles and halted in a small valley. It was late in the evening, and both were powder-grimed, dust-covered and exhausted, but by no means conquered.

"What do you think of this Billy," asked Tom.

"What do you think was the answer?"

"Dun'no."

"They've about got enough of us."

"Should think so."

"It was a glorious fight, Tom."

"You bet it was, Billy, an' one could well afford to cave in in such a scrimmage as that. What will you do, Billy? Leave the country?"

"Not by a jug full."

"Surrender?"

"Not much."

"Get a pardon from the governor?"

"Not by my askin'."

"What then?"

"Reorganize."

"The band?"

"Yes."

"Good!"

"You like the plan?"

"You bet I do."

"Some of the boys escaped?"

"Yes."

"Have you any idea how many?"

"No, but several."

"They will come to us."

"You bet they will."

"And all be true grit as ever?"

"You can depend on 'em, Billy, to the death."

"We must hunt 'em up, Tom."

"How'll you go about it, when they are scattered fur and wide?"

"Wait here until they come up to us. When it is known the old band is to be reorganized they will flock to our standard."

The Kid did not miscalculate his men. That very evening he picked up four who had escaped the fight, and the next day six more. With a force of ten, he robbed a ranch, fifteen miles from Lincoln, and stopped the mail coach, deliberately robbing the passengers.

He, as usual, gathered about him a band of outlaws equally bad as the former.

About this time Axtell was removed from the governorship of the territory, and Col. Lew Wallace appointed in his place.

A weaker man for the occasion could not have been selected. Wallace evidently intended to do right, but was too easily influenced. Chisum was one of the most wealthy and influential men in the Territory, and wealth and influence is sure to capture a governor.

Chisum went up to Sant[a] Fe, and represented to the new governor that he had been very badly imposed on. His stock had been stolen and his employees slain. He represented that Billy the Kid was but a child, and that what he had done, the boy believed he was doing in self-defense, or as an officer of the law.

The naturally romantic mind of the old governor took in all that was said by the astute villain.

Here was a boy who possessed one of the greatest virtues, bravery, and he lost sight of the crimes he had committed. A proclamation was issued, pardoning all the parties engaged in the Lincoln county outbreak, and commanding them to lay down their arms and go home in peace.

The generous governor included in his pardon even army officers who had been engaged in the outbreak.

Nothing could have been more absurd or outrageous than the allusion to army officers; putting them on a level with cow-boys, thieves and plunderers. Col. Dudley was exasperated beyond measure, and he denounced the governor in round terms.

The Lieut. Colonel Dudley and Marion Turner had only been engaged in enforcing, or attempting to enforce the execution of a writ, issued from a court of justice.

Scarce had the trump of peace been sounded than Mrs. McSwain determined to prosecute the murderers of her husband, and recover damages for the home that had been destroyed.

Oscar Chapman was a shrewd unscrupulous attorney in Los Vegas, yet a man with considerable reputation as a lawyer. She employed Chapman to prosecute the criminals, and procure damages for the destruction of her property.

Chapman came over to Lincoln and began to promptly stir up the strife anew. He was loud in his denunciations of Marion Turner, Col. Dudley, and all engaged in the effort to capture the Kid.

Silas Rodgers was a man honest and upright after the fashion of frontiersmen. He was brave, and had shot two or three in brawls, but was not regarded as quarrelsome.

One day he met Chapman in a saloon. Chapman had been drinking, and was uttering the most bitter anathemas against every one opposed to Chisum and McSwain.

There is no doubt but that old John Chisum was at the bottom of the new trouble.

Rodgers had been a drover under the employ [of] Murphy, Dolan & Co., and was one of Marion Turner's posse. He was not pleased with the turn affairs had taken, and could ill brook such language.

"They are all cattle thieves and murderers," said the lawyer, bringing his fist on the table with a crash.

"Who are thieves and murderers?" demanded Silas Rodgers, his brow growing dark.

"Turner and his cut-throats, who murdered McSwain," replied the lawyer.

"Be careful ye legal rooster how ye flop yer wings around me, I was one o' them chaps. I was with Turner."

"You was, you ugly owl. I am going to hang you for a contemptible thief."

"Look'ee here, you mutton head son o' a race of liars, do you intend to call me a thief?" cried Silas

"I do."

"Then you are a liar."

"You cowardly bull stealer, do you tell me I lie?" shouted the lawyer, bracing himself in front of Silas with some difficulty; determined to be brave if he died for it.

"I do," Silas answered.

"Take that."

"Spat," came the open hand of the lawyer against the sun-burned cheek of the herder. This is something no herder will endure.

Silas' hand clutched his pistol, and reeling and smarting under the blow, he snatched it from his belt.

Click, click—bang! went the weapon before any one could interfere.

With a groan Chapman sank to the floor, a corpse.

When Governor Wallace heard of the death of Chapman he was so incensed that he arose with all the power and majesty of a little terri-torial official with a tin ear, and went down into Lincoln County. He outlawed Turner, his posse and all the officers of the law that had been fighting Chisum and McSwain, the Kid, and the train of demons they had under them.

To make his gubernatorial act still more outrageous, the weak-minded governor had Turner, Rodgers and eleven others put in irons. Even the brave Colonel Dudley was relieved of his command, and put under arrest. Thieves rejoiced, but honest people were indignant.

CHAPTER VIII. TURNER'S PERSECUTIONS

Through the intrigue of old John Chisum and manipulations of Gov. Lew Wallace, who now seemed fully identified with the bandits, twenty-one indictments were found against Marion Turner for murder, arson and cattle stealing.

For forty days and nights he and his companions lay in jail. They were then brought before the court. Thank Heaven, the territorial court and jury were either more intelligent or more honest than the governor!

After a lengthy trial, in which Billy, the Kid, now clothed with all the rights of a peaceful citizen, appeared as chief witness, they were all acquitted.

When the jury returned a verdict of not guilty in Turner's case, a shout of joy went up from the audience, or the honest part of it.

Old John Chisum was the very picture of a fiend incarnate.

"You will find we are not through with you yet," said Chisum to Turner before they left the court-room.

"You old cow-stealer, if you had your just deserts you would be in the penitentiary!" said Turner.

"Be careful, Marion Turner, how you talk," said Billy the Kid, who stood near Chisum. "You have escaped us once, but this thing is not over with yet."

"You cowardly little thief, if you had only had the spunk you assume, and stood your ground up on the Pecos, I would have cut your throat, and rid the world of a curse!"

With an oath, Billy snatched his pistol, but before he could use it half a dozen pairs of hands snatched his arm, and tore it from him.

"Never mind, Billy," said Chisum, as they walked away, "we will be even with him yet, never fear."

The two left the court-room, arm-in-arm, and it is certain that the Kid spent that night with Chisum.

From that time forth persecutions in every conceivable manner began against Turner. His cattle were stolen, horses poisoned, and worse than all, a thousand lies were circulated to poison the public mind against him.

Thief, perjurer, and murderer, were soon among the mildest epithets addressed to him. Turner bore it all with meekness.

He was indicted in every court and paid out over six thousand dollars attorney fee, besides the loss of time.

Turner became attached to a beautiful girl, to whom he gave his warmest affections.

His love was returned. Chisum set ardently to work with all the ferocity and determination of a devil to break the young hearts.

The young lady's name was Hattie Phillips, and she was living with Surgeon Appel of the Ninth cavalry. The surgeon was a cousin of hers, and was evidently an unprincipled man; at least his subsequent acts proved it.

To him Chisum applied with all his devilish determination to ruin Marion Turner.

"Do you know this man your cousin is to be married to?" asked Chisum.

"Turner? do you mean Marion Turner?"

"Yes it is he I am talking about."

"I am not intimately acquainted with him, and I do not know that my cousin is to marry him," the surgeon replied.

"Well she is, surgeon, and the fellow is a perfect scamp," said Chisum.

"I cannot believe it, Mr. Chisum; he has been here frequently, and seems a gentleman. I—I beg your pardon, but you must be mistaken."

"I am telling you the square truth; the fellow has been indicted for murder, arson and theft, and almost every offense known to the criminal calendar."

"But was he not acquitted by a jury?" asked the surgeon.

"By a jury, yes, but it was a packed jury of the worst kind. Do you not know that Governor Wallace outlawed him?"

"No."

"Well it is true. I tell you, surgeon, that I would give five hundred dollars myself rather than have the scoundrel marry your cousin. This may seem strange to a man who is not related to either party; but I am interested in your cousin, and do not wish to see her come to ruin."

"Do you know that it is their intention to be married?"

"I do," said Chisum, for a faithful ally of his had eavesdropped the young couple, and knew the hour that ceremony was to take place.

"When are they to be married?"

"On the morning of the 27th of September, at the hotel in Lincoln."

"Well, I will just balk that little game," said the surgeon, "by sending her to her uncle Frederick C. Godfrey in Michigan."

"Do not do that yet," said the old villain, who had a more develish plan on foot. His design was to publicly humble and crush his enemy. "Wait until the 27th, then come forward and claim your relative—she is under age—and prevent her marriage then and there. Besides, the scoundrel can be indicted for marrying a minor without the consent of her parents or guardian. How old is Miss Phillips?"

"Just sixteen."

"Good; if he attempts to marry her, we will have him fast."

The old villain went away chuckling at the thought that he was on the road to vengeance.

In the meanwhile the lovers, with bright prospects in the future, were making arrangements for their nuptials.

The glorious day of their wedding dawned. Happy bride in prospective, and equally happy groom. The sun arose bright and clear in the heavens, and the hour of the ceremony drew slowly on.

Sweet Hattie Phillips never looked more bewitching than when decked in her bridal robes. On the evening before she had slipped away from her cousin's house, and gone to the hotel. At the hour she was dressed and awaiting the arrival of her soon to be husband.

Marion Turner never looked more brave than at that hour, when he entered the room where the beautiful Nettie was awaiting him.

Never will Nettie forget that hour, that moment. Though torn from the manly breast she loved so well, and borne across plains, mountains, and dark rolling rivers, yet that picture of manly beauty can never fade from her memory.

Though slanderous tongues have lied about Turner, until his fair fame is pointed to her blacker than Satan, yet she cannot forget how grand, how noble, he looked on that occasion.

With a little cry of joy she arose to meet him.

"Oh, Marion, Marion, have you come at last?" she said.

"I have, my darling Nettie; am I not on time?" he answered.

"I suppose you are, but oh! I am so nervous to-day. I feel that something awful is going to happen to us."

"Have no fears of anything, my dear. I am with you, and no one shall harm you. We will soon be one in law, and then I will protect you with my life."

"But those dreadful men, of which there are so many, who I believe would murder you; they may kill you at any time."

"My little darling, what makes you so uneasy to-day? this day of all others, when you should be happy? Our wedding day."

"I cannot say, Marion; but oh, my dear Marion, I do so fear that man Chisum, and that bad-looking boy, that always hangs around with him."

"Have you seen Chisum lately?" asked Turner.

"He has been conversing with my cousin, Surgeon Appel, for several days."

"The old thief is hatching up more mischief," said Turner, reflectively. "He ought to be in the penitentiary."

At this moment the attendants entered with the announcement that all was ready.

A more beautiful pair, one of manliness and courage, and the other of womanly sweetness, was never married in New Mexico.

The ceremony was said that made them one. At two, a banquet was prepared, and the few guests invited seated at the table. The cook of the hotel had done his best, and the table fairly groaned under its load of good things.

The bride and groom were seated, and the other guests had taken their places about the table.

A messenger came to the groom to announce that a stranger wished to see him. Turner arose and, chancing to glance out of the window, saw the yard filled with negro soldiers. At the door he met old John Chisum.

"What does this mean?" he demanded.

"It means," replied Chisum, with a hideous grin on his ugly face, "that Surgeon Appel has come after his cousin. She is under age, and he is to take her away."

Turner endeavored by every means to avoid a scene, and have the surgeon and the two companies of the 9th cavalry go away, but entreaties were useless.

The bride who, becoming alarmed, had approached her husband, was seized. Turner began to resist, but was seized by twenty negro soldiers, and held fast.

"Oh, my darling husband, do not let them take me away Do not—do not!"

What husband would not exert himself on such an appeal? The soldiers of the 9th cavalry were large powerful men, but he hurled them aside like so many children.

Once he had approached, and fought his way so near his wife, as to touch her hand, but he was seized and hurled to the earth, while she was hurried away. The last that Turner ever heard of that beloved voice, was:

"Oh, my husband, my darling husband, do not let them separate us."

She was dragged away from Lincoln, and sent to her uncle, Fredrick C. Godfrey, in Monroe county, Michigan. They placed her in a seminary, where she remains to this day.

Her husband is in New Mexico, a sad wreck of what he once was.

CHAPTER IX. THE KID'S ATTEMPT ON COL. DUDLEY

After the acquittal of Turner and his men at the trial in Lincoln, the Kid was strongly advised by his friends to leave the country. He reluctantly consented, though it was plain to be seen that he had by no means given up his ideas of lawlessness

"There is one scoundrel I am determined to kill before I leave," said Billy one day to his former employer, John Chisum.

"Who do you mean?" asked the cattle king.

"Col. Dudley, the man who brought down the Digger soldiers from Fort Stanton to capture me."

"Do not think of such a thing, Billy, but go away at once. Another desperate act of blood, and even the influence of myself and Gov. Wallace cannot save your neck."

The Kid hung his head in sullen silence, and remained thus some time. Then, arising to his feet without a word of reply, he went away.

"That young demon is a born murderer," said old Chisum, as the murderer and desperado left.

It was not the natural goodness of heart on the part of Chisum, that he desired to save the life of Col. Dudley. The old reprobate had been mixed up with so much of the Kid's devilment, he began to fear that honest men would rise up in their might to put him out of the way, on some new outrage of that little demon.

Col. Dudley, whom Gov. Wallace had had arrested for his assistance in the attempt to capture the outlaws at the McSwain house, was undergoing a trial at Fort Stanton. A court martial, or court of inquiry, was investigating his case.

Judge Ira E. Leonard, formerly of Missouri, but now of New Mexico, had been employed by Mrs. McSwain to conduct the prosecution against

Dudley, as being accessory to the murder of her husband, and burning her house. Judge Leonard, at the time a resident of Las Vegas, was accompanied to Fort Stanton by John McPherson, chief of police of Las Vegas.

McPherson had been with Quantrel[1] during the war, and was himself a desperado. He was a short time after killed by some of the roughs of Las Vegas.

As he and Leonard were sitting in their room one night, during the Dudley trial, discussing the probabilities of a conviction, there came a tap at their window.

"What can that mean?" asked Judge Leonard, naturally a little nervous.

"I do not know," said McPherson, "but I will open the shutter and see."

"Do not, do not, for the world," cried the frightened lawyer. "Some armed desperado may be out there to shoot us down."

The judge lived in constant dread, during the trial of Col. Dudley, lest some of the desperadoes should become offended and seek his life.

McPherson, who, to use a phrase common in the West, "had been there," had no such fears.

"Oh, bosh, judge," he said, "don't be so timid as to be afraid of your shadder," and he rose and swung open the shutter.

The small form of Billy the Kid leaped nimbly through, into the room.

"Helloa, Billy, is that you?" said the lawyer, somewhat reassured.

"It certainly is," the boy replied, with that devilish smile playing on his thin face which always appeared when he meant murder.

"What do you want here Billy?" asked McPherson.

"I come to put an end to this trial," he said. The young fellow had a belt about his waist, which literally bristled with knives and revolvers.

"Who with—Dudley?" asked McPherson.

"Yes."

"How?"

"I came to kill the scoundrel."

"Oh! Billy, you must not think of such a thing," said the lawyer.

"But I will; I'll shoot him. Which room is he in?"

Dudley was in the room just across the hall at this moment, in consultation with his attorneys, and there was some danger of his carrying out the threat.

"Why do you wish to kill him, Billy?" asked McPherson, with a coolness that was necessary on such an occasion.

"He is a scoundrel, and too mean to live," was the Kid's reply.

"There are so many scoundrels in this world, that one cannot kill them all."

"But he tried to kill me."

"We are now trying him for that offense, and if convicted he will be hung, which will certainly be more pleasant," said Judge Leonard.

"No, but he will be acquitted just like Turner and his gang."

"No, no, we have all assurance of a conviction," said the lawyer, hoping to get rid of the little desperado.

"But I can end it all right here, just by killing him and getting it over at once."

"No, no no!" cried Judge Leonard, "an attempt of that kind would create a sympathy for him, and we could not convict him at all. If you desire me to successfully prosecute the cases against him and his followers, you must be on your good behavior. I can do nothing if such an attempt was to be made."

"If I can get one crack at him with my revolver, I don't care whether he is convicted or acquitted."

"But be reasonable, Billy; you are not the only one interested in this."

"It is the wish of all that I kill him."

"You must not do so."

" But I will."

"You must not."

"Where is he?"

"I do not know," answered the terrified lawyer, "but do not think he is in this house."

"I believe he is. I saw him come here not an hour ago."

"You must have been mistaken."

"No, I am not. He is in that room right across the hall. I'll just step in there, and in half a minute can put an end to a three weeks' trial."

"Heavens, boy, you must not do that!" cried the almost frantic lawyer.

"No, Billy," said McPherson. "Listen to reason. You are friends to us, and you do not wish to do anything that will get us in trouble. Don't you see if you should go from here at this hour of the night to the room of Col. Dudley, and kill him, we would be implicated?"

"But he must die!" cried the youth, becoming somewhat infuriated. "He murdered my men and killed my old boss, Alec McSwain. By —— I will kill him for that if for nothing else."

A new thought entered the mind of the lawyer, and it doubtless saved Col. Dudley's life.

"Billy," he said, "just wait a moment, and let me reason with you on this. Did you love McSwain, your old boss?"

"I did; better than ever I loved father, brother, or relative," was the reply.

"Do you love his widow?"

"More than my own mother."

"Would you do anything to injure her?"

"No, not to save my own life; but she wants him killed. I'll kill him just for her sake."

"Just wait a moment," said the lawyer, who, having regained all his coolness and self-possession, had his wits thoroughly about him.

"No, no, no! I cannot wait. Let me kill him, and I will come back and talk it over afterwards."

"Sit down, Billy, in this chair, and let me tell you something of which you have never thought. Don't be in a hurry; Colonel Dudley will not leave where he is to-night."

"But I must kill him."

"But wait until I reason with you. You love Mrs. McSwain?"

"I do, I swear it!" said the desperado, taking a seat near the lawyer.

The lawyer now had him safe. It was the power of a cultured, logical mind over an ignorant desperado, and when once left to reason education always conquers.

"You would not do anything to injure her?"

"Not to save my life," he repeated.

"If it would be better for you not to kill Dudley than to kill him, you would not do so?"

"But she wants him killed."

"You are mistaken, Billy," the lawyer answered, with a smile. "You remember her husband was killed?"

"Yes, and I'll kill him for that."

"Wait, wait! you remember that Dudley helped to burn her house, and made her homeless?"

"Yes, and I swear I'll kill him for that."

"Hold on, just wait. He has made her penniless and homeless."

"And he shall die for it!" cried the youth, starting up.

"Wait, wait," said the lawyer, smiling serenely again. "Do you want to keep her homeless—do you want to make her a begger for life?"

"No,"—sitting down again.

"She has civil suits for damages against Dudley and others, by which we hope to recover sufficient to make her at least comfortable. Now, if you should kill Dudley before this is done, there would be a sympathy for the murdered man, and Mrs. McSwain's last hope would be gone."

The reasoning was so clear and piercing that it even penetrated the thick skull of the Kid.

The lawyer followed it up with logical reasoning, until Billy was convinced that the death of Col. Dudley would be detrimental to the interest of his friends, and left by the same means he had entered.

Dudley was informed of the Kid's attempt on his life. At the trial the lieutenant-colonel was acquitted.

CHAPTER X. A LIFE OF OUTLAWRY

After quitting the hotel in Lincoln, the Kid mounted his horse and galloped away to the Staked Plain, where old John Chisum had a ranch. Chisum was there at the time, and Billy demanded a thousand dollars for services he had rendered him.

Niggardlyness was added to the other evils of old John Chisum, and he refused the moderate sum.

A quarrel ensued in which the Kid came very near taking the old reprobate's life, but was finally induced, partly through fear, and partly through influence of friends, to quit the ranch.

He was riding along the road in an aimless manner, when he again came upon his friend and partner, Tom O'Fallaher.

"Well, Billy, what now?" asked Tom.

"Old Chisum an' I have had a row," replied the Kid.

"What, you and he split?"

"We have."

"What about?"

"He owes me, and won't pay."

"Why blast his mug, take cattle enough to pay you."

The idea had never struck the Kid before. It was capital, and just the thing.

"I'll do it," he said. "We will organize the old band again, and prey upon his cattle. The old scoundrel, after all we have done for him, to be thrown aside for some new favorite."

"The old band and the good old times. The dashing down on ranches, and moonlight raids again; hip, hurrah for the jolly old band!"

The two rode along together.

"Do you know where the boys have scattered?" asked the Kid.

"The most of them are prowling about Lincoln and Fort Stanley."

"I will lay about Staked Plains, and do you make your way to Lincoln and Fort Stanley. Tell the boys of our rallying place. As soon as we have a dozen we will commence business."

Tom went as directed, and the Kid slept that night on the ground. The next day Tom returned with ten desperadoes of the old band.

The greeting was warm, and they at once swore allegiance to the new organization. That very night they swept down on the herds of Chisum, and drove away three hundred fat cattle. They had half the night to travel, and made good time. When dawn came they looked back and saw twenty or thirty horsemen in pursuit.

The Kid determined to give them battle, and hurrying the drove a mile or two further on, they came to a halt in a low piece of ground.

Dismounting they placed their horses in front of them, and with cocked rifles awaited the approach of the pursuers.

"Them chaps was once our friends, Billy," said Tom.

"What care we for that," replied the Kid. "They are all a set of —— scoundrels, and ought to be killed."

The pursuers saw the herd ahead, and with wild shouts came on at full speed.

Coolly the Kid's men awaited their approach.

A volley of keen rifle shots rang out upon the air, and half a dozen of the pursuers plunged headlong from their horses.

The outlaws were armed with repeating-rifles and double-barreled shot-guns. The pursuers halted and fired a volley, which swept over the Kid's brigands on account of their being on low grounds.

Again a sharp volley from the outlaws rang out, this time bringing both men and horses to the earth.

The pursuers bolted.

Billy took advantage of the momentary check and cried:

"Mount quick!"

Instantly every man was in the saddle.

"Charge!"

With the rein in their teeth and a pistol in each hand, they swept down like an avalanche on the discomfited pursuers.

"Crack, crack, crack!" rang out the revolvers, sharp and keen, each bearing a death shriek with it.

The herdsmen of Chisum turned and fled, leaving half their original number dead or wounded on the plain.

The wounded were put to death.

An incident here will show the heartless cruelty of the Kid.

Among the wounded was George Dye, a former friend and acquaintance, who had remained true to the interest of John Chisum. His thigh was broken and his horse killed. The horse, in falling, fell on the sound leg of Dye, thus pinning him to the earth.

In this condition he was found by the Kid.

In vain Dye implored the desperado to spare his life, and called to his recollection the many days they had spent together, and their former friendship.

"It's no use to talk of that, George," said the Kid, with his murderous smile; "you make too good a mark where you lie." He cocked his pistol as he spoke, and aimed at his head.

"Oh! Billy, Billy," cried the terrified wretch, "for God's sake don't shoot me!"

"Hold your head still, George, so I will not disfigure your face much, and give you but very little pain."

The words were spoken in that cool, determined, bloodthirsty manner, as only the Kid could speak.

Billy's men, knowing the former good friendship that had existed between Billy and George, supposed he was only having some sport at his friend's expense; George evidently thought so too, for he ceased to struggle and avoid the aim, but with a fixed smile on his face gazed the Kid in the eye.

A moment the revolver was held with a breathless silence.

"Crack!" rang the shot. George Dye's head fell upon the grass alongside his dead horse. The fatal bullet had pierced his forehead.

The Kid's force increased to twenty-five men, and he embarked on a career of lawlessness never before known in the annals of crime. How many murders he committed, how many cattle he stole, how many daring deeds of deviltry he performed, will never be known, until the dark deeds of cow-boys, congressmen, governors, thieves, lawmakers and law-breakers, are laid bare to the world.

• • •

The stage-coach running from Silver City to Lincoln was one night stopped by a dozen armed desperadoes, in February, 1881.

The first intimation the driver had of any one in the road was a tall, powerful man leaping out, and grasping the leading horses by the bits. He had half drawn his pistol, when a cold ring of iron was laid against his cheek.

Turning, he beheld Billy the Kid sitting on the seat by his side. The young outlaw had in the confusion ascended unperceived to the box, and now sat with cocked revolver pointed at his head.

"Surrender, sir!" said the Kid in his sharp, clear tones; "if you make an effort of resistance, I will shoot you dead in you[r] tracks."

The driver now knowing his danger, concluded it would be best to remain quiet. He was acquainted with Billy, and knew his deadly character.

For once, the robbery was effected without bloodshed.

The coach had been stopped in a dark mountain pass, and was instantly surrounded by a dozen ruffians.

Two or three torches were lighted and the passengers ordered to alight. The mail bags were ripped open, and money taken from them. Then two or three express packages containing money.

Among the passengers was a dark-eyed girl, from eighteen to twenty years of age. She was beautiful, and calmly awaited her fate. Others were crying and bewailing their sad fate, but she was calm. Some were begging to retain a portion of their treasure, but the robbers were relentless and every thing was taken.

As Billy was passing in front of the young lady he paused and gazed at her sharply.

"Nettie—Nettie Jones," he said, "is that you?"

"It is," she said, with a smile, extending her pure innocent hand, to grasp the blood-stained palm of the outlaw. 'This is Billy the Kid, who was once in Silver City."

"Yes, who was in jail over there," he replied, "and whom you aided to escape. Nettie, I am glad I have met you; these men are all mine, and you shall be my queen."

The beautiful face turned pale at this assertion, and she began to implore him to allow her to go on. She offered every valuable she had, and promised to send him more.

"No, no, my dear," he responded, "you are the richest jewel I could find, I will give you up for none."

"Oh, Billy, for Heaven's sake, for the kindness I once rendered you, allow me to go."

The Kid swore Nettie should be his wife, and when the stage rolled on, she was left behind with the outlaws.

CHAPTER XI. CAPTURE AND ESCAPE

The last atrocious act of Billy the Kid aroused the public against him more than all the murders he had committed. Pat Garret, Deputy Sheriff of Lincoln County, organized a posse to meet the desperadoes who were being chased by a body of citizens, under Jones, of Silver City, determined on the recapture of his daughter Nettie.

The bandits were so closely pursued that Nettle escaped, wandered for two days in the forest and prairie, and was found by her father's party, half famished and insane. She was taken home, but died in a few weeks from a fever, brought on by ill-treatment and exposure. Finding that the outlaws were encamped in a small bottom, Pat Garret descended on them one night

His men were furious, and poured in a fearful volley, which killed half the outlaws. Tom O'Fallaher was among the slain, and Billy the Kid made prisoner.

"You infamous black-souled murderer," said Garret, as he put the irons on his prisoner, "you shall swing for some of your devilment."

"Never fear," said the Kid; "they dare not harm me. I have too many friends in New Mexico for them to permit me to suffer death. We will escape."

Upon his arrest, the Kid promptly applied to Chisum, whom he had of late been fighting, and various other persons, for aid. But for once the young murderer found himself deserted by all. Even the romantic old Lew Wallace failed to come to his relief. He was taken by Pat Garret to Mesilla, where he was tried, found guilty of murder in the first degree, and sentenced to be hanged in the town of Lincoln.

One beautiful May-day the town of Lincoln was thrown into a state of excitement, by the information that the notorious outlaw, Billy the Kid, was in the village.

Numbers flocked to see him, and none could believe that the pale-looking boy, with his mild blue eyes, delicate frame, and sweet, sad face, was the noted outlaw and desperado.

Billy was under a strong guard, heavily ironed, and in charge of Deputy-Sheriff Bell.

"Is that little fellow the great outlaw?" asked one citizen of another.

"He is, and he is terrible."

"Bah! that little cuss [never] hurt anybody!" said a big bully from Texas.

"He is the most dangerous man in all New Mexico," said a by-stander who had known Billy.

"That poor little fellow going to be hanged?" sighed a lady, as she paused to look upon him.

"Yes," answered Bell, who had Billy in charge. "He is a monster, and has been condemned to suffer death."

"Oh, dear me! do let him go! He is so young, so beautiful to die."

The officer smiled, and said that was something he could not do. "You might appeal to the *governor* though," he added, with some contempt. "He pardoned him once, and might do so again."

The lady, not understanding the meaning of the officer's expression, turned to a neighbor to express her sympathy for the poor little fellow who was soon to suffer death.

In the meanwhile the doomed youth had been sitting on the portico of an old house with an armed guard near.

"I can convey him to the jail," said Deputy Sheriff Bell to the guard. "There is no danger of any one attempting to rescue him."

"But he is so desperate, will you not be afraid of him?" asked one of the guard.

"Afraid of that little fellow, no," replied the deputy sheriff with a laugh. "Why, I could hold him if he should attempt to escape, even if he was free."

"We can go with you, if necessary," said one of the guard.

"It is but a block to the jail, and will not be necessary," was the assuring answer of Bell.

"Then keep your eye peeled," said one of the guard as they both wended their way toward a saloon.

"Never fear," was Bell's answer, with a light laugh.

The prisoner sat, during the discourse, between the officer and guards, apparently indifferent, yet drinking in every word. He formed a resolution that eclipsed the most daring act of any desperado on earth.

"Come, Billy," said the deputy, "we must go around to your new quarters."

The Kid arose apparently with some reluctance, descended from the porch, and started with Bell out into the street.

As soon as the street was reached, he turned upon Bell with the ferocity of a tiger, struck him over the head with his handcuffs such a blow as to confuse and stun him. The Kid then, manacled as he was, snatched a pistol from Bell's belt, and shot him dead.

The shot was heard by Robert Ohlinger, who was a deputy United States marshal, and who had been a member of Turner's posse.

No sooner had the Kid shot Bell than he armed himself with the deputy's double-barreled shot-gun and revolver.

Robert Ohlinger with gun in hand, came running around the corner of the house to see what had happened.

The Kid, seeing him coming, coolly cocked one barrel of the shot-gun, and cried:

"Hello, Bob!"

Ohlinger paused a second, thunderstruck in amazement. That moment's delay cost him his life.

Bang! went the shot-gun in the hands of the Kid, and a whole charge of buckshot was poured into the unfortunate man's heart.

Thus in thirty minutes, ironed as he was, the young demon had committed two murders.

The people who witnessed the daring act were paralyzed with terror. His daring and audacity was not over yet.

The young monster then went back to the portico of the old house, where the dead men had been guarding him, and defied the town. No one dared oppose him, or make any effort toward his recapture.

He made one man knock his irons off, and covering another with the death-dealing shot-gun, ordered him to saddle a horse that was standing in the street This done, he deliberately walked out, mounted, and galloped out of town, in the presence of the whole population.

CHAPTER XII. THE END OF THE KID

So desperate, remarkable and successful had been the plan of escape of Billy the Kid, that the more superstitious regarded him as immortal. Wonderful stories were afloat as to his vanishing into air, and that soldiers had driven their sabers through his body without injuring him.

He was called a wizard, a spook, a devil, anything that was supernatural and horrible.

So common had become the belief that he could not be killed by a bullet of lead, that some of the hunters run bullets of silver to shoot him.

But there was one who did not believe the Kid was immortal.

That man was Deputy-Sheriff Pat Garret, the only man in New Mexico who had been able to capture him, since he had commenced his wild, daredevil career.

The Kid had sworn to kill Pat at sight, on account of the death of Tom O'Fallaher, his partner.

Garret knew that the little demon would make his threat good, unless some means were taken to prevent it.

He must either leave the country, or kill the Kid. Pat had no thought of doing the former. He was a man of too much nerve and personal pride to think of such a thing. He bid farewell to his family, and armed with a short repeating rifle and a pair of revolvers, set out to find the Kid. A meeting was sure to be bloody, and end in the death of one or the other.

One afternoon, as Pat was walking along the hanks of a creek, he met a Mexican with whom he was acquainted, named Riaz.

"Senor Riaz, do you know where the Kid is?"

The Mexican smiled, and asked:

"Does Senor Americano want to see the Kid?"

"I do."

"What for does the Senor want to see him?"

"Riaz, we are friends; by telling me where I can find Billy the Kid, you will save my life. I must be where I can see him, and he not me."

"Billy is one desperate man; he kills all who tells on him. If he finds out I give you information, he'll kill me."

"He shall never know it, Riaz. You are familiar with the Kid, and know where he will be likely to sleep to-night."

The Mexican reflected a moment and then said:

"He sleeps to-night at the house of Pete Maxwell."

Pete Maxwell's house, or ranch, was a rough adobe affair, with earthen floor, near Fort Sumner.

This was on the 14th day of August, 1881. Pat further ascertained from the Mexican that the Kid never went near the house until midnight, and that he left before daylight in order to avoid detection.

A short time before midnight Garret went to Maxwell's house, and found the door open, but the building deserted. He went in and concealed himself in the dark corner, behind Maxwell's bed.

Here he waited with breathless anxiety, resting upon one knee, his rifle cocked.

A little after midnight the door of the house opened and the Kid entered.

Instantly discovering, in spite of the darkness, that some one was in the room, he leveled his pistols at Garret, demanding in Spanish:

"*Quien est? Quien est?*"

The delay of asking was fatal.

"Crack!" went Pat Garret's rifle, before the sentences were fairly out of his mouth. The bullet pierced his heart, and Billy the Kid, the terror of New Mexico, lay a lifeless corpse, while his blood dyed the dirt floor of Pete Maxwell's dark adobe hut.

Thus died the youngest and greatest desperado ever known in the world's history.

A reporter for one of the Western papers, who knew him, says:

"In personal appearance the Kid was anything but a desperado, or monster. He was very small and slender, being but about five feet two inches high, and not weighing over one hundred and twenty pounds. He had a plain, pleasant face, with thin sharp features, blue eyes, and light hair. He was calculated to make friends, and, strange as it may seem, left many who sincerely mourned his death. One of the best men in the Territory said:

"I couldn't help feeling sorry, when I heard that boy was killed."

"He was a splendid horseman and a dead shot. At his death he was nearly twenty-two years of age."

With proper culture, Billy the Kid might have made his mark in the world. His wonderful energy and remarkable bravery, had they been directed in the right channel, might have placed him high on the pinnacle of fame, instead of giving him an early and ignominious grave.

(THE END.)

CHAPTER TWO

A True Sketch of "Billy the Kid's" Life

Charles A. Siringo

Hot on the heels of Don Jenardo's *True Life,* a small posse of dime novels about Billy the Kid galloped into print. The first, its preface dated July 15, 1881, by its author, Edmond Fable, was *Billy the Kid, the New Mexican Outlaw; or, The Bold Bandit of the West,* which claimed on its title page to be "A True and Impartial History of the Greatest of American Outlaws, His Adventures and Crimes Committed in the West, The History of an Outlaw Who Killed a Man for Every Year in His Life." Published in Denver, it appeared on newsstands during the first week of September 1881. Later in the year it was followed by John W. Morrison's *The Life of Billy the Kid, a Juvenile Outlaw.* Early in 1882, Morrison's Sensational Series published three more titles: *Billy the "Kid" and His Girl; Billy the "Kid" and the Cowboys;* and *Billy the "Kid" No. 2.* These were the "yellow-covered cheap novels" containing the "thousand false statements" that Pat Garrett claimed he had been impelled to correct by writing the "true" story in his *Authentic Life of Billy the Kid.*

In point of fact, the dime novels were little more than ephemera; Garrett's book was a complete failure and probably sold only a few hundred copies. It was not until 1885, with the publication of Charles A. Siringo's *A Texas Cow Boy,* that the Kid's metamorphosis from small-time rustler to boy bandit king took place. A huge bestseller, *A Texas Cow Boy* was reprinted in many different editions and remained continuously in print for more than forty years (according to Siringo, a million copies were sold during his lifetime, chiefly by hawkers on railroad trains). While much of his account faithfully follows the Upson-Garrett version, there are enough variations, notably his garbled version of a story about the Kid's kindness to a sick man (an apocryphal tale probably based upon an experience related by John Meadows) and the eyewitness information from the Tularosa "ditch war" prisoners, to suggest his having done a little, albeit inaccurate, research while adding some flourishes of his own, such as the stock black soldier who talks like the end man in a minstrel show or the "fact" that Olinger and Bell deserved hanging even more than Billy did.

More than perhaps any other writer, Siringo was responsible for disseminating to a wide audience many of the undying myths associated with the life of Billy the Kid—that he killed a black soldier in Fort Union and a blacksmith in Silver City, that he became a fugitive "adept at cards and horse stealing," that he swore vengeance against the murderers of Tunstall (all of whom he had killed before the war ended), that he played the piano during the siege of the McSween house, and all the rest of it. These "facts" in Charlie Siringo's unpretentious little book would remain unchallenged for almost half a century. Some people still believe them.

[T]he following sketch of [the "Kid's"] short but eventful life was gleaned from himself, Ash Upson and others. The circumstance connected with his death I got from the lips of John W. Poe, who was with Garrett when he fired the fatal shot.

Billy Bonney, alias the "Kid" was born in New York City, November the 23rd, 1859; and at the age of ten he, in company with his mother and stepfather, Antrim, landed in the Territory of New Mexico.

Mr. Antrim, shortly after his arrival in the Territory opened up a restaurant in Santa Fe, the Capitol, and one of his boarders was the jovial old Ash Upson, my informant, who was then interested in a newspaper at that place.

Often when Ash was too busily engaged about his office to go to dinner, Mrs. Antrim would send it by her little merry-eyed boy, Billy, who was the pride of her life.

Finally Ash sold out and moved to Silver City, which was then booming on account of its rich mines. And it wasn't long until Mr. Antrim followed and opened up another eating house there, with Ash as a boarder again. Thus it will be seen that my informant was just the same as one of the family for quite a while.

The "Kid's" first man, as told to me by himself, was a Negro soldier, in Ft. Union, whom he shot in self-defense.

His next killing was a young blacksmith in Silver City whom he killed in a personal encounter, but not according to law, hence it was this scrape that first caused him to become an outcast; driven from pillar to post, out of reach of a kind mother's influence.

It was a cold stormy night when he, after kissing his mother's pale cheeks for the last time on this earth, rode out into the darkness, headed west for the wilds of Arizona, where he soon became an adept at cards and horse stealing.

Charles A. Siringo, Boise, Idaho, in 1907. Probably more than any other early writer, cowboy detective Siringo was responsible for propagating the "legend" of Billy the Kid. J. Evetts Haley Collection, Haley History Center, Midland, Texas.

He finally landed in the City of Chihuahua, Old Mexico, with a pocket full of Arizona gold. Here he led a gay life until one night when a bullet from his trusty revolver sent a rich Mexican monte-dealer to his long and happy home.

The next we hear of him is in the friendly land of Texas, where he remained in retirement until the spring of 1876, when he drifted across the lonely Guadalupe mountains into Lincoln County, New Mexico, then the outlaw's Paradise.

At Lincoln, the county seat, he hired out as a cow boy to a young Englishman by the name of Tunstall.

In the spring of '78 Mr. Tunstall was killed by a mob, headed by a fellow named Morton, from the Reo Pecos.

The "Kid" hearing of his employer's foul murder, rode into Lincoln from the Tunstall ranch to learn the full particulars concerning the killing. He and the young Englishman were warm friends and before leaving the ranch he swore vengeance against every one of the murderers.

Arriving in the Mexican Plaza of Lincoln the "Kid" learned that Morton and crowd had pulled back to the Reo Pecos. So he joined a crowd composed of the following named parties: R. M. Bruer, J. G. Skurlock, Charlie Bowder, Henry Brown, Frank McNab, Fred Wayt, Sam Smith, Jim French, McClosky and Johnny Middleton, and started in pursuit. This was just the beginning of the "bloody Lincoln County war" which you have all read so much about. But it is said that the "Kid" killed every man connected with the murder of his friend before the war ended.

Billy was caught in a great many close places during the six months' bloody encounter, but always managed to escape, as though possessed of a charmed life. There is one of his hair-brea[d]th escapes I wish to relate, just to show how cool he was in time of danger.

He and about a dozen of his men were housed up at lawyer McSween's in Lincoln, when thirty-five of the Seven River "warriors" and two companies of United States Soldiers under command of Col. Dudly of the Ninth Cavalry, surrounded and set the large two-story building on fire, determined to capture or kill the young outlaw.

The house was burning on the south side from whence the wind came, and as the fire advanced the little crowd would move further north, into an adjoining room. There was a fine piano in the parlor, the property of Mrs. McSween, who was absent, and on this the "Kid" played during the whole time, "just to amuse the crowd outside" he said.

John Henry Tunstall, San Francisco, February 26, 1876. Author's Collection.

Finally everything was wrapped in flames but the little kitchen which stood adjoining the main building on the north, but still the coarse music continued to sail forth out onto the night air.

At last the blaze began to stick its fiery tongues into the kitchen. Then the music ceased, and the little band, headed by the "Kid" made a bold dash for liberty, amidst the thick shower of hot lead. The balance can be described best by quoting a negro soldier's words, he being nearest the kitchen door when the dash was made: "I jes' tell you white folkses dis nigger was for getting away from dah, kase dat Billy-goat was shooten wid a gun and two six-pistols all bofe at de same time."

The "Kid" and Tom O'Phalliard were the only ones who came out of this scrape unhurt. Mr. McSween, owner of the burned building was among the killed. He had nine bullets in his body.

Late that fall when the war had ended, "Kid" and the remainder of his little gang stole a bunch of horses from the Seven River warriors, whom they had just got through fighting with and drove them across the Plains to the Texas Panhandle, at Tascosa on the Canadian, where they were soon disposed of at good figures.

After lying around the little town of Tascosa for nearly a month, squandering their surplus wealth on poor whisky and Mexican women, they, with the exception of Fred Wayt and Henry Brown who struck east for the Chickisaw nation where the former's mother and two half-breed sisters lived, pulled back to Lincoln County, New Mexico, to continue their lawlessness.

From that time on, the "Kid" made a specialty of stealing cattle and horses, although he would kill a man now and then, for what he supposed to be a just cause. Let it be said right here that the "Kid" was not the cruel hearted wretch that he was pictured out to be in the scores of yellow-back novels, written about him. He was an outlaw and maybe a very wicked youth, but then he had some good qualities which, now that he is no more, he should be credited with. It has been said and written that he would just as soon shoot an innocent child as a mule-eared rabbit. Now this is all wrong, for he was noted as being kind to the weak and helpless; there is one case in particular which I can prove:

A man, now a highly respected citizen of White Oaks, was lying at the point of death in Ft. Sumner, without friends or money, and a stranger, when the "Kid," who had just come into town from one of his raids, went to his rescue, on hearing of his helpless condition; the sick man had been placed in an old out-house on a pile of sheep skins. The "Kid" hired a team and hauled him to Las Vegas, a distance of over a hundred miles, himself, where he could receive care and medical aid. He also paid the doctor and board bills for a month, besides putting a few dollars in money in the sick man's hand as he bid him good bye.

This circumstance was told to me by the sick man himself, who at the time was hale and hearty, on hearing of the "Kid's" death. While relating it the tears chased one another down his manly cheeks, to the end, at which time he pulled out a large red handkerchief and wiped them away.

After the "Kid's" capture at Stinking Springs, he was lodged in jail at Santa Fe, and the following spring taken to Mesilla, county seat of Dona Ana county, and tried before Judge Bristol for the murder of Sheriff Brady, during the Lincoln county war.

He was sentenced to be taken to Lincoln, and hung on the 13th day of May. On the 21st day of April he was turned over to Pat. Garrett, who, being sheriff, was to see that the law was carried out.

There being no jail in Lincoln, Garrett used his office, which was up-stairs in the two-story court house, to guard the prisoner in. Robert Ollinger and J. W. Bell, two men who should have been hung before William Bonney was born—judging from reliable reports, were secured to do the guarding.

The morning of April 28th, Garrett was making preparations to go to White Oaks, when he told the guards to be very watchful as the pris-oner, not having but a few more days to live, might make a desperate effort to escape.

Ollinger who hated the "Kid," they having fought against one another in the Lincoln County war, spoke up and said: "Don't worry Pat, we'll watch him like a goat." So saying he unlocked the armory, a small closet in the wall, and getting out his double-barrel shot gun, put eighteen buck-shot in each barrel. Then setting it back, remarked, at the same time glancing over in the opposite corner at the "Kid" who was sitting on a stool, shackled and hand-cuffed: "I bet the man that gets them will feel it!" The "Kid" gave one of his hopeless smiles and said: "*You* might be the one to get them yourself."

After Garrett left, the two guards had five more prisoners to look after. But they were allowed to wear their pistols, for fear of being mobbed by a crowd of Tulerosa Mexicans who had chased them into Lincoln. They had given themselves up to Garrett more for protection than anything else. They had killed four Tulerosa Mexicans, in a hand to hand fight, the day before, hence the mob being after them. One of those prisoners was a young Texan by the name of Chas. Wall, who had received two almost fatal bullet wounds in the fracas of the day before. It was from this young man, Mr. Wall, whom I became personally acquainted with afterwards, that I received my information from, in regard to the "Kid's" escape, etc.

About five o'clock, that evening, Ollinger took the armed prisoners across the street, to the hotel, to supper, leaving Bell to guard the "Kid."

According to what the "Kid" told after his escape, Bell became interested in a newspaper, and while thus engaged, he slipped one of his hand-cuffs, which he could have done long before if the right chance had been presented, and made a leap towards his guard, using the hand-cuff as a weapon.

Bell almost fainted on looking up from his paper. He broke for the door after receiving a stunning lick over the head with the hand-cuff. But the "Kid" was right at his heels; and when he got to the door and started down stairs the "Kid" reached forward and jerked the frightened man's pistol which still hung at his side, he having never made an effort to pull it. Bell fell dead out in the back yard, near the foot of the stairs, with a bullet hole through his body.

"Kid" then hobbled, or jumped, his legs being still shackled, to the armory and kicking the door open secured Ollinger's shot-gun, which contained the eighteen buck-shot in each barrel. Then springing to an open window, in an adjoining room, under which the other guard would have to come to get up stairs, he waited patiently for his "meat," as he termed it.

He hadn't waited long though when Ollinger, who had started on hearing the shooting, came trotting under the window. "Kid" called in a pleasant voice: "Hello, Bob!" Robert looked up, but just in time to receive eighteen buck-shot in his breast. The "Kid" then walked out onto the balcony, fronting on Main street, and emptied the other barrel into the dead body of Ollinger. Then breaking the gun in two over the balcony railing he threw the pieces at the corpse, saying: "Take that you s— of a b-h! You will never follow me with that gun again!"

This proceeding was witnessed by nearly a hundred citizens nearly all of whom sympathized with the "Kid," although they didn't approve of his lawbreaking. There was a few of his bitter enemies in town, though, but they soon hunted their holes, each one trying to pull the hole in after him, so as to be hid from the outside world.

After being supplied from the armory with a good Winchester, two colts "45" pistols and four belts of cartridges, he ordered a file thrown up to him, which was done without ceremony; he also ordered the deputy County Clerk's pony and saddle brought out into the street, which was also done in double quick time.

The shackles being filed in two he danced around on the balcony quite a while, as though he was the happiest mortal on earth.

As he went to mount, the firey pony, which was being held out in the street, and which had once belonged to him, broke loose and ran back to the stable. But he was soon brought back, and this time held until the "Kid" was securely seated in the saddle.

After bidding everybody in sight adieu he rode slowly towards the setting sun, the Winchester still gripped in his right hand. But when he arrived at the end of Main street he pulled off his hat, and waving it over his head, yelled at the top of his voice: "Three cheers for Billy the Kid!" Then putting spurs to the pony he dashed out of sight.

After traveling about four miles west he turned north-east across the Captain mountains, towards Ft. Sumner.

About the first of July, Garrett, who hadn't hunted much for "Kid" since his escape, received a letter from a Mr. Brazil, who lived near Ft. Sumner, informing him of the "Kid's" presence in that vicinity.

Garrett after answering the letter, asking Mr. Brazil to meet him at a certain spot on a certain night, secured the services of John W. Poe, one of the whitest and bravest men in the Territory, and taking his Deputy, "Kip" McKinnie along, struck out for "Sumner" to capture the Kid if possible.

The little party of three arrived at the mouth of Tayban Arroyo, on the Reo Pecos, where Garrett had written Brazil to meet him, about dark on the night of July 13th. They waited there all night and Mr. Brazil failed to show up.

Mr. Poe being a stranger in that country, and not known in the Post, Garrett sent him to the town, a distance of five miles, to try and learn, by keeping his ears open and mouth shut, of the "Kid's" whereabouts, while he and "Kip" would meet him at "Sunny-side" a ranch seven miles above "Sumner."

About sundown Poe met his two companions, at Sunnyside, but was no wiser than when he had left them. Garrett then concluded that they would all ride into the town and if Peet Maxwell was at home he could maybe get some information from him.

Arriving in an old orchard back of the Maxwell mansion about ten o'clock that night, they tied their horses and crawled around to the front of the building.

There was a long porch on the south side of the house and about midway was Peet's room, the door of which opened onto the porch. Garrett knew where the room was, and there they headed for.

On arriving in the front yard opposite the door of Peet's room, which was wide open, the night being very hot, Garrett told his companions to lie flat down in the grass while he slipped into the room.

He found Peet asleep, but awakened him. He then laid down by the side of Peet, and they began talking.

Back of the Maxwell house was an adobe cabin in which lived an old Mexican Peon. The Mexican had gone to bed, and by a greasy looking table sat the "Kid," who had just come in from the hills. He had pulled off his boots to rest his tired feet, and was glancing over a newspaper.

Throwing down the paper he told the Peon to get up and cook him some supper, as he was very hungry. Being told that there was no meat in the house he picked up a butcher-knife which was lying on the table, and said: "I will go and get Peet to rustle me a piece." He started without either hat or boots.

While walking along on the porch, butcher-knife in hand, he discovered the two men out in the grass, and, drawing his pistol, asked in Mexican: Quien es? Quien es? (Who's there? Who's there?) Not getting an answer, the boys thinking he was one of the Peons, he backed into the door of Peet's room, and then turning towards the bed, which was to the left of the door, he asked: "Peet, who is that out there?" Not receiving an answer again, and being suspicious of some one being in bed with Peet, he began backing towards the opposite side of the room, at the same time asking: "Who in the h—l is in here? Who in the h—l is in here?"

Peet whispered to Garrett: "That's him, Pat." And by that time the "Kid" had backed until the light shone full upon him, through one of the south windows, giving Garrett a good chance to make a center shot.

Bang! Bang! went Garrett's pistol. The first bullet took effect in the "Kid's" heart, while the next one struck the ceiling.

The remains of what was once a fond mother's darling were buried next day in the old dilapidated Military Cemetery, without a murmur, except from one, a pretty young half-breed Mexican damsel, whose tears, no doubt, has dampened the lonely grave more than once.

Thus ended the life of William H. Bonney, one of the coolest-headed, and most daring young outlaws, that ever lived. He had dwelt upon this earth just 21 years, seven months and 21 days.

CHAPTER THREE

Billy the Kid: The True Story of a Western "Bad Man"

Emerson Hough

Emerson Hough was born in Newton, Iowa, on June 28, 1857. He received a bachelor of philosophy degree at the University of Iowa in 1880 and, at the urging of his father, read law and was admitted to the bar in 1883. Following an unhappy romance with a fickle young woman, he decided to try moving to New Mexico. He joined a law firm at White Oaks, where he also worked as a reporter on the town's newspaper, the *Golden Era*. In 1886 he returned to the Midwest, working on newspapers in Iowa, Ohio, and Kansas while also submitting articles on hunting and fishing to outdoors magazines. By 1889, when he was appointed manager of the Chicago office of *Forest and Stream Magazine*, he already had a regular column in the *Saturday Evening Post*. His first book, *The Singing Mouse Stories*, was not a success, but two years later, in 1897, his fortunes changed when *The Story of the Cowboy* appeared. In 1902, his greatest commercial success, a historical novel called *The Mississippi Bubble*, was published. He followed it in 1905 with *Heart's Desire*, a novel inspired by his sojourn in New Mexico.

It was at this juncture that he took another shot at telling the story of Billy the Kid (the first had been in a chapter titled "Wars on the Range" in *The Story of the Cowboy*). It was one of the more unsympathetic essays that followed Garrett's *Authentic Life* and Siringo's *Texas Cow Boy*, and it was all the more surprisingly inaccurate in view of the fact that Hough had known many of the participants in the Lincoln County War personally, including Pat Garrett. But even with Garrett at his elbow, he preferred folklore to fact.

Hough would go on to later write *The Story of the Outlaw*, which corrected some (although by no means all) of the more blatant howlers in this piece, including the tale of the Kid stabbing a man to death when he was fourteen, or killing seven Mexicans "just to see them kick"; and the claim that four hundred men were killed in the Lincoln County War, and that although "all sorts of promises of pardon were offered to him," the Kid turned them all down. He renders Olinger's name as "Orrendorf" and Chisum's as "Chisholm," and he locates Billy's

61

grave at Las Cruces and the Maxwell house in the Peñasco valley south of Lincoln. His Billy is an unrepentant monster who "killed because he liked to do so. By the time he was sixteen, the groan of a victim, the sight of his writhings upon the ground, had ceased to affect him. He was a boy, but what a terrible boy! With the down not yet upon his face, he was a murderer time and time again. Not all the wild West has ever produced his equal in sheer inborn savagery." They don't write 'em like that anymore.

There is a legend of home and mother connected with the earlier stages of the saga of Billy the Kid, perhaps the most thoroughly bad of all the bad men ever known in the really bad times of the West. History has it, with what accuracy let us not inquire too closely, that when Billy the Kid was yet a boy, not more than fourteen years of age, some one addressed to his mother a disrespectful remark. This was in Arizona, and at a time when resentments were swift and deadly. The story goes that the boy drew a knife, fatally stabbed the man, and then fled the country. From that time Billy the Kid became an outlaw, and an outlaw he remained for the seven years which completed the span of his short life.

To-day there is a little lowly heap of earth located at Las Cruces, New Mexico. To the curious stranger some idle native may, now and again, point out this little grave and explain, with a certain pride, that Las Cruces possesses the final resting place of the worst bad man that ever infested the Southwestern border. An ancient Mexican, who sometimes shows this grave to visitors, once made the cautious remark regarding its occupant that, had he lived, he would probably have turned out to be a bad man.

"And how old was Billy when he died?" asked one curious stranger.

"Twenty-one, señor," replied the ancient. "He was but twenty-one. He died, almost one might say, before he fully began to live."

"You say he was bad?" remarked another stranger.

"He is said to have killed many men."

"How many? How many, *amigo,* had this man killed at the time he himself died?"

"He had killed," replied the ancient Mexican, "twenty-one men, one for each year of his age, may the saints defend us," said the Mexican. "He was a good man, and very kind to poor people. Yet, had he lived, he might, according to the opinions of some, have turned into a bad man."

It is true, in the opinion of some, indeed of many, Billy the Kid might have become a fairly dangerous sort of person had he lived to attain mature years. The record of his "killings" is correctly given by the ancient Mexican. He had, indeed, killed twenty-one men in admitted record at the time of his own death. Most bad men develop later in life. There might be a twinge of regret, from a philosophical standpoint, that Billy did not live longer and more fully work out the problem which seemed to be assigned to him by fate.

Such a career as that of Billy the Kid could only have been the product of a peculiar environment. In this work-a-day epoch of the world we can scarcely understand or appreciate the peculiarities of that environment, or realize that it existed within the borders of American civilization not more than a double decade ago. Yet it was less than twenty years ago that Billy the Kid found his end. It was not twenty-five years ago that the vivid and bloody drama, in which he held the centre of the stage, was finding its enactment under the serene blue sky of Arizona and New Mexico.

Consider a land still Spanish in all the essential elements of its civilization, a land not yet acquainted with any modern transportation, a land more distant from the heart of America than is Central Africa today. Imagine a population imbued with all the old Spanish disregard for human life—a disregard not paralleled even in the wildest of the half-savage communities of the Northern cattle trail and mining ranges; a population composed partly of Indians, partly of Mexican half-breeds, or "Greasers," in some part of pure Mexican blood, and in the dominant minority made up of those vigorous Anglo-Saxon souls, half lawless and all reckless, who have ever represented America upon the frontier to the limit of the time when we might be said to possess a frontier. What brought the American population to the Southwestern frontier twenty-five years ago it would be bootless now to ask. There were a thousand reasons for a thousand men. The reckless, the brave, the courageous, the desperate, the careless, the criminal—all these blended indifferently in the heterogeneous mass which represented the society of the time and region. Among them all there were but few unused to scenes of strife and bloodshed, or unprepared to render the stern accounting of weapons in the settlement of any difficulty with a fellow-man. Of women there were but few entitled to the name of womanhood, and of civilization, as we understand it, there was nothing. Churches and schools were unknown. There was no social fabric. These wild men had left the settlements, had broken away from the compact of society, and had founded a new, wild land of their own, where they lived each for himself, each sufficient unto himself, and all scorning the surrender of personal rights to the social machine. Of courts there were none worthy of the name.

No man who has spent his life in civilized communities can have any idea of the character of such a place and time, where there is no social body, no machinery of the law, no personal surrender. Therefore, we must apply to the problems of that time standards entirely foreign to those with which we are accustomed to weigh the problems of our own time and place. In the Southwest of that time, it was literally every man for himself. No one could expect protection for himself or his property except as he was able to exact it. Physical indifference to danger was the price of one's continuance upon that soil. A coward had no footing there. Wild, lawless, riotous, ignorant of restraint and scornful of any law, the dominant population of the Southwest lived on after its own fashion, a fashion which we shall never see again in America, and of which, even at the time, America remained in total ignorance. The railroad, it is true, had passed through the sandy deserts on its transcontinental flight; yet for hundreds of miles on each side of the railroad there reached and rolled out the low, dark mountain chains, the wide river valleys, the sandy, brown, undulating foot-hills, mile after mile, league after league; an unknown land, smiling, calm, and with a fascination all its own, the fascination of sheer savagery. To-day, were one an absconding bank cashier, or the murderer of a friend, it is in these low, brown foot-hills, and in the piñon-covered slopes that he might best search out a hiding-place.

Into this little-known region, subsequent to the Civil War, there pressed a few men, the skirmish line of those prospectors who have conquered the Rocky range, and the advance guard of those hardy cattlemen who have subdued the lower reaches of the cattle lands. All through the Civil War men of the Southwest were too busy to take account of their flocks and herds. The cattle multiplied all over the land, all over Texas, New Mexico, in a thousand flats and valleys of the Southwest. Then the Americans, tired of killing each other, went back to the shops and farms, the flocks and herds. Millions of unclaimed cattle ranged an unmeasured area in the Southwest. The best man was he who could, with his own branding iron, put his claim upon the greatest number of these "mavericks." A cow had little value in those days, and the round-ups were inexact. It might have been that such big stockholders as the Chisholms, in southeastern New Mexico, had a herd of forty, fifty, or sixty thousand cattle. They themselves did not know. The stranger journeying on foot, or in the saddle, made little question if he needed meat. He shot the fattest yearling he could find, and no one cared, for there was enough for all. It was a land of plenty, a land of inexactness, careless of metes and bounds, not knowing, and indeed not needing, any law.

It was in this land, a land where law was still unknown, and where human life had no value, that Billy the Kid set up his own home, after that time when he first found the brand of Cain upon his brow. He fled, as the story goes, into old Mexico, but left there for reasons similar to that which first caused his flight. Then he worked north and east into the wide and unknown regions of New Mexico, more especially that Pecos Valley which was for so long time the empire of the free riders of the far Southwest.

Now, by what inner workings of the human mind let us not seek to ask, Billy the Kid all at once found himself past the point of all that consideration which usually enters into the plans of man-killing man.

We may theorize or speculate as we like regarding the evolution of the bad man. Scientists may tell us of degenerates and that sort of thing to-day. At the time of Billy the Kid, the title of degenerate was not yet known. Had you asked any citizen of the far Southwest why Billy the Kid was as he was, he would probably have told you that it was because he was born so. He was not embittered by any early disappointments. He was never crossed in love, and, indeed, of love in its true form he was perhaps all his life in ignorance. He was an animal, pure and simple; an animal born with a cat soul, blood-thirsty, loving to kill. There you have it, and as to the reasons for it, let others answer.

Billy the Kid killed because he liked to do so. By the time he was sixteen, the groan of a victim, the sight of his writhings upon the ground, had ceased to affect him. He was a boy, but what a terrible boy! With the down not yet upon his face, he was a murderer time and time again. Not all the wild West has ever produced his equal in sheer inborn savagery. Once he and some friends, in the old-time Lincoln County War, rode upon a party of Mexicans who had camped near the trail not far from Seven Rivers. There were seven Mexicans in the party, all inoffensive, all strangers, and all certainly innocent of any crime whatever against the Kid and his companions. Yet the latter as they rode by drew their revolvers, and calmly and with exacting skill shot down every member of the party. Questioned as to his motive for this act, Billy the Kid later replied that they had shot the Mexicans "just to see them kick." With a man like this, it is obvious that ordinary reasons and ordinary limitations fail. Surrounded by all the crude wealth that here lay to each man's hand, it was likely that Billy the Kid and the kindred souls whom he drew about him would soon fall to appropriating that which pleased them, rendering no account to any man. It seemed to them that they had fully as good right to the branded or unbranded cattle as the man who owned the branding iron; in which attitude, perhaps, they were not far from correct. To the cattleman, however, stern, hardy, and tenacious of that upon which he bad set his hands, this matter could not fail to have a different aspect.

Witness now that long and fearful Lincoln County War, one of the bloodiest wars, for its size, ever known in the history of mankind, and one regarding which there is less information obtainable of reliable sort than ever was known regarding any war on earth. In short, the cattlemen and the cattle thieves drew apart into two factions. Each hired men for its cohorts, the cattlemen paying five dollars a day, with expenses and ammunition; the cattle thieves, for the most part, paying nothing at all, except the hope of division of rewards in the day of victory. It came about that no man who rode the range in New Mexico might tell the disposition of a stranger whom he chanced to encounter upon the trail. If you were for the thieves, and you chanced to be sure of the nature of your interlocutor, whom you knew also to be a thief, it was very well. But, suppose an employee of the cattlemen met a stranger on the trail, and that the stranger was so unlucky as to guess wrong, and declare that he was one of the party of Billy the Kid? It was his mistake, and he paid for it with his life.

Scores and scores of corpses, hundreds of them, nearly four hundred of them, as near as the tally could be made, dotted the piñon-covered slopes and the sandy brown foot-hills of New Mexico alone in this bloody Lincoln County War. Governor Lew Wallace of New Mexico tried to put an end to this war. It was said that he ordered out troops and asked them to take a cannon or so down into the Pecos Valley and so stop these riots. This talk of the cannon caused Homeric merriment among all the lawless souls of the bloody Pecos.

By the time he was eighteen years of age, Billy the Kid was a king. He had at his back a score of retainers, each man a perfect horseman and a splendid shot with the revolver. They rode as they listed. They needed no robber cave, no mountain fastness. They lived openly upon the land, stopping where they liked and eating as they pleased. The Mexican women scared their children with the name of Billy the Kid. As for the Kid himself and his party, they quartered themselves as they liked at every ranch where they found it convenient to stop. The answer to any argument offered was a pistol shot. Yet they gave rude largess out of other people's goods. They laid the land under tribute, and they kept it under terror. They needed no habitation or occupation. America never saw a situation so savagely remote from all human obligations as this which the Kid imposed upon his provinces, from Las Vegas to El Paso, and even farther south, into the region tributary to the Spanish arms.

As to the personal doings of the Kid himself, their story would fill a book, indeed has filled more than one book of more or less veracious chronicle. Thus the centre of the Kid's realm might have been said to be in the neighborhood of White Oaks, in Lincoln County, a little mining community which was undertaking to make a living on the strength of one or two rich discoveries of gold; which, however, rapidly pinched out as the veins were followed down. Around this White Oaks region there stretched a large area of country more or less suited for cattle-raising. The Kid and his companions found this region well enough to their liking, and they lived upon it, sweeping now here, now there, like a pack of hungry wolves, as their fancy or their needs dictated.

Perhaps there may still be traceable, in the country between the Pecos and the Rio Grande, something of the old tales, though such stories were writ upon wax in the frontier history of the West. You may, perhaps, still hear of that brave young man at White Oaks, who refused to do the bidding of the Kid's gang one night, and who was shot four or five times before he could get to his arms. Thus sorely wounded, he ran across the street to the tent where he lived, still seeking for his own weapon. He was pursued and shot down again, but with that terrible and vital refusal to submit to death which now and again shows itself among strong men stirred to rage, he would not yet give up to die. One of the gang trod upon his neck with his foot as he lay there upon the ground, and thrusting the muzzle of a Winchester rifle into his face, gave him the shot which finally ended a superb manhood. Or perhaps some ancient Mexican may show you, in the village of Lincoln, the little adobe building where the Kid and his gang were once besieged by the other side of the forces in the Lincoln County War. He may tell you how they fought from room to room and how at length they won escape. He may also show you, high up upon the mountain side which rises back of the court-house at Lincoln, a certain huge rock. Here, he will tell you, lay six long hours of a hot summer day a poor fellow who had his back broken by a shot from a needle gun held in the hands of one of the Kid's gang, within the adobe on the main street of Lincoln. The forces of the besiegers were scattered along the mountain side, and this poor, unknown soldier undertook to run from cover in an attempt to get behind this rock, whence he felt quite sure he could command the windows of the adobe. This and similar stories you may find, or at least could find, twenty years ago, at the time when the writer made his home in that locality. They may be glossed over now, or exaggerated, or palliated. Time does very much. But not all the years of all the time that ever is to be will disclose all the stories of the skeletons which lie, deep slumbering in their last sleep, among the piñon-covered hills.

One night the Kid's gang rode down into the village of White Oaks, then a straggling little camp, half canvas and half adobe. It had always seemed to them a diverting pastime to fire at the lights in the tents or houses as they rode swiftly down the street, and upon this evening they followed their usual custom. It chanced, however, that but a few days before there had come down from Kansas the first women ever seen in the camp, two females who, we may be sure, were frightened enough when they heard the crashing of the window panes and the rattling of the pistol shots without. The chivalry of American manhood now rebelled. It was determined that the women of the place must be protected.

Having had their sport, and consumed their whiskey as they liked, Billy the Kid and his gang rode rapidly out through the low hills toward the Pecos Valley. They were followed by a little party of citizens headed by a self-elected leader known as Carlyle. A few hours' ride from the town, the Kid and his band pulled up at a wayside ranch house where there was a well, the latter a rare thing in this arid region. They were besieged in this ranch house by Carlyle and his men, who drew a thin line about them as closely as the piñon trees offered shelter. Carlyle himself, having read of such things somewhere in the articles of war, resolved to carry a flag of truce up to the besieged and inquire what terms would be accepted. His handkerchief brought him safely to the door, and as he reached the door it was opened. He was caught by the wrist and jerked swiftly within. His friends never met him again alive.

Late in the afternoon, when every one was cold, hungry, and well-nigh exhausted in the besieging line, Carlyle attempted an escape. He sprang through a window and ran as hard as he could for cover. What hope had he before the steady muzzles which covered him as he ran? Hardly a shot fired after him missed him, and he fell dead in the sand in the shallow wheel tracks of the trail. The besieging army then went back to White Oaks, and the party of Billy the Kid, when they were ready, rode on upon their way.

One by one, one after another, the "killings" of Billy the Kid increased and multiplied. No one called them murders, for murder was a word unknown upon the border at that time. A shooting matter was sometimes called a "difficulty," but usually it was called a "killing," for shooting affairs practically always terminated in a fatal manner. The little pistols of the East were things unknown. The regulation forty-five-calibre, eight-inch barrel, single-action Colt's revolver was the universal weapon, and constant practice made every man practically master of a great degree of skill. With a pair of these heavy guns strapped low to his legs, a man in good practice in the swift pulling of the revolver made a dangerous antagonist to engage in any acrimonious argument. The victims of Billy the Kid rarely made much argument. Of him it was said that he always shot first and looked for the explanations afterward. Perhaps he killed a great many men under a misunderstanding of the facts. If so, it is not of record that the matter ever troubled his conscience. As to the law, he was the law. The theory of evolution—the survival of the quickest—that was the law of the far Southwest. Compared with this land, the doings of the collegiate northern ranges are as the transactions of babes and sucklings. If you seek a bloody country, search the Pecos, or among the piñons of the Capitans, the Sacramentos, the Oscuras, the Carrizos. Here there was an empire of crime and bloodshed which, for half a genera-tion, remained hidden and unknown to reading mankind. The telegraph wire, the printing press, the interviewer, and the recorder were things unreckoned in the scheme of life.

There is always the apostle of the new day. Naturally the Anglo-Saxon civilization was destined to overrun this half-Spanish civilization. Witness now the apostle of this new civilization, a solemn, long-legged man known as Pat Garrett. Reputed among his fellow-men to know nothing of that quality denominated fear, and to be actuated always by a sense of right and fairness, Pat Garrett was of the description known as a "white man" or a "square man." There was a rumor that Pat Garrett would be the best sheriff to elect. The platform was simply this: We must elect a man who can kill Billy the Kid. Pat Garrett took it under advisement. Meantime the Kid was troubled not at all. He sent word to Pat that he understood the situation, but that he could not come in and surrender, according to the wishes of Governor Wallace, even though all sorts of promises of pardon were offered to him; as indeed they were. Pat returned Billy word that, if he were elected sheriff, he would have to kill him. Billy agreed that this was the case, but said it did not matter.

Once upon a time the officers of the law had taken Billy the Kid, and taken him alive and unharmed. It was much such a case as that of the ranch-house episode, in which Carlyle was killed, with this exception, that the besiegers were better equipped and had plenty to eat, while the Kid and his party were out of food and water. They had their horses inside the adobe, and mounting, rode out, but rode into such a coil of rifles and revolvers that they were willing to dismount and give it up. Billy was taken as a prisoner to the town of Las Vegas, and the citizens of that community, hearing of his arrival, received him joyously and with a rope. The officers had much ado to protect their prisoner. As for Billy himself, who sat chained to a car seat, he thought that his time had come, and his only request was that the officers would give him a couple of six-shooters and turn him loose in the crowd. He was not lynched, however, and lived for another day.

In connection with his captivity there is chronicled one of the most cold-blooded and brutal acts of which he was ever guilty. He was taken to Lincoln, the county seat of Lincoln County, a little straggling hamlet situated on the Bonito River, not far below the old military post of Fort Stanton, which was erected to guard the Reservation of the Mescelero Apaches. In charge of the little wild beast were two worthy deputy sheriffs, known as Orrendorf and Bell, and with the generosity of big-natured men, they treated their prisoner kindly and with a certain good-fellowship. They kept him under guard in a room above the court-room, which was located in the largest building of the place, fronting upon the single street, and serving alike as jail, courthouse, post-office, and grocery store, besides furnishing a few rude offices for the County officials. One day, about noon, Orrendorf stepped across the street to the local eating-house to get his lunch, Bell being left to guard the prisoner. As Billy had promised to behave himself and had thus far given no trouble, Bell treated him with a certain amount of confidence. Billy made some pretext which induced Bell to release the shackles upon one of his hands. Billy had not yet been shackled again at the time when Bell, turning around carelessly, leaned out of the open window. Like a cat Billy crept up behind him, and doubling his hands together, swung down the iron manacles with all his might, striking Bell on the back of the head. Stunned, he fell half forward upon the window sill, and upon the instant Billy snatched Bell's revolver from the holster and shot him with his own weapon. The report of the shot was heard across the street, and Orrendorf came hurrying to see what was going on. Like a flash Billy had sprung into the next room and caught up a double-barrelled shot gun, which was lying among others on the table, part of the machinery of the law at that day and place. As Orrendorf opened the little gate at the corner of the court-house in his haste to find out what was going on, Billy ran to the window and shot him dead with the shot gun. He was now master of the court-house and of the town of Lincoln, and, indeed, once more of Lincoln County. He went out to the front of the building, and sat calmly down on the edge of the porch, and for some time worked with a file, until at length he had cut away the manacles from his hands. He had plenty of firearms now, and be sure he kept them close at hand while he was laboring. All this time there was a man in the eating-house across the street with a loaded Winchester rifle, and two or three times this man raised the gun and took a bead on Billy through the window. He had not the nerve to shoot. He knew that if he missed Billy, his life would be forfeited, either then or at some future day. No one could tell in those communities who was, or who was not, a friend of Billy the Kid.

Having freed himself from his incumbrances, Billy walked up and down upon the porch in front of the court-house a few times, dancing a sort of jig for joy. He thought nothing of the two corpses which lay close beside him. At length he deemed that it was time to set about his further journeying. A horseman was seen coming down the road, mounted upon what seemed a fairly good young horse. Billy drew a bead on him as he came up opposite the courthouse, and commanded him to dismount. The rider was a young man by the name of Burt, the son of a prospector then located at White Oaks. Billy took the horse and headed south. A

Lincoln, New Mexico, ca. 1904. Robert G. McCubbin Collection.

couple of weeks afterward the horse was found near the yard of Burt in the town of White Oaks, minus its saddle and trailing a lariat. No one knew how far it had gone in the meantime, or who was the man to bring it back to its original owner. This is perhaps the only act of gratitude or generosity that Billy the Kid ever showed in his long career of crime.

The riotings, the cattle-thieving, horse-stealing, and man-killing of Billy the Kid and his gang now broke out again all up and down the Pecos Valley, from Seven Rivers almost as far north as Las Vegas. There could hardly be said to be any regular courts in Lincoln County, or any actual enginery of the law. What that country needed—and the level-headed citizens of the land knew it perfectly well—was not so much a court as a Man. The sheriff, he was to be the law. "If we can get Pat Garrett to serve," so said these men of the Capitans and the Bonitos and the Carrizos, "then we will see an end of Billy; unless—"

It was about 1880 to 1882 that the mining discoveries of that region began to bring in a new population. The territory was ashamed of the blot on its reputation, although few men outside of the residents of the territory knew anything about the blot. Not wanting was that territory in many stern and cool-eyed men. The process of the law resolved itself into a man-hunt. One by one the members of the Kid's gang were killed. Not more than half a dozen remained, and these, under the increasing influx of American population, now resolved to take their flight into the more congenial clime of old Mexico.

This, be it remembered, was subsequent to the time when Pat Garrett had accepted the office of sheriff, including that sombre duty by reason of which he knew the office had been tendered to him. It was not a challenge from Pat Garrett to Billy the Kid. There was nothing personal about it. Simply Civilization, new come upon the land, had sent its challenge to Savagery; the law had issued its ultimatum to the lawless. Pat Garrett cared nothing for the pay and nothing for the glory. He accepted his office because be thought it was his duty to this civilization and to this law. He stood for the new order of things. Billy the Kid clung steadfastly to the old order. Each knew, and each so declared to the other, that one man or the other must go down.

The problem was how to get at Billy the Kid, now grown very old in cunning; since by this time he was past twenty years of age. All the country-side was concerned in this contest. Not only over that strip of sand and mountains three hundred miles long by a hundred wide, which, roughly speaking, made the extent of the Kid's immediate domain, but all over the Territory of New Mexico, the question of Billy the Kid was the question of the hour. Among the new men, the miners and the recent cattlemen, the sentiment was clearly against Billy. Among the old timers, and especially the Mexican population, no man could tell what was the sentiment, and no man dared to guess, where the penalty of a wrong guess would have been that of his own life. Billy mingled his acts of barbarity with acts of generosity and kindness. He never took anything from a poor man, but, on the contrary, with true bandit nobility, took from the rich in order that be might give to the poor. Hence the ignorant villagers, the swarthy goat-herders and shepherds of that sun-kissed land looked upon him almost as a divinity. He might have been at such and such a *placita* the very night before. Certainly the owner of the house where he had slept would be blandly polite, yet absolutely ignorant of the existence of any such a man as Billy the Kid, reputed to be a cow-thief and a man-killer. No information of reliable source could be gathered regarding his whereabouts. The governor issued to him renewed proclamations of amnesty if he would come in and force his gang to stop their depredations. Billy the Kid had no stomach for surrender. He himself knew that he had sinned beyond forgiveness. He knew that he must dree his own weird.* He must work out his own bloody problem. He sent word, as one general to another, that he would never again be captured, that this time he would stay out until he was killed.

And this is how the little tiger at last found his end. He and the scant remainder of his gang were on their way across the line into Mexico, when Billy finally made the fatal mistake of his lifetime. It was all about a woman. It became known, in what way it would be violating Pat Garrett's confidence to state, that upon a certain night Billy the Kid would be at the ranch house of one Maxwell, far down to the south of Lincoln, in the Rio Peñasco country, it being his purpose there to say good-by to a sweetheart, a Mexican girl. At last the little ruffian was located, pinned down to a certain time and place; for it was considered sure that he would not violate this promise.

Pat Garrett, with two deputies, appeared quietly at Maxwell's ranch house on the evening specified. They were not announced, for they were

---

Editor's note: A Scottish saying: "submit to his own destiny."

taking no chances in regard to the confidential nature of any information, and they argued that the fewer in possession of their own knowledge the better for every one concerned. It was a bright moonlight night, so that objects could be plainly discerned for some distance. Garrett left his two deputies at the gate, close to the door of the ranch house. He himself slipped into the main room. He found Maxwell in bed. Arguing that, if he would permit a visit of this sort to his place, he would also inform the visitor in case he had opportunity, Garrett commanded the ranchman to lie quietly in bed where he was. He enforced this demand with an alternative which had sufficient weight. He then stepped back of the bed where Maxwell lay, and in order to keep the latter quiet, he rested one arm across him, and with the other kept his own pistol handy.

Pat Garrett was a good shot with the heavy six-shooter. Once, while some of us were practising with pistols, Pat Garrett, at a distance of some ten or twelve yards, put five bullets from his six-shooter into a postal card which was nailed against a tree. "Now I will be particular," said he, "and shoot the stamp mark off the corner"; which latter he did practically as stipulated. This hardly reads like some of the weird stories of Western pistol work, but it was the best shooting any man present had ever seen done with the "grown-up" six-shooter. There was very good chance, therefore, that at a range of a few feet Pat Garrett's aim would be effective in this midnight interview, even though the light were poor and Maxwell's attitude uncertain.

Along toward midnight a horseman rode up and stopped his horse not far from the ranch house. He came through the gate where the two deputies were sitting. In order not to make any noise, this horseman kicked off his boots, so that, as he actually stepped over the threshold of the door, he stood with his boots in his left hand. This surely was a moment of mortal danger and of mortal terror to the two deputies who held guard without. They were saved, by Providence alone knows what of change in the mental action of this little fiend, who was now playing the last act of his red drama. For the first time and the only time in his life, Billy the Kid entertained a suspicion, and failed to shoot first and ask his explanation afterward. He looked with a certain doubt upon the two figures squatted down in the semi-darkness.

"*Quien es?*" (Who is it?) he asked.

"*Amigos*" (friends), one of the deputies had strength enough left to utter. He knew perfectly well who the little man was, standing there at

The gun Pat Garrett used to kill the Kid, a Colt's SA Frontier Model .44-40, serial number 55093. James H. Earle Collection.

the door, with his boots in his hand and the muzzle of his revolver now pointing toward him hesitatingly.

Now the figure of Billy the Kid standing thus, half hesitating, in the moonlight at the open door, perhaps with some vague softer thought of love and good-by in his soul, just as there had been a thought of home and mother at the beginning of his career, presented an object visible enough at a distance of a few feet to any one within the room. The long left arm of Pat Garrett held Maxwell tightly to the bed. His own long legs slowly uncoiled as he rose up from his place, crowded between the bed and the wall. The Kid heard some sort of sound behind him, and quick as a flash he whirled, hesitation no more a part of him. It was too late. The aim of Pat Garrett, even thus in the half-dark, was accurate as ever. Billy the Kid, his face toward the firing, fell forward into the room. Yet so quick was his own mental and muscular action that he had, before receiving his death-wound, fired his own shot in reply. Garrett fired again as the Kid fell. Thus there were three shots in all fired, but of these only two were ever located: the first shot, which killed Billy, and the shot from the Kid's revolver, which went high and lodged in the wall above the bed.

It was all over. The rest of the gang dispersed. Peace reigned along the Pecos. The cattlemen counted their own herds, the miners went safely over the devious trails among the Capitans, the Sacramentos, the Carrizos, and the Bonitos. The day of law set on apace, and one more of the wild regions of America ceased to be lawless. Today Pat Garrett, prosperous ranchman, quiet, gentle, and singularly reticent regarding anything having to do with Billy the Kid, lives at Las Cruces, in the far Southwest. At last accounts he was still a sheriff, and a very good one. Near him is the grave of Billy the Kid, one of the worst of the outlaws of the West, and certainly bad as man could be. As the grave received him, he was a short, undersized little man, with legs none too good, and the habit of a riding man. His eyes were bluish gray. His chin, so far from being broad and strong, was narrow and pointed. His teeth were large and projecting, the teeth of a carnivor[e]. Providence alone knows through what miscarriage in the eons of evolution the soul of some fierce and far-off carnivor[e] got into the body of this little man, this boy, this fiend in tight boots and a broad hat. He died at the age of twenty-one. A man for every year—indeed, had Billy lived, he might have grown to be a bad man!

CHAPTER FOUR

Billy the Kid: A Man All "Bad"

Arthur Chapman

Arthur Chapman (1873–1935), an early-twentieth-century American poet and newspaper columnist, is best remembered today for his poem "Out Where the West Begins." He was born in Rockford, Illinois, in 1873, and lived there until 1895, when he married and moved to Chicago. After three years as a reporter for the *Chicago Daily News,* he relocated to Denver, where he was a reporter and columnist for the *Denver Republican* for fifteen years. One evening in 1911, deadline looming, Chapman was racking his brain for material to fill his "Center Shots" column when he saw a press item reporting that the governors of western states were arguing about where the West began, with some saying the Mississippi River, and others insisting that it was the Alleghany Mountains. Struck with a sudden idea, Chapman scribbled his famous poem "Out Where the West Begins." He finished it in time to beat his deadline and still catch the 6 o'clock streetcar home for dinner.

From 1916 through 1919, he was managing editor of the *Denver Times,* and from 1920 until his death in 1935 he worked as a special writer for the *New York Herald-Tribune.* He authored two books of poetry: *Out Where the West Begins and Other Western Verses* in 1917 and *Cactus Center* in 1921. He also wrote *Mystery Ranch* (1921), *John Crews* (1926), and *The Pony Express: A Record of a Romantic Adventure in Business* (1932). His son John (1900–1972) also became a well-known journalist, renowned as "Old Frostface" because of his acerbic reviews during his reign as a noted New York theater critic from 1930 to 1950.

Published the same year as the Emerson Hough article (and suffering from the same sort of purple prose), Chapman's piece purports to dissect the legend while actually propagating it, a shade more accurately in some instances—the theft from the Chinese laundry and the chimney escape from jail are featured rather than the teenage stabbing—and madly wrong in others, such as making Bob Olinger a member of the posse that captured the Kid at Stinking Springs, or the Kid wantonly murdering three Chisum cowboys. Following the example of his dime-novel predecessors, Chapman's Kid killed Mexicans just to see them kick, "the only white man who slew out of pure wantonness." "His desire was to kill, and it seemed to make little difference to him whether he killed in the most cowardly manner or whether he boldly faced the weapons of his enemies." It was Chapman who first gave wide currency to the apocryphal story of Judge Warren Bristol's sentencing the Kid to be "hanged by the neck until you are dead, dead, dead" and Billy defiantly responding, "And you can go to hell, hell, hell!"

Chapman returned to the subject of the Lincoln County War and the Billy the Kid legend in the same magazine six years later. "A Cowboy War" had John Chisum and his cowboys (all hired guns from Texas) preying upon the herds of honest ranchers, who rallied around two fine young men, James Dolan and John Riley. When Tunstall was killed, his father gave McSween $30,000 to bring his son's murderers to justice, with a reward of $1,000 for every member of the posse convicted or killed. The rest of the piece closely follows this one, except in its assertion that the cost of the war was $1 million. One thing that Arthur Chapman did write, however, resonates as vibrantly today as it did a century ago, and that is his description of Billy the Kid as "wholly the most unaccountable figure in frontier history."

It is one of the anomalies of Western life that a pale, slender, high voiced, light-haired, and altogether effeminate individual named William Antrim, sometimes called Billy Bonny, and generally known as *Billy the Kid,* should be the worst desperado in the history of the frontier. Yet, in considering the so-called "bad men" of the West, his name must stand forth as the superlative of badness. Some of the gun-fighters of frontier days killed in self-defense, and others killed when they were in liquor or inflamed with anger—but *Billy the Kid* was the only white man who slew out of pure wantonness. Three of his victims—Mexicans they were—he bowled over "just to see them kick," as he laughingly explained afterward. If he had a grudge against a man he never harbored it long, but simply confronted his victim and slew without making explanation. Only sturdy John Chisholm bade defiance to Billy to the end of. the desperado's red career, and only one man ever proved himself a quicker shot—Patrick F. Garrett, one of the nerviest sheriffs that ever served in the days when the Southwest needed nervy men in that office.

Billy the Kid was only twenty-one years of age when he gasped out his life at the feet of his most implacable foe, and it was known that he had killed one man for every year of his existence. In early boyhood he was a New York street waif, from where he was sent to Silver City, New Mexico, where a stepfather volunteered to make him a worthy member of society.

But at the mature age of fifteen, Billy quarreled with his stepfather—one of the few quarrels in which *The Kid's* pistol did not speak the final word—and the youth left home, becoming a waiter in a hotel at Silver City. Soon Billy was convicted of stealing supplies from the hotel larder, and clothes from a Chinese laundryman. He was put in jail, but the jailer little reckoned with the budding desperado in his charge. Billy worked his slender form up through the chimney and made his escape.

It was not to be his last successful jail-break, for no desperado since the days of Jack Sheppard showed *The Kid's* wonderful faculty of turning the devices of locksmith and the watchfulness of guards to naught. After his escape from the Silver City jail he began life anew as a blacksmith's apprentice at Camp Apache. But one day he quarreled with the black-smith. The apprentice shot the forge-master dead and made his escape. Thereafter Billy's ways were the ways of the desperado, for at last he had reached the proud distinction of having a price put on his head.

At the time of Billy's first essay in supreme crime the Lincoln County Cattle War was making Southwestern New Mexico a delectable place for gentlemen who cared not so much for clear consciences as for well-notched gun-handles. This war was waged between the horse thieves and cattle rustlers on one side and cattle owners on the other. A few bold cattlemen had entered the Pecos country with their herds, despite the fact that in so doing they were invading the haunts of men who had been driven out of the more settled portions of the territory by sheriff's posses and vigilance committees. One class determined to despoil the other class of its herds and to drive it out of Lincoln county, and the other class determined to fight for its range. A guerrilla warfare went on for two years and upwards, and Emerson Hough, in his "The Story of the Cowboy," estimates that two or three hundred men on both sides lost their lives in the long series of assassinations.

Chief among the stock owners was John Chisholm, whose brand was on thousands of range cattle. Billy worked for Chisholm a short time, but soon he had his inevitable quarrel with his employer. It was over a question of wages, Billy claiming that Chisholm had not squared their account. Only the fact that Chisholm was surrounded by a guard of hard-fighting cowboys, with reputations as "killers," kept him from assassi-nation when he and the young desperado parted. As it was, Billy managed finally to exact a terrible penalty from Chisholm. It is more than likely that *The Kid* swore his vendetta against Chisholm and other cattle owners simply as a matter of course instead of a punctilious affair of principle. Billy would naturally take sides with the rustlers who were making life miserable for honest men in Lincoln county. He soon became a leader of the desperate crew and was in the thick of many of the deadly encounters that took place during the curse of the "war." It is estimated that he put a round dozen of notches on his gun-handle during this fiercest of range feuds, every notch representing a human life. Two of his victims were a sheriff and his deputy, who had driven him and part of his gang into an adobe house.

The name of *Billy the Kid* became such a terror in the Southwest that the people of Lincoln county cast about for the right sort of a man to literally camp on the trail of this outlaw and rid the world of his presence. For this sole purpose Pat Garrett was elected. Garrett, who is now Collector of Customs at El Paso, and who looks mildly bored when anyone mentions *Billy the Kid,* had earned a reputation as a man who never wasted speeches or lead. Cool headed at all times, skilled in handling firearms and thoroughly acquainted with the habits and haunts of the ruffians of the Southwest, the tall, easy-going Garrett was elected to try conclusions with the desperado. It was not an enviable task this, to essay to overmatch a man who knew the desert as [the] average matinee idol knows his Broadway, and whose "gameness" matched his ferocity, but Garrett undertook the responsibility with open eyes. He invaded the territory of *Billy the Kid* and carried out his plans so cleverly that he succeeded in trapping the desperado.

Organizing a posse of twenty-five determined men, many of whom had lost friends at the hands of *The Kid,* Garrett set out after his man. Bob Ollinger, who was as brave, faithful and skilled a man as ever hunted a desperado in frontier days, and a deputy named Stewart, were Garrett's lieutenants. On *The Kid's* side there was a resolute band, including Billy Wilson, Dave Rudabaugh and Tom Pickett, these three being almost as desperate criminals as their beardless leader. Garrett's posse divided in two bands, the larger, consisting of fifteen men, being headed by the sheriff and his two lieutenants. Garrett's party succeeded in bringing *The Kid,* Billy Wilson, Tom Pickett, and one other at bay in an old cabin at Stinking Springs. The outlaws fastened their horses near the cabin and fortified the place. Garrett stationed his men about fifty yards from the cabin behind some natural rock fortifications, and at 3.30 o'clock in the afternoon the battle opened. A continuous fire was kept up on both sides. The posse kept well under cover and none of Garrett's men was hurt, but one of the outlaws was killed by a bullet that penetrated the cabin door. About twilight, when their ammunition ran low, the outlaws made a break for liberty. *The Kid* stole out, to where the horses stood, intending to lead them to the cabin where all could mount and ride away. He succeeded in getting the bunch as far as the door, when one of the animals was killed, falling against the entrance in such a way that it was partially blocked. Billy once more took his stand with the besieged, but, when the posse began to surround the house with the intention of firing it when it became dark, the outlaws concluded to surrender. Dave Rudabaugh stepped out in the dusk and held up his hands, shouting as he did so that he surrendered. Billy Wilson and Pickett followed, and all were securely shackled hand and foot and taken to Las Vegas.

When it became noised about Las Vegas that *Billy the Kid* was made captive, a mob soon formed. Garrett had anticipated a lynching, and had put his prisoners in a box car, over which he, Ollinger, Stewart and their little band stood guard. Three hundred Mexicans and whites swept down upon Garrett and his men, demanding the prisoners. The sight of *The Kid,* who shook his manacled hands at the crowd and begged Garrett to "turn him loose with a brace of pistols," inflamed the mob to fury. The train could not move for an hour, but during that long sixty minutes Garrett and his bold deputies, with weapons drawn, held the mob at bay. Could the crowd have laid hands on the outlaws, short work would have been made of them, but every man in the mob knew the temper of Pat Garrett and the men at his back, and the train finally pulled out with the desperados unscathed.

The outlaws were duly tried, and *Billy the Kid* and Rudebaugh were sentenced to be hanged, the latter for having murdered a jailer at Las Vegas the year before, in an attempt to rescue some imprisoned partners in crime. The judge, in pronouncing sentence on *Billy the Kid,* made it impressive by declaring severely:

"And you are sentenced to be hanged by the neck until you are dead, dead, dead!"

Whereupon the boyish prisoner laughed in the judge's face and chanted in mockery:

"And you can go to hell, hell, hell!"

Not for an instant did *The Kid's* confidence desert him. Though shackled hand and foot and guarded day and night, he was constantly on the watch

Stinking Springs, New Mexico, as it looks today. The group at the center of the photograph is standing on the site of the stone cabin where the Kid was captured. Author's Collection.

for a chance to make his escape. When the day of his hanging was but two weeks distant, Billy saw his chance. The redoubtable Ollinger, who was one of *The Kid's* guards, was eating supper at a coffee house across the street. Another deputy, J. W. Bell, guarded *The Kid* while the desperado ate. In order to permit Billy to carry the food to his mouth, both handcuffs had been fastened to one wrist. Bell relaxed his vigilance an instant, when within striking distance of his prisoner. Quick as thought Billy's manacled hand came down on the deputy's head, stretching him out, half stunned. Snatching Bell's pistol, Billy shot the deputy through the body, the man staggering to his feet, and lurching down the back stairs, when he fell dead in the yard. Ollinger heard the shot and ran across the street. As he entered the jail yard someone called his name. Just as the deputy looked up and saw *The Kid* at a window, Billy fired Ollinger's own shotgun, which was heavily charged with buck-shot. Ollinger fell dead, and Billy broke the weapon across the window sill, crying: "There: you won't corral me with that any more."

Warren Henry Bristol, the judge who sentenced Billy the Kid to death. Photograph by William H. Brown. Courtesy Museum of New Mexico, negative no. 8815.

Kicking open the door to an adjoining room where the weapons were kept, Billy gathered up six rifles and a number of revolvers. Then he forced the first person he met to break the shackles from his legs and bring up a horse. Taking a Winchester and four revolvers, Billy rendered the rest of the weapons useless and rode away.

At the time of *The Kid's* escape, Sheriff Garrett was at White Oaks. On his return to Lincoln he at once took the trail in search of the man who had killed his faithful assistants. But in the meantime Billy's ever-ready revolver was playing havoc on the borders of Lincoln county. Soon after his escape from the Lincoln jail, *The Kid* killed one William Matthews and a companion, whom he encountered in the desert. Such was the tribute of fear levied by the outlaw that he was practically sure of securing food and shelter, no matter where he turned. Nor were people likely to give out information concerning his whereabouts, for the reason that, if it ever came to the outlaws' ears, it was equivalent to a death warrant. Now camping with sheep-herders in the desert, now appearing at some round-up camp, and again walking boldly into some settlement *The Kid* remained in Lincoln county for weeks, laughing at Garrett's efforts to trace him.

One day *The Kid* turned up at one of the Chisholm cow-camps. He had not forgotten his old feud with the cattle king of the Pecos. Three of the cowboys were at a fire, cooking supper, and twenty yards away Barrett Howell was hobbling a cow pony. Billy rode up to Howell and asked him if he worked for John Chisholm. On being answered in the affirmative, *The Kid* shot the cowboy through the head, at the same time crying, in his high-pitched voice: "Well, there's your pay."

The cowboys at the fire sprang to their feet, as they saw their comrade fall, but Billy's revolver spoke twice more and two of them fell dead. Then, covering the remaining cowboy with his revolver, Billy shrilled this message:

"You tell John Chisholm he owes me money. I'll credit him with five dollars on the bill every time I kill one of his men. If I kill him the account is wiped out."

In July, 1881, after Billy had been at large some two months, Sheriff Garrett heard that *The Kid* had been seen in the vicinity of Fort Sumner. Accompanied by two deputies, Garrett remained in the vicinity of Fort Sumner a week, but information about *The Kid* was hard to get, in view of the bonds of terror in which the desperado held the entire community. One night, after vainly watching a suspected house until midnight, Garrett suggested that a call be made on Peter Maxwell, who lived in one of the old buildings at the fort, and who was brave enough to tell what he knew about *The Kid's* whereabouts. Garrett stepped into Maxwell's room to talk to him, while his deputies sat on the porch in the bright New Mexican moonlight. Soon a man, clad in shirt and trousers, and carrying a knife in one hand and a revolver in the other, hurried toward the building, and as he stepped on the porch, cried:

"*Quien es? Quien es?*" ("Who is it?")

One of the deputies, having no idea that this could be *Billy the Kid,* told him to put up his gun and not be alarmed. At the same time he rose and walked toward Billy, but, lithe as a cat, the desperado leaped through the open doorway into Maxwell's room.

Something—probably the sixth sense said to be given to all hunted things—told Billy that all was not right in the room. Coining into the dark from the bright moonlight he could not make out objects distinctly, consequently he could not see Garrett sitting at the foot of the bed. Coming to the edge of the bed, and putting his hand on the coverlet within a few inches of Garrett, Billy asked Maxwell:

"Say, Pete, who are those fellows out there?"

Garrett recognized the voice as that of *Billy the Kid,* and slipped his holster around so he could get at his revolver. At the same time Billy caught sight of the figure on the bed. Covering Garrett with his revolver, he sprang backward, crying: "*Quien es?*"

The instant's pause was fatal to *Billy the Kid,* for almost before the Spanish words had dropped from the desperado's lips, Garrett's revolver had spoken. *The Kid* fell to the floor, shot through the heart, his revolver being discharged by his convulsive movements as he fell.

The qualities that caused Pat Garrett to be known as the coolest head in the Southwest were shown in this encounter. As he fired, Garrett leaned to the left, thinking that he could get Billy's bullet in the right side. "That would give me a chance to get another shot at him," explained the sheriff grimly.

As soon as the shots were heard, the deputies outside called Garrett's name, but again the presence of mind of the born gun fighter was manifested. Garrett did not answer, thinking that perhaps his gasping foe on the floor was not fatally wounded, and that the sound of the sheriff's voice would give *Billy the Kid* a chance to get in an effective shot.

Could a Lombroso* have studied this mere boy, who seemed to have been born with a tiger's blood thirst, no doubt science would have received

---

Editor's note: Cesare Lombroso (1836–1909) was an Italian criminologist who evolved the theories—put forward in his books *The Delinquent Man* (1876) and *The Man of Genius*

an interesting contribution. Without a spark of pity for his numerous victims, and with no fear of his enemies in his heart, *Billy the Kid* presented a peculiar phenomenon. His desire was to kill, and it seemed to make little difference to him whether he killed in the most cowardly manner or whether he boldly faced the weapons of his enemies. Few men have been *The Kid's* equal with the revolver, and none ever made a more terrifying record with that universal weapon of the frontier.

Dying, as he had lived, like a wild beast, this beardless, soulless youth who had about him none of the attributes that usually gain the Western desperado a certain sort of admiration, must remain wholly the most unaccountable figure in frontier history.

(1888)—that criminals belong to a distinct anthropological type, and that genius springs from some form of physical or mental illness.

CHAPTER FIVE

Billy the Kid

Harvey Fergusson

Harvey Fergusson (1890–1971) was born in Albuquerque, New Mexico, and developed very early an abiding interest in the history of his native state. After graduation from Washington and Lee University in 1922, he remained in the East for ten years, covering the political scene for a series of Washington, D.C., newspapers. During that decade, he became friendly with H. L. Mencken, a powerful arbiter of literary taste who encouraged him to try his hand at fiction. Working for nearly two years, mainly at nights and on weekends, Fergusson completed *The Blood of the Conquerors*, a novel set in twentieth-century Albuquerque, and Mencken was instrumental in getting it published in 1921.

Although his roots were in the West, Fergusson clung throughout his writing career to his perception of himself as an eastern intellectual. As a result, there is an almost schizophrenic rift between his "eastern" works—*Modern Man: His Belief and Behavior* (1936) and *People and Power: A Study in Political Behavior in America* (1947), the novels *Capitol Hill* (1923), *Women and Wives* (1924), *Hot Saturday* (1926), *Footloose McGarnigal* (1930), and *The Life of Riley* (1937); and his historical novels of the West—*Wolf Song* (1927), *In Those Days* (1929), *Rio Grande* (1933), *Grant of Kingdom* (1950), and *The Conquest of Don Pedro* (1954).

After the publication of his first novel, Fergusson moved to New York City, where he churned out formula material for mass-market periodicals to support his "serious" writing. He later worked as a screenwriter in Hollywood and remained thereafter in California. Although he continued to write until his death, he was unable to find publishers for much of his work, because, he believed, his style did not accommodate writing about "misery, violence, and perversion, the unholy trinity of publishing success."

In 1924, H. L. Mencken and critic George Jean Nathan, editors of the magazine *Smart Set*, launched a new literary publication, *The American Mercury*, envisioned as a lively forum for serious criticism and wit. From its inception, it featured contributions by the most important writers in the United States, and it became one of the publishing success stories of the 1920s. An article on Billy the Kid seems an unlikely one for Mencken to have commissioned Fergusson to write; perhaps he wanted to encourage his protégé's writing, or perhaps Fergusson just needed the money. The article that follows appeared in June 1925 and thus qualifies as an example of Fergusson's less serious writing. Relying heavily on Garrett's *Authentic Life* ("one of the fairest gems of frontier literature") and sprinkling the story with liberal helpings of guesswork, omission, and invention, he appears to have intended mainly to build up Billy (rather as Garrett did), in order to more permanently dispose of him. As the article shows, Fergusson believed that the Kid's fame had not persisted and that he enjoyed none of the "posthumous eminence" of such bandits as Jesse James. "Billy the Kid died at the right time," he concludes. "The brief day of the hero-bandit in the Southwest was over." This just one short year before Walter Noble Burns would appear upon the scene: Could ever man have been more wrong than Fergusson was?

Who remembers Billy the Kid? He is no more than the echo of a name today, but in his time he stalked in glory across the front pages, and during the Lincoln County War in New Mexico he was almost a national hero. The New York *Sun* even had a war correspondent in attendance upon him. When he was shot by Sheriff Pat Garrett, a few years later, he got another turn in the red and amber spotlights. Everyone who could read knew that he had killed twenty-one men, "not counting Indians," before his own death at the tender age of twenty-one. He had many admirers who regarded him as a wronged and heroic man. A San Francisco daily published an editorial demanding that Garrett be jailed for killing him, and other papers criticized and reviled the officer. Garrett replied by writing and publishing a "Life of Billy the Kid," devoted chiefly to an account of his own herculean exploits on the border and to a blistering diatribe against his critics. It remains one of the fairest gems of frontier literature. A melodrama, portraying Billy as a promising youth ruined by evil companions, was written and put on the boards; I saw it in the West as late as 1913. An enterprising fellow, whose name I forget, made a living for years by exhibiting a skeleton, alleged to be that of the bandit, at ten cents a look. Hundreds of thousands paid their dimes to gape at it. Billy had in a high degree all the qualities which impress the imaginations of simple men. And yet, for some strange reason, his fame has not persisted. Certainly he enjoys no such posthumous eminence as Jesse James, for instance, although he was a far more gallant and engaging figure. The James brothers were hard-headed business men who made crime pay. Billy was a quixotic romantic, who cared nothing for money.

He lived and died an idealist. He began his career in murder to avenge an insult to his mother, and lost his life rather than leave his sweetheart. He had in immense measure that uncompromising vanity which makes human destiny spectacular, and, according to Rochefoucauld, is the chief difference between heroes and ordinary men.

Moreover, he was the key figure of an epoch—the primitive pastoral epoch in the history of the West, which began after the Civil War and ended with the completion of the first trans-continental railroads in the early eighties. It has been the subject of much romancing, but of little patient investigation. Here, then, briefly sketched, is the career of a man who was who typical of it.

II

William H. Bonney was born of Irish parents on the East Side of New York in 1859. For reasons unknown his father moved with his family to Coffeyville, Kansas, where he died. The widow went to Colorado, where she married a man named Antrim, and with him went first to Santa Fe and later to Silver City, New Mexico, then a boom mining town, lawless and full of saloons and dance-halls. Mrs. Antrim ran a restaurant and Billy ran wild on the streets. Antrim comes into the picture as a disapproving step-father, who gave Billy many a thrashing and earned his hatred. But for his mother Billy had a jealous and worshipful affection.

He himself always claimed to have been driven from home by Antrim, but the immediate cause of his departure was an insult offered his mother on the street by a tipsy man. Billy, then about sixteen years old and small for his age, attacked the man with a rock and was saved from a severe thrashing by a friend named Ed Moulton. Later, in a saloon, Moulton got into a fight with the same man when Billy was present. Moulton seemed to be getting the worst of it when Billy intervened with a pocket-knife and the Berserker fighting spirit which was later to make him the most feared man in the Southwest. He killed his man by stabbing him in the heart, and departed the saloon with a yell of defiance, brandishing his bloody blade. He got out of Silver City accompanied by a boy a year older than himself named Jesse Evans. Both riding one pony with a sore back, they reached Fort Union, where they were fed by the soldiers and also obtained from them an old army rifle and a six-shooter of the cap-and-ball type used in the Civil War. So accoutered, they set out to master the world.

After several days of hungry wandering, they encountered three Apache Indians traveling with a herd of twelve ponies and a load of peltries. The boys asked for food and were curtly refused. Instantly, the newly acquired armament came into play, three Indians perished and the ponies and peltries changed hands. This, so far as I can learn, was the only murder Billy ever committed for gain. The contemporary chroniclers, such as Garrett and Siringo, pass it over as a mere boyish lark. The only popular solution of the Indian problem at that place and time was to slaughter the Indians.

The ponies and peltries were quickly converted by the boys into gauds and armament of the sort locally esteemed—high heeled riding boots and silver spurs, *chaparejos* with silver buttons, wide white hats and silken bandanas, good Winchesters and six-shooters. The first model of the Winchester carbine came into the world, like the six-shooter, just about the time Billy needed it. He was now, at seventeen, a bad man full blown, with his life in his hands, a gun on his hip and a world without law to roam in. He was beginning already to discover the two facts upon which his subsequent career was based—that he had more skill with a gun than most men and that most men are cowards. He had tasted the wild intoxication of battle. He fought, later on, for many causes, but always he fought primarily for love of battle.

Billy at this time had already reached his full growth. He was five feet, eight inches tall, and slim and muscular. He had very small, almost effeminate feet and hands, and was fond of elegant raiment. His features were aquiline and rather good, except that he had two very large and prominent front teeth. His hair was curly brown and his eyes blue-gray, with the hot hazel specks in them which often mark the man of gore. He was a bright fellow, with Irish wit, and an inveterate smiler. He always smiled when fighting. The gleam of his buck-toothed grin illumined many a man's last sight of earth.

About this least known period of his career many tales are told that have a romantic, apocryphal flavor. He is described as rescuing a wagon-train of immigrants from the Comanches, charging the savages with an axe, felling five of them, and completely demoralizing them with his demoniacal yells. Again, cornered by Apaches, in the mountains, he is said to have escaped by scaling a cliff the Indians were afraid to attempt. One tale represents him as making a record ride of one hundred and twenty-five miles in one night to deliver a friend from jail single-handed.

It is interesting to note that in this last exploit he is said to have been fed
and furnished with fresh horses by Mexican peons. The peons remained
his friends to the last, and he could not have survived so long without
them. They fed and hid him and gave him news of his enemies. He, in
turn, gave them money by the handful when he had it. Like Robin
Hood, he befriended the poor.

The story of his famous ride is probably at least partly authentic. Of
the other sagas of his early prowess it can only be said that many tell
them, but that none of them can be traced to Billy's own lips, for he was
always reticent. What seems certain is that he made his living for several
years without the indignity of work by playing monte and faro in the
towns of the border and especially in Sonora, in Old Mexico. With a
Mexican gambler named Melquiades Segura he would invade a town,
play furiously for high stakes, generally win, get into a quarrel, kill a
man, and then get out. Most of his killings were thus in fair fight, as fair
fight was understood on the border, and over games or women, for he
was a famous lover. There were many men like him in the Southwest of
that day—professional adventurers of the dance-halls and faro tables.
Most of them talked big and fought little. But Billy killed. He was always
crossing the border on a fast horse, leaving a dead man and a panting
posse behind. But one by one, as order penetrated that wilderness, his
old haunts were closed to him. So he rode East, broke, to meet some
friends who had promised him a job in the Pecos valley. And thus he
came to the scene of those gaudy exploits which give him his bloody
place in the history of the Southwest.

III

Most of the Pecos country then was a cattle range for one John
Chisum (or Chisholm), who claimed some sixty thousand head of stock
under the jingle-bob brand. Here it is necessary to understand the state
of the cattle business at that time and in that country. The first long-
horned herds had been brought north from Old Mexico into Texas
before the Civil War. During the war these herds ran wild and were forgotten. Afterward, when the great western push of discharged soldiers
and bankrupt Southerners began, they belonged to any man who put his
brand on them first. Since they were worth about three dollars a head,
branding mavericks was a legitimate and laborious way of getting a start

in life. But once a number of forehanded men had large herds under brand, they looked with hostility upon new-comers with hungry branding-irons. They could not patrol their half-wild herds adequately, and so their calves and yearlings tended to fall to some other man's rope and to wear his mark. So began the battle between the cattle barons and the rustlers which lasted a quarter of a century. Each side believed it was in the right; law was laid on the shelf. Only gradually did the word rustler become synonymous with thief. Only gradually did property win its inevitable triumph.

Chisum was the cattle baron of the Pecos, one of the first in the South-west. He had for allies a lawyer named McSween and a young Englishman named Tunstall. Tunstall was a leader in the long procession of well-born British younger sons who went to the Wild West to sink capital in the cattle business and hunt grizzlies and buffaloes. He bought an interest in Chisum's ranch, but proceeded at once to forget business and devote himself to sport. He was a big, hearty, red-faced boy, stupid, honest and well-meaning. With his background of orderly English country living, his instinctive faith in law and the right thing, he was pitifully unqualified to cope with the subtle and dangerous men of the border. He knew there was trouble between Chisum and the Murphy-Dolan company of Lincoln, New Mexico, but he never thought of it as anything that menaced his own safety.

Murphy and Dolan ran a store in the town of Lincoln, which was the county seat of Lincoln county, then about as large as Pennsylvania and as wild as central Africa. They were the backers and creditors of all the small cattlemen and rustlers who were the natural enemies of Chisum. They gave leadership to the men who argued that Chisum was "hogging the range." Chisum, in turn, accused them of branding stock that should have been his.

The Chisum faction also had headquarters in Lincoln at a store owned by Tunstall and McSween. The bad feeling between the two groups was brought to a fighting climax by a lawsuit—itself unimportant as lawsuits always were then. Suits and warrants were used liberally by both sides, but were merely pretexts. Both were meanwhile hiring cowboys, always chosen for their skill as fighting men. That was where Billy the Kid came in. His fame as an artist in homicide was sufficient to get him a job, first with the Murphy-Dolan faction. But before any real trouble came up he one day met in a saloon the young Englishman, Tunstall, and the two

John Chisum, Denton, Texas, ca. the 1860s. At one time the financial ally of
Tunstall and McSween, he was prominent among those who got Pat Garrett
elected sheriff on a ticket to get rid of the Kid. Robert G. McCubbin Collection.

formed an enduring friendship. There is no doubt that Billy had the
capacity to win the regard and confidence of men of many kinds. He has
ancient friends living today who defend him hotly and make plausible
excuses for all his crimes. Nearly always, indeed, he had some devoted
follower to whom he was bound by an unspoken pact of mutual loyalty—

Jesse Evans, Segura the gambler, and then, strangest of all, this young Englishman. The immediate result of their meeting was that Tunstall offered Billy a job, not as a fighting man but as a cowpuncher, for Tunstall probably was one of the few in Lincoln county who expected no bloodshed. Billy accepted, thereby switching from Murphy and Dolan to their enemies.

For some months he and Tunstall worked and hunted together. Meanwhile Murphy and Dolan were gathering a posse of thirty gunmen, all properly sworn in as deputy sheriffs, to collect the claim they held against McSween and Tunstall. Suddenly, the war swept down without warning on the Rio Feliz ranch, where Tunstall, Billy and two other cowboys were riding the range. When Billy and the other cowboys saw the enemy coming, they put spurs to their horses and shouted to Tunstall to follow. They knew what was in the air. They knew that the long-brewing storm was about to break and that four men had no chance against thirty. But Tunstall, the aristocrat, refused to run. Frank Coe, a friend of Billy who still lives near Lincoln, says that Billy stopped to argue with his friend, but that Tunstall was serenely stubborn. He was a law-abiding Englishman, minding his own business, and he had wronged no man. He felt sure he was safe.

"You fellows go on," he said. "They've probably got it in for you. I'll stay and talk to them."

Billy and his companions went—straight for the tall timber, low on their horses' necks. Looking back they saw the group sweep down and cluster about Tunstall, who out-topped them all on his imported thoroughbred. There was a moment of deliberation, and then six-shooters whanged, the posse swept on, and Tunstall and his mount lay dead on the prairie.

According to some accounts of this incident, Billy was away chasing wild turkeys when the posse came down on Tunstall. But the facts are probably as Coe tells them. Billy may have believed that Tunstall really was safe. Whatever the facts, his rage at the death of his friend was a thing he never got over. Ever afterward he carried a notebook in which he wrote down the names of all the members of the posse as fast as he could learn them, and he told everyone that if he lived long enough he would get them all. He did get five or six of them, and this yearning for blood vengeance seems to have been the leading motive of his short subsequent career.

The murder of Tunstall was the opening skirmish of the struggle which figures briefly in footnotes of western histories as the Lincoln

James J. Dolan and Lawrence G. Murphy, 1871. Their explosive reaction to John Tunstall's mercantile challenge resulted in the Englishman's death and fueled the Lincoln County War. Robert G. McCubbin Collection.

Benjamin Franklin "Frank" Coe with wife Helena Ann "Ella" Tully, son Wilbur, and daughter Annie, ca. 1890. Coe was one of the Tunstall-McSween "Regulators"; he survived the Lincoln County War to become a local celebrity. Paul Family Collection, courtesy Lillian Bidal.

County War. It was a guerilla warfare of small mounted bands battling for the possession of forlorn cattle herds in a wilderness of mountain and desert. Each side had men who had been made deputies by complaisant sheriffs, and each carried warrants for its enemies, but there was really no law in the contest, nor, indeed, in the land. The important thing is that Billy the Kid, at the age of nineteen, became the leader and field marshal of the Chisum-McSween faction, and that he missed no chance to pump lead at the men who had murdered Tunstall. Two of them were captured and sent under guard to prison. Billy was in charge of the guard. The men never got to jail alive. Billy said they tried to escape. Another man was waylaid and shot down by Billy and several of his followers. Yet another was surrounded in a house and killed after a long siege. Billy was a hired gunman doing murder for wages, but he picked his victims from the list in his pocket. According to Coe, all he ever said about Tunstall was: "He is the only man I ever worked for that gave me a square deal."

The Lincoln County War went on for more than a year. It reached its climax when the Murphy-Dolan army surrounded Billy and his gang in the building in Lincoln where McSween lived and also had his store. An open siege was maintained for several days, right across the street from the court-house. Troops were sent from Fort Stanton to quell the riot, but they stood by and did nothing. Finally the building was set on fire and the besieged made a break for liberty. Several of them were shot down, but Billy and a few of his followers got away. McSween the lawyer was among those killed. This was his first taste of battle with bullets instead of words. He sat in a helpless daze throughout the siege, unable to believe that such things could happen. When the word came to make a break for it, he ran straight toward the enemy and fell riddled.

General Lew Wallace, the author of "Ben Hur," had just been appointed governor of the territory of New Mexico with extraordinary powers. He was devoting the lucrative leisure of his post chiefly to the composition of a romance about imperial Rome, but he now brought himself back to reality long enough to take cognizance of the fact that a state of war existed within his jurisdiction. He visited Lincoln and studied the situation. What was he to do? The execution of justice in the legal sense would have required hanging half the county. Seeing that this was impracticable he tried to settle the war in the grand manner by proclaiming amnesty for all who would agree to lay down their arms and keep the peace. Most of the combatants were glad to comply. Only one man, indeed, flatly refused the amnesty, and that was Billy the Kid. He had a personal interview with General Wallace, who was immensely surprised to find the celebrated desperado a slim youth with a broad good-humored grin. Billy declined the governor's mercy with smiling politeness.

The reasons he gave were various. He had more enemies than any other man in the country and if he settled down to a peaceful life he would lay himself open to them. Moreover, two of his killings had been on United States government property—an Indian reservation and a hospital site—and he believed, or professed to believe, that he would be arrested by the federal authorities in spite of the amnesty of the territorial governor. It was on these federal warrants, in fact, that he was finally taken to jail. Thus the reasons he offered to Wallace were plausible enough. But there was also another: if he accepted amnesty he would no longer be Billy the Kid, the most feared man in the Southwest. He would be just one more cow-puncher. His life of battle and fame would be over. Now, as always, he did the spectacular thing. He rode away from Lincoln with his gun on his hip, thumbing his nose at all the world.

For a year or more thereafter Billy was at the height of his glory—a perfect specimen of the bandit as hero. With a troop of followers he went about the country stealing whole herds of cattle and horses with almost perfect impunity. He and his confederates would round up a herd, drive it a few miles and sell it. It was often sold for a fraction of its value, and usually then got back to its owner. In effect, Billy levied a cash tribute on the live stock industry. He did not forsake his old haunts. He still drank in the saloons of Lincoln and Fort Sumner, often with the very men he robbed. He was more than ever a flame among the girls, including some who belonged to the first families. He was not an outlaw in any proper sense of the term, but a distinguished member of society, the most feared and admired man of his time and place.

Fear of his deadly skill with firearms was of course a large element in his power and eminence, but genuine admiration for him was another. Many substantial ranchmen fed and housed him. Some of them, perhaps, did so in return for immunity from his raids, but others regarded it as an honor to have Billy the Kid for a guest. The humble Mexicans were his friends now as ever, and when hard put he could always count on sharing the beans and mutton of some sheep-herder.

IV

But the Southwest was changing. Men and money were pouring into it. The cattle business was being capitalized and incorporated. The forces that make for law and order were strengthening. The men at the heads of the new cattle companies determined to get rid of Billy. Posses were organized to find him and finish him. Unluckily, they always came back without him. The fact was that even money could bring forth no man who was willing to stand up in the open and shoot it out with Billy the Kid. They would chase him a while for a price, but when a clash threatened they always found reasons for coming home. There was a fine comic quality about some of these chases. In one of them a posse of a dozen men pressed Billy and several of his band so hard that the bandits took shelter in a deserted house and prepared to give battle. They were surrounded and the stage was set for slaughter. But the weather was cold and the pursuers had brought nothing to eat. It seems not to have occurred to them either to build a fire or to send for provisions. Instead they held a council and agreed unanimously that it was best to call it a day and go home. They went back to Lincoln and gathered in a saloon—to tell each other what they would have done if the weather had been better.

That same night Billy the Kid rode into Lincoln, put up his horse at a livery-stable, entered the same saloon, and loafed about for a quarter of an hour. No man spoke a word to him or looked him in the eye. He was ignored as completely as though he had worn a cloak of invisibility. There was only one man in the place who was honest enough afterward to admit that he had seen Billy and had been too scared to move as long as the bandit was in the room. Before this boy of twenty the mighty fighting men of the border were as skittish as cotton-tail rabbits. They were all loath to die—and an encounter with Billy meant sure death to someone, for his professional skill was now at its height. He could bring a six-shooter into play just a little faster than any other man of his time.

But his enemies kept on seeking a man brave enough to tackle him, and finally that man was found. He was one Patrick F. Garrett, and he took the job of sheriff in Lincoln county with that avowed purpose. Garrett was a native of Louisiana, and one of the many Southerners who had left ruined plantations to come West after the Civil War. He was six feet four inches tall, silent, truculent and resolute. His memory is not revered by the old-timers, because, although he killed many men, he killed nearly all of them from cover. He was careful and deadly. He seems to have taken the job of getting Billy because he was politically ambitious and believed that he could thereby win fame and favor where favor counted. For the details of the hunt there is no room here, but they showed plainly that Garrett planned either to ambush the Kid or to take him otherwise by surprise. He executed one ambuscade and killed one of Billy's followers, but the Kid was saved by the fact that he had dropped back to borrow a chew of tobacco.

It was the treachery of a friend that finally led to Billy's capture. A rancher named Brazil, who had been feeding and housing him, went over to Garrett and led him to a deserted house where the Kid and three companions were camped. It was surrounded, and the siege was a real one this time. Garrett dug himself in, taking no chances, and sent for a wagonload of provisions. With a skill almost equal to Billy's own he shot away the tethers of the bandits' horses, and then dropped one of the animals in the doorway of the house, so that a sortie was impossible.

Billy and his followers then surrendered, without the chance of firing a shot, to save themselves from death by starvation and cold.

The others came out scared and grave, but Billy seemed in high spirits. He ate a large meal and laughed and joked with his captors, talking over all the details of his pursuit and capture as though it had been a friendly game they were playing. His fine saddle mare he presented to a member of the posse to whom he had taken a fancy, with the remark that he probably wouldn't be taking any horseback exercise for quite a while. Leg-ironed and hand-cuffed, he was hauled away to prison, absolutely undaunted, as though he had known he was on the way to the most spectacular moment of his career.

Lincoln lacked a jail, and Billy was confined in an upper room of the old two-story adobe court-house. None of its doors would lock securely, but he was ironed hand and foot and two armed men were set to guard him. One of these, Bell, was a good-natured fellow, glad to earn a few dollars by what looked like an easy job. The other, Ollinger, was a bitter enemy to Billy and a choice specimen of the bad man at his worst. A born killer, he had earned his living chiefly as a deputy sheriff, and had a reputation for killing men under arrest on the pretext that they had tried to escape. He was proud of his dangerous reputation and spared no pains to look his part. He wore his hair long, had long ferocious moustachios, and was one of the few men of the time who carried a knife at his belt as well as a gun. Billy had a great contempt for him, which he often and eloquently expressed, and Ollinger hated Billy. He now took delight in sitting before his prisoner with a shotgun loaded with buckshot, cursing and taunting him.

"You just try to get away once, you goddam little Irish gutter snipe! All I want is one crack at you with this old smoke wagon . . . "

Billy smiled and held his peace. His smile was based on a discovery he had made—that he could get his small and supple hands out of the hand-cuffs whenever he wished.

V

He waited until one noon, when Ollinger had locked up his shotgun in an adjoining room and gone across the street to dinner. He then persuaded Bell to bring him a newspaper and under cover of it he got his hand-cuffs off. Still concealing his hands under the newspaper, he asked Bell to take him downstairs on a natural plea that could not well be denied. Bell marched him out with a six-shooter at his back and started to march him in again. When they reached the steps, which had a turn in them, Billy suddenly leaped ahead and out of sight. He kicked down the door of the room where Ollinger had locked up his shotgun, seized a six-shooter which lay on the table and got back to the head of the stairs in time to meet Bell coming up. As always, he shot first and Bell fell dead. Billy then got the shotgun and went to the window, where he waited for Ollinger to come across the street. When he did so, Billy called to him, and then, as Ollinger looked up, shot him with both barrels, savagely broke the shotgun and threw the pieces into the street. "There, you son-of-a ——" he shouted. "You won't follow me around with that gun any more."

All Lincoln now knew that Billy had killed his jailers, but the one street of the little town was as deserted as though a plague had taken the last inhabitant. Not even a head was poked out a window while Billy sat on the porch, whistling and smiling after his cheerful fashion as he filed off his leg-irons. When this was done he summoned an old man who acted as janitor of the building and made him bring a saddle horse. Mounted and armed and free once more, he rode up and down the street several times, defying all and sundry to come and get him. As no sign of life showed, he rode away, stopping at the edge of the village to give a Mexican a message for the owner of the horse to the effect that he would either pay for it or send it back.

The natural and expected move for him now was to cross the border into Old Mexico and safety. For reasons which were never explained, Garrett gave him every opportunity to do this. Although put under a good deal of pressure to take Billy's trail, he did nothing for more than a week. He probably felt that if Billy would cross the border and stay on the other side it would save both of them a great deal of trouble. But Garrett was now pestered by a rumor, which gradually grew into a certainty, that Billy had not really skipped. He was hanging around Fort Sumner to see a girl there.

Why Billy staid must remain a mystery. He ought to have known that he would be hunted to the death. But he was in love with this pretty daughter of a ranchman, and he risked his life nightly to see her. He was a romantic fellow, foredoomed to be a fool for women. Moreover, he was also a man of enormous vanity and of a self-confidence much swollen by his easy triumphs.

Soon Garrett, urged on by public opinion, went to Fort Sumner to investigate a report that the Kid was in hiding there. He went after dark and very quietly, with two companions. These he stationed on the porch of the suspected ranch-house while he went inside to talk with the ranchman, whom he found in bed. Forbidding his host to make a light, he sat down at the foot of the bed and began a low-voiced conversation.

The ranchman was a weak, good-natured fellow and a firm friend to Billy. Garrett tried to persuade him to tell where Billy was hiding and he professed not to know.

As a matter of fact, Billy was in another room of the same house, which his friend had placed at his disposal. He had just come in and had taken off his boots. He was hungry. There was a small stove in the room and he determined to awaken his friend, get the key to the meat-house, where the usual quarter of beef hung, and cut himself a steak to broil. In his sock-clad feet he went softly out upon the porch and toward his host's room. In the dark he almost stepped on Garrett's guard. He whirled around, gun in hand, and backed away from them, calling out in Spanish: "Who are you?" Getting no answer, he backed into the room and turning, asked his host, whom he could not see in the dark: "Who are they, Pete?"

Garrett recognized the voice. His six- shooter belched red in the dark, and Billy went over backward, shot through the heart just as he pulled the trigger of his own gun, shooting a hole in the wall.

Destiny was thus hard on Billy the Kid at the last, for he died with his boots off, in the dark, without a chance for his life. It was still harder on Garrett. Instead of reaping praises he was denounced loudly, not only for the way he killed Billy but for killing him at all. A tale was widely current and is still believed by many in that country that he hid under the bed where Billy's girl lay waiting and killed the Kid as he came to a rendezvous. When he ran for sheriff again he was defeated. In a rage he sold out land-holdings that would have made him a millionaire and moved to other parts. There he was shot in the back and killed by one of his many enemies.

Billy the Kid died at the right time. Within a year the railroad reached New Mexico, and less than a decade later it was almost as tame as any State in the Union. The brief day of the hero-bandit in the Southwest was over.

CHAPTER SIX

A Belle of Old Fort Sumner

Walter Noble Burns

Within a year, Harvey Fergusson's question "Who remembers Billy the Kid?" was comprehensively answered by a Chicago newspaperman, Walter Noble Burns, in his 1926 book *The Saga of Billy the Kid*. "Gray-beard skald at boar's-head feast when the foaming goblets of mead went round the board in the gaunt hall of Vikings never sang to his wild harp [a] saga more thrilling than the story of Billy the Kid," he enthused, and proceeded to make it so. Despite its many failings—shaky facts, invented situations and dialogue, the complete omission of such events as the Dudley Court of Inquiry and the killing of Jim Carlyle—it became an immediate bestseller, in the process triggering off an industry of movies, books, and magazine and newspaper articles that has continued to the present day.

Although others would later interview many of the participants in the Lincoln County War more thoroughly and record them more accurately, Burns was the only writer who ever talked with Paulita Maxwell. What she said convinced him that she had been the love of the Kid's life and he of hers, but he "was unable to write it frankly," as he wrote to lawman Jim East, "because my publishers were afraid any such statement might lay them open to a libel suit. So I had to soft-pedal [it in] my chapter called 'A Belle of Old Fort Sumner' [and] let Paulita, now Mrs. Jaramillo, deny it. I was sorry I had to do this but the publishers insisted and there was no way out of it."

Even though Burns could not write it the way he wanted to, he still contrived to present Paulita's affectionate portrait of the Kid in a way that strongly suggests—by his naming of Paulita's three "candidates" for the "honor" of being the Kid's inamorata, and most particularly in its final paragraph—that her feelings were the very opposite of what she was saying, in the process comprehensively disposing of the still widely held misconception that she was a "Mexican señorita."

To his conclusion that Paulita was indeed the Kid's last love, however, one observation must be added: that nowhere among Burns's papers at the University of Arizona is there so much as a page of notes relating to this conversation, let alone a full transcript. So we are left to wonder: Are these loving recollections truly the words Paulita Maxwell spoke, or did Walter Noble Burns give his considerable imagination free rein and simply invent them?

Billy the Kid was a youth of many light affairs, but he loved but one woman. This at least is what the Southwest has believed for nearly fifty years. His love for her was his soul's one clear drop of poetry. On his way to hell, it gave him his one vision of Heaven. Concerning the identity of his sweetheart, there has been much speculation. She lived in old Fort Sumner—that much is certain. When, later on in his story, Billy the Kid escaped from Lincoln, it is generally conceded he could have got quickly into old Mexico where he would have been safe from pursuit. Life and liberty beckoned him across the Rio Grande. But the love in his boy's heart longed for his sweetheart and he headed straight for Fort Sumner. For the one woman of his dreams he risked his life in his life's most desperate chance. For love of her he died.

Mrs. Paulita Jaramillo of *New* Fort Sumner, who in her youth was Paulita Maxwell, daughter of one of New Mexico's famous families, throws much interesting light on this old sweetheart romance. She and Billy the Kid were friends, and the friendship of this good, pure girl was a gracious influence in his life.

Time has dealt gently with Mrs. Jaramillo. No one would be so ungallant as to inquire how old she is, but it may be whispered that in 1881, when Billy the Kid met death in her home, she was a blooming girl of eighteen. Streaks of gray have only begun to show in her coal-black hair; when she smiles, the suspicion of a dimple still shows in the olive smoothness of her cheeks, and there is a sparkle in her black eyes that age has had no power to dim. It is easy to fancy her as the dashing beauty she is said to have been when she was the belle of old Fort Sumner.

Mrs. Jaramillo unites the blood of Spanish hidalgos and American pioneers. Lucien B. Maxwell, her father, was a friend and companion of Kit Carson, and at one time was reckoned the richest man in the Southwest. He was a native of Illinois and settled in New Mexico when the country was still a part of old Mexico. He married Señorita [Ana Maria de la] Luz Beaubien of noble ancestry, tracing back to the aristocracies of France and Spain. She was the daughter of Charles Hip[p]olyte Trotier, Sieur de Beaubien, a Canadian, who embarked in the commerce of the

Paulita Maxwell, ca. 1915. The Kid's sweetheart as she probably looked when she told her story to Walter Noble Burns. Robert G. McCubbin Collection.

Santa Fe trail and settled in New Mexico in 1823. Her mother had been Señorita [Maria] Paula Labata [Lovato], descended from a family that came to the New World soon after the conquest of Mexico by Hernando Cortez and arrived in New Mexico in the wake of Oñate's pioneers. So Mrs. Jaramillo has, as her intimate background, the proudest family traditions in all that part of the country. . . .

You find Mrs. Paulita Jaramillo in her own little cottage in the outskirts of the town. If the day is pleasant, she will perhaps be sitting in a rocking chair on her porch, working an embroidery or crocheting a mantilla. . . . With an air of frankness, Mrs. Jaramillo tells you the name of the woman who, she declares, was the sweetheart whose fascination drew Billy the Kid to his death. Mrs. Jaramillo's answer to the conundrum that has intrigued the Southwest for almost half a century has, even at this late day, a certain piquant interest; but it is charitable, and perhaps wise, not to rake this ancient bit of gossip out of the ashes of the past. The woman Mrs. Jaramillo names has been dead many years.

"Billy the Kid, I may tell you, fascinated many women," Mrs. Jaramillo continues. "His record as a heart-breaker was quite as formidable, you might say, as his record as a man-killer. Like a sailor, he had a sweetheart in every port of call. In every *placeta* in the Pecos some little señorita was proud to be known as his *querida*. Three girls at least in Fort Sumner were mad about him. One is now a respected matron of Las Vegas. Another, who died long ago, had a daughter who lived to be eight years old and whose striking resemblance to the famous outlaw filled her mother's heart with pride. The third was his inamorata when he was killed.

"Fort Sumner was a gay little place. The weekly dance was an event, and pretty girls from Santa Rosa, Puerto de Luna, Anton Chico, and from towns and ranches fifty miles away, drove in to attend it. Billy the Kid cut quite a gallant figure at these affairs. He was not handsome but he had a certain sort of boyish good looks. He was always smiling and good-natured and very polite and danced remarkably well, and the little Mexican beauties made eyes at him from behind their fans and used all their coquetries to capture him and were very vain of his attentions.

"We had quite a bevy of pretty girls in Fort Sumner. Abrana Garcia, Nasaria Yerbe, and Celsa Gutierrez had a Spanish type of beauty that you associate with castanets and latticed balconies and ancient courtyards filled with the perfume of oleander. They were very graceful dancers, too, and with these three, I think, Billy the Kid danced oftenest. Manuela Bowdre, Charlie Bowdre's wife, was a dark, glowing, slender little creature of high spirits. Poor girl, it broke her heart when Charlie Bowdre was killed by Pat Garrett and his man-hunters. But time mends broken hearts and Manuela married Lafe Holcomb, a cow-puncher, and was living over in the Capitans when I last heard of her. Juanita Martinez, Garrett's first wife, and Apolinaria Gutierrez, his second, were sparkling young women, who had the charm of gaiety and light-heartedness and were always surrounded by admirers at our dances. Juanita was the sister of Don Juan Jose Martinez, who still lives in new Fort Sumner. Everyone loved her and mourned for her when an unkind fate changed her bridal gown into a shroud three weeks after her wedding. Garrett was more fortunate in his second love affair. Soon after his marriage to

Apolinaria Gutierrez, he moved to Roswell and I saw little more of him or his wife, but I always understood they were very happy together.

"You doubtless suspect our Fort Sumner dances were not very fashionable affairs. Well, perhaps not; but they were great fun. The girls were not burdened with wealth and did not get themselves up in expensive and elaborate toilets. But in their simple gowns, made by themselves for the most part, with perhaps a red rose in their black hair or a bunch of blossoms at their waist, they were alluring enough to set any man's heart going pit-a-pat. Nor were they unskilled in the subtle graces and diplomacy of the coquette. They knew how to use their black eyes to good advantage, and they were adept in the old-fashioned Spanish art— gone now from the Southwest—of making their fans talk when their tongues were silent. I will venture it would be hard to find at modern balls and cotillions more spirited or graceful dancers than our Fort Sumner girls. No orchestra concealed behind palm fronds played for us, but we had very good music; generally six pieces—violins, guitars, clarinets, and sometimes a tambe or Indian drum.

"It might surprise you to know that our dances were extremely decorous. Everybody attended them, old and young. We girls of Fort Sumner were not accustomed to dueñas, but with our mothers and grandmothers looking on at our merriment, we were quite well chaperoned. There was no drunkenness, no rowdyism. Our men would not have tolerated anything of the kind for an instant. The men did not wear evening clothes, but they lived up to the old West's traditions of chivalry. I suppose you are amazed that an outlaw and desperado like Billy the Kid should have been a favoured cavalier at our dances. But in the code of those days, any man who was courteous to a woman was considered a gentleman, and no questions asked; and, as there was little law in the country, an outlaw who measured up to this simple standard was as welcome at Fort Sumner's social affairs as anybody else. . . .

"An old story that identifies me as Billy the Kid's sweetheart," says Mrs. Jaramillo with an indulgent smile, "has been going the rounds for many years. Perhaps it honours me; perhaps not; it depends on how you feel about it. But I was not Billy the Kid's sweetheart. I liked him very much—oh, yes—but I did not love him. He was a nice boy, at least to me, courteous, gallant, always respectful. I used to meet him at dances; he was, of course, often at our home. But he and I had no thought of marriage.

"There was a story that Billy and I had laid our plans to elope to old Mexico and had fixed the date for the night just after that on which he was killed. There was another tale that we proposed to elope riding double on one horse. Neither story was true and the one about eloping on one horse was a joke. Pete Maxwell, my brother, had more horses than he knew what to do with, and if Billy and I had wanted to set off for the Rio Grande by the light of the moon, you may depend upon it we would at least have had separate mounts. I did not need to put my arms around any man's waist to keep from falling off a horse. Not I. I was, if you please, brought up in the saddle and plumed myself on my horsemanship.

"Billy the Kid, after his escape at Lincoln, came to Fort Sumner, it is true, to see a woman he was in love with. But it was not I. Pat Garrett ought to have known who she was because he was connected with her, and not very distantly, by marriage. The night the Kid was killed, Garrett asked Pete Maxwell why the Kid was in Fort Sumner. Pete shook his head and said he didn't know. But he merely wanted to save Garrett embarrassment. He knew and I knew. I was standing beside Pete's chair at the time and I would have answered Garrett's question if Pete, by a look, had not warned me to keep my mouth shut.

"But if I had loved the Kid and he had loved me, I will say that I would not have hesitated to marry him and follow him through danger, poverty, or hardship to the ends of the earth in spite of anything he had ever done or what the world might have been pleased to think of me. That is the way of Spanish girls when they are in love."

CHAPTER SEVEN

Billy ("The Kid") Bonney

N. Howard (Jack) Thorp as told to Neil McCullough Clark

Cattle rancher and poet Nathan Howard "Jack" Thorp (1867–1940) was described by his publisher as "a Carl Sandburg of the Southwestern range," but the author of "Little Joe the Wrangler" was hardly that. Thorp was born in New York, the third son of a wealthy lawyer, but his life changed in his teens when his father lost all his money. Passing up on college, Jack visited his brother Charles's ranch in Nebraska and fell in love with the West. Eventually he became a rancher himself. Weighing in at two hundred pounds plus and 6'2" tall, he was renowned for his prowess at rodeos and as a bronco-buster, although he was never a regular performer. His special field of intellectual interest was cowboy songs and singing cowboys.

From his early twenties, Thorp collected songs from every cow camp and lonely ranch he visited, and when he had enough of them, he tried to interest a publisher. When no one expressed any interest, he published them himself in 1908 as *Songs of the Cowboys,* which appeared in an expanded edition from Houghton Mifflin in 1921. Another book, *Tales from the Chuck Wagon,* also failed to find a publisher, so he printed it himself in 1926. It is clear that he was a born storyteller, but apart from a few articles, that was about the sum of his writing.

In the last years of his life, Thorp collaborated with editor-turned-freelance writer Neil McCullough Clark to write an autobiography, from which the following chapter is excerpted. Like most of his ranching contemporaries—and unlike most of the writers of the time—Thorp (who had served as New Mexico state cattle inspector from 1913 to 1918 and knew something about the cattle business) considered Billy the Kid little more than a small-time rustler and his death as "good riddance." Having talked with Pat Garrett, George Coe, and Charlie Siringo to get a fix on his subject, he set out to challenge the Kid's "hero" status in general and his killings in particular. In doing so, he produced one of the first credible critiques of the legend; sadly, he died before the book appeared in print.

I

Of all the New Mexico "bad men," William H. Bonney, known as Billy the Kid, is by far the most famous. Sixty years after his sordid death, native women still scare their children by telling them "Bilito" will come and get them if they don't behave. Armchair adventure hounds halfway around the world scare themselves under their reading lamps over lurid accounts of his alleged exploits. His career has even been put in the movies, and from now on he will probably be pictured in the public mind as two-gun Robert Taylor.

There seem to have been about as many contradictions in Billy's character as in that of "Bad Man" [also known as "Outlaw Bill"] Moore—he was part good and part bad, like most of the rest of us. But the most curious thing about Billy is not what he actually was, in the flesh, but the steps by which his reputation grew so that he is now transformed into the kind of person the thrill-hungry public imagines him to be. He is not history any more, but legend, romanticized out of all likeness to the gun-totin', rambunctious, carefree cowboy kid that his friends and enemies knew, and he has become a sort of super-hero. It is hard, maybe impossible, to separate the truth about him from falsehood, the facts from the fiction. However, that is what I have tried to do, and in this chapter I aim to examine some of the evidence concerning a very curious phenomenon in the history of the West.

Actually, Billy the Kid was just a little, small-sized cow- and horse-thief who lived grubbily and missed legal hanging by only a few days. He killed, or took part in killing, several people; but his killings were more often on the order of safe butchery than stand-up-and-fight-it-out gun battles. He took part in a range war on the losing side. He died, not in a blaze of glory, but like a butchered yearling, shot down in the dead of night in his stocking feet, when he was armed with a butcher knife and, possibly, though not certainly, with a six-shooter. Yet for all that, romance does cling to his name. Half a dozen books about him have been written and published. The town of Lincoln, New Mexico, thrives on his memory. And many people regard him as a sort of super-Robin Hood of the range, a daredevil of matchless courage, haloed by smoke wreathing upward from fogging guns. He makes a fascinating study in the technique and psychology of literary and national hero creation. Many have told the facts about Billy. Few have agreed about them. The heavy shadow of the "hero" tradition has made unconscious liars of some; others have lied about him on purpose, loading the public with tall tales to satisfy the appetites of listeners greedy for shudders and blood.

I, of course, did not know Billy. He died too young. His bones had been mouldering in the dust of old Fort Sumner for nearly ten years when I first laid eyes on the sunny flats and mountain ranges beyond the Pecos where the bloody events in which he shared, took place. But I knew Lincoln County intimately, and I knew many of those who knew him, including Sheriff Pat Garrett, who fired the shot that killed him; George Coe, who rode and bunked with him for months when matters were at their worst; Charlie Siringo who, although he knew Billy only slightly, wrote a small and highly-colored book about him; and many more. To most of those who knew him, Billy was no hero. To some, he was a good friend and a likable companion. Others considered him no better than any other brand-blotting thief, and a coward besides. The truth seems to lie somewhere between these extremes, as it usually does in judging the characters of people. But it is the growth of the hero myth that I am particularly interested to examine, thinking it might shed light on the deification of certain other "heroes" in our modern world, such as Adolf [Hitler] of Berchtesgaden and John Dillinger.

The Kid's background was certainly colorful. The years that made his fame were spent on or near the Pecos River, which well deserves its other name, the River of Sin. The Pecos rises in the Sangre de Cristo Mountains at an elevation of ten thousand feet, and after cascading down rocky slopes wild with pine, aspen, and juniper, breaks out into the flat country near old Fort Sumner. Thence toward the south it threads the old cattle range of the Chisums, and on into Texas, finally entering the Rio Grande in a rocky gorge north and west of Del Rio, not far from Judge Roy Bean's town, Langtry. For several hundred miles the Pecos passes through a country almost destitute of trees, meagerly fed by five rivers from the west that have their origin in the Guadalupes, and by two from the east— Pintada Canyon, and Alamogordo Creek. The very name of the river came to stand for murder, for when the freebooters of the valley killed a man, they were said to have "Pecos'd" him, meaning, tied stones to his dead body and rolled it into the river. Three races, Indian, Spanish, and English, with a scattering of French and others, met, mixed, and fought in this valley. It is likely that the country that became Billy the Kid's playground, is richer than any other in the West in tales of lost mines, buried treasures, cattle wars, bloody violence, and mysterious happenings.

No one, for example, has ever explained the mystery of the three human skeletons found on the upper Pecos, together with their guns, saddles, and camp equipment, and a buckskin bag full of nuggets and placer gold. The guns were ancient cap-and-ball pistols, and two shots had been fired from one of the guns, one shot apiece from each of the others. Nor has anyone, presumably, ever found out where the bandits buried the gold they took when they robbed the stagecoach a few miles east of the Pecos River. The bandits, lost in a blind canyon, were overtaken promptly and killed near the river, but the stolen gold was not on them. Nor does anyone have an accurate record of the number of bloody battles that were fought at or near the site of the Pecos Pueblo, first between Plains and Pueblo Indians, and later between the Pueblos and the Spaniards.

A little to the west of the river stands the tragic Sierrito Bernál, now called Starvation Peak, where a wagonload of emigrants fled when attacked by Indians. Besieged there constantly by the Indians, without food or water, all starved to death. This area, too, and the whole country from Las Vegas to Santa Fe, was the stronghold of *Vicente Silva y sus Quarenta Bandidos*—night riders who wore long white sheets with red daggers embroidered on the back, and who, when they rode into a town four abreast and a hundred strong, always left behind some victim of their vengeance, his corpse perhaps not being found for months.

Old Fort Sumner, on the east side of the Pecos, was founded in 1862, expressly to prevent bloodshed on the Bosque Redondo Indian Reserve, where thousands of bloodthirsty Apache and Navajo Indians had been placed. Two companies of cavalry had their barracks here.

In the town of Roswell, further down the river, Sheriff Charles Perry, in order to keep the peace, had to kill three men in one day, while at Eddy (now Carlsbad) certain hard characters murdered the sheriff in broad daylight.

Two miles south of Eddy was a collection of saloons and dance halls, populated by the riffraff and outcasts of Eddy, the place being known as Phoenix. One of the houses here was run by a man named Barfield, who "fell from under his hat" when shot from the outside through the window. Across the street was a place run by Ed Lyalls and his wife,

Nellie, frequented by a gang who paid for their liquor with stolen cattle. I stopped at Lyalls' place once for a few minutes on the way back to my ranch on Black River, and while I was there, two strangers rode up. They sat down at the faro table and proceeded to lose their money—maybe a couple of hundred dollars. One of them whipped out his gun and covered the dealer, the other covered the lookout man. They raked in the entire bankroll, backed out, mounted, and fled. I learned later that one of the two was the notorious John Wesley Hardin, who was afterwards killed in El Paso. The name of his companion I never learned.

Further south, at the junction of the Black River and the Pecos, was Red Bluff, near which the Butterfield stagecoaches were held up so often that the government finally established a camp of soldiers near the point of the Guadalupes to protect travelers.

These are only a few of many happenings that gave the River of Sin its reputation, and it was against such a bloody background that Billy the Kid played his part as a fighting cowboy and became a legend to scare the papooses. The man himself was a good deal less of a fellow than the legend; and it's the man himself I mean to try to put together from the authentic pieces that are left.

The original published source material about Billy is contained principally in five books, as follows: Pat F. Garrett, *The Authentic Life of Billy the Kid* (1882; 2nd ed., 1927); John W. Poe, *The Death of Billy the Kid* (1919); Chas. A. Siringo, *History of Billy the Kid* (1920); George W. Coe's autobiography, entitled *Frontier Fighter* (1934); Miguel Antonio Otero, *The Real Billy the Kid* (1936). It is significant that with the exception of Garrett's book, which appeared about a year after Billy's death, all of these have been published within the last twenty-one years, about forty years or more after Billy's death. For almost forty years the hero myth had little printed matter to feed on, and it was dormant or dying, and possessed only an antiquarian interest. Soon after the [First] World War, however, the coals of interest began to show red again, and finally burst into flame. Old-timers, once given to obstinate silence about what they had seen, grew talkative, and began to tell what they remembered or thought they remembered.

The principal peg on which public interest was hung, of course, was the "fact," so called, that this beardless youth who died when he was little more than twenty-one, had killed "twenty-one men, not counting Indians"—a man for every year of his brief life. Armchair appetites demanded good stories about this matchless character, and supply has a tendency to follow demand in the fiction business as well as in the cow business. The stories became better and better, taller and taller, maybe Old Truthful himself would be ashamed to own interest in some of them. Old Truthful, I might say, was a character with a claim in the Guadalupe Mountains, who was famous for handling facts in a free-and-easy style. One of his stories had to do with a bear fight he allegedly fought with a huge old silvertip with an eight-foot tail. Attacked by Old Truthful himself, his little dog, and a swarm of bees all at once, the bear took refuge in a fifty-gallon barrel that Old Truthful brought along to gather honey in. Her tail stuck out the bunghole, and Old Truthful tied a knot in it, thereby attaching the barrel permanently to her tail; and the bear left camp quick. The next time Old Truthful saw that bear, he said, was about a year later. She still had the barrel on her tail, and what's more, she had two cubs with her, and each one of them had a gallon keg on its tail.

"No, sir!" Old Truthful remarked after telling this yarn, "I don't go to town often. I like ter live up here. Yer see, there's a bunch that jest sets around the store with their feet wrapped around nail kegs, an' they're always tellin' lies. They make me so mad!"

Billy, the cow thief, the occasional killer, the buck-toothed desperado, became more and more a "hero" in the stories. Final deification came with *The Saga of Billy the Kid,* by Walter Noble Burns, a book in which a cook-up of fact and fiction was served with a literary sauce nicely calculated to please the palates of thousands of readers whose only range-riding was done in pipe smoke. There have been other publications claiming to give "the facts," which actually have only enhanced and embroidered the legend. That legend has now grown to such a size that it will not be ignored, even by those who know it to be about nine parts fiction to one part fact.

To appraise the substance on which this shadowy hero structure has been built, I have gone over all the evidence again, and here present results and conclusions.

II

Authentic knowledge of Billy the Kid, insofar as we have it, is confined to the last four years of his life. He rides out of the shadows of a nomadic boyhood, into the sunlight of intense and recorded action, in the year 1877. What he had done in the eighteen years of his life up to then, is largely conjecture. There is some evidence that Billy himself knew how to spin a good yarn about his past, and was not unwilling to have people think that he had done some pretty bloody and impossible things in the course of his travels. Many a cowboy did as much. And Billy seems to have known, as some women know, that "a past" can often be an asset—if you are not too explicit about the details. Many of the killings attributed to him are supposed to have taken place in that unlighted past, beyond proof or investigation. The story of that period is told, allegedly, in the first seven chapters of Garrett's *Authentic Life,* and most later writers have blindly followed his account, without recalling all of Garrett's reasons for writing the book.

It's a tall tale, as Garrett spins it. Before he was eighteen, Billy is credited with having ended the mortal agony of (a) a man who insulted his mother, (b) three Indians on the Chiricahua Apache Indian Reservation, (c) a "soldier blacksmith," (d) a monte dealer in Sonora, Old Mexico, (e) a monte dealer in Chihuahua City, (f) about fourteen Mescalero Apache Indians who had attacked an emigrant train, and (g) an uncounted number of Apaches near a spring in the Guadalupe Mountains. The flavor of these episodes, admittedly largely imaginary, is shown by the words attributed to Billy just before the Guadalupe Indian killings. To his lone companion, he is supposed to have remarked: "I believe a little flare-up with twenty or thirty of the sneaking curs would make me forget I was thirsty while it lasted, and give water the flavor of wine after the brigazee was over." That might be the way dime novels talk, but not cowboys.

During this period of his life, Billy is pictured as dropping in occasionally at towns where he was known, just to jeer at officers of the law who feared him, and "to watch their trembling limbs and pallid lips as they blindly rushed to shelter." But the author hedges occasionally on the authenticity of the events he is describing, for he says of one killing, "Billy never disclosed the particulars of the affair"; and of another, "The date and particulars of this killing are not upon record, and Billy was always reticent in regard to it." The truth is, of course, that Garrett was building up this desperado for purposes of his own. Sheriff Garrett, you remember, killed Billy in the dead of night, when out with two deputies to capture and return him to a condemned cell.

A chance shot fired by Garrett,
A chance shot that found its mark;
'Twas lucky for Pat the Kid showed plain,
While Garrett was hid in the dark.

The West approved the kind of peace officer who gave even a desperate gunman a chance, and Garrett was always a little on the defensive in regard to the manner of Billy's death. His claim was, "If I had not shot him when I did, I would not be here to tell the tale." So he was interested in using any and every device he could find, to play Billy up as a super-gunman. In presenting an autographed copy of his book to Territorial Governor Miguel Otero (later the author of *The Real Billy*), Garrett said of his volume: "Much of it was gathered from hearsay and 'made out of whole cloth.'"

Garrett himself, be it noted, did not do the actual writing of his book. That was the work of M. A. (Ash) Upson, an old newspaper man who is said to have boarded with Billy's mother in different towns. With a subject such as he had here, when he was not held down to earth by facts of which either he or Garrett had sober personal knowledge, Upson just loosed the bridle and let old Pegasus sunfish and windmill. Billy's name, he soaringly said, "will live in the annals of daring crime so long as those of Dick Turpin and Claude Duval shall be remembered. This verified history of the Kid's exploits, with all the exaggeration removed, will exhibit him as the peer of any fabled brigand on record, unequalled in desperate courage, presence of mind in danger, devotion to his allies, generosity to his foes, gallantry, and all the elements which appeal to the holier emotions."

That's pretty loud screamin' for *any* eagle!

I think it is permissible to dismiss as unproved, and probably untrue because incredible, most of the killings supposedly done by Billy before he became a participant in the Lincoln County War. What remains? There is a list of eleven killings, more or less charged against Billy in that strange uprising which helped plenty to brand the Pecos as the River of Sin. Did Billy do these eleven killings? And if so, were all or any of them "heroic"? Let's see.

(1) The first two of the eleven killings charged to him were those of Billy Morton and Frank Baker. The exact truth of the Morton-Baker affair will now never be known. It was one of the earliest incidents involving

actual bloodshed in the Lincoln County War. The history of that war is much too complicated and obscure to dwell on in a single chapter here. It's enough to say that it was born of range and trade rivalries and involved what is known as the Murphy-Dolan faction on one side, and the Tunstall-McSween faction on the other.

The Murphy-Dolan faction was the natural one for a gun-slinging tough like Billy the Kid to side with. Under the leadership of Jim Dolan, it represented political control and corruption, was allied with rustlers, grafters, and any who cared more about money than honesty. Such an outfit needed fellows who were prepared to steal cattle, blot brands, dry-gulch enemies, and otherwise do the devil's business on the range. And Billy did side with them. They were his first employers in Lincoln County. He played with their marbles, and maybe they paid him some wages. The big mystery is why he ever quit them for the other side. But quit them he did, and the reason may have been the personality of John Tunstall, the Englishman. Tunstall and Billy, somehow, seem to have been greatly attracted to one another right from the start, perhaps because they were such completely opposite types and their backgrounds were so different. Billy was a product of the raw frontier, and knew more about the inside of saloons, gambling halls, and *tendejons* than other kinds of inhabited buildings. Yet with it all he seems to have been possessed of a certain personal charm. Tunstall, by all accounts, was a cultured and educated Englishman of wealth. When they met, the spark of friendship was struck. George Coe tells of being in Lincoln one day, and asking Tunstall about Billy. He quotes Tunstall's reply:

"George, that's the finest lad I ever met. He's a revelation to me every day, and would do anything on earth to please me. I'm going to make a man out of that boy yet. He has it in him."

If these were not Tunstall's exact words, they undoubtedly reflect accurately his feelings, for Coe tells the truth about what he saw and remembers—and about what he didn't see, he keeps still. This remark of Tunstall's doesn't make a "hero" of the lad, but it does show him in a favorable light.

Now, the very first blood shed in the war was that of John Tunstall. He had come to Lincoln and opened a store which cut into the business of the store owned by the Murphy-Dolan crew, partnering in this and another enterprise with a man, Alexander A. McSween, who had displeased and defied that bunch. He had bought ranch interests and conducted himself on the range in an upright manner, which was calculated to bring him into conflict with their crooked operations. So, capping a series of events, Tunstall was waylaid and killed. Billy the Kid was working for Tunstall then. Just where Billy was at the time of this killing is a matter of dispute. He seems to have been just around the next hill shooting wild turkeys, but no one knows for sure. At any rate, the Tunstall killing was the shot heard round the range that set other Lincoln County guns to blazing.

Two days after the event, a group of Tunstall's friends carried his body to town. Four miles south of Lincoln, six Spanish-American workmen stood in a field of grain belonging to Señor Charles Fritz, and watched the procession pass. A youngster among them, Julian Chavez, listened to his elders (*hombres grandes*) discuss the event, and heard them express the opinion that it was an affair concerning American houses exclusively, and that probably the Mexican population would not be drawn into it at all. Many years later, in a naive longhand narrative recording his recollections of those days, Julian remarked that he himself of course had no opinion in the matter then, since he was a youngster and a young boy did not have opinions— *"Yo no tube opinion, pues estaba Joben, y las muchachas no tienen muchas opiniones."* But he discovered soon that the opinion of his elders was far from correct.

Bill Bonney and others swore vengeance on Tunstall's killers. The Lincoln County War was on, and nearly everybody in the region was drawn into it, either actively or passively, on one side or the other.

An unofficial posse, of which Billy the Kid was a member but not the leader, captured Morton and Baker, two men who were connected with the Tunstall killing. The posse started with them toward Lincoln, but the captives never got there. The story usually accepted is that for some reason they made a break to escape, presumably when one member of the posse, who was suspected of favoring their cause, was shot. Pat Garrett gives Billy the Kid all the blame for killing Morton and Baker. In one of these highly purple passages of his book, he (*via* Ash Upson) says: "The Kid wheeled his horse. All was confusion. He couldn't take in the situation. He heard firearms, and it flashed across his mind that perhaps the prisoners had in some unaccountable manner got possession of weapons. He saw his mortal enemies attempting to escape." And so on. "Twice only," Garrett dramatically declares, "his revolver spoke, and a life sped at each report."

Thrilling enough, if true. But it seems to be perfectly certain that Garrett was merely making up a good story, the way he wanted it, out of an event of which he had no first-hand knowledge, knowing that because of the peculiar circumstances, his account was not likely to be contradicted publicly by any of those who did have first-hand knowledge. George Coe, who knew Billy the Kid more intimately than Garrett ever did, said of the same event, "No one knows the details, but it is evident that . . . Baker and Morton . . . put spurs to their horses and made a desperate attempt for liberty only to fall, riddled with bullets, a few seconds later." He says that all the mention Billy ever made to him about the affair, was: "Of course you know, George, I never meant to let them birds reach Lincoln alive." "Billy," he adds, "did not seem to want to talk about it."

Let's sum up. There were eleven members of the posse. All of them, except the prisoners, were heavily armed; the prisoners weren't armed at all, and they died. It requires a pretty big stretch of credulity to believe that when they fell dead, the only bullets in their bodies were those of nineteen-year-old Billy the Kid, who was not even the leader of the posse. In any event, were those killings the kind to make a "hero's" reader proud of him? Did they reveal the dash and daring of a resourceful, courageous soul endowed with all the elements which appeal to the holier emotions? Or were they more on the order of butchering a couple of range steers?

(2) Another allegedly daring killing laid at Billy's door was that of "Buck-shot" Roberts. Garrett did not witness this killing either, but his hearsay account of it has a fine air of gallantry, dash, and derring-do befitting a knight of the range, a cowhand with lance atilt. The encounter took place at Blazer's sawmill. Once again Billy the Kid was a member of a large posse, and Roberts, the victim, was alone.

"As the party," says Garrett, "approached the building from the east, Roberts came galloping up from the west. The Kid espied him, and bringing his Winchester on his thigh, he spurred directly towards Roberts as Brewer demanded a surrender. Roberts' only reply was to the Kid's movements. Quick as lightning his Winchester was at his shoulder and a bullet sang past the Kid's ear. The Kid was as quick as his foe and his aim more accurate; the bullet from the rifle went crashing through Roberts' body, inflicting a mortal wound."

That's the way a "hero" and his worthy opponent ought to meet and do battle to the death! The only trouble is, that's not what happened; in fact, it's nothing like what happened.

George Coe was there. He and Billy the Kid were temporarily members of the same gang. His shattered right hand from which the trigger finger is gone, is evidence to this day* of his participation in the Blazer's Sawmill fight. Dr. Blazer ran a sort of roadhouse, and the party of twelve men, one of them being Billy the Kid, arrived and ate lunch there, two of their number standing guard because they were expecting trouble. While the main bunch was eating, trouble arrived—Roberts on a bay mule. The fireworks did not start at once. Roberts dismounted and told one member of the party, whom he knew personally, that he wanted to speak to him, walked around the house and sat down in an open doorway. Meanwhile, others of the party conferred and decided Roberts, who was known to be after their scalps for a reward that had been offered by the opposing faction, had better be "arrested." Dick Brewer, the party's leader, asked who would go around the house and get him. There were three volunteers, Charlie Bowdre, George Coe, and Billy the Kid, *in that order* and in that order they started around the house, guns in hand and cocked. Bowdre called on Roberts to surrender.

"Not much, Mary Ann!" he replied. All the accounts agree that those were his actual words.

Bowdre had the drop, but Roberts and he fired almost instantaneously. "Bowdre's bullet," says Coe, "struck Roberts through the middle, and Roberts' ball glanced off Bowdre's cartridge belt, and with my usual luck, I got there just in time to stop the bullet with my right hand. It knocked the gun out of my hand, took off my trigger-finger, and shattered my hand." Bowdre's bullet, and his alone, was the one of which Roberts died. But he did not die at once, and before he finally passed out, he put up a very game fight. He took refuge in the room in the door of which he had been sitting, and from here he picked off and killed Dick Brewer, and wounded another member of the posse. Billy the Kid, according to Coe (who throughout his book tells only what he saw without elaboration), had slight part in the episode beyond being third in a party of three aiming to "arrest" Roberts.

Again the facts of a battle, in which one man was ranged against twelve, hardly seem to show Billy up as "hero" size.

(3) A third affair laid to Billy was a double killing—that of Sheriff Brady and his deputy, Hindman, on the main street of the town of Lincoln.

---

*George Coe has died since this account was written. —N. M. C.

Garrett, who generally makes out a case for Billy's dare-deviltry and courage when he can, calls this "a crime which would disgrace the record of an Apache." It occurred a few days before the killing of "Buckshot" Roberts. The sheriff of Lincoln County at that time was a certain Major Brady. All events of the Lincoln County War were backgrounded against a relatively passive and pacific, but by no means disinterested, native Spanish population; and their judgments of the principal figures involved in the conflict are not to be disregarded. Many of the Spanish people, for example, thought highly of Billy the Kid, and he is said to have liked them too, and it has been claimed that of all the people he is supposed to have killed in New Mexico, not one was a pure-blooded Spanish-American. Many of the Spanish people thought well of Major Brady, too. To quote once more from the manuscript of Julian Chavez, this sheriff was held by the Mexicans to be an honorable citizen and very much the gentleman (*muy caballero*), partly perhaps because he was married to a Mexican woman of the Bonifacia family. "I knew all of his family," Julian writes— "*yo conosi a toda su familia.*" However, Jim Dolan is supposed to have undermined the Major's sterling character simply by giving him a paid-in-full receipt for eight hundred dollars, to clear off the balance of the mortgage on the Major's home, and thereafter "*el buen hombre se doblego, y se presto a serbir ordener*"—the good man became deceitful, and put himself out to obey Murphy-Dolan orders without question. "*Sabe Dios,*" exclaims Julian, "*Que tontas bacilasiones*"—God knows why men do such things!

Major Brady is supposed to have held warrants for the arrest of several of the alleged killers of Morton and Baker. So a group of the dead Tunstall's friends went to the town of Lincoln on April 1, 1878, and lay in wait for him behind an adobe wall surrounding Tunstall's store. They knew his habits, and expected him to ride along the main street at about the time they took up their positions.

How many lay in ambush behind the wall is reported variously. George Coe says there were five; others say there were eleven. One of them, at any rate, was Billy the Kid.

The sheriff failed to come past as expected. Hence, a man was sent to the lower end of town to pretend that he was drunk and shooting bottles off the shelves. News of this speedily brought the sheriff along Lincoln's one main street. With him were his deputy, George Hindman, and the clerk of the circuit court, Billy Matthews. As they passed the adobe wall, the ambushed "heroes" let them have it. Brady was killed instantly, Hindman lived barely an hour, and Matthews, though wounded, got away and lived to tell the tale.

Billy the Kid was credited with these murders. Garrett in his book does not come right out and say whose bullets killed whom. He does call the murder "a most dastardly crime on the part of the Kid," leaving the hasty reader to conclude that Billy did it all, or at least engineered it. But Governor Otero reports Garrett as saying to him later that "he doubted if the Kid had even fired at Brady," giving as his reason that he hated Billy Matthews and would naturally have tried to get him first, and Matthews was the one of the three who got away!

We shall never know the truth. There was no science of ballistics then to measure bullet markings microscopically, and photograph them, and to say past all doubt that a certain fatal bullet came out of a certain gun. Did any bullet from Billy's gun come anywhere near any one of the three victims? Nobody can say for sure. Was his bullet only one of many that entered their bodies? Was somebody else's bullet straighter and more deadly? No one knows. But the nature of the crime speaks for itself. It was butchery from the ambushed protection of an adobe wall, and even a ruse was necessary to entice the victim to the spot. If that's "heroism," maybe somebody will be erecting a monument one of these days to every paid killer hired by Al Capone.

(4) Next we come to the killing of Bob Beckwith.*

I know of no reliable testimony denying that Billy did this killing. Most people think he did. Probably he did. The blood was shed in the turmoil of a general conflict.

Consider the circumstances. A major battle was fought between the two warring factions in the town of Lincoln, and was the culminating action of that war. Fifty or more partisans were engaged on both sides. The United States Army got into it too, in the person of a certain Colonel N. A. M. Dudley, commander of neighboring Fort Stanton, who seems to have acted in a role unlike that usually adopted by the Army. He came with a detachment of soldiers and a gatling gun, parked the

---

*According to the Chavez manuscript, which seems worthy of belief on this point, this man's real name was Roberto Becues. Julian's spelling is never to be taken positively for gospel; however, he knew the man personally, and declares him to have been a half-breed, the son of a Mexican mother and an American father— *"mislo hijo de Mexicana y de Americano."* —N. M. C.

military in the main street, and saw to it that the "right" side (the side he favored—the Murphy-Dolan partisans) got the breaks.

The McSween residence, in which Billy the Kid and a number of others held the fort, was fired and burned. While attempting flight from the burning building, Alexander McSween, who never carried a gun and did not on that occasion, was shot and killed. Beckwith, or Becues, an enemy partisan, rushed forward waving a pistol and yelling, so it is said:

"I killed McSween. I've won the reward."

"Yes!" cried Billy the Kid, who was still inside the burning building, "you won the reward all right." And shot him between the eyes, "killing him dead."

Maybe almost anybody under the circumstances would have done as much. Still, give the Kid all the credit the deed deserves.

(5) Billy was supposed to have added another notch to his gun by killing a bookkeeper, Morris J. Bernstein, employed at the Mescalero Indian Agency.

As Garrett tells it, Billy and a bunch of his pals rode up in plain sight of the agency and began stealing some horses, which in the nature of things was a fool thing to do. Bernstein witlessly said he would go and stop them, and though warned, tried it, and that sounds like another fool thing. To Bernstein's order to Billy to desist, says Garrett, "the only reply was from the Kid's Winchester."

Siringo copies the story from Garrett, and embroiders it, calling the killing the Kid's most cowardly act. Gratuitously, Siringo adds that the Kid's excuse for shooting Bernstein had a strong Hitlerian flavor—"He didn't like a Jew nohow."

What were the facts? They seem to be perfectly clear. George Coe again was there, and has told the tale. He says that their party consisted of six or eight Mexicans, and four Americans—Hendry Brown, Billy the Kid, Fred Wayte, and himself. Their object, he affirms, was not horse-stealing, but to discover what had happened to the body of Dick Brewer, their former leader, after "Buckshot" Roberts had shot him in the battle of Blazer's Mill. When they were within a mile or so of the Indian Agency, Coe says, he and the other three Americans decided to go to the far side of the canyon for a drink at a spring. Now, the spring was out of the shelter of the trees, and the Mexicans, who were scared, refused to go. While the four were in the act of drinking, shots were heard. The four Americans mounted three horses, Billy's horse having run away at the first shot, and raced for cover. When they reached cover and came up with the Mexicans, they learned that a party of five riders had approached, and the Mexicans had desperately opened fire, killing one. The dead man was Bernstein.

It is a matter of record," Coe points out, "that the Kid was accused of this killing, tried for the offense and acquitted. Several writers have attributed this murder to him as one of the most blood-curdling crimes of his career. Since I was present at the time, I can testify that he had nothing whatever to do with it." So passes another "notch."

(6) Now we come to the sordid saloon killing of Joe Grant. Again the credit for the blood spilled, if it can be called any credit, seems justly due to Billy. Grant was a Texas tough who apparently had it in for Billy, and Billy heard of his intentions and threats. One day Billy entered a saloon in Fort Sumner with a group of cowmen whom he had invited in for a drink. Grant was there already, and he was mean drunk. He made a lunge and grabbed a fine ivory-handled pistol from the scabbard of one of the men who entered with Billy, putting his own in place of it. Billy, who was ostensibly friendly with Grant, asked for a look at the pistol. Grant stupidly handed it over. Examining it, Billy saw that there were only three cartridges in the gun, and he whirled the chambers so that when next fired, the hammer would fall on a blank. He handed the pistol back to Grant, who thereupon got noisy behind the bar, began breaking the glassware, called Billy a liar, turned his gun on him, and pulled the trigger. Of course nothing happened, since the gun had been "fixed." Meanwhile, the Kid deliberately pulled his own gun, fired, and Grant fell dead.

Was this a "hero" act? Heroes supposedly fight fair. And these dice were loaded, so that Billy could hardly lose. Maybe Grant needed killing. But to me, the manner of his killing looks more like butchery than heroism.

(7) Jimmie Carlyle was a young blacksmith who had "hundreds of friends and not one enemy," according to Pat Garrett. "He was honest, generous, merry-hearted, quick-witted, and intelligent." And Billy the Kid killed him.

With three members of his cattle-stealing band, the Kid had been trapped by a posse in the roadhouse of Jim Greathouse. The posse called for a surrender. There was a parley, in the course of which Greathouse went to the posse for a talk, and stayed as a hostage while Carlyle, who was a member of the posse, went unarmed into the roadhouse to talk to the outlaws. It was agreed that if Jimmie was harmed in any way, Greathouse would be killed. Several hours passed. The time when Carlyle was to have returned passed. According to one story, some member of the posse fired a gun, and apparently Carlyle thought that Greathouse had been killed and his own life was now forfeit. Anyhow, he made a rush for the window, and leaped through it, taking sash, glass, and all. Billy fired at him, wounding him, and while he was trying to crawl away on hands and knees, Billy deliberately polished him off. During the melee, Greathouse escaped.

Again Billy's gun was notched by the murder of an unarmed, desperate man. The act of a "hero"?

(8) And now we come to Bell and Ollinger, Billy's last two killings—if he killed them both.

Pat Garrett, in the course of events, had been made sheriff. The main figures in the Lincoln County War had been killed off, and the "war" had degenerated into a ragtag-and-bobtail affair. Billy the Kid was now a notorious cow thief, a pest and a neighborhood blight, operating over eastern New Mexico and western Texas, and it was part of Garrett's job to get him and end the pestiferous pilfering. Garrett eventually captured Billy, very tamely, at Stinking Springs, and landed him in jail. Tried on the charge of murdering Sheriff Brady, Billy was convicted, and was sentenced to be hanged on May 13, 1881. He was lodged in an upper room in the old Lincoln County Court House, and because this building was a very poor excuse for a jail, Billy was leg-ironed and hand-cuffed, and was guarded day and night by Deputy Sheriff J. W. Bell and Deputy Marshal Robert W. Ollinger.

On April 28, a little over two weeks before he was to be hanged, Billy escaped. Both of his guards were killed.

How did it happen? Everybody knows the weaknesses and frailties of human observation. I read about a fatal automobile collision in which two newspaper reporters and a magazine editor, all trained to observe expertly, were passengers in the cars involved, yet there were seven different eyewitness versions of what actually happened, and no two were near enough alike to enable a jury to return a verdict placing the guilt. It is not strange that no one knows exactly how Billy made his escape, since the two guards were killed, and no one else is known to have been on the spot, and Billy, having flown, was not doing much talking for publication.

The Old Court House at Lincoln, New Mexico, scene of the Kid's escape on April 28, 1881. There were no stairs then. Robert G. McCubbin Collection.

All stories, however, agree that Ollinger had taken some other prisoners across the road to supper, leaving Bell alone with Billy. Garrett's version is that Billy asked to be taken to the latrine, which was downstairs and outside in the jail yard. On the way back, he says, Billy ran ahead of Bell upstairs, broke into the room containing the jail's arsenal, obtained a six-shooter, and shot Bell who was coming up the stairs. Garrett doesn't say who told him that this was what happened—maybe he just "deduced" it. George Coe's version is that Bell and Billy were playing cards while Ollinger was away; that Billy dropped a card as if by accident, and when Bell stooped to pick it up, Billy drew Bell's gun from its scabbard and threatened him with it; that Bell made a lunge to escape, and Billy shot him. Charlie Siringo rather spectacularly claims that Billy had starved himself so he could get one hand out of his handcuffs, and that on the fatal evening Bell was facing him reading a newspaper; that Billy released his hand, swung the cuffs and stunned Bell, grabbed the deputy's gun, and shot him. Martin Chavez, a friend of the Kid's, is quoted by Governor Otero as saying that a line had been drawn down the center of the room and Billy had been warned to stay on his side of it; but he deliberately crossed over and taunted Bell, and when the latter was off guard, grabbed his pistol. Others, nameless, say that a confederate on the outside shot Bell, that Billy did not do it.

Be all that as it may, Bell was killed, and for lack of any eyewitness accounts, we can only guess and conjecture how it happened. Anyhow, Billy took advantage of his death. He next seized a double-barrelled shotgun, and fired both barrels into the body of Ollinger when the latter rushed across the street to see what was up. Billy then is said to have called for a file and a horse, and after freeing himself, made good his escape. No killings were credited to him after that. And less than three months later, on the night of July 13, 1881, he himself was shot to death in the dark by Pat Garrett in Pete Maxwell's bedroom in old Fort Sumner.

So the tale of the killings is told. What does it add up to? What must we conclude? Was Billy the brave lad and noble "hero" that he has been made out to be? Did he really kill as many men as he was reported to have killed?

I think not. Nowhere near as many. As I read the record, it is fairly certain that he killed the half-breed Beckwith, Grant, Carlyle, and Ollinger. Probably he killed Bell too. That makes five. I think some of his bullets may have lodged in the bodies of Morton and Baker, Brady and Hindman, but whether his bullets alone would have been enough to kill, no one can say. Definitely, he did not kill Roberts and Bernstein. Of the nine in whose killing Billy conceivably may have had some share, three were shot down when unarmed: Morton, Baker, and Carlyle. Two were killed from ambush: Brady and Hindman. One, Grant, was murdered after Billy had tampered with his victim's gun to make sure of an easy killing. That leaves three, and three only, whom Billy met on tolerably even terms: Beckwith, Bell, and Ollinger, and he killed them when his own life was in deadly danger. Such an analysis certainly removes a good deal of the glitter from the "hero" halo.

III

How, then, did the "hero" legend grow? In large part, apparently, it grew spontaneously out of the public's never-ending desire for a hero, and the mists and shadows that gather over all persons and events with the passing of time. There's a glamor about the cowboy's life, that is heightened by the thoughts of risks and dangers boldly met. It's hard to dramatize events without actors. Every play needs a hero. Billy the Kid has been cast in that role, and with the passage of time the facts have been distorted to make him fit the role according to the way we'd like to have had him be. Maybe the Robin Hood legends grew in the same way. Maybe a lot of "heroes" were just as insubstantial stuff in actual life. The Lincoln County War was a pretty sordid chapter in the history of the range, but it was nevertheless backgrounded against romance and color. There were hard- riding cowboys who were not afraid to fight hell itself for the lives and property of their friends, and the thought of them has always stirred the blood of arm-chair adventurers. Billy the Kid, a cow-country tough, happened to be enrolled on the "good" side in the Lincoln County War. He was admired by the likable and upright Tunstall. Perhaps his own insinuations about the unproved notches on his gun helped the stories about him to circulate. The fact that he died young was in his favor. The stories grew by what they fed on.

An important factor, too, was Pat Garrett. Probably a psychoanalyst would have a highfalutin word for him. I believe that Garrett felt a need to justify himself to himself and to the world. Governor Otero in a casual paragraph remarks: "In spite of the money and prestige which Pat Garrett secured for his services in killing the Kid, Tom O'Folliard, and Charlie Bowdre, the author has always felt that he regretted it."

Garrett and Billy had been good friends. But Pat killed Billy, and he was on the side of the law when he did it. As I said before, he always claimed that he had to do it; that Billy would have killed him if he hadn't killed Billy. But did Billy have a gun when Pat shot him? Pat always maintained that he did have. And John W. Poe, one of his deputies on that occasion, who later became president of the Citizen's National Bank of Roswell, in the reputable brief account which he wrote of Billy's death, said that Billy was carrying a six-shooter. But it was close to midnight when they met. The seeing wasn't good. Billy was admittedly in his stocking feet and almost completely undressed. And the first people to enter Pete Maxwell's bedroom after the shooting of Billy the Kid—Jesus Silva and an old Navajo Indian woman named Deluvina—both declared positively that Billy had no pistol.

Once more, who knows? The facts are clouded and the reports differ. Was Garrett secretly aware that he had shot an unarmed man? Did he purposely build up his victim in the book he sponsored and the stories he told, in order to justify himself? I knew Garrett, but I can't be sure of the answers to my own questions. Certainly he did build Billy up.

I first met Garrett at a wagon camp at the point of the White Sands, in New Mexico, when he came over to arrest a fellow. That was in 1889 or '90, eight or nine years after the dramatic killing of Billy. Garrett was a tall, slim, rawboned officer, with a black mustache and a very pleasant manner. I met him often afterwards at Santa Fe, Tularosa, Las Cruces, and elsewhere, and got to know him well. He was a rough-and-ready customer, a great lover of poker, with a good enough record in a hard line of work. He was made sheriff of Lincoln County on the theory that he would clean up Billy the Kid and other outlaws and cattle thieves; and he did that. But I have the impression that the rest of his life was haunted by ghosts from the Lincoln County War. In fact, it may have been one of these "ghosts" in the flesh that finally ended him, for he too died of a gunshot wound, under circumstances never fully explained. I think secret doubts about his own actions troubled him, and I believe he was driven to make Billy the Kid a more-than-life-size villain in order that Pat Garrett might be able to look Pat Garrett and the world straight in the eye. It's a curious and not impossible thought that he may have made the Kid a "hero," in order that he, the "hero" killer, might sleep easy at night!

IV

If he was not a "hero," then, what sort of chap was Billy the Kid?

We have the testimony of a lot of people that in certain moods he was a friendly and likable lad, with a sense of humor and a good singing voice, that he was undersized physically, with hands little larger than a woman's, a graceful dancer, polite and respectful to women, generally neat in personal appearance, and that he neither drank nor smoked to excess. Charlie Siringo met him at Tascosa, in Texas, in the late fall of 1878, when the Kid was over there disposing of a bunch of stolen horses, and Charlie writes:

"I found Billy the Kid to be a good natured young man. He was always cheerful and smiling. Being still in his 'teens, he had no sign of a beard. His eyes were a hazel blue, and his brown hair was long and curly. The skin on his face was tanned to a chestnut brown, and was as soft and tender as a woman's. He weighed about one hundred and forty pounds, and was five feet, eight inches tall. His only defects were two upper front teeth, which projected outward from his well shaped mouth."

George Coe says that when Billy bunked with him, most of one winter, he helped with all the chores and domestic work—"And I could not have asked for a better friend or companion."

Was he a wonderful shot? The testimony indicates that he was pretty fast with a gun, and coolheaded in using one in an emergency. Siringo has this to say: "While loafing in their camp, we passed off the time playing cards and shooting at marks. With our Colt's .45 pistols I could hit the mark as often as the Kid, but when it came to quick shooting, he could get in two shots to my one.*

Garrett's testimony was somewhat similar. Asked by a newspaper reporter whether the Kid was a good shot, he replied, "Yes, but he was no better than the majority of men who are constantly handling and using six-shooters. He shot well, though, and he shot well under all circumstances, whether in danger or not."

---

*In a personal letter written to me from Venice, California, September 22, 1927, Siringo said in part: "I have known a few men who could shoot two pistols at the same time with accuracy. But Billy the Kid was not a two-gun man. John Wesley Hardin was." —N. M. C.

George Coe, according to his cousin, Frank Coe, was the best shot among the Tunstall-McSween men. Frank Coe is quoted by Governor Otero as follows: "When he could take plenty of time for aiming, George hit the mark, and in hunting he always brought down more game than all the rest of the party put together. The Kid, however, was by far the quickest with a pistol; he could empty all six chambers of a revolver while an ordinary man was firing his first shot. He never seemed to take aim, but appeared to have an instinctive control."

George Coe, in the 220 pages of his book, makes little or no mention of Billy's shooting skill, except to say in one place that the Kid while spending the winter with him, did become quite expert as a deer slayer. Once at a shooting match, Coe tells, Billy was beaten by some buffalo hunters, and to get even with them, challenged them to a match with his friend—George Coe. Billy bet his last dollar on Coe, and won a dollar a shot until he banked eight dollars. If Billy had been a super-marksman, Coe undoubtedly would have mentioned the fact. His friends say he was good enough, but no wizard.

If he was likable, there are many things to show that Billy was not above saving himself at the expense of others, and in property matters he was shifty or worse. Siringo relates an exploit which he says was told him by the Kid himself. The government had given a gang of Mexicans a contract to put up a lot of hay at twenty-five dollars per ton. As they drew their pay, Billy who was an expert at monte, won it from them at cards. When the government contract was completed, Billy's source of money gave out, and he didn't like that. "With his own hands," Siringo says, "he set fire to the haystacks one windy night." The government had to let another contract at a higher price for more hay, and again Billy was on hand to win the money from the haymakers. There seems to be some reasonable doubt whether sharp practice of that kind is altogether "heroic." Also, there are records of occasions when stolen cattle were sold, and Billy allegedly kept the bulk of the proceeds, giving his partners little or none of it.

And it seems as though Billy's action was deliberately despicable, or downright cowardly, on the night when his friend and partner, Tom O'Folliard, was shot and killed by Garrett's posse. Billy was riding to town with several friends. He sensed danger, and ducked. As George Coe, reporting the incident from hearsay, put it: "By a clever ruse he avoided them (Garret and his posse). He left his gang about a mile from

Tom O'Folliard in his late teens, ca. 1875. He became the Kid's buddy and staunchest supporter. He died in front of the guns of Pat Garrett's posse at Fort Sumner on December 19, 1880. Robert G. McCubbin Collection.

town and rode in by another route"—leaving them to "take it!" Garrett's account of that incident is different:

"With all his reckless bravery, the Kid had a strong infusion of caution in his composition when he was not excited. He afterwards told me that as they approached the building that night he was riding in front with O'Folliard. As they rode down close to our vicinity, he said a strong suspicion arose in his mind that they might be running into unseen danger.

"'Well,' I said, 'what did you do?'

"He replied—'I wanted a chew of tobacco bad. Wilson had some that was good and he was in the rear. I went back after tobacco, don't you see?' and his eyes twinkled mischievously."

A few minutes after going back for his chew of tobacco, thus taking his own hide out of the zone of danger, guns blazed out of the blackness, and the Kid's good friend, Tom, riding in front, received a mortal wound.

Billy, according to Garrett's report, declared that if ever he were taken prisoner by the law, it would be a dead man that the law got. "The Kid," says Garrett, "had sworn that he would never give himself up a prisoner and would die fighting even though there was a revolver at each ear, and I knew he would keep his word." Yet at Stinking Spring, after spending a cold night and day in an old stone shack, Billy and his three companions never fired a shot when Garrett and his posse built a fire and cooked supper outside. "The odor of roasting meat was too much for the famished lads who were without provisions. Craving stomachs overcame brave hearts."

No! Making all allowances, I think Billy the Kid was short weight for a hero. But the legend has grown past stopping. Even those who denounce him, now, merely add volume to his fame.

CHAPTER EIGHT

The True Trail of Billy the Kid

Alvin Rucker

Tennessee-born Alvin Rucker (1879–1934) was raised in Missouri, where he studied law at the University of Missouri but failed to graduate. He worked in banking for a decade before becoming a newspaperman, and joined the *Daily Oklahoman* in 1913. Over the next twenty years, according to his obituary in that newspaper on March 8, 1934, he won a reputation as "the encyclopedia of Oklahoma" and was said to be "personally acquainted with more Oklahoma territory, more Oklahoma history, and more Oklahomans than any other politician or newspaper man."

His remit as a reporter seems to have been as wide as he cared to make it. He "retraveled the 'Trail of Tears.' He made a flesh and blood man of Sequoyah . . . he wrote of the Rosses and the Boudinots, the Choteaus on the Verdigris, the hoary old rocks of the Wichita, the beauties of Black Mesa, the true story of Geronimo."

Had he written his own headline for it, Rucker might well have titled the piece that follows "Newspaperman Fearlessly Seeks Truth: The Real Facts of the Billy the Kid Story." Obviously prompted by the success of Burns's *Saga of Billy the Kid*, and intending to pen something of a corrective to that "romance," he somehow still manages to sensationalize the Kid's story. To beef up his historical credibility, Rucker borrowed heavily from the 1927 version of Garrett's *Authentic Life*, edited by Maurice Garland Fulton; nowhere else could he have obtained the details of the Fritz insurance policy, Lew Wallace's correspondence with the Kid, and Dudley's report on the July 19 fight at Lincoln, because Fulton was the first to publish them.

To his credit, Rucker went the extra mile by following the Kid's trail through New Mexico, and he even made an effort to get closer to the historical facts by talking to George Coe, who supplied some interesting background information not available elsewhere. His survey of the Lincoln County War and its partici-pants—completely missed by later bibliographers and writers—also included biographical material on the likes of John Middleton, Henry Brown, Fred

Waite, and Jim French, which would likewise remain undiscovered for more than sixty years.

Despite these plusses, however, when he wanders out from under Fulton's historical umbrella, he reveals a very shaky grip on the backstory and some equally wobbly geography—for instance, making both McSween and Tunstall British and having them arrive in Lincoln together in 1876; dating the Brady assassination April 18, 1878; putting ten thousand Mescalero Apaches on the reservation at Fort Sumner; having fifteen hundred people living in Lincoln; claiming that there was "not a mile of railroad in New Mexico"; and having the Rio Grande form the western boundary of Lincoln County. Despite Rucker's good intentions, his Billy the Kid remains largely the same dime-novel character that Ash Upson and all the others had made him, but his article was an important step in the right direction, and others would follow his lead.

Oklahomans who speed over the wonderful highways, traversing the mountains of the southern half of New Mexico in quest of interesting places to visit, rush through a country drenched with romantic history, in the making of which some of Oklahoma's restless children of a forgotten day played tremendous parts. It is the land of Billy the Kid and the cattlemen's war—a war in which the souls of 200 knights of the plains were sent to dusty death.

Talk with any old resident of that section and you soon hear mentioned such names as Fred Waite, John Middleton, Jim French, Henry Brown, Billy the Kid, Pat Garrett and Killing Miller—all in some way connected with Oklahoma, and with the cattlemen's war in old Lincoln county, New Mexico.

It was the cattlemen's war in old Lincoln county, New Mexico, that concentrated on the western stage a group of characters the like of which had never before been seen and never since. All up and down the fertile Rio Pecos valley, from old Fort Sumner on the north to the Rio Grande on the south, and in the Bonito, Hondo, Ruidoso, Tularosa canyons and around the base of the Sierra Capitan mountains and in the Seven Rivers country there are scores of forgotten graves in which rest all that remains of a restless breed of men—victims of the cattlemen's war. It was a cattleman's war, but it was a cowboy's fight.

New Mexico historians long ago despaired of writing the history of their commonwealth without alluding to William Bonney, universally referred to throughout the southwest as Billy the Kid, but like Banquo's ghost the restless spirit of the Kid would not [lie] down, and today his picture hangs on a wall in the old Governors' palace at Santa Fe, N. M. Billy the Kid, leader of the fighting forces of one faction in the cattlemen's war, long ago evolved from the character of an outlaw into a historic personage in New Mexico history. Public sentiment in southern New Mexico has changed from condemnation to sympathy for Billy, with the lapse of years. To use a modern slang phrase, the Kid is regarded as the "goat" of that bloody, private war. The idea of a youth becoming a fugitive from justice at the age of twelve years, because of a killing in the defense of his mother, and then being so buffeted by fate and chance during the next nine years, during which he killed more than 20 men, appeals to the sympathy of a generation of New Mexicans not financially or otherwise interested in the cause of the cattlemen's war. Governor Lew Wallace's amnesty, unconditional to the cattle kings who were proprietors of the private war, and to nearly all their fighters in the ranks, was conditional to Billy the Kid. The cattlemen's war got under way with skirmishes in 1876 and reached its climax two years later in the street of Lincoln, county seat of Lincoln county. During the two years the war was in progress, the law, when invoked at all, was used merely to give color of legality to deeds of violence. Following the fight in Lincoln President Rutherford B. Hayes took a hand, removed Governor Axtell because of the partisanship he had shown and appointed Lew Wallace as governor of New Mexico territory, with extraordinary powers to be used in bringing peace to distracted Lincoln county. Governor Wallace's amnesty applied to all except those under indictment. The Kid was under indictment for several things—in fact for nearly every misfortune that had befallen the opposition.

George Coe, a genial old man and one of the few survivors of the Lincoln county war waggishly expresses the situation as follows:

"The Murphy crowd controlled the public officers in Lincoln county and could get warrants for anybody for anything. It got so that every time a rifle shot was heard in the canyons, or on the plain, a warrant was sworn out for Billy the Kid and the rest of us. They would just leave blank the name of the person imagined killed, and the first time they heard of a body being found anywhere, they would fill in that man's name."

The Lincoln county war was a fight between two groups of cattle and business men, the bone of contention being highly valuable beef contracts with the federal government. New Mexico was created a territory

in 1850, two years after the area was obtained from Mexico as a result of
the war with Mexico. At the time of acquisition the area was populated
largely by Mexicans. Discovery of gold in California resulted in New
Mexico soon being over-run with American miners who operated in the
mountains. The federal government undertook to round up the warlike
Mescalero Apaches and other turbulent tribes and concentrate them on
a reservation in the Mescalero mountains, in southern New Mexico, to
obviate conflicts between the invading white miners and the Indians.
Soon the government had 10,000 warlike Indians on the reservation
and Fort Stanton was established to watch over them.

Fort Stanton was in Lincoln county, which, at that time embraced
nearly all of the southeast quarter of the present state of New Mexico.
The county was approximately 200 miles square. It was necessary for the
government to feed the Indians and that created an enormous demand
for beef. Old Lincoln county was bounded on the west by the Rio Grande
river and on the east and south by Texas. The western two-thirds of the
area of Lincoln county was made up of mountain ranges, deserts and
semi-arid flats. The east one-third of old Lincoln county was composed
of the western edge of the staked plains which extended eastward across
the Texas panhandle. There was not a mile of railroad in New Mexico,
the nearest cattle shipping points being at Dodge City, Caldwell and other
railroad points in southwestern Kansas. At the close of the Civil war, L. G.
Murphy and Emil Fritz, two Union soldiers, were mustered out at Fort
Stanton and they promptly set up a sutler's store at the fort and sold goods
to Indians, soldiers, and Mexicans. In 1867 John Chisum, founder of the
city of Paris, Texas, contractor and cattleman, moved 10,000 head of cattle
into Lincoln county, New Mexico, and grazed them in the fertile Rio
Pecos valley in the eastern one-third of Union county. The Rio Pecos
valley afforded the sole extensive, well-watered grazing area in Lincoln
county. Chisum established headquarters at Bosque Grande, a magnificent grove of cottonwood trees about 20 miles north of the present city
of Roswell. Soon the post office of Roswell was established and an adobe
cow town developed. Chisum prospered to such an extent that he soon
owned nearly 100,000 head of cattle, grazing on the free ranges of the
Rio Pecos valley. Four miles south of the adobe town of Roswell there
was a great spring and to that place Chisum moved his headquarters,
and there built a large adobe home, surrounded by all the outbuildings
and trappings that go to make up baronial headquarters, sold cattle to

the government agents at Fort Stanton, and delivered them by driving the herds up the beautiful Hondo, Bonito, Tularusa, Ruidoso, Feliz and other canyons through which crystal clear streams of mountain water rushed eastward to join the Rio Pecos. The Spaniards who named the canyon streams in southern New Mexico gave to them names that literally described. Rio Bonito means "Pretty river"; Rio Ruidoso means "Noisy river"; Rio Feliz means "Happy river"; Rio Penasco means "Rocky river." Those canyons come down from the Rocky mountains and extend east. They form natural chutes through the Sierra Blanca, Sacramento, Guadalupe and other mountain ranges in the western two-thirds of old Lincoln county.

While John Chisum was prospering in the cattle business in the Rio Pecos valley, Murphy and Fritz were having trouble as operators of the sutler's store at Fort Stanton. Questionable practices caused the government to cancel their sutler's permit and they promptly moved ten miles east to the county seat town of Lincoln in the Bonito canyon, where they built a large two-story store building and opened a general merchandise store. Lincoln county, large as it was at that time, contained a citizen population of only 2,500 and of that number 1,500 lived in Lincoln, at that time an adobe town, most of the buildings being low with flat roofs, and used as residences, eating houses, gambling dens, saloons and forms of vice vocations. Two other elements soon appeared to swell the population of the town of Lincoln—miners from the played-out mines around Silver City in the southwestern part of New Mexico, and the irrepressible American "nester." The miners prospected the mountain sides and the nesters settled in the canyons. The canyons in the old Lincoln county area are scarcely a mile wide, and usually not more than a half mile wide. A rifle bullet can be fired from one mountain side to the opposite mountain side. There is just enough valley floor in each canyon to provide room for a rushing mountain stream, a narrow bench of tillable land and a trail or road. The cattle and wagon trails of the old days have been supplanted by splendid automobile highways, and Ruidoso canyon today is given over in places to fashionable public and private summer resorts.

The early-day nesters filed homestead claims on the narrow strips of canyon-floor land, built small dams across the streams and diverted the water to the bench land where it was used for irrigation purposes, the principal crops being fruit, vegetables and alfalfa. By pre-empting the waterfront canyon land, the nesters had the exclusive use of unlimited cattle range on the flanks and tops of the mountains.

The old county seat town of Lincoln, with its motley population of cattlemen, cowboys, Indians, gamblers, saloon and restaurant keepers, was strung out for more than a mile in Bonito canyon, the rear of the buildings on the north side overhanging the Rio Bonito. The road formed the sole street in the town—there wasn't room in [the] canyon for an additional street. Murphy and Fritz erected their big two-story building on the south side of the canyon road and well toward the west end of town. Other stores existed, but the Murphy-Fritz store, because of its size, became known as the "Big Store." It was destined to play a tremendous part in the Lincoln county war, and in the lives of many men. Lumber for floors and sills in the building was sawed from pine trees on the mountain sides of Tularosa canyon 30 miles southwest across the mountains and was transported on burros through mountain passes to Lincoln. The lumber was sawed at what is still referred to as "Dr. Blazer's mill." Doctor Blazer was a young dentist who cast his fortune in Lincoln county, New Mexico. He abandoned his profession and devoted his time to accumulating land, cattle and money, and he succeeded. His son still lives on the old home-place. Blazer's mill was destined to be the scene of one of the battles engaged in by Fred Waite, Jim French, John Middleton, Billy the Kid, George and Frank Coe, R. M. Brewer and others.

In the town of Lincoln, Murphy and Fritz prospered as merchants and undertook to branch out into the cattle business. They took into partnership J. J. Dolan, a cowboy who was to have charge of the cattle business. The nesters had pre-empted the watered canyons and John Chisum's great herds were monopolizing the Rio Pecos valley, 50 miles to the east. Absence of a more suitable place forced Murphy and associates to graze their herd on the sparsely watered Carrizozo flat, and lava beds 20 miles west of Lincoln. Murphy had become the Warwick of Lincoln county and that made him a tremendous political factor in New Mexico politics, as Lincoln county comprised one-fourth of the entire area.

He formed a political and business alliance with Thomas B. Catron, United States district attorney and president of the First National Bank at Santa Fe, capital of New Mexico, and was accepted into full fellowship as a member of the "Santa Fe political ring." Through Murphy's influence Catron became interested in cattle ventures in Lincoln county. Murphy was now deeply intrenched. He controlled the local public officials, he had intimate financial and political relationship with Catron, the federal prosecutor; when pressed for funds he borrowed money from Catron's bank; he established himself socially at Fort Stanton and through that means obtained highly profitable beef contracts; he elected William Brady, a cowboy, sheriff of Lincoln county and when in need of emergency funds with which to carry on his business, he borrowed from Sheriff Brady the Lincoln county tax funds collected and held by the sheriff. Murphy's influence with the Indian agency official at Fort Stanton was such that John Chisum was completely horned off so far as beef contracts were concerned, and Chisum was forced to drive his herds across the staked plains then through what is now western Oklahoma to Dodge City, Caldwell and other cattle shipping points in southwestern Kansas.

There was only one fly in Murphy's coffee—he didn't have enough cattle with which to supply the beef contracts at Fort Stanton, and the nearest supply was the vast herds of his rival, John Chisum, in the Pecos valley, 60 miles distant. Murphy made a strategic move. He moved his herd from the sparsely water[ed] Carrizozo flats into the lower part of the Rio Pecos valley, and quartered the herd in the Seven Rivers country, an area which for ten years had been monopolized by John Chisum, cattle king of the Rio Pecos valley. It was free range and belonged to anyone else as much as to Chisum.

The Seven Rivers area is about fifteen miles north of the present city of Carlsbad. It was there that the cow town known as Seven Rivers developed. It became the hangout of Murphy's cowboys in the Rio Pecos valley, and the rendezvous of Murphy's dragoons, known as the Seven Rivers Warriors, headed by Jesse Evans, 19 years old, and who until a year before, had been childhood companion of Billy the Kid. The Seven Rivers Warriors were cowboys, who at times worked for Murphy and at other times operated on their own hook by driving off detached bunches of Chisum's cattle and selling them to Murphy, who added them to his herd and resold them to the Indian agency at Fort Stanton.

Today a fine federal highway passes within a mile of the site of old "Seven Rivers" adobe town and its neglected cemetery. There is nothing on the Seven Rivers townsite except old sloughed-down adobe buildings which once housed saloons and eating places, and thousands of pieces of whisky bottles, and used revolver shells. Such was the condition that prevailed in Lincoln county, New Mexico, when the year 1876 dawned. In that year Alexander A. McSween, a British subject by birth, and John H.

Tunstall, another British subject by birth, following different paths found their way to Lincoln. McSween hung out his "law shingle," and Tunstall, who was wealthy, entered the cattle business, establishing a ranch on the Rio Feliz in a canyon about twenty miles southeast of Lincoln. John Chisum took the inexperienced newcomers under his wing. He threw legal business to McSween and instructed Tunstall in the cattle business. The three became personal and business friends. McSween and Tunstall, at Chisum's suggestion, erected a large general store in Lincoln and embarked in the mercantile business in opposition to Murphy & Company, Tunstall furnishing most of the money. McSween and Tunstall also organized the Lincoln County bank, the first bank in Lincoln county. Their square dealings drew to them nearly all the nester trade in the canyons.

George Coe, veteran of the Lincoln county war, still lives in Ruidoso canyon and has lived there for more than a half century. While pointing out historical places in connection with the Lincoln county war, he described pre-war conditions as follows:

"I and my cousin Frank, who still lives down the canyon, were nesters. We had filed homestead claims on canyon valley land that fronted the Ruidoso and the Hondo rivers and nearly all the other water-front land in the canyons had been filed upon by other nesters. We were undertaking to till the canyon land and run cattle on the mountain sides. Murphy hated the nesters and by charging exorbitant prices for goods tried to force us to give up and leave the country so that he could obtain possession of the well-watered canyons for his cattle. His prices were so high I quit trading with his store and so did nearly all other nesters. We went ten miles farther to the sutler's store at Fort Stanton to trade until McSween and Tunstall started their store in Lincoln, and then we traded there. Some of the nesters owed Murphy so much they were nearly reduced to peonage. That was how I incurred Murphy's enmity. Murphy owned Sheriff Brady body and soul and could get warrants for anybody he wanted arrested. Most of us were mere boys, very few of us 21 years of age. One of Murphy's schemes of driving people out of the country was to bring about their imprisonment at Lincoln. Then an opportunity would be afforded for escape, and usually the one under arrest took advantage of the opportunity and fled the country. The old jail at Lincoln was simply an adobe shack with a wooden door. The court house was the long adobe building that still stands at the east end of Lincoln and the adobe jail stood back of it. Sheriff Brady's son was jailer at the time the war broke out. If he wanted a prisoner to escape he simply walked away from the court house, from which he was supposed to watch the jail door, and if the prisoner wanted to escape, all he had to do was push hard on the jail door, and break the lock. The absence of the jailer from the vicinity of the jail shack was always regarded as the signal that it was all right for the prisoners to break out, or for some friend to come along and break open the door from the outside. If the sheriff had a prisoner he really wanted to keep, he placed an armed guard around him, night and day, in a room, or sent him to the military prison at Fort Stanton, ten miles west. The Murphy crowd formed the elite of society in Lincoln and the Lincoln social set and the army set at Fort Stanton were on an intimate social basis. The Murphy set would give balls in honor of the Fort Stanton military officers and balls would be given at Fort Stanton in honor of the Lincoln social set. That enabled Murphy to have soldiers at his beck and call until President Hayes, through Governor Lew Wallace stopped the practice."

Emil Fritz, one of Murphy's original business associates, died while on a visit to Germany in 1874. Nothing was done until 1876 toward settling the estate. In that year, the year of McSween's advent in Lincoln county, McSween was employed by Fritz heirs to look after their interest. McSween discovered that Fritz had carried a $10,000 life insurance policy, the policy being in the possession of Murphy. Murphy refused to surrender this policy, claiming that Fritz owed him a large sum of money. McSween found that the policy had been put up by Murphy to secure an open account of less than $1,000 in Santa Fe. McSween paid the debt and obtained the policy. He went to New York and hired a law firm there to assist in collecting the policy. The [New] York lawyers collected the money and deducted $3,852 for their fee, turning $7,148 over to McSween. McSween deducted $4,095 as his fee, leaving $2,052 due to Fritz heirs. Instead of turning that amount over to them, he placed it in a bank to his own credit. The Fritz heirs in Lincoln county consulted with Murphy and as a result a warrant was sworn out for McSween, and attachment was levied on the McSween & Tunstall store in Lincoln and on cattle and horses belonging to McSween & Tunstall as partners, and even on horses and cattle belonging exclusively to Tunstall.

While McSween was in the east in the summer of 1877, Jess Evans and his Seven Rivers warriors raided Tunstall's ranch and stole a bunch of Tunstall's horses. When Tunstall returned he forced Sheriff Brady to arrest them. Brady placed the thieves in the adobe shack jail in Lincoln from which he helped them escape, and they promptly returned to their hang-out at Seven Rivers.

Murphy openly bought cattle and horses plundered by the Seven Rivers warriors from the Chisum-McSween-Tunstall group, and encouraged his own cowboys to raid the enemy herds, justifying the action on the grounds that Chisum's enormous herds swept over and absorbed small Murphy herds. Here is how George Coe explains the situation:

"Unquestionably some of Murphy's cattle grazing on the range did mingle with Chisum's big herds, and Murphy used that as a pretext for the wholesale plunder of Chisum herds. Chisum realized his big herds contained cattle belonging to Murphy and other small drovers. Invariably before starting on a drive to market, Chisum would notify all other cattlemen of his intention and tell them to cut out their cattle. That was a cow country custom. Murphy would not respond. He wanted an excuse to plunder, as he knew that for every steer he lost to Chisum, he would eventually get 100. Chisum would hold up his herds for several days, then drive them to market. Chisum's herds did contain Murphy cattle, but it was Murphy's own fault. He was willing that the situation should be that way, as it provided him with an excuse for wholesale raiding."

All the elements, except the presence of Billy the Kid, that went to make up the cattlemen's war, were now present.

William Bonney, known throughout the southwest as Billy the Kid, was born in New York City, Nov. 21, 1859. Two years later the Bonney family moved to Coffeyville, Kan., where the father died, the mother moving to Colorado where she married a man named Antrim, and from Colorado the family moved to Santa Fe and then to Silver City, New Mexico. Mrs. Antrim aided the family income by keeping boarders while in Santa Fe and while in Silver City. The few facts known concerning the Kid's early life were preserved by Ash Upson, a newspaper man who boarded with Mrs. Antrim in Santa Fe and then in Silver City. Upson later became postmaster at the adobe town of Roswell, Lincoln county, and was serving as postmaster there during the Lincoln county war. He later lived with Pat Garrett, who, as sheriff of Lincoln county, killed Billy the Kid, and immediately after the killing of the Kid, Upson assisted Garrett in assembling all the known facts concerning the Kid and publishing them in pamphlet form. Garrett, in assembling and printing the facts, was actuated primarily by a desire to present his side of the story, for he was openly accused of all

forms of cowardice in killing the Kid. All of the many romances that have
been written around the life of Billy the Kid are largely rhetorical embell-
ishments and distortions of Garrett's simple statements of facts. Garrett,
in describing the battle in Lincoln, mentions the fact that bullets fired
into the McSween home struck piano chords and caused the instrument
to give out discordant sounds. That unsensational incident of the battle is
invariably distorted by Billy the Kid saga writers into such florid passages
as "During the fight Mrs. McSween encouraged her wild garrison by
playing inspiring airs on her piano and singing rousing battle songs, until
the besieging party, getting the range of the piano from the sound, shot it
to pieces with their heavy rifles."

Another Billy the Kid saga writer describes the incident as follows:

"Mrs. McSween's eyes rested sadly on her piano. Flame reflections
were leaping and dancing in its polished depths. It was fated to destruction. A few hours more and it would be a wreck buried under flaming
debris. She threw herself upon the stool at the keyboard. She still had
hope—hope in Billy the Kid and his fighting men. They were battling
desperately in their last ditch. A war song might inspire them to still more
heroic courage. It might turn defeat into victory. With one last brave
swan-song before the ultimate silence, the piano yet might save the day.
At once she plunged into the stirring bars of 'The Star Spangled Banner.'
Facing death the men felt the lift and thrill of 'O say, can you see,' etc."

Garrett is authority for the statement that. Mrs. McSween was not in
the building, as she and two women friends left before the firing started.

During the time Billy the Kid lived in Silver City, New Mexico, he had
a boy playmate, Jesse Evans, who like Billy was destined to play an important part in the cattlemen's war. . . . Jesse was about two years older than
Billy. When Billy was 12 years old he killed a man in Silver City, as the
outcome of a slighting remark about his mother. He cut the man to
death with a pocket knife. The Kid fled to Fort Bowie, Ariz., where he eked
out a living by hanging around saloons and gambling houses, becoming
an expert gambler and a fluent speaker of the Spanish language. It was
in Arizona that he learned to ride and rope, and drifted into the voca-
tion of a cowboy, becoming famous for horsemanship, dexterity with lariat
and accuracy with rifle and revolver. Billy and his boy companion killed
Apache Indians and robbed them of their horses and packs. While dealing
monte in Fort Bowie, a drunken soldier refused to pay his gambling losses
and in the argument slapped the Kid to the floor; he shot the soldier

dead and fled to Mexico, where he killed a Mexican gambler and was chased by a Mexican posse back into the United States.

Shortly after the Kid crossed the Rio Grande river, the Kid met his boyhood friend, Jesse Evans, and the two embarked upon stock raids on both sides of the Rio Grande, which resulted in the death of eight persons. Near Mesilla, a dreamy adobe town 30 miles north of El Paso, Billy and Jesse met a band of cowboys. They were the Seven Rivers Warriors, and Jesse was well acquainted with them. Among the Seven Rivers Warriors were William Morton, James McDaniels and Frank Baker, who were destined to play prominent parts in the Lincoln county cattlemen's war. The "warriors" explained to Billy and Jesse the situation in the Rio Pecos valley and assured them they could make money there. Billy and Jesse joined the Warriors, and went to the Pecos valley, where they immediately began raiding the Chisum-Tunstall-McSween herds, selling the stolen cattle to Murphy. That was in the summer of 1876. Billy was 17 years old; Jesse was 19 and each was an expert cowboy, gambler, marksman and cattle rustler. Shortly after Billy joined the Seven Rivers Warriors he met Tunstall, whose herds he had plundered. As a result of that meeting he went to work on Tunstall's Rio Feliz ranch about 20 miles southeast of Lincoln. The Kid and Tunstall became fast friends, Tunstall being the first man who Billy regarded as standing in the relationship of a parent. Through Tunstall, Billy became acquainted with McSween and Chisum. It was Billy's duty to herd and guard Tunstall's cattle and horse herds from the depredations of his former companions, the Seven Rivers Warriors and Murphy's cowboys. It was while working for Tunstall that Billy became acquainted with Frank and George Coe, cousins, and with Fred Waite, Henry Brown, John Middleton and Jim French, all youthful cowboys employed at times by the Tunstall-McSween-Chisum group.

Fred Waite was born and reared at Paul's Valley, Okla., where he was related to the Smith Paul family and where he has relatives still living, Mrs. Milas Laster being his sister. Waite fought throughout the cattlemen's war under the leadership of Billy the Kid, and when Gov. Lew Wallace issued the amnesty in November, 1878, Waite laid down his arms, returned to Oklahoma where he studied Chickasaw law, was admitted to the bar, became a member of the Chickasaw legislature and then attorney general for the Chickasaw nation. He died in middle life, a substantial and highly honored citizen. His former law partner is still practicing law in Pauls Valley.

John Middleton, who fought throughout the cattlemen's war on the McSween-Tunstall-Chisum side, accepted the terms of Gov. Lew Wallace's amnesty and returned to Oklahoma with Waite and Henry Brown. In Oklahoma, Middleton and Brown went north to Caldwell, Kan., where they became acquainted with the Colcord family. Middleton at that time was still suffering from a rifle bullet wound, through the chest, just below the heart. The Colcords nursed him back to health and he married Birdie Colcord, sister of Charles E. Colcord, destined at that time to become one of the wealthiest men in Oklahoma. The Colcord family took an interest in Henry Brown and helped obtain for him the appointment of deputy city marshal for Caldwell, Kan., at that time a turbulent frontier town. Brown proved an efficient deputy and became city marshal. During his police officer service in Caldwell he killed four men in the discharge of his duty. Brown, however, hearkened to the call of wild life, and with his marshal's badge still pinned on his breast, led a band of bank robbers into Medicine Lodge, Kan., killed George Geppert, cashier, and Wiley Payne, president of the Medicine Lodge Valley bank and all were promptly shot or hanged by a posse. Jim French returned to Oklahoma at the close of the cattlemen's war, joined Belle Starr's gang of outlaws, and after her death operated with Cherokee Bill and Bill Cook. He was killed while holding up Reynolds & Co.'s store in Catoosa, Okla., being shot twice through the neck by Colonel Irwin, store manager, whom French had mortally wounded.

● ● ●

Beginning in the summer of 1878, conflicts between the opposing bands of cowboys were so frequent and deaths and cattle thefts so common that they ceased to excite interest. It was the murder of John H. Tunstall, February 18, 1878, that precipitated wholesale fighting and swept aside such semblance of law as had been administered by Murphy's office holders. The Murphy crowd had obtained a writ of attachment for McSween's property as part of the suit to collect the money due on the Emil Fritz life insurance policy. William Morton, ranch foreman for Murphy, was commissioned deputy sheriff by Sheriff William Brady to levy upon the property. Morton assembled his cowboys, levied upon the McSween-Tunstall store in Lincoln and then rode to the Tunstall's ranch on the Feliz, ostensibly to look for cattle and horses in which McSween might have an interest. R. M. Brewer, Tunstall's foreman, informed the posse that McSween had no interest in any of the stock on the Tunstall ranch, and in the absence of Tunstall, refused to allow the posse to go peaceably through the herds. Brewer told Morton that if he would return alone in a few days he could go through the herds and inspect brands. Morton and his posse returned to Lincoln and reported to Murphy and Sheriff Brady. Tunstall, who had been in Lincoln when the posse rode to his ranch, learned of the incident and went to the ranch, where he instructed Brewer to allow the posse, if it returned, to levy upon the cattle and said the matter would be settled in court. Tunstall, accompanied by Billy the Kid, John Middleton and R. M. Brewer and another cowboy, started to drive to Lincoln a bunch of horses which Tunstall was anxious to remove from the operation of the attachment writ. After they had left the ranch with the horses, the Morton posse, composed of a score of cowboys, including the Seven Rivers Warriors, arrived at the ranch, levied on the cattle, but found Tunstall and the horses gone. It was agreed that the Seven Rivers Warriors, headed by Morton, should try to overtake Tunstall and the horses, and the remainder of the posse should herd the cattle. When the Morton posse overtook Tunstall, he and John Middleton were riding along in charge of the horses, Brewer, the Kid and the other cowboy being on a distant hillside chasing a flock of wild turkeys. Morton called to Tunstall and the latter stopped. Middleton sensed the impending danger and fled, calling Tunstall to follow. Tunstall, however, stood still and handed his revolver to Morton, when the latter came up. Tom Hill, one of the Seven Rivers Warriors, rode up and shot Tunstall dead. Tunstall's horse was then killed and the two bodies were left where they fell. The posse then rode back to the ranch and reported to the larger posse that Tunstall had resisted arrest and had been killed as a necessity.

News of the killing of Tunstall spread throughout Lincoln county and the population was immediately divided into two hostile camps. Each side sought to invoke the aid of law and in the roundup Federal Prosecutor T. B. Catron arrested and jailed John Chisum at Las Vegas on the charge that he was illegally connected with a packing house deal at Little Rock, Ark. Chisum probably welcomed the imprisonment as it safely removed him from the seat of war. As the sheriff's office was in the hands of a Murphy man, the Tunstall-McSween-Chisum elements were hard pressed

in obtaining warrants for the arrest of the slayers of Tunstall. A justice of
the peace finally issued warrants for the arrest of the slayers, and it was
placed in the hands of R. M. Brewer, Tunstall foreman, for execution,
Brewer being appointed special constable for serving the warrant.

Brewer assembled his cowboys, Billy the Kid, Jim French, John Middleton, Charley Bowdre, Henry Brown, Doc Scurlock, William McCloskey
and Sam Smith. All members of that posse except Brewer, who was killed
shortly afterwards, and McCloskey, became known as "Billy the Kid's
crowd." The posse started southeast for the Seven Rivers country about
100 miles distant, where the Seven Rivers warriors hung out. In the Seven
Rivers area the posse flushed five Seven Rivers warriors, William Morton
and Frank Baker being captured after their horses had been shot. Morton
and Baker took refuge in an arroyo but surrendered after a skirmish
and with the understanding that they were to be safely delivered to
Sheriff Brady at Lincoln. The promise was made, but not kept.

The posse and prisoners rode north to Chisum's South Spring ranch
four miles south of Roswell, and stayed all night. From there the march
was continued to Roswell, where Morton mailed a letter to an eastern
friend, in which he set forth his suspicions as to his outcome. It was in
that letter that the name of many of the men who later became Billy the
Kid followers, were set forth and their identity established. The posse,
instead of taking the prisoners to Lincoln, turned onto a side trail and
Morton and Baker were shot to death at Agua Negra (Black water hole).
The posse reported that Morton had grabbed a revolver from McCloskey;
had killed McCloskey and then accompanied by Baker had sought to
escape, and that they had been killed as a necessity. The Brady element
promptly obtained warrants for arrests of members of the Brewer posse,
but when the grand jury met it ignored the killing. As Brady held the
warrants, notwithstanding the grand jury had ignored the killing, the
Brewer posse members could not safely remain around Lincoln, and the
posse took to the field in search of other members of the Seven Rivers
Warriors, for whom the Brewer posse held justice of the peace warrants.

George Coe, while standing by the graves of R. M. Brewer and "Buck-
shot" Roberts at Blazer's mill a few days ago said:

"I like everyone else in Lincoln was drawn into the cattlemen's war. I
and my cousin Frank were nesters who had filed on homestead claims
in the Ruidoso canyon, and for that reason we were among those whom
the Murphy crowd were trying to drive out. I had quit trading at the

Murphy store in Lincoln and was patronizing the Sutler's store at Fort Stanton, ten miles west of Lincoln. Nearly all the other nesters were doing likewise. Frank Freeman, a young nester living in the canyon south of here, always stopped over at my place while making the journey to and from Lincoln and Fort Stanton. He reached my place one night and left early next morning for Fort Stanton, by the way of Lincoln. I did not expect him to return for several days as Fort Stanton was about 30 miles distant across the mountains. The next morning, however, Freeman returned and was excited. He said that he had killed a negro soldier who insisted on eating at the same table with him in a Lincoln restaurant and had been arrested by Sheriff Brady. The sheriff, however, regarding Freeman as a nester, turned him over to a squad of negro soldiers instead of putting him in jail or sending him under civilian escort to the military authorities at Fort Stanton. The soldiers got a rope, put Freeman on a horse, and rode up the canyon looking for a tree to hang him from. It was then night. The soldiers found a tree on the south side of the Rio Bonito but could not with ease throw the rope over the lower limb. At the suggestion of a sergeant they decided to cross the Rio Bonito where suitable trees were plentiful. The Rio Bonito was swollen and the horses floundered in the swift mountain current. Freeman took advantage of the situation and plunged from the horse into the torrent. The soldiers fired at random in the dark, but failed to hit Freeman, and he escaped across to the mountains and made his way to my place. He said that it was useless to return to his own place as the soldiers would go there in search of him, and that he had nowhere else to go. He said that he was going to hide in the mountains and depend on me to carry food to him. I took care of him in that way for several days. Sheriff Brady and a posse came across the mountains one day and arrested Doc Scurlock, another canyon nester, on suspicion that he had been harboring Freeman, and then came to my place and arrested me. Brady put me on a sharp-backed pony behind Scurlock, tied his feet and my feet beneath the horse's belly, tied Doc's hands to the horse's neck and tied my hands around Doc's body. The trip across the mountains to Lincoln took two days. Rain fell; the ropes shrunk and Doc and I suffered terribly.

"We told Brady to shoot us, if that was his intention, and put us out of our misery. He didn't shoot us—he just made us ride that sharp-backed pony all the way across the mountains to Lincoln. He put us in jail and our bond was fixed at $1000 each. Isaac Ellis at that time ran the Ellis hotel. He was a wealthy old man. He and I had come across the plains together when we came to Lincoln county a few years before. Brady took Doc and me to Ellis and told us to have Ellis go our bond. He left Ellis and me in a room to talk it over. I told Ellis I did not want him to go my bond but I did want him to give me and Doc two Winchester rifles, four belts of ammunition and two saddle horses. Ellis at that time, like everybody else in Lincoln, had plenty of rifles. He had at least 20 stacked in the room in which we were talking. Brady had confiscated my fine Sharp's rifle for which I had paid $56 and had also taken my revolvers. Ellis wanted to go our bonds instead of furnishing the requested rifles, ammunition and horses. I told him that all Brady wanted to accomplish was to liberate me on bond and scare me so bad that I would leave the country. I had as much right in the country as Brady and his owner, Murphy, did; I hadn't run into the country to get away from the law and I wasn't going to run out. Ellis and I talked so long that Brady and his deputies got restless and took us back to jail. They abused us terribly. They gave us an opportunity to escape that night, thinking that we would leave the country and abandon our claims. A day or two later, R. M. Brewer, Billy the Kid, Fred Waite, John Middleton, Henry Brown and several other members who formed the Brewer posse that held justice of the peace warrants for the Seven Rivers Warriors, rode up the canyon and stopped at my place. I told them how Sheriff Brady had treated me and Doc and I swore that we would kill Brady at the first opportunity. Billy drew a white-handled revolver from a scabbard and laughingly remarked that he would bet me the revolver against 5 cents that he would beat me to the killing of Brady. A few days later the posse again came by my place and Billy told me that he had won the wager, as he had killed Brady. He and others related how they had ridden into Lincoln and killed Sheriff Brady and George Hindman, court clerk, and had driven Jimmie Matthews, deputy sheriff to cover. I threw up my hat and told the posse that from then on I could be counted as a member. If Sheriff Brady is in hell, I hope the devil makes him ride a sharp-back pony up and down the hills of hell for all eternity."

The killing of Sheriff Brady and the court clerk was the most audacious of the many killings attributed to members of the Tunstall-McSween-Chisum faction. Lincoln, the county seat, was a Murphy stronghold. Its streets were filled at all times with Murphy cowboys and other members and sympathizers of the Murphy faction. The sheriff and other public officials owed their elections to Murphy and his wish was their highest law. Into this enemy nest, on the morning of April 18, 1878, rode the Brewer posse composed of Brewer, Billy the Kid, John Middleton, Fred Waite, Charlie Bowdre, Jim French, Frank McNabb and Tom O'Folliard. Back of the McSween-Tunstall store was an adobe corral, the east part of which projected beyond the store building. The old corral still stands after the lapse of 50 years. The walls are nearly head-high. The Brewer posse rode into the corral, and one of the members was sent to the Ellis hotel, several hundred yards east, with instructions to start a disturbance so as to attract Sheriff Brady from the Murphy store at the west end of town.

Warren Bristol, district judge, had sent word from Mesilla that he would not undertake to hold court in distracted Lincoln county until the reign of anarchy which prevailed had been ended. He said that he feared for his life and the lives of others who might undertake to attend court. Sheriff Brady, accompanied by J. B. Matthews, deputy, and George Hindman, court clerk, were discussing at the Murphy store the advisability of starting to the courthouse to announce that the regular session of district court would not be convened. While they talked a Mexican rushed up and reported that a member of the Brewer posse had dared invade Lincoln and was at that time in the Ellis hotel bar creating a disturbance.

Brady, Matthews and Hindman shouldered their rifles and started to the east end of town for the dual purpose of announcing that court would not be held, and arresting the member of the enemy posse who had dared invade town alone and create a disturbance. The McSween-Tunstall store building stood about half way between the Murphy store at the west end of town and the Ellis hotel and courthouse at the east end of town. As Brady, Matthews and Hindman passed from in front of the McSween-Tunstall store they were in range of the Brewer posse behind the corral wall. The Brewer posse gave Brady, Matthews and Hindman a rifle blast and Brady fell dead, his body riddled with bullets as he was the especial object of the posse's wrath. Hindman fell mortally wounded and Matthews, unwounded, ran behind an adobe house on the south side of the street. The Kid and Fred Waite jumped over the corral wall and ran into the street for the purpose of obtaining Brady's and Hindman's rifles and revolvers. Matthews stuck his head from around the corner of the adobe building, behind which he had taken refuge, just as the Kid was stooping over to pick up Brady's weapons. Matthews cut down on the kid, the Winchester bullet knocking Brady's rifle from the Kid's hand and plowing a furrow in the Kid's side. The Kid and Waite ran back and jumped over the corral wall, joined the other members and the entire posse rode out of town, crossed the mountains into the Ruidoso canyon, and went to George Coe's place.

George Coe, in describing the posse's movements during the next few days, said:

"The Murphy men, of course, immediately circulated a pack of lies and said that after the posse left my place, it headed west in Ruidoso canyon for the purpose of waylaying and killing Judge Warren Bristol and District Attorney Rynerson, in case they should decide after hearing of Sheriff Brady's death, to ride to Lincoln from Mesilla and take charge of things. That may have been the purpose of the Brewer posse when it rode up to my ranch, but if so nothing was said about it to me. The Brewer possemen told me about the killing of Brady and Hindman and said they were going to ride around until things settled down in Lincoln. They said that they hoped that the man appointed to succeed Sheriff Brady would be neutral and would not allow Murphy to use the office as an instrument of revenge. I told them that some horse thieves had been operating in the Ruidoso canyon, and we got my cousin, Frank Coe, and all of us rode up the canyon looking for the horse thieves. We reached Doctor Blazer's mill about noon and made arrangements to eat dinner at his house. When dinner was ready, all members of the posse except John Middleton and I went inside to eat. Middleton and I were left on guard outside. While the other boys were eating, Doctor Blazer told them that he had heard that Murphy had offered a reward of $100 apiece for scalps of McSween-Tunstall-Chisum men and that 'Buckshot' Roberts had notified Murphy that he was going out to look for scalps. While they were talking, Middleton and I saw a strange man ride up on a mule. He had a Winchester rifle and two revolvers and two belts filled with ammunition. John and I had never seen him before. We called to the boys in the house and when Frank came out he recognized Roberts, as Roberts had been to his house to a dance a short time before that. It was all very plain then to us. Roberts had taken the posse's trail out of Lincoln; had followed it to my place and then had followed us to Doctor Blazer's place. Roberts was the bravest and most brazen killer I ever heard of. We learned later that in Texas he had potted five rangers just as he hoped to pot us, and killed them all. His name was Alexander but he was called 'Buckshot' because of the amount of lead he carried in his body as the result of his many fights. Frank and Roberts sat down right there on that door sill and began talking. Each had his rifle across his lap.

"Frank told Roberts he could consider himself under arrest. Roberts wasn't a bit scared. He simply said that he didn't consider himself under arrest. Brewer listened to the conversation and concluded that it was going to take more than one man to make Roberts give up his guns. Brewer came around the corner of the house and called for volunteers. Charles Bowdre said he would go; the Kid said he would go; I said I would go, and others trailed along. Bowdre was in the lead as we turned the corner. He threw his pistol down on Roberts and told him to throw up his hands. Roberts had his Winchester in his right hand and fired from the hip, just as Bowdre pulled trigger. Roberts's bullet cut Bowdre's cartridge belt loose and hit my right hand, knocking off the front finger and smashing my hand to pieces. Bowdre's bullet went through Roberts's stomach and he fell back against the door, which flew open. Roberts got into the house and opened fire through the door and window. We ran to cover in such a way that we had the house completely surrounded. Roberts shot John Middleton through the breast, the bullet entering just below the heart. Blazer's sawmill was right over there about 300 yards from the house. The firing continued for a long time. Roberts pulled a bed up by the window; stretched his wounded body out on it and fired every time he saw anybody to shoot at. Finally he quit firing, and Brewer peeped over a sawlog. As he did so, a bullet from Roberts's rifle tore the top of his head off. It was one man fighting 15 and the one man won although he died from his wound. Middleton's wound through the chest and my shattered hand demanded attention. We decided that Roberts couldn't live long and that it was foolish to risk more lives in finishing him. We got our horses and rode into the hills, one of the men taking Middleton on his horse. We figured it wouldn't do to go back to my place, as the soldiers would come out looking for us when they heard where we were. We laid out in the mountains and around springs for several days. The other boys rustled food for Middleton and me and also got a bottle of carbolic acid. That acid was all the medical attention we received. I began practicing shooting with my left hand and finally could shoot as well as ever. Middleton recovered but he was never strong. When we left the scene of the fight we called to Doctor Blazer and asked him to bury Brewer's body. He said he would, and did.

He buried Brewer and Roberts side by side right over there on the hill side. Let's go up there and I will show you."

While leaning over the rickety fence around the grave, "Uncle George" related the following story:

"When Brewer was killed, Billy the Kid assumed leadership of the posse. Not long after the fight here, we decided to visit the place and see where Doctor Blazer had buried our captain Brewer. We didn't have much else to do except ride around and look for Murphy men. McSween kept us well supplied with ammunition and we could always get something to eat from the nesters and in Chisum's cow camps. The day we started back here to visit Brewer's grave, I was acting captain at the Kid's suggestion as I hadn't learned to shoot left handed very well. We got to a spring on the Indian reservation. Some of the boys wanted a drink. I directed some of the boys to stand guard on the hill while the others went to the spring. While we were at the spring, a bunch of men rode up. The men on the hill commanded them to halt, and general firing followed in which an agency employee named Bernstein was killed. As usual, a lot of lies were told on us. It was said we were trying to steal horses. The agency men may have thought we were but we were not. We had all the horses we needed, and could [get] more for nothing from our friends. Bernstein worked for Murphy before he joined the Indian agency. When Bernstein fell, his men gathered around his body and we rode away in the timber. We didn't visit Brewer's grave then as we figured the soldiers would be after us soon."

Following the killing of Sheriff Brady by the Brewer posse there was an interval in which Lincoln county was without a sheriff and anarchy reigned. McSween tried his hands at Murphy's game of combining politics and ranching and induced the county commissioners to appoint John N. Copeland as sheriff. That enraged the Murphy men and they gave to McSween a demonstration of the far-reaching political influence they wielded as a unit of the Santa Fe political ring. They appealed to Governor Axtell and he promptly removed Copeland from the sheriff's office and appointed George W. Peppin, a Murphy man, as sheriff. Under Peppin's regime killings and all other forms of crime became so rampant that President Rutherford B. Hayes took a hand and removed Governor Axtell from office, appointing Lew Wallace as governor.

It was while Axtell was governor and Peppin was sheriff that the battle in Lincoln occurred—a battle which swept the McSween element out of the picture; brought about the interference of President Hayes; the

PROCLAMATION

BY THE GOVERNOR.

For the information of all the citizens of Lincoln County I do hereby make this Public Proclamation.

First---John N. Copeland, Esq., appointed Sheriff by the County Commissioners, having failed for more than thirty days to file his bond as Collector of Taxes, is hereby removed from the office of Sheriff, and I have appointed GEORGE W. PEPPIN, Esq., Sheriff of Lincoln County. This has been done in compliance with the laws, passed at the twenty-second session of the Legislative Assembly, relating to Sheriffs.

Second---I command all men and bodies of men, now under arms and traveling about the county, to disarm and return to their homes and their usual pursuits, and so long as the present Sheriff has authority to call upon U. S. troops for assistance, not to act as a sheriff's posse.

And, in conclusion, I urge upon all good citizens to submit to the law, remembering that violence begets violence, and that they who take the sword shall perish by the sword.

S. B. AXTELL,
Governor of New Mexico.

Proclamation by Governor S. B. Axtell appointing George W. Peppin sheriff of Lincoln County. Facsimile of the original in the National Archives. Photograph by the author.

removal of Governor Axtell and Sheriff Peppin; the appointment of Lew
Wallace and the issuing of his amnesty to nearly all participants in the
war. Immediately after the appointment of Peppin as sheriff a large posse
took the field in search of McSween men. The posse went to Chisum's
South Spring ranch, four miles south of Roswell, and there found the
Kid and his followers barricaded in the Chisum home, a huge adobe
building of a score of rooms. The sheriff's posse realized the futility of
ousting the Kid and his followers from the protection of the thick walls;
gave up the attempt, and after leaving scouts to watch, returned to Roswell.
The McSween men boldly rode from the Chisum ranch into Lincoln, 45
miles away, where they took up quarters in the McSween residence, a big
adobe structure which because of its size has been described as a castle.
The McSween residence was by far the largest residence in Lincoln. It
stood adjacent on the west to the McSween store. Not a vestige of the
building remains today. Its adobe walls were nearly two feet thick and
invulnerable to rifle bullets. It had a flat roof with a high adobe cornice.
The old McSween store still stands in Lincoln today and is unchanged in
appearance. The heavy wooden, metal-lined shutters with which McSween
provided the windows are still in place. A few hundred yards east of the
store stands the old circular rock fort, built for the purpose of offering
protection to Lincoln citizens against warlike Apaches. The fort originally
was much higher than it is today. It was a tower divided by several floors,
on which the besieged could lie and through portholes fire at the enemy.
Today a later-day building stands between the old McSween store and
what remains of the old rock fort. Invasion of Lincoln, the Murphy stronghold, by the McSween men was an insult that could not be ignored by the
Murphy men. It was the second time McSween men had been so brazen.
When word spread through Lincoln that the McSween men were in town
and quartered in the McSween residence the Murphy clans gathered at
every point of vantage—in neighboring adobe buildings, in the old rock
fort and on the mountainsides south of Lincoln from which they poured
a steady stream of lead into the McSween house and store from heavy
Sharpe rifles and Winchesters. A messenger was hurried off to Fort Stanton
by the Murphy men, and Lieut. Col. Nathan Dudley, ever faithful to his
social friend Murphy, responded by trotting out his soldiers, two companies
equipped with two cannon. A McSween follower got through the line
and carried word to the McSween cattle camp across the mountains and

McSween, at the head of a band of cowboys, rode into Lincoln and they entrenched themselves in adobe houses from which they could return fire. McSween and several Mexicans during the night slipped into the McSween residence and store. George Coe, describing the invasion of Lincoln by the McSween men and the fight, said:

"The Murphy men had been riding over the country harassing us, attacking McSween and Chisum cow camps and plundering the herds. We had as much right to be in Lincoln as did the Murphy men. Except for Murphy's influence with the court officials and soldiers, both side[s] were on the same basis. Murphy could get all the warrants he wanted for us. As a matter of law the warrants were not worth any more than confederate money, but they gave color of legality to anything Murphy wanted done. With the exception of the warrants Brewer got from the justice of the peace at the time Tunstall was murdered we didn't have any warrants, as the public officials were Murphy tools and we would have been shot to death if we had gone in to get warrants. We knew that we were free-born American citizens and that most of us hadn't done anything except file on claims which we had a right to do. When the Murphy posse left the Chisum ranch south of Roswell, we decided to ride into Lincoln, where we had a right to go, and if the Murphy men wanted us we would be handy. We took up quarters in McSween's own home and store. Mrs. McSween was not in her home the morning the fight started. She was at a neighbor's house. Before the fight ended, after the Murphy men had set fire to the building, Mrs. McSween made the hazardous trip back to the building to get some important papers and personal belongings and left. The enemy did not fire at her as she entered or left the building.

"Each side had plenty of ammunition. McSween carried a big stock of cartridges which we used, and the Murphy men got all the cartridges they wanted from the Murphy store about a quarter of a mile down the street. The firing started when a Murphy deputy sheriff came up to the McSween home and shouted out that he had warrants for Billy the Kid and most of the others. The Kid shouted back 'We've got warrants for every Murphy man that helped kill Tunstall,' and then the firing started."

When Colonel Dudley arrived he trained his cannon on the McSween buildings and approached close enough to command the McSween men to quit firing. McSween wanted to know why he didn't train his cannon on the Murphy men and command them to quit firing also. That angered

Dudley and he replied that if we fired another shot he would open fire on us with his cannon.

"McSween told Dudley that he, as an army officer, had no right to use government troops to aid a personal friend, and that an investigation of his conduct would follow if he fired a single shot," said Coe.

"That must have put old Dudley to thinking, for he didn't fire, and the battle went on. Right back of the McSween buildings was the Rio Bonito and then came the range of mountains on the north side. Murphy men couldn't fire at us from that side, the north side, as the mountains on that side were too far away for accurate shooting. As a result we didn't watch the north side. During the fighting a Murphy man slipped around to the north side, crept along under the shelter of the Bonito banks and then got up to the north wall of the McSween home. With some coal oil he set fire to the building. From then on we had fire to fight as well as Murphy men. The fire was on the outside of the thick adobe walls and burned slowly. Our men couldn't fight it until it ate through the adobe blocks. The fire drove our men from one room to another as the walls fell. It was then that bullets began striking the piano chords which the newspaper and books writers describe as Mrs. McSween playing the piano to cheer us on."

On the night of the fifth day of fighting the fire had so closed in on the McSween men in the residence that there was nothing left to do except flee. The McSween men bolted from the two buildings, made their way across the Bonito, and took refuge in the mountains north of town. During the fighting the McSween men lost Bob Beckwith, one of the Seven Rivers Warriors and Lusio Montigo, a Mexican, and a man named Crawford. Montigo was killed while going down the mountain side to get a drink of water at a spring in the valley. Crawford, while firing from the top of a mountain on the south side of the road, was hit by a bullet fired by Billy the Kid from a Sharpe's rifle, his body rolling entirely down the mountain side. McSween's dead were buried at the foot of the mountains in a cemetery, the remnants of which still remain.

On the north side of the Bonito, about four miles west of Lincoln, there is still living today an aged Mexican whose last name is Salazar. He was one of the McSween men wounded when the dash was made from the burning building. Through an interpreter he explains concerning the fight:

"I was hit here, here and here and fell over unconscious. It was night. When I regained consciousness there was a big crowd of Murphy followers drinking and dancing around the burned building. I guess they thought I was dead. After the crowd left I crawled away and got to a friend's house and was finally moved secretly to old Fort Sumner, about 100 miles northeast, where I recovered."

According to George Coe there were about 15 McSween men in the McSween home and store during the fighting.

"Nearly all of the original Brewer posse, except Brewer and John Middleton, were in the two buildings. We had left Middleton at Chisum's ranch as he was still suffering from the bullet wound received during the fight with Buckshot Roberts at Blazer's sawmill. After the fight in Lincoln we hid in the mountains north of town until daylight, as we were afoot. Through our spyglasses we looked down on the scene of our fight. The Murphy faction had looted the McSween store of its stock of goods. That's why they hadn't set fire to the store building. They wanted to get the goods, and they did."

Colonel Dudley made the following official report of the fight which he had witnessed:

"Men who have the reckless courage to attack a building in bright midday, its walls forming a perfect protection against any modern rifle fire to its inmates, pierced as the castle of McSween's was with scores of loop holes for rifles on every side and angle, to say nothing of the flat roof protected by a perfect wall of defense, and for hours hugging the walls exposed to the fire not only from the loopholes but from the roof and adjacent buildings held by McSween's men, charging this position across a space perfectly exposed to the fire of the McSween men for a distance of nearly 300 yards are not of a character to be easily induced to abandon a course they believe is only half completed. A similar remark can be made of the party holding this structure for five days, the last nine hours gradually retreating from one room to another as the heat compelled them to do what no amount of leaden missiles from the rifles of the attacking party could do, and for one hour finally, all huddled in one room, nearly suffocated by the flames, some, as it is claimed, preferring to be burned rather than surrender to the sheriff's posse. More desperate action than was exhibited on this unfortunate day by both sides is rarely witnessed."

That fight broke the McSween war forces. Tunstall and McSween, the principal financiers of one side of the war, were dead and the McSween dragoons were disorganized. Their source of ammunition and money was gone. President Hayes took a hand and removed Governor Axtell, appointing Lew Wallace as governor, with extraordinary power to restore peace to Lincoln county. Governor Wallace at that time was writing his famous book "Ben Hur—A Tale of the Christ." He divided his time between writing and effecting peace. He was inaugurated Oct. 1, 1878, and on November 13, following, issued an amnesty to all combatants on each side, except those under indictment. There were questionable warrants out for nearly everybody on each side, but Billy the Kid was under grand jury indictment for the killing of Sheriff Brady. The amnesty let out the rich, influential cattle barons and practically all their followers, but did not apply to the waif of the plains, Billy.

It was the old story, old as government itself, "plate sin with gold and the strong lance of justice hurtless breaks; clothe it in rags, a pigmy's straw does pierce it." Chisum, Murphy and all the other wealthy owners of the war were in the clear, and so were their followers, except the Kid, who had been fighting Chisum's battles. Chisum not only quit, but he repudiated the chief of his faction's fighting force and refused to aid him financially or otherwise. He even denied that he had ever enlisted the Kid in his cause or had accepted his services. Like King John of old, he held to the theory that it is the curse of kings to be attended by underlings who mistake hints for authority. Chisum soon left the country until the strife blew over.

The Kid and his followers, following the fight in Lincoln, gathered up horses wherever they could find them and all went to old Fort Sumner, 80 miles north of Roswell. At Fort Sumner Frank and George Coe quit Billy and went to Colorado, and Jim French quit and returned to Oklahoma. Billy, Fred Waite, John Middleton, Henry Brown, Charlie Bowdre and Doc Scurlock started to Atascosa, cattlemen and cowboy capital of the Texas panhandle, 50 miles north of the present city of Amarillo, with their drove of horses. En route, Scurlock and Bowdre quit, and . . . Middleton, Waite, Brown, O'Folliard and the Kid went on. At Atascosa, Waite, French and Middleton quit and returned to Oklahoma and tried to induce the Kid and O'Folliard to quit. The Kid argued that he couldn't quit, as he was not included in the amnesty, for he was under grand jury indictment and that he had no place to go if he did quit. He and O'Folliard sold the herd of horses and returned to Fort Sumner, where they rejoined Scurlock and Bowdre, and sustained themselves by plundering John Chisum's herds. The Kid, Bowdre and Scurlock each claimed that Chisum owed them for fighting for him, and on that grounds justified the cattle stealing they carried on. The Kid and his followers, with the death of McSween and the desertion of Chisum, had lost the status of a posse, and had become simply cattle and horse thieves.

In February, 1879, Billy the Kid and Tom O'Folliard entered Lincoln and ran into Jesse Evans, James J. Dolan, one of Murphy's business partners and Edgar A. Waltz, brother-in-law to Thomas B. Catron, one of Murphy's business and political friends, and William Campbell, a Dolan cowboy. A parley followed in which all agreed to forget the past and be friends. Mrs. McSween, who had left the country, sent a lawyer named Chapman to Lincoln to salvage whatever was left of her husband's estate. As Chapman passed the group, Campbell shot him dead. The Kid and O'Folliard did not renew the feud, as they considered that the war was over so far as they were concerned.

Gov. Lew Wallace, at Santa Fe when he learned of Chapman's death, laid aside the pen with which he was writing "Ben Hur" and journeyed 200 miles overland to Lincoln, in an effort to prevent a fresh outbreak of the war. Governor Wallace, on arriving, wrote the following letter to the Kid:

Lincoln, March 15, 1879

W. H. Bonney:

Come to the house of old Squire Wilson (not the lawyer) at nine o'clock next Monday night alone. I don't mean his office but his residence. Follow along the foot of the mountain south of the town. Come in on that side and knock at the east door. I have authority to exempt you from prosecution if you will testify to what you say you know.

The object of the meeting at Squire Wilson's is to arrange the matter in a way to make your life safe. To do that, the utmost secrecy is to be used. So come alone. Don't tell anybody—not a living soul where you are coming or the object. If you could trust Jesse Evans you could trust me. (Signed) LEW WALLACE.

The Kid kept the appointment. Governor Wallace told the Kid that if he would surrender; testify before a military court of inquiry concerning Colonel Dudley's use of the federal soldiers in aiding Dudley's personal friend Murphy; testify before a grand jury relative to the murder of Mrs. McSween's lawyer, Chapman, by the Murphy crowd, and then stand trial for the murder of Sheriff Brady and the killing of Buckshot Roberts, he,

Governor Wallace, would pardon him in case of conviction. The Kid agreed to Governor Wallace's proposal, but made the condition that there should be a fake arrest instead of a voluntary surrender on his part, as he was fearful of the new role he was about to play. The fake arrest was arranged for a near day. On March 20, 1879, the Kid sent General Wallace the following letter:

San Patricio, Lincoln County

March, 20, 1879

General Wallace:

I will keep the appointment that I made, but be sure and have men come that you can depend on. I am not afraid to die like a man, fighting, but I would not like to die like a dog, unarmed. Tell Sheriff Kimbrell to let his men be placed around the house and for him to come in alone; and he can arrest us. All that I am afraid of is that in the Fort we might be poniarded or killed through a window at night, but you can arrange that all right. Tell the commanding officer to watch Lieutenant Goodwin (he would not hesitate to do anything). There will be danger on the road of somebody waylaying us to kill us on the road to the fort. You will never catch those fellows on the road. Watch Fritzes, Captain Baca's ranch and the brewery. They will go to Seven Rivers or the Jacarilla mountains. They will stay around close until the scouting parties come in. Give a spy a pair of glasses and let him get on the mountain back of Fritzes and watch, and if they are there, there be provisions carried to them. It is my not place to advise you, but I am anxious to have them caught, and perhaps know how men hide from the soldiers better than you. Excuse me for having so much to say and I will remain, Yours truly, W. H. BONNEY.

P.S. I have changed my mind. Send Kimbrell to Guiterez's ranch just below San Patricio one mile, because Sanger and Ballard are, or were, great friends of Campbell. Ballard told me yesterday to leave, for you were doing everything to catch me. It was a blind to get me to leave. Tell Kimbrell to come before 3 o'clock, for I may not be there before.

The fake arrest took place, and the Kid testified before the military court of inquiry relative to Colonel Dudley's use of the troops, and before the grand jury relative to the murder of Mrs. McSween's lawyer, Chapman. He pleaded not guilty to two murder charges against himself and his trials were set for hearing at Mesilla, Dona Ana county, in the southwestern part of New Mexico. The Kid had been promised that he would not be put in the adobe shack jail, but would be held guard in a suitable residence or hotel. He was finally allowed to roam unattended around the streets of Lincoln and was permitted to carry his rifle and revolvers for self-protection. As a result of the Kid's testimony before the grand jury, Dolan, a Murphy partner; Jesse Evans and Campbell were indicted for the murder of Mrs. McSween's lawyer, Chapman.

While under arrest the Kid became fearful that he would be assassinated because of his testimony before the grand jury and military court, and he heard rumors that Governor Wallace could not or would not pardon him. He left Lincoln with Tom O'Folliard, persuaded Doc Scurlock and Charley Bowdre to join him, and the four went to old Fort Sumner where they embarked upon wholesale horse and cattle stealing, driving their stolen stock to a spring south of Los Portales, about 40 miles east of Fort Sumner.

Pat Garrett, an ex-buffalo hunter and Chisum cowboy, established a ranch adjacent to Chisum's South Spring ranch in the Pecos valley. Garrett had a brother-in-law, Barney Mason, Garrett and Mason having married Mexican sisters, with relatives and friends around Fort Sumner, 80 miles north of Roswell. Garrett was well acquainted with the Kid. Mason and the Kid ran around over the country together. John Chisum, J. C. Lea and other cattlemen of the Pecos valley decreed that the Kid should be suppressed, and decided upon Pat Garrett as the best man for the job. They backed Garrett for sheriff of Lincoln county and he was elected. Garrett immediately set about planning the Kid's capture. The Kid continued to associate with Mason until the Kid became suspicious that Mason was acting as a stool pigeon for Sheriff Garrett, Mason's brother-in-law. Posses were continually scouring the country for the Kid and his crowd. Ranchmen, through friendship and fear, tolerated the Kid and he experienced no trouble in obtaining food. Scattered throughout the ranch country of New Mexico one sees, even today, small one-room rock and adobe buildings. During the cattle days those buildings were shelters for cattle and sheep herders. The buildings were nearly invariably close to a spring or clear-water stream. Those buildings furnished emergency shelters for the Kid and his fellow cattle thieves. About 20 miles east of old Fort Sumner, there stands today an old ranch house, known as the Wilcox-Brazil place. Close by is a spring and grove of cottonwood trees. It was one of the Kid's retreats. Brazil and Wilcox overheard the Kid and his crowd planning to attend a dance in old Fort Sumner. There were two girls in old Fort Sumner whom the Kid liked very much. One was related to Pat Garrett and Barney Mason by marriage, and the other was a daughter of Pete Maxwell, wealthiest sheep rancher in the Pecos valley. Maxwell was an aristocratic Mexican. Brazil, when he learned that the Kid's crowd planned to attend the dance at old Fort Sumner, sent word to Garrett and a posse immediately rode into Fort Sumner and concealed themselves in a building on the road the Kid and band would traverse. They posted a guard and played cards until the guard announced that the Kid's crowd was approaching. Garrett, Mason and other members of his posse went out on the porch, backed against the wall and concealed themselves as much as possible behind sets of harness hanging on the wall. As the Kid's crowd rode up to the porch, Garrett and his men called to them to halt and an instant later fired, O'Folliard falling dead from his saddle.

Garrett's posse had fired at the leader, thinking he was the Kid. It was Tom O'Folliard. The others fled back to the Wilcox-Brazil ranch, and sent Brazil to Fort Sumner next day to obtain information as to the whereabouts of Garrett's posse. When they obtained the false information Brazil imparted they moved east about 20 miles to another spring known as Stinking Spring, where there was a rock sheepherder's building. Brazil sent word to Garrett and he and his posse rode to the building under the cover of night and surrounded it. At daybreak, Charley Bowdre passed out of the door with a bag of oats, to feed three horses tied to the rafters of the building. Garrett and his men fired and Bowdre fell mortally wounded, dying a few minutes later. One of the three horses moved in front of the door and Garrett shot it dead, and then the halters with which the other two horses were tied were shot loose and the horses walked away, leaving two horses and three men inside the building, with the door blocked by a dead horse. The weather was bitter cold and after an all-day siege the Kid and his companions surrendered with the understanding they would not be shot. Garrett took the Kid to Santa Fe for safe keeping, placing the others in other jails.

The Kid was taken to Mesilla and tried during the March term of court, 1881, for the killing of Buckshot Roberts, acquitted, and immediately tried and convicted for the murder of Sheriff Brady, execution being set for March 13, 1881, at Lincoln. When taken to Lincoln, the Kid was placed in a large room on the second floor of the Murphy building and an armed guard placed over him night and day. As a protection against the Kid's escape through connivance with guards, Garrett appointed two personal enemies of the Kid, J. W. Bell and Robert W. Ollinger, as guards. While Ollinger was absent, eating supper one afternoon across the street, the Kid asked Bell to take him to the lavatory downstairs, which Bell did. The Kid was handcuffed and his feet shackled. On the way back upstairs, the Kid got a short distance ahead of Bell, made several long leaps up the steps, burst open the door of the room in which the guards kept emergency supplies of weapons, obtained a revolver, went back to the head of the stairs and killed Bell as the latter was rushing up the steps to overtake him. The Kid then returned to the armory room, obtained Ollinger's double-barrel shotgun, which Ollinger had placed in the room while on his way to supper. Ollinger, while eating across the street, heard the shot that killed Bell and rushed out of the restaurant building. From an upstairs window on the east side of the building, the Kid called Ollinger's name, and as Ollinger looked up, the Kid fired a load of buckshot into his body, and Ollinger fell dead. The Kid then got on an upper porch, fired the second load of buckshot into Ollinger's body, then broke the gun across the porch railing and threw it down at Ollinger, shouting "Take that to hell with you; you won't follow me any more with it." He returned to the armory room, obtained a rifle, two revolvers and ammunition and then under the threat of death compelled an old man to bring a file with which he filed away his handcuffs and shackles. The old man was then compelled to catch and saddle a horse in a nearby corral, and two hours following the double murder the Kid rode from Lincoln, free and unfollowed, the citizens terrified into inaction.

Garrett never disclosed the sources of all his information concerning the fact that the Kid was in the vicinity of Fort Sumner. Gossips later claimed that Maxwell, fearful that his daughter would run away to old Mexico with the Kid and become his wife, sent word to Garrett that the Kid was around Fort Sumner and that if Garrett wanted him he had better come at once. Others suggested that Garrett obtained from his relatives at Fort Sumner the information that the Kid was around the old fort. Shortly before the Kid was killed, he told a friend that although he had already killed 21 men, he hoped he lived long enough to make it 24 by killing Pat Garrett, Barney Mason, to whom the Kid referred as "that traitor Barney Mason[,"] and Gov. Lew Wallace. Garrett, in his printed statement, shortly after he killed the Kid, asserted that his going to Fort Sumner in quest of the kid was the result of information from several sources, and that his going into Maxwell's bedroom where he killed the Kid, was almost accidental. He exonerated Pete Maxwell from any complicity in laying a trap for the Kid. On the night of July 14, 1881, Garrett, with two companions, arrived at old Fort Sumner and after concluding that the Kid was not to be found, approached the Maxwell home, a very large army building that had been sold to Maxwell. Leaving his companions in Maxwell's yard, Garrett in the dark, entered Maxwell's bedroom, sat down at the head of the bed, about 10 o'clock, and asked Maxwell if the Kid had been around. Before Maxwell could explain, the Kid, carrying a butcher knife in his right hand and his revolver in his left, tipped into the dark room and said to Maxwell, in Spanish, "Who is that?" his reference being to the two men whom he had seen outside on the porch. Under the circumstances Maxwell was afraid to reply, and the Kid approached the head of Maxwell's bed and again asked "Who is that?" the reference still being to the two men outside. The Kid then was within two feet of Garrett, but in the darkness the Kid did not realize Garrett's presence. Maxwell, instead of replying to the Kid's questions, whispered to Garrett "That's him" and in the darkness Garrett fired. The bullet drilled straight through the heart, and the soul of Billy the Kid with all its imperfections, took flight. He was 21 years old. Garrett was accused of firing from under the bed, and from back of the head of the bed, but his own statement of his position when he fired savors more of the truth.

As Garrett had been in the room several minutes his eyes had become accustomed to the darkness and he could see the Kid's silhouetted form in the room. The Kid, having stepped in from bright moonlight outside into the dark room, could not see Garrett. "After he asked the question 'Who is that?' the first time and not receiving an answer from Maxwell, the Kid approached the head of Maxwell's bed until he was within two feet of me," said Garrett. "Apparently he then saw my form or intuitively felt my presence, for he jumped back toward the far corner of the room, from which he could shoot either at me or at anyone entering the door. As he jumped back he asked the question again, and I fired and threw myself to the floor and fired a second shot, the latter going wide of its mark. The Kid doubtless died without knowing who it was that shot him."

Peter Menard Maxwell, ca. 1870–75. It was in his bedroom that Pat Garrett killed the Kid on July 14, 1881. Robert G. McCubbin Collection.

After the Kid had been killed it developed he had been in a neighboring Mexican house and had crossed to the Maxwell house for the purpose of cutting a steak from a beef hanging on the porch, and that accounted for his having the butcher knife. He was in his sock feet. As he stepped on to the Maxwell porch he saw the two strange men and backed into Maxwell's room to inquire as to their identity.

His body was stretched out on a work table in an outbuilding that night, and buried in the old military cemetery the next day, where it still reposes beside the bodies of his former companions Tom O'Folliard and Charlie Bowdre, both of whom Garrett had killed. A short distance from the grave lies the body of Pete Maxwell, in whose bedroom the Kid was killed. Until a few years ago the Kid's grave was without a marker. Today there is a small metal marker bearing the simple inscription "Billi" the spelling indicating the marker was placed by a child or a Mexican unfamiliar with spelling English words. The old work table on which the body of Billy was stretched is still in use in the Maxwell family, about a mile from the cemetery. The killing of Billy the Kid immortalized Garrett in frontier history and literature. When [Theodore] Roosevelt became president he appointed Garrett to the position of inspector of customs at El Paso on the Mexican border. Mrs. McSween, widow of Alexander McSween, now lives at White Oaks, one of Billy's old hangouts, and one of Pat Garrett's daughters, a highly talented blind musician, lives there also.

CHAPTER NINE

The Individual Song: "Billy the Kid"

D. K. Wilgus

D. K. Wilgus (1918–1989)—his first name was Donald, but he preferred to be known, both professionally and personally, as "D. K."—pioneered the chronicling of the development of popular musical forms, such as blues and country-western, as an important part of American culture. A native of Columbus, Ohio, and a graduate of Ohio State University (1941–1954), he was the first to plead "hillbilly" music's case for academic respectability, and he led the way in the teaching of Anglo-American folk song as a rigorous academic subject. He taught at Western Kentucky University (1950–1963), where he founded and edited the scholarly journal *Kentucky Folklore Record*. His *Anglo-American Folksong Scholarship since 1898*, published in 1959, remains the definitive overview of the subject to this day. The remainder of his academic career (1963–1989) was spent at the University of California, Los Angeles, where he established and served as first chair of that university's Department of Folklore and Mythology, and where he also edited the magazine in which the article that follows was published. He died suddenly on Christmas Day 1989, just three years after his marriage to folklorist and writer Eleanor Long-Wilgus, with whom he had been planning many new projects. In this fascinating examination of the origins of what many believed—and many more still believe—to be an authentic folk song, more or less contemporary with the Kid's life, Dr. Wilgus convincingly demonstrates that "The Ballad of Billy the Kid" actually owes its complete existence—as do so many of the myths about him—to Burns's *Saga*.

The preceding articles in this special John Edwards Memorial Foundation issue of *Western Folklore* have dealt with a considerable portion of the materials involved in the study of commercialized folk music. The study of an individual traditional song in twentieth-century North America—if it has any connection with the commercial media—involves all of these materials and all of these skills. To these must be added all of the other materials and skills necessary in the study of traditional song. And because of the scattered and "primitive" state of the resources, the study is inevitably a cooperative undertaking. For the production of this article I am indebted to more individuals for more information than I am able to credit in the notes.

The student of an individual song is first confronted with the task of identifying his material in the commercial media. In the area of commercial recordings, discographies are label, company, or performer oriented. A discography which provides a title index is a bit unusual, and anyone who has worked with traditional songs knows the difficulty of identifying a song by title. Even a relatively wide knowledge of alternate titles and tendencies in titling is not enough, as I can testify on the basis of my lucky accidents in finding materials. As a very simple example, one can recognize that "Bury Me Out on the Prairie" is a title for "I've Got No Use for the Women"; but "Bury Me Out on the Prairie" does turn up as a title of "Bury Me *Not* on the Lone Prairie" or "Dying Cowboy" (Laws B 2).[1] Short of listening to all recorded and unrecorded performances, one can only exercise his utmost ingenuity.

Gaining access to the material, before or after identifying it, is a serious problem. Although one can do fair work on discography and attendant problems without listening to every recording, viewing every disc, reading every folio, one cannot study an individual song without the actual examples of its appearance in the media. I do not think I have to detail the difficulties involved, since we know that one does not go to one's friendly research library expecting to find the materials. And, unfortunately, one cannot expect to find all the materials even in the John Edwards Memorial Foundation.

In choosing an example of the problems and rewards in the study of an individual song, I have had to limit myself carefully, and shall limit myself even more in the presentation of the material I have chosen. Had I decided to discuss "John Henry," I should have to concern myself with at least 400 commercial sound recordings alone, not to speak of other commercial materials, of the materials recorded from noncommercial tradition, and of the extensive scholarship previously devoted to the ballad. In order to avoid producing anything approaching the proportions of a monograph, I have chosen to discuss "Billy the Kid," dealing only with sixteen commercial recordings, in addition to song folios, folksong collections, and some unpublished material.

There are a number of ballads purporting to tell the story of "Billy the Kid," whatever his true name might have been.[2] The one with which I am concerned has been reported most widely; in fact it is the only one which seems to have any real traditional status.

1. I'll sing you a true song of Billy the Kid,
        I'll sing of the desperate deeds that he did;
    Way out in New Mexico long, long ago
        When a man's only chance was an old forty-four.

2. When Billie the Kid was a very young lad
        Out in Silver City he went to the bad;
    Way out in the West with a gun in his hand—
        Altho but twelve years old, he killed his first man.

3. Fair Mexican Maidens play guitars and sing
        A song about Billie their boy-bandit king;
    How ere his young manhood had reached it's sad end
        Had a notch on his pistol for twenty-one men.

4. On the very same night when poor Billie had died—
        He said to his friends, I am not satisfied
    There were twenty-one men I have put bullets through
        And Sheriff Pat Garrett must make twenty-two.

5. Now this is how Billie the Kid met his fate,
        The bright moon was shining, the hour was late—
    Shot down by Pat Garrett who once was his friend,
        The young outlaw's life had now come to its end.

6. Down in Pecos Valley all covered with green
        Out in "Hell's Half-acre" three graves can be seen;
    Where Tommie and Charlie and Billie now lie,
        Their trail of blood ended, they all had to die.

7. There's many a young man with face fine and fair
        Who starts out in life with a chance to be square;

But just like poor Billie, he wanders astray,
    And loses his life in the very same way.

Rev. Andrew Jenkins
1-20-27

(This song was taken from true life of Billie the Kid, as read and studied from the newspapers and other reading matter.)

The above text was furnished by Mrs. Irene Spain Futrelle, now of Mableton, Georgia. Mrs. Futrelle is the stepdaughter of the late Andrew Jenkins of Atlanta, newsboy-preacher, pioneer "hillbilly" radio and recording artist, and composer of many songs now accepted as traditional by folklorists. And it can be shown that the origin and dissemination of "Billy the Kid" roughly parallels that of Jenkins' better- known "The Death of Floyd Collins" (Laws G 22).[3]

Like the Floyd Collins ballad, "Billy the Kid" was commissioned by Polk C. Brockman, the Atlanta, Georgia, "scout" for recording companies as well as an independent entrepreneur. And, as in the case of "Floyd Collins," Brockman chose the Rev. Andrew Jenkins to execute his desire. But in this instance we have even more firm evidence. On 20 December 1926 Brockman wrote to Jenkins:

> The attached will no doubt interest you. I have been trying to get some dope together with which to compose a song on "Billy the Kid." I hope you will keep the attached and study it over very carefully and within the next few days I hope to have a book on the subject of this young desperado, also some first-hand information from people out in Texas. As soon as I receive anything further I will send it on to you.[4]

The "attached" was a "flyer" advertising the Book of the Month Club selection of Walter Noble Burns' *The Saga of Billy the Kid* (Garden City, New York, 1925). Brockman must have sent Jenkins the book, for Mrs. Futrelle recalls that they did use a book—and "Blind Andy" could read, though with difficulty.[5] By 1 January 1927 Jenkins and Irene Spain had produced the text and tune of "Billy the Kid."

A question immediately arises as to whether Andrew Jenkins and Irene Spain were actually composing a new song of Billy the Kid, or revising a

traditional song. We have, I think, more documentary evidence than I can
recall in any similar instance. We do not, unfortunately, have a manuscript
of the text, only a number of typescripts which Mrs. Futrelle has made over
the years. We have a manuscript of the tune, and I have as well a manuscript of a tune which the composers decided not to use. I have not been
able to recognize the accepted melody as an analogue of a traditional
tune—though such a recognition would be somewhat beside the point.

The text could not have been composed on the basis of the "flyer," but
every bit of information used can be found in Walter Noble Burns' volume
(pages 54–55, 59, 61, 64–65, 72–73, 184–187, 280–283, 290ff.), with the
possible exception of the account of Mexican maidens playing guitars and
singing a song of Billy. But Burns does mention (pages 186–187) Mexican
girls and music in connection with Billy; and in the "flyer" is included the
statement: "Mexican girls sing to their guitars songs of 'Billee the Keed.'"
Even more telling is stanza six of the Jenkins typescript, dealing with "Hell's
Half Acre." Burns devoted an entire chapter to the "acre." No mention of
the "acre" appears in later variants of "Billy the Kid" (and all variants of the
ballad are "later") because, as we shall see, the stanza was omitted from the
popularization of the ballad.

Nothing remotely resembling Jenkins' text was reported before 1927—
a fact which is not so important as that echoes begin turning up soon
thereafter. For example, a poem by Henry Herbert Knibbs in *Songs of the
Lost Frontier* (Boston and New York, 1930)[6] includes:

> So Young Billy Bonny he came to his end,
> Shot down by Pat Garrett who once was his friend . . .
> . . . . .
> Each year of his life was a notch in his gun,
> For in twenty-one years he had slain twenty-one.
> . . . . .
> And so ends the true story of Billy the Kid.

One might not make too much of these "echoes," since they seem
commonplace; but the "end/friend" rhyme is certainly more than coinci-
dental. Not commonplace, however, is a version collected by Austin E. Fife
from Hollywood stuntman Chuck Haas, who claimed to have learned it
from Wyatt Earp.[7] Assuming the informant's veracity, we recall that Wyatt
Earp lived until 13 January 1929[8] and could have heard the Jenkins ballad.

In the absence of other evidence, the Haas text seems to be an expansion and localization of Jenkins' ballad, for the differing material is unique.

To return to the chronology of the Jenkins ballad: the completed material must have been sent to Brockman about February 1927. The successful exploitation of "The Death of Floyd Collins" must have prompted him to give this ballad also to the "citybilly" Marion Try Slaughter, better known as "Vernon Dalhart." And Brockman must have forwarded the ballad with considerable dispatch, for Dalhart recorded it for Brunswick Records 15 February 1927, for Okeh Records 21 February 1927, and for Columbia Records 1 March 1927. These performances—Brunswick 100 and Okeh 45102 as Vernon Dalhart, and Columbia 15135-D as Al Craver—are virtually identical. They all employ the two-strain tune composed by Irene Spain, but omit stanza six of the Jenkins typescript (possibly because of the lack of symmetry involved in setting seven stanzas to the two-strain tune), which never appears again. From a test pressing of one of the recordings, a transcription was made for copyright registration 17 March 1927, words and music by Andrew Jenkins, arranged by Irene Spain, registered in the name of Polk C. Brockman.[9] As printed in two song folios,[10] the transcription is relatively sophisticated musically, but textually faulty. In fact, the text must have been transcribed by someone with a bad ear for Southern speech and no knowledge of Billy the Kid.

1. I'll sing you a true song of Billy the Kid,
    I'll sing of the desperate deeds that he did,
    Way out in New Mexico long, long ago,
    When the man's only chance was his own forty-four.

2. When Billy the kid was a very young lad,
    In old silver city he went to the bad,
    Way out in the west with a gun in his hand,
    At the age of twelve years there he killed his first man.

3. There Mexican maidens play guitars and sing,
    A song about Billy their boy bandit king,
    How weird is young manhood that reached it's that end,
    And the notch on its pistol for twenty-one men.

4. 'Twas on the same night when poor Billy died,
    He said to his friends I'm not satisfied,

There are twenty-one men I have put pullin thru,
And share it that Garret must make twenty-two.

5. Now this is how Billy the Kid met his fate
The bright moon was shining the hour was late
Shot down by that Garret who once was his friend
The young outlaw quite had come to his end.

6. There's many a man with feet fine and fair
Who starts out in life with a chance to be square
But just like poor Billy he wonders afraid
And looses his life in the very same way.[11]

On 12 April 1927 Vernon Dalhart, who operated as a free agent, recorded "Billy the Kid" for the Victor Recording Company. In the take issued as Victor 20966 he made one error—or change—in that he sang "there he first killed his man" instead of the "there he killed his first man" on previous recordings. In 1934 in John and Alan Lomax's *American Ballads and Folk Songs*[12] was printed "Billy the Kid" as transcribed from Victor 20396. As Victor 20396 is a recording of piano solos by Hans Barth, one assumes a misprint for 20966. However, it must be noted that in Alan Lomax's *Folk Songs of North America*[13] a variant transcription is printed, credited to *American Ballads and Folk Songs* and "As sung by Frank Crummitt." As far as I have been able to determine, Frank Crumit (correct spelling) never recorded the ballad for Victor, nor for any other recording company. The transcription in *American Ballads and Folk Songs* faithfully records "he first killed his man," though omitting "there." Furthermore, only the first strain of the tune is transcribed.

If we wish to follow the influence of the important Lomax version on subsequent tradition, we have little to go on. "He first killed" can easily be reversed to "he killed his first"—and Alan Lomax does so in *Folk Songs of North America*. The omission of the second strain might seem more crucial. Unfortunately, Irene Spain's second strain with its minor progressions might be expected to disappear in American folk tradition. The second strain has actually survived in professional tradition, at least, for it occurs exaggerated in a recording by the Sons of the Pioneers[14] and somewhat worn down in Marty Robbins' more recent *Gunfighter Ballads and Trail Songs* (Columbia CL 3581/CS 8158). On the other hand, recordings by

Tex Ritter,[15] Bill Bender,[16] The Willis Brothers,[17] Paul Clayton,[18] Jimmie Driftwood,[19] and Dave Frederickson[20] (who thinks he learned the song from the radio) are one strain, as is Woody Guthrie's recomposition.[21] One might well expect a recording from the urban folksong revival, such as that of Oscar Brand,[22] to be one strain, but a version printed in a song folio of recording artist Jules Verne Allen in 1933,[23] *before* the Lomax transcription, has only the first strain.[24] I have never heard a traditional performer sing the second strain, and the only other published two-strain version I know is that in Beatrice Landeck, *Git on Board,*[25] which significantly credits both Vernon Dalhart and the M. M. Cole Publishing Company, to which Brockman assigned copyright in 1941.

In this brief study I do not pretend to have examined all the materials that must exist from professional and nonprofessional tradition. I have not been able to hear Bobbie Gentry, Capitol 2788, or Buddy Starcher, Starday 460; and have not seen the copy in Mr. and Mrs. George German, *Cowboy Campfire Ballads* (1929), or in *Fun with Poetry.* But one can conclude on the evidence that "Billy the Kid" has had an active and not completely stable life in *professional* tradition. Bill Bender's text (Stinson SLP 37) is a significant variant which is the source of the text in Bill Clifton's *150 Old-Time Folk and Gospel Songs* (ca. 1957, 40). In Sterling Sherwin's *Saddle Songs*[26] a relatively standard text (credited to "The Texas Troubadour") is set to a new two-strain tune. Carson Robison's "Billy the Kid" in *Carson Robison's "Buckaroo" Song Book*[27] is a text only slightly related to Jenkins' and again set to a different tune.

The relatively small number of variants from oral tradition I have been able to examine[28] are closely related to copies found in print or on commercial recordings. For example, *Cowboy Songs,* published by *Hobo News* (New York, n.d.), and *Popular Cowboy Songs* (probably from the same press) contain a corrupt text which turns up identically on a ballet in the Stella M. Hendren Collection[29] and in the Virginia WPA Collection.[30] (Yet the Virginia informant stated, "I think I learned it from my aunt. I've known it for a long time.") Of course the text in the printed copies suggests a traditional source—it seems a ballet text to me—and subsequent information may alter the conclusion as to the limited domestic tradition of the ballad. But we should rather turn to a matter of simple justice, particularly in light of rather slender record of this ballad as "traditional."

The composition of Andrew Jenkins and Irene Spain was sold to Polk C. Brockman, presumably for $25, the "going rate." Andrew Jenkins and Irene Spain lost the monetary rights to the song. And they also lost credit for the composition after the early recordings and the M. M. Cole folio publications. In the world of professional hillbilly the song has been treated as P.D. or given a fictitious credit (e.g. "York" on Starday) for financial reasons. In the world of folklorists and librarians the song became traditional with its inclusion in *American Ballads and Folk Songs*. This is certainly a tribute to the genius of Andrew Jenkins and Irene Spain. But I must point out that as of 18 March 1954 "Billy the Kid" was copyrighted in the name of Andrew Jenkins, and to this date [1971] no payments have been received from the productions of Burl Ives, Marty Robbins, Paul Glass and Irene Singer, or anyone else who has profited from publishing or performance. In this paper I am paying what tribute I can to the author and composer, with the hope that something more substantial may result.

NOTES

1. L G. Malcolm Laws, Jr., *Native American Balladry*, 2d ed. (Philadelphia, Pa., 1964).

2. For a survey of information and misinformation about "The Kid," see Ramon F. Adams, *A Fitting Death for Billy the Kid* (Norman, Oklahoma, 1960).

3. D. K. Wilgus, "Folksong and Folksong Scholarship: Changing Approaches and Attitudes. The Rationalistic Approach," in *A Good Tale and a Bonnie Tune*, Publications of the Texas Folklore Society no. 32 (1964), 229–232; reprinted in *Folksong and Folksong Scholarship* (Dallas, Texas, 1964), 31–34. Archie Green, "Hillbilly Music: Source and Symbol," *Journal of American Folklore* 78 (1965): 218.

4. Quoted from copy of letter now in my possession.

5. Mrs. Futrelle's latest discussion of the circumstances of composition was in a taped interview with Archie Green, Judith McCulloh, and Lewis Wills, 9 November 1969. Mrs. Futrelle has, however, related essentially the same story in other interviews and correspondence in my possession. For aid in gathering material on the Jenkins family I am also indebted to Fred Hoeptner and Ed Kahn.

6. Reprinted in Austin E. and Alta S. Fife, *Cowboy and Western Songs* (New York, 1969), 266–268. I am indebted to the Fifes for making available to me other materials relative to "Billy the Kid."

7. Ibid., 265–266.

8. Stuart N. Lake, *Wyatt Earp: Frontier Marshal* (New York, 1959), 306.

9. Library of Congress E659098. Letter to Mrs. Irene Spain Futrelle, 19 June 1967. Copy now in my possession. I have not seen the photostat deposited.

10. *"The Kentucky Wonder Bean"*: Walter Peterson Sensational Collection of Mountain Ballads and Old Time Songs (Chicago, c. 1931; reprinted 1941 [?]), 22; *Hamlins Singing Cowboy: Sensational Collection of Mountain Ballads and Old Time Songs. KOMA, Oklahoma City, Okla.* (Chicago, c. 1933), 22.

11. A text collected by Herbert Halpert in New York, 10 August 1938, contains somewhat similar "corruptions," but the alterations are probably independent. (Text in Fife Collection, Utah State University, FAC II 464.)

12. (New York), 137–138. The same material is reprinted in the collectors' *Cowboy Songs* (New York, 1938), 141–142.

13. (New York, 1960), 387.

14. Vocalion and Okeh 04136, Harmony 1033 and HL 7317; matrix LA 1487, recorded 21 October 1937.

15. Capitol 20037 in album BD 14, released 30 October 1945; matrix CAP 634-3A, recorded 7 May 1945.

16. *Traditional Songs of the Old West*, Stinson SLP 37, 10" LP. The recording probably came from a previously unissued matrix of the United States Recording Company.

17. *The Willis Brothers in Action*, Starday SLP 163, 12" LP. (There is another issue by the Willis Brothers, Hilltop JM 6035, I have not as yet obtained. The 12' LP is probably a "supermarket" issue taken from the Starday session.)

18. *Wanted for Murder*, Riverside RLP 12-640, 12" LP.

19. *How the West Was Won*, RCA Victor LSO-6070, 12" LP.

20. *Songs of the West*, Folkways FH 5259, 12" LP.

21. *Cowboy Songs* (with Cisco Houston), Stinson SLP 32. The Guthrie version is collated with the "traditional" (Jenkins) version by Pete Seeger and Jack Elliot on *The Badmen*, Columbia L2S 1012, 12" LP.

22. *Badmen and Heroes*, Elektra EKL-16, 10" LP; EKL-129, 12" LP.

23. *Songs of the Range* (San Antonio, Texas), 162–63.

24. Other one-strain forms of the tune in print can be found in Satis N. Coleman and Adolph Bregman, *Songs of American Folks* (New York, 1942), 110–111; Burl Ives, *Song in America* (New York, 1962), 202–203; and Paul Glass and Louis C. Singer, *Songs of the West* (New York, 1966), 28–29. The one-strain tune printed by the Fifes in *Cowboy and Western Songs*, 265, and credited to "Pat Patterson, commercial recording" is almost certainly derived from the Al Craver, Columbia 15135-B disc. Patt Patterson does not seem to have recorded the ballad, and he set the text in *Songs of the Roundup Rangers* (New York, 1933), 6–7, to a different one-strain tune. The transcription in the Fife's volume apparently illustrates the independent transcription of but one strain of the full tune.

25. (New York, 1944, 1950), 42–43.

26. (London, 1948), 3–5.

27. (New York, 1940), 60–61.

28. Including Dee Donahue, Logan, Utah, 1958, Fife Collection. FAC I 644; Blanche Silvey, Hopkinsville, Kentucky, 1965, Western Kentucky Folklore Archive, UCLA, T7-128.

29. No. 685, Fife Collection.

30. Etta Kilgore, Wise, Va., 1940. (Bruce A. Rosenberg, *The Folksongs of Virginia: A Checklist of the WPA Holdings, Alderman Library, University of Virginia* [Charlottesville, Va., 1969], no. 97.)

PART TWO

Legend into History

CHAPTER TEN

New Light on the Legend of Billy the Kid

Philip J. Rasch and R. N. Mullin

Like so many others, Philip J. Rasch became interested in the Kid after reading Burns's *Saga*. In 1949 he struck up a correspondence with Toledo, Ohio, oil company executive Robert N. Mullin, a longtime Kid aficionado, and jointly (although not always together) they set out to research the background of the (then) shadowy "man named Antrim" who was said in Pat Garrett's *Authentic Life* to have married the Kid's mother.

The outcome of that research was truly a major breakthrough, documenting for the very first time the fact that the Kid's real name was Henry McCarty, that the "man named Antrim" who had married his mother in Santa Fe was William Henry Harrison Antrim, and that Henry had a brother named Joe, or Josie. During the following year, Rasch and Mullin went on to locate documents that became and remain to this day the primary foundation stones in the true story of Billy the Kid: the 1874 obituary of Catherine Antrim, the 1877 newspaper account of the Kid's killing of Francis P. Cahill, and the November 1930 death record of Joseph Antrim in Denver. Almost incidentally, they also found newspaper items as early as April 1879 claiming that the Kid came from New York State, establishing the provenance of that "information," and explaining its appearance in everything written about the Kid from the dime novels of 1881 onward.

Persistent, outspoken, and astonishingly disciplined, Phil Rasch would go on to become the preeminent Lincoln County War historian of his generation, but his blunt, sometimes even antagonistic approach to the topic was at variance with, and eventually anathema to, the manners and methods not only of Bob Mullin but also of older, more conservative pioneers such as William A. Keleher and Maurice Garland Fulton. If it ever bothered him, Rasch gave little sign of it; and anyway he hunted better as a lone wolf. Between this early effort and his death in 1995, he went on to produce more than 170 articles—papers, as he called them—which together constitute a unique documentation of New Mexico and Arizona outlaw-lawman history in the latter half of the nineteenth century.

It can confidently be said that the article which follows marked a sea change—literally, a profound and notable transformation—in Billy the Kid studies, which has continued to reverberate to the present day.

The generally accepted account of the early life of Billy the Kid is based on information given to Garrett[1] and Otero[2] by Ash Upson, an individual not noted for his devotion to fact. Their readers will recall that Upson, who claimed to have lived with the Kid's family in Santa Fe and in Silver City, related that early in the summer of 1862 William H. Bonney, Sr., his wife Katherine and their two young sons, William H. (born November 23, 1859) and Edward (born in 1861) left New York City for the West. After the father's death in Coffeyville, Kansas, the widow and her children joined a wagon train going to Pueblo, Colorado, where "she married a man named Antrim." The Antrims ran a restaurant–boarding house in Santa Fe in 1863, but in 1868 moved to Silver City. In the book that he wrote for Garrett, Upson stated that by 1882 Antrim was the only surviving member of the family.

The historical fact that Silver City was not laid out as a town site until after the first rich silver strike in 1870 casts considerable doubt upon the accuracy of this chronology. Further, the investigator will quickly find that there is no documentary evidence to support any of Upson's statements. The Clerk of Manhattan reported that there is no mention of a William H. Bonney in the recorded births for the years 1859 and 1860. Coffeyville has no records of deaths for as far back as 1862; in fact the old Osage Indian village known as Possum-town was not incorporated by its few white inhabitants until 1871. The records at Pueblo for the year 1862 do not list a marriage between William Antrim and Katherine Bonney.

About three years ago the writers became interested in the shadowy figure of the "man named Antrim." Ignored as he was by the Kid's various biographers, it seemed possible that a study of his life might throw some interesting side lights on the Kid's early years. This study has turned out to be decidedly profitable and has led to the discovery of hitherto unpublished facts which completely discredit the Upson account. The biography of Antrim will be published later; it is the purpose of this paper to set forth and to document a new thesis as to the origin and the early years of Billy the Kid.

During the Civil War, William Henry Harrison Antrim served in Company I, 54th Regiment, Indiana Volunteers. In later years he stated that after receiving his discharge he lived at Indianapolis, Indiana, until 1869. The Antrim family then moved to Kansas and he resided at Wichita until 1872. In the latter part of 1872 or the first part of 1873 he married Catherine McCarty, a widow with two sons, in the Presbyterian Church in Santa Fe. These statements may be found set forth in a series of papers which he filed with the Bureau of Pensions in support of his claim for a pension for his Civil War services. They are now in the files of the Chief Archivist, War Records Branch, General Services Administration, National Archives and Records Service.

In the Book of Marriages "A," pages 35 and 36, of Santa Fe County there appears the notation that on March 1, 1873, the Reverend D. F. McFarland united in matrimony William H. *Antrum* and Mrs. Catherine McCarty, both of Santa Fe. Witnesses are listed as *Hary* Edmonds, Henry McCarty, Joseph McCarty, Mrs. A. R. McFarland and Miss Katie McFarland. The records at the First Presbyterian Church in Santa Fe show that on March 1, 1873, the Reverend McFarland married William H. *Antram* to Mrs. Catherine McCarty. Witnesses are given as Harvey Edmonds, Mrs. A. R. McFarland, Miss Katie McFarland, Henry McCarty and Josie McCarty.

From other sources there is ample evidence to identify Henry McCarty as Billy the Kid, and some of them make it clear that the account of the Kid's New York origin was not one of Upson's inventions.

The first published mention of this fact that the writers have been able to uncover is contained in the *Rio Grande Republican*'s report of the Kid's death. The paper says quite simply "the Kid was born in New York State and his true name was McCarthy. . . . He was 23 years old." Articles published in the *National Police Gazette*[4] and by John W. Morrison[5] that same year agree that the Kid lived in New York City and that his name was Michael McCarthy.

In 1902 the *Silver City Enterprise* published an interview with former sheriff Harvey H. Whitehill, who is quoted as saying:

> Early in his career he changed his name to Billie Bonney in order to keep the stigma of disgrace from his family. Billie's right name, you know, was Henry McCarty and he was born at Anderson, Indiana.[9]

The writers have devoted considerable time and effort to this phase of the problem. They have found mention of McCartneys, McCartys, McCarthys and McCartheys among the male residents of Anderson in

William Henry Harrison Antrim, ca. 1873. This may very well have been a
wedding photograph; it was on March 1, 1873, that Antrim married Catherine
McCarty in Santa Fe, in the process becoming stepfather to her two sons,
Henry and Joseph. Philip J. Rasch Collection.

pre–Civil War days, but they have been unable to tie any of them in with the Kid and his family. Unfortunately, the vital statistics were among the Madison County records destroyed in the 1880s. Sheriff Whitehill's impression that Billy had been born in Anderson may have arisen from knowledge of the fact that William Antrim was born near that town.

Mr. Gilbert Cureton, of Silver City, has furnished the writers with copies of interviews with several of the old settlers recorded by Mrs. Helen Wheaton some years ago. Mr. Louis Abraham told her:

> I went to school with Billy the Kid. . . . I helped bury Billy's mother. . . . I always knew Billy as Henry McCarty. His stepfather's name was Anthrum and sometimes he went by that name.

In 1932 the *Silver City Independent* carried a report of an interview with Anthony B. Connor, brother of Mrs. Richard Knight, both now deceased. Connor said in part:

> Antrim boarded at the Knight home, and with him was his son Joe Antrim and Billy McCartney, his stepson who afterwards became known as Billy the Kid. Billy sometimes was known as Billy Bonney, his mother's name before she married Mr. Antrim.[7]

(It should be noted at this point that Antrim never had any children of his own.)

In 1949 Mrs. Maude B. Stratton told Mr. William V. Morrison that:

> She knew the Whitehills and the Hennessy family. They knew the Kid as McCarty, or McCartney. They knew his brother, Joe, who was the youngest.[8]

In 1951 the *Silver City Daily Press*[9] published an interview with Chauncey O. Truesdell, who claimed that as a boy he had known the Kid and that the latter had lived briefly at the Truesdell home. Mr. Truesdell was interviewed by one of the writers [Mullin] on January 9, 1952, at which time he stated in part:

> I was eight years old when I arrived at Silver City from Santa Fe. . . . This was in 1871. Mr. and Mrs. Antrim and their sons, Joey and Henry, arrived a little later. . . . [Mrs. Antrim] was sickly and died after they had lived there a little while. My mother nursed her before she died. She told my mother her name was McCarthy before she

married Mr. Antrim and Mr. Antrim was Joe and Henry's step-father. I never heard the name Bonney until afterward. After Henry left town, some people that knew him in Silver City saw him other places and said he called himself "Bill Bonney." It was the same boy, all right; they knew him well.

For the sake of the record, it should be mentioned that there are stories around Silver City to the effect that Mrs. Bonney was a widow when she came there and that the Kid's real name was Henry McCarty (McCarthy, McCartney), with seduction implied as the explanation. One lurid but wholly false bit of local folklore insists that Billy killed his first man because the latter recognized Catherine Antrim as the notorious Kate Bender!

It will have been noted that whenever the above quoted individuals refer to the Kid's brother, they give his name as Joe, mention of whom also appears in the marriage records. This name is confirmed by Mrs. Robert K. Bell[10] and other informants. Evidently Upson was exercising his imagination in giving it as Edward. The Antrim MSS. indicate that Joe was alive at least as late as 1901, which disproves Upson's statement that by 1882 only Antrim himself remained alive.

It has proved difficult to recover any of the background of the Kid's family. Even within his own lifetime he was well on his way to becoming a legend. Thus when he was captured by Garrett and brought into Las Vegas on December 26, 1880, Dr. Sutfin, proprietor of the Grand View Hotel, assured his guests that "Billy was a Chicago bootblack whose mind became inflamed by reading dime novels."[11]

Don Jenardo's *The True Life of Billy the Kid,* reputed to be the first complete narrative of the life of the Kid, was originally published August 29, 1881, just a few weeks after his death. It asserts that the Kid's true name was William McCarthy and that he was born in the state of New York in 1859 or 1860. Jenardo specifically adds that the location of his birthplace as the City of New York is a mistake.[12] Unfortunately, the State of New York Department of Health was not organized on a permanent basis until 1880, and its records prior to that date are very incomplete. It has no information on William Bonney or Henry McCarty.

Writing in 1908, J. E. Sligh, who claimed to have been a resident of Lincoln County during the troubles there, stated that Billy's father was a soldier stationed at Fort Bayard, where he died, leaving a widow and three children.[13]

Charles Siringo, alleging that he had got his information from the Kid himself and from several individuals who knew him, including Garrett and Upson, repeats the traditional Upson account.[14]

Maurice Fulton, the leading authority on the Lincoln County troubles, has recovered part of a serial life of the Kid which ran in the *Las Vegas Optic* in the latter part of 1882, the author being unknown. The writer of the series purports to have interviewed the Kid personally and to have learned that he was born in County Limerick, Ireland, about 1859. His father's name was Williams. After the death of the father the Kid, his mother and her two daughters moved to Canada. In 1869 she married "an old reprobate named Antrim" in Nova Scotia and soon afterwards the family moved to New Mexico.[15]

Hendron states that it is generally accepted as fact that the Kid was born in New York City on November 23, 1859. He adds that the Kid's mother was of French extraction, was known as Gene, and had run off to New York with a man who never married her but who was the father of William Bonney.[16] (Louie Abraham, who knew Mrs. Antrim personally, described her as "a jolly Irish lady.")

According to Mary Hudson Brothers, Antrim told her father that his wife thought her first husband "was one of those killed by Apaches in the first strikes in the Pinos Altos district."[18] Pinos Altos is a gold mining community six miles from Silver City. The first strikes were those led by Mangas Coloradas in 1861, but it would appear more likely that this statement refers to the attacks by Victorio's warriors in 1869. However, Mrs. Mildred York contends that Mrs. Brothers is actually reporting the life of Dad Russel rather than of William Antrim.[19]

This welter of information and misinformation is most confusing. It is disappointing to find that the Antrim MSS give very little information on the background of Mrs. Catherine McCarty Antrim and her family. They state that her first husband had been a man named McCarty, who had died in New York City and who had no military service known to Antrim. This is, of course, not quite the same thing as saying that this mysterious individual was the father of the boy known as Henry McCarty, but it strongly suggests that certain of the versions listed above may be tentatively eliminated from serious consideration.

The Upson story goes on to assert that when Billy was twelve he attacked a ruffian who had insulted his mother and was saved from a beating by Ed Moulton. Later when Moulton was in a fight, this same individual attempted to strike him from behind, whereupon Billy killed him with a knife and had to flee for his life.

This story will not stand up under analysis. There is in the Library of the Museum of New Mexico a manuscript signed by Jim Blair, son-in-law of Ed Moulton, in which he states

> Billie the Kid never did kill anyone in Silver City. That story is all false. The story of him killing a man over Ed. Moulton is positively not true. Mr. Moulton never would read an article about Billie because he would become angry for he said "They write so many lies about that boy, and I know the ones are false about his killings in Grant Co."[20]

Connor, Abraham, Truesdell, Whitehill and every other Silver City informant the writers have ever met or seen quoted flatly deny that Billy ever killed a man in Grant County. They all agree that the Kid's troubles in Silver City started after the death of his mother.

So far as the writers know, no one has ever questioned Sheriff Whitehill's statement that he was the first officer ever to arrest the Kid. Catherine Antrim died of tuberculosis on September 16, 1874, after having been confined to her bed for the last four months of her life.[21] Whitehill did not become sheriff until some time in 1875. Since the Kid is definitely known to have been in Lincoln County in 1877, it would seem to be established that his first arrest took place between 1875 and 1877, and in any event after the death of his mother. The arrest by Whitehill was for theft, not for murder, and he refers to the Kid as having been just over fifteen at the time.[22] Reportedly there is extant a letter written by Connor which states that this event occurred in 1877.

Billy is quoted as having told his friends in Lincoln County that he was driven away from home by "the tyranny and cruelty of his step-father."[22] Obviously this conflicts with the account of his having to leave because of killing the man who insulted his mother, and both stories appear to be only romantic efforts at self-justification. Whitehill states that "the boy's mother died, and with his brother he was left to the care of his stepfather, who lavished upon them almost a mother's care."[24] Dick Clark affirmed that "Mr. Antrim was good to his step-children, there being two boys."[25] Bickerstaff has recorded a conversation with

Dan McMillan bearing on this subject. McMillan related that he worked with Antrim in the mines at Chloride Flats.

> Mr. Antrim was called out of the mines one day to talk to his son who said the matter was urgent. When he returned he told Dan that his boy had gotten himself in a great deal of trouble and he had given him all of the money he had on him at that time and told him to leave town.[26]

This does not sound like the action of a cruel stepfather. Neither does it sound like the sort of advice Antrim would have given a twelve year old child, though he may well have suggested it to an eighteen year old youth.

The evidence presented above completely destroys Upson's "history" of the McCarty-Antrim family, but at the same time it raises more questions than it answers—questions to which the writers as yet have no answers to offer.

There is no doubt but that the Kid called himself Bonney—letters written by him and signed with that name are still extant. But why that name in particular? Was it simply an alias selected more or less at random, as Whitehill's statement would suggest? Could it have been his mother's maiden name? Or are the Silver City folk right in their contention that Billy was an illegitimate child? The fact that Mrs. McCarty had tuberculosis suggests that she may have emigrated to New Mexico for her health. Certainly such a trip and the subsequent life on the rough frontier would have been a difficult prospect for a sick woman. Various versions of the story of Billy's boyhood refer to Coffeyville, Kansas. There is evidence that about the time in question a man named Bonney owned farm land near Coffeyville. It is possible that Catherine and her children lived there with him. Antrim might have felt that there was nothing to be gained by resurrecting an old scandal in his pension application. In his old age when the family spoke of his having been married "Uncle Will would change the subject quick."[27] May we read any significance into this, or are we being viciously unfair to the memory of a virtuous woman who is no longer here to defend herself?

It would appear to the writers that certain lines of further investigation are clearly indicated. First, a search should be made of the New York

City directories, census lists, etc., to determine whether this family of McCartys can be located therein. Second, an attempt should be made to determine whether there is any record of a man named Bonney actually having been associated with Mrs. McCarty. Third, if Joe Antrim was alive at least as late as 1901, there must be scores of people still living who knew him. Some of these might have valuable data to contribute.

The writers plan to continue their researches along the lines indicated above. It would be greatly appreciated if readers who have information on any of these subjects would get in touch with them through the Editor of *The New Mexico Folklore Record.*

NOTES

1. Pat F. Garrett, *The Authentic Life of Billy the Kid* (New York, 1927).

2. Miguel Antonio Otero, *The Real Billy the Kid* (New York, 1936).

3. *The Rio Grande Republican,* July 23, 1881.

4. "Billy the Kid," *National Police Gazette,* XXXVIII (August 13, 1881), 203.

5. John W. Morrison, *The Life of Billy the Kid, a Juvenile Outlaw* (New York, 1881).

6. *Silver City Enterprise,* January 3, 1902.

7. *Silver City Independent,* March 22, 1932.

8. William V. Morrison, Personal communication, March 17, 1952.

9. *Silver City Daily Press,* May 23, 1951.

10. Mrs. Robert K. Bell, Personal communication, July 13, 1952.

11. Albert E. Hyde, "The Old Regime in the Southwest—the Reign of the Revolver in New Mexico," *Century,* XLI (March, 1902), 690–701.

12. Don Jenardo (John W. Lewis), *True Life of Billy the Kid,* Happy Hours Brotherhood Reprint No. 5 (Fisherville: Ralph W. Cummings, 1945).

13. J. E. Sligh, "Billy the Kid," *Overland Monthly,* LII (July, 1908), 46–31.

14. Charles A. Siringo, *History of Billy the Kid* (Santa Fe, 1920).

15. Maurice G. Fulton, "Apocrypha of Billy the Kid," *Folk-Say, A Regional Miscellany,* B. A. Botkin, editor (Norman, Oklahoma, 1930).

16. J. W. Hendron, *The Story of Billy the Kid* (Santa Fe, 1948).

17. Louie Abraham (as told to Betty Totty), "Billie the Kid." Unpublished manuscript in the files of the New Mexico Writers Project, Santa Fe.

18. Mary Hudson Brothers, "The Stepfather of Billy the Kid," *New Mexico Magazine,* XXVIII (October, 1950), 22ff.

19. Mildred York, Personal communications, July 24, 1952, and August 4, 1952.

20. Jim Blair (as told to Frances E. Totty), Unpublished manuscript in the files of the New Mexico Writers Project, Santa Fe.

21. *Silver City Mining Life,* September 19, 1874.

22. *Silver City Enterprise,* January 3, 1902.

23. Garrett.

24. *Silver City Enterprise,* January 3, 1902.

25. Dick Clark (as told to Mrs. W. C. Totty), Unpublished manuscript in the files of the New Mexico Writers Project, Santa Fe.

26. *The Mustang,* April 14, 1950.

27. R. C. Hollinger, Personal communication, May 30, 1951.

CHAPTER ELEVEN

Billy the Kid: The Trail of a Kansas Legend

Waldo E. Koop

Joseph W. Snell, former director of the Kansas State Historical Society, and co-author with the late Nyle H. Miller of *Why the West Was Wild*, once described Waldo Koop (1920–1990) as "one of the finest amateur researchers I've ever known." It was an opinion shared by many fellow researchers, not to mention the many local, state, and national organizations with which Koop came into contact. During his working life, most of it spent with the Boeing Company in Wichita, Kansas, where his skills as an engineer were highly valued, Koop developed a lifelong interest in the Old West, which eventually led him to conduct original research into the rich history of frontier Kansas. His wife, Bette, and his children shared his interests and encouraged him to pursue them. He was unique in his methods, in that he "scanned" newspapers and documents and often included seemingly trivial material in his notes that invariably proved invaluable later on.

Koop's discovery and documentation of the when and the where of the Antrim family's sojourn in Wichita was and remains a landmark contribution to Billy the Kid research, and it deservedly earned Koop nationwide attention. The next subject to attract his interest was gunman-gambler "Rowdy Joe" Lowe, but he elected to turn over most of his research material for that project to Joseph G. Rosa, who continued the research and later (retaining Koop as co-author) published a book on the subject, *Rowdy Joe Lowe: Gambler with a Gun* (1989). At the time of his death, Koop was exploring the life and background of Kansas gunfighter Jim Curry, a veteran of the Beecher's Island fight, and renowned as the man who (very nearly) shot Wild Bill Hickok. Waldo Koop was seventy years of age when he died on April 23, 1990, following a long illness.

Few characters of the frontier have brought on as much speculation in the literature of the Southwest as the youthful desperado who traveled under the alias of Billy the Kid. Perhaps the mystery which has surrounded him and his antecedents has stirred the fancy and the imagination of the many persons who have delved into his background. At last count, upwards of four hundred publications dealing with the Kid have been recorded. Most of these have attempted to shed some light on his boyhood, but, for all practical purposes, all have failed. Surely if one knew more of the Kid's boyhood, the development of the legends surrounding him might be explained, and in that pursuit an amazing amount of effort has gone downstream as historian after historian has tried to retrieve the early years of the desperado before he materialized on the New Mexican scene.

Most of those who have made these attempts have been led astray by the statements of a man who ought to have had the facts regarding those lost years. But that man, Marshall Ashmun Upson, for reasons of his own, chose not to release them, choosing instead a curious mixture of fact and fiction. Thus was born much of the legend of Billy the Kid's early life as a Kansas resident, a legend which had its basis in fact, but not as Upson told it.

Marshall Ashmun Upson, better known as Ash Upson, was a veteran newspaperman, a member of a profession usually expected to record the current contemporary events with some degree of accuracy. For a short period, too, Upson had been a boarder in the home of the Kid's mother and, without doubt was in a favorable position to have learned much about the Kid's boyhood in Kansas, certainly more than he told. Considering Upson's knowledge of the Kid's background, it was natural that Pat Garrett drafted him into the project of setting to print the Kid's life story. Garrett's motive for the project is not entirely clear. Perhaps he was aware that his final and fatal bullet had marked a significant milestone in New Mexican territorial history, and felt the need for a lasting record of events. If so, the book published under his name failed of its purpose, particularly in regard to the subject's early life. Or perhaps Sheriff Garrett saw an opportunity to reap an additional financial harvest through the sale of *The Authentic Life of Billy the Kid*. From all that can be learned, the book also failed of that purpose.

In the book's introduction, Garrett and Upson avowed that the purpose was to correct the myriad false accounts of the Kid's life then being published elsewhere. Time and the untiring efforts of succeeding historians have proven the failure of their effort in that direction also. Certainly the efforts of serious students into the life and ways of New Mexico's legendary Kid have turned up enough evidence to refute thoroughly the use of the word "authentic" in Garrett's titling. But that evidence is mostly of a negative nature, particularly in regard to the Kid's boyhood, all of which leaves a puzzling set of clues for those who would retrace his trail across the frontier.

Let's double back briefly to pick up the trail as Upson left it, for, inaccurate as it is, Garrett's and Upson's statement should be considered as a starting point. Upson detailed the nativity and 4 early years of the Kid by designating him William H. Bonney, born in the city of New York on November 23, 1859. Upson volunteered little information about the Kid's father beyond stating that he had died in Coffeyville, Kans., soon after the family allegedly emigrated there in 1862. The mother, described only as Kathleen, then took her two sons to Colorado where she met and married a man named Antrim. In 1868, Upson declared, the family moved to Silver City, N. M.

At that point in the narrative, the researcher might better dispense with Upson's doubtful assistance along Billy's trail, for at Silver City the Kid, then known as Henry McCarty and Henry Antrim, began to leave footprints of a more reliable nature.

Upson, then, left precious little for the researcher to go on, even if what he had stated had been true, and for eighty-odd years, little progress has been made from that point. In recent years, a major breakthrough was scored when it was discovered that the "man named Antrim" had married the Kid's mother, not in Colorado, but in Santa Fe, N. M. That discovery, credited to Robert N. Mullin, also helped to firmly identify the Kid's mother as Catherine McCarty, the stepfather as William H. Antrim, and the elusive Kid as Henry McCarty.[1]

But even with that discovery which dated the marriage March 1, 1873, the back trail from Santa Fe led nowhere. But just as surely as Henry McCarty, alias the Kid, had died under Garrett's guns, Henry had experienced a boyhood life somewhere, and in that somewhere, there had to be records of his passing. Coincidentally, just as the Kid's legend was beginning to take shape and the seed of newsman Upson's effort was being planted, another newspaperman was setting down that record. As if to show that truth can often be stranger than fiction, that newsman also bore the given name of Marshall—Marshall M. Murdock, founding editor of the pioneer Wichita *Weekly Eagle*, of Kansas.

Col. Marsh Murdock's words, until now, have escaped the questing eye of Kid researchers, for nowhere in the reams of print devoted to the Kid have they before been repeated as a clue to the locale of his early years. But Col. Marsh knew whereof he wrote when he stated in his columns of August 11, 1881:

> "Billy the Kid," an account of whose tragic death we published two weeks since, formerly lived in Wichita, and many of the early settlers remember him as a street gamin in the days of longhorns.[2]

At this late date Col. Marsh's statement might tempt the unknowing to relegate it to a category of similar items which appeared in newspapers over the country for everywhere editors were claiming the Kid as a product of their own municipalities.[3] Some of this was, no doubt, sensationalism, for Billy the Kid was good copy. But to those acquainted with Col. Marsh Murdock's journalism, the word "sensationalism" never, never applied. One of the most dependable of the frontier editors, Murdock was a con- servative conservative. In this particular instance Murdock was repeating the facts as related to him by what must have been an authoritative and dependable source. Henry McCarty's boyhood in Wichita during the "days of longhorns" is clearly indicated by other records.

Of course, the doings of one so young as eleven-year-old Henry seldom are a matter of record. However, the Kid's boyhood can well be traced by the deeds of his mother, the widow McCarty. The earliest known record of her Kansas transactions may be noted in various entries in Sedgwick county deed records which indicate that on September 12, 1870, Mrs. Catherine McCarty was given title to a vacant lot on Chisholm (now Market) street in the city of Wichita.[4] Numerous other entries were found, too numerous in fact, for inclusion here, but all dealt with the real estate purchases of Catherine McCarty. Of further interest are the entries which reveal that in February of 1871, William H. Antrim was given title to neighboring lots on Chisholm street.[5] All of these entries, indicating modestly extensive holdings in what was then the very hub and center of the village's business district, give an entirely different view of the legendary picture of an impoverished widow barely able to make ends meet for a family of two growing boys.

The location of a residence can be assumed from another entry which shows that on June 28, 1871, William Antrim deeded to Catherine McCarty the lots on Chisholm street which he had previously purchased and "the building on lot 75, Court (now Main) street."[6]

The obvious inference is that Mrs. McCarty was owner of the lot on which was located the building owned by William Antrim, and in this transaction, Antrim was transferring ownership of the building to Mrs. McCarty. An 1873 panoramic sketch of Wichita, accurately detailed on known buildings, shows a two story structure of frontier hotel proportions standing on the site.[7] Other evidence indicates that the widow McCarty operated a laundry in the building while most likely the living quarters were on the second floor. On March 15, 1871, the editor of the Wichita *Tribune* brought out his salutatory edition, and in giving free "puffs" to various local businesses, commented:

> The City Laundry is kept by Mrs. McCarty, to whom we recommend those who wish to have their linen made clean.

Col. Marsh Murdock's comment referring to Henry McCarty as a Wichita street gamin, leads one to believe that the principal residence of the widow McCarty was within the city in connection with her "City Laundry," but eleven-year-old Henry had opportunity to spend part of his time in the surrounding country for the widow reached out to take into her real estate holdings a quarter section of land located just northeast of the village. Here records of the land reveal the most significant details yet presented about the early life of Henry McCarty, alias Billy the Kid.

On March 25, 1871, Catherine McCarty presented herself at the United States Land Office in nearby Augusta, Kans., and there lay claim to land described as the northwest quarter of section twelve, township twenty-seven south, range one east. As a part of the Osage trust lands, the quarter section was offered for sale to qualified persons at a price of $1.25 per acre. The widow McCarty paid the total sum of $200 in full.[8]

To support her claim and qualifications, William H. Antrim submitted a sworn statement, which because of its highly significant implications, is presented in full.[9]

LAND OFFICE, Augusta, Kansas, March 25, 1871

> In the matter of the application of Catharine McCarty of Sedgwick County, Kansas to purchase the northwest Quarter of Section No. 12 in Township No. 27 South, in Range No. 1 East, under the provisions of the Joint Resolution of Congress approved April 10, 1869, for the disposal of the lands ceded by the Osage Indians under the Second Article of the Treaty of September 29, 1865.

Personally appeared the said Catharine McCarty and offered proof in support of her application, as follows, viz: William Antrim of lawful age being duly sworn, deposes and says: I have known Catharine McCarty for 6 years last past; that she is a single woman over the age twenty-one years, the head of a family consisting of two children, a citizen of the United States, and a bona fide settler upon the foregoing described land, which she seeks to purchase, having settled thereon about the 10 day of August, 1870; on or about the 10 day of August, 1870 he built a house upon said lands, 12 by 14 feet, 1 story high, board roof, 1 door and 2 windows. She moved into said house with her family and effects on or about the 4th day of March A.D. 1871, and has resided in said house and upon said land to the present time, and that she has made the following additional improvements on said land: She has about 7 acres enclosed and in cultivation. She has 640 rods hedge row about 7 ft. wide. She has posts and rails on ground for further fencing. She has a well 12 ft. deep. She has 57 fruit trees set and growing. She has an outdoor cellar 6x8 ft. covered with earth and timbers. I estimate the value of improvements at from $250 to $300 dollars.

Wm. H. Antrim

Sworn to and subscribed before me this 25th of March, AD. 1871

W. A. Shannon, Receiver

Fredrick Daily of lawful age being by me first duly sworn according to law deposes and says, I have known Catharine McCarty for the ten months last past and know of my own personal knowledge that the allegations herein contained are substantially correct and true.

Fredrick Daily

Sworn to and subscribed before me this 25th day of March, 1871

W. A. Shannon, Receiver

"I have known Catherine McCarty for six years last past." And because of those words—the sworn statement of William Antrim in 1871—history's

whole concept of the Antrim-McCarty relationship is due a drastic reappraisal. Made at a time when Antrim was under no duress, there is no apparent reason why his statement should not be accepted at face value. In 1871, Antrim's words would not have been repressed by the shadow of scandal, for the escapades of the Kid were yet to come. Too, in order to qualify his acquaintanceship with Mrs. McCarty in support of her land claim, he would not have felt compelled to claim such a long term acquaintance had it not been so.

William Antrim's words date his liaison with the widow McCarty back to 1865, and with the knowledge of his whereabouts during that time, the trail of the McCarty family can be further followed, for the movements of the Antrim clan are much less obscure than those of the McCarty family.

William Henry Harrison Antrim was born on December 1, 1842, at Huntsville, Madison county, Ind[iana]. The 1850 United States census for that county indicates he had three brothers and one sister. The father's occupation was listed as merchant, but three years later he was the proprietor of a leading hotel (the Railroad House) which was situated opposite the courthouse in Anderson.[10] In 1862, William Antrim served a three months' enlistment in Co. I of the Fifty-Fourth Indiana Infantry, a service which later provided the basis for a pension claim.[11] By 1867, Antrim had taken up residence at 58 Cherry street, Indianapolis, and was employed as driver and clerk for the Merchant's Union Express Company whose headquarters were at 42 and 44 East Washington street.[12]

At this point there came about the acquaintanceship with the widow McCarty under circumstances yet unknown. Possibly the delivery of an express parcel to the widow's residence afforded the circumstance which brought together the not unattractive widow and Antrim. For at least one year, 1868, her residence was at 199 North East street within a few blocks of the express company's headquarters and in the same general area as Antrim's residence.[13]

Though a search was made in Indianapolis directories from 1858 through 1870, only one Mrs. Catherine McCarty was found and she in 1868. Whether she moved to a neighboring area or was for some similar reason omitted in the other annual compilations is not known. As was the usual practice, minor children were not listed and there was no other person noted at the address of Catherine McCarty.

Yet the single glimpse into the Indianapolis years of Henry McCarty and his mother is one of significance, for it provides the answer to a long unexplained riddle—the identity of Billy the Kid's father. It has been stated that the Kid's father died in Coffeyville, Kans[as], about 1862 but most historians are aware that Coffeyville did not exist as such until ten years later. To make matters more difficult for the researcher, the given name of the senior McCarty was either unknown or withheld. William Antrim provided a more concrete knowledge of the Kid's father in a statement made to the Bureau of Pensions in 1915. Yet Antrim's statements were cautiously evasive in referring to the McCarty family members and he prefaced his remarks with a precautionary, "This is not of my own knowledge." Of the elder McCartys he said, "She was married to McCarty, date not known, died in New York City, date not known, no other marriage, no military service that I know of." In answer to the question asking for the names and birthdates of all of his children, he may have executed an adroit sidestep when he said, "We had no children. My wife had two boys, one died in the eighties, and the other I have not heard from in fourteen years."[14]

Antrim's evasiveness is understandable, for he would not have desired to resurrect an old scandal. In later years, he was to be even more evasive on the subject of the McCarty family, for when questioned about that part of his experiences, he would quickly change the subject.[15]

In 1868, however, Catherine McCarty was more candidly inclined when she gave to the compilers of the Indianapolis city directory the information that she was the widow of Michael McCarty. Appearing in such terse simplicity, that single clue to the elusive identity of the legendary Kid's sire has a singularly anti-climactical aspect in the face of the years of effort which has gone into its search.

There is not much room for doubt that Michael McCarty, wherever he may have lived and died, was the father of Billy the Kid. Antrim's deposition to the effect that he had known Mrs. McCarty during his years of residence in Indianapolis, the single directory reference to *any* Mrs. Catherine McCarty during this period, the telling fact that this registrant was also a widow, and the proximity of her residence to Antrim's and the place of his employment all militate toward this conclusion and it would require a remarkable belief in coincidences to support any other.

Efforts to learn more about Michael McCarty have resulted only in the elimination of some likely candidates. Casting aside all preconceptions caused by the statements of Ash Upson, William Antrim and others, a researcher is offered a number of likely avenues to explore. The probable time of Michael McCarty's death suggests that he may have been a Civil War casualty despite the statement of Antrim. One Michael McCarty enlisted at Indianapolis in the Fifth battery of the Indiana Light Artillery and died in November, 1863, of wounds received at the battle of Chickamauga.[16] Nothing in his service record reveals that he had dependents. The disposition of several months' pay due him is left in doubt. The Surgeon in Charge of the general field hospital at Chattanooga, Tenn., detailed the few possessions he left: one hat, one blouse, one pair of trousers containing a pipe, a wallet with fifty cents in change and a three cent postage stamp—but no dependents.

The state of New York furnished a total of twenty-seven individuals named Michael McCarty for military service but it is not known how many of these were casualties and the task of winnowing that mass of material must await a more propitious time and circumstance. So the pursuit of Michael McCarty has at least temporarily ended in a stalemate and, for the time being, he must be left to rest in the peaceful anonymity which has been his for the past century.

With the record of Billy the Kid's early years properly oriented in time and place, one can retrace his steps as he moved westward to his New Mexican destiny and here and there one can reconstruct the life and scenes he must have experienced as little Henry McCarty.

Starting at the beginning of what is now the known record, it seems probable that the widow McCarty and her two sons, Henry the elder, and Joseph the younger, came to Indianapolis some time prior to 1865. Their probable point of origin was New York City, but this cannot be definitely stated for there is the recollection of Harvey Whitehill to be considered.[17] Whitehill had known the Kid and his mother at Silver City, and in 1902 he stated that Henry McCarty was born at Anderson, Ind[iana]. However, no support for Whitehill's statement has been found.

At Indianapolis came the friendship with William Antrim, a relationship which continued there for some years. It must have been an exciting day for little Henry when his mother announced that the family was moving west with "Uncle Billy" to what was then considered the frontier.

From the standpoint of the researcher who would attempt to trace the McCarty family, the timing of the move to Kansas was unfortunate, for it appears that the family left Indianapolis in the spring of 1870 just before the enumeration for the decennial census began. An unsatisfactory search through partially illegible census records turned up nothing conclusive in regard to the McCartys and William Antrim. The trip to Kansas was begun about June, 1870, and at their destination the census enumeration had just been completed. Antrim's deposition for the land claim and the statement of Fredrick Daily places their arrival some time shortly before the first of August.

Wichita was then not much more than a cluster of picket shanties on the east bank of the Little Arkansas river near its junction with the Arkansas. There was no railroad line into the town at that time, but it lay directly on the route of the cattle trail to Abilene and a freighting route from Fort Harker to Fort Sill. A business district was developing along what is now Main street north of Central avenue and it was in this area that Catherine McCarty purchased several lots and opened her City Laundry.

It was a colorful era for the city of Wichita and must have been a fascinating one for little Henry McCarty who was having his first taste of frontier life. No doubt he had looked forward to meeting western plainsmen and Indian scouts and here he had his first opportunity. Capt. David Payne, later of Oklahoma fame, but better known as "Old Ox-Heart" in the 1870's, was a familiar sight on the streets and if Henry asked for a tale of Indian fights, it would have been typical of the big-hearted Payne to spare the time for it.[18]

Capt. Allison J. Pliley, one of the Beecher Island survivors, was another of the plains scouts who had recently settled at Wichita. Just at the time of Henry McCarty's arrival there, he may have been too busy to notice the buck-toothed youngster. On the 27th of July, Pliley's friend and partner, "Uncle Jessie" Vandervoort, was murdered by George P. Murray in a claim dispute and it was Pliley who captured and brought in the murderer the next day.[19]

Shortly after his preliminary hearing, Murray escaped from the rickety local calaboose and a vengeance-determined Pliley saddled up and provisioned himself for a long pursuit. Over two months later, after a chase which must have been a classic in determined and persistent trailing, Pliley caught up with his man in the Creek Nation. Murray opened fire at sight of Pliley but missed. Pliley's answering shots were more accurate and Murray was buried on the prairie. Pliley returned to Wichita to display Murray's horse and six-shooter as evidence of his death and it must have been a wide-eyed Henry McCarty who heard the tale of Pliley's vengeance for the murder of his friend.[20] Perhaps this was Henry's first lesson concerning the obligations a frontier code placed upon the remaining friends of a murder victim, a lesson which he later applied after the death of his own friend, John H. Tunstall.

A short distance down the street from the McCarty laundry was the town's leading hotel, the Harris House, presided over by handsome Jack Ledford, another likely subject for Henry's interest. Ledford had married a prominent village belle and was becoming a popular citizen in spite of rumors of lawlessness in connection with army scouting days in northwestern Kansas. In November, 1870, Ledford had been elected sheriff of Sedgwick county but for some unexplained reason the election was declared void and another man was appointed to the office.[21]

Ledford found his former career a difficult one to turn his back upon, just as Henry McCarty also did later. On February 28, 1871, United States Deputy Marshal Jack Bridges, accompanied by Scout Lee Stewart and a twenty-five man detail of the Fifth Infantry arrived in Wichita with orders for the arrest of Ledford. It was reported that there was bad blood between Ledford and Bridges over an earlier difficulty and on this occasion Ledford refused to be taken but stepped from an outbuilding—shooting. Bridges was severely wounded; Ledford was killed in the Main street fracas.[22] If little Henry McCarty was not an eyewitness, one can be reasonably sure that the sound of gunfire brought him to the scene before Ledford expired.

Possibly this outbreak of six-shooter promiscuity so close to the McCarty home was the occasion that brought about his mother's decision to remove Henry from the ranks of the street gamins, for within four days she had packed her belongings and moved into the outlying claim cabin which William Antrim had erected for her.

For a while, things must have been quite busy around Henry's new home for there was the business of putting in the spring crops and a half mile row of hedge seedlings to set out. Come St. Patrick's Day, Henry was probably assigned the task of cutting up the seed potatoes for planting, and together with assisting "Uncle Billy" in the tasks of finishing the fencing, well curbing and storm cellar, Henry probably had little time to keep his ear cocked for the sound of six-shooter excitement on the town streets. Once a day, the El Dorado-Wichita stage passed near the McCarty claim and Henry could wave and shout a greeting to driver Bill Brooks. All in all, it was probably a new and pleasant experience for the boy and one wonders if in later times Billy the Kid did not wish himself back on the McCarty claim at Wichita's edge, regretting the events which had removed the family from the home Antrim had established for them.

In some of the literature dealing with the Kid, the stepfather has been described as a ne'er-do-well who spent most of his life in fruitless wandering and prospecting and his character has suffered some undeserved disparagement because of remarks credited to the Kid himself— a most doubtful source, even if the Kid actually made them. A new look at the Antrim-McCarty relationship should provide at least a partial vindication of the much-maligned Antrim. It is apparent that at Wichita Antrim was making a sincere and hard-working attempt to establish a home for the widow McCarty and her two sons. The erection of a cabin may have been a requirement to prove actual settlement, but the digging of a well and storm cellar and the planting of hedges and fruit trees went far beyond such a requirement and were plainly the acts of a man intending to establish a family homestead.

Antrim's letters to his parents living at Indianapolis must have reflected his satisfaction with conditions at his Kansas home for in the spring of 1871 the Antrim family (consisting of the parents, a daughter and a son, James Madison Antrim) joined William at Wichita. While circumstances forced William to move on, the Antrim family remained there for some years. James Antrim was a Wichita citizen for over twenty years and a popular and well- liked policeman.

William Antrim's efforts to provide a home for the McCartys point to an early desire for a marriage with the widow and one cannot help but wonder about the reason for what seems to have been an inordinately long courtship. The evidence also points to Catherine McCarty as the procrastinating partner but reveals no reason for her delay. If one could again cast aside all preconceptions about the reported death of the McCarty family head, and for the moment consider that Mrs. McCarty's Indianapolis directory listing as "widow of Michael" may have been merely an expedient explanation for her unattached status, one is struck by the bare possibility that the widow herself may not have been sure of her first husband's fate and that she may have been waiting the proverbial seven years before deciding that a spouse who had *disappeared* must be considered dead.

Antrim's home building efforts might have come to fruition but for a turn of fate which changed his and the widow's plans. Sometime in the late spring of 1871 the acquisition of property in and around Wichita came to an abrupt end and both parties began to dispose of their real estate. It is not difficult to reconstruct the reason, for one can imagine the signs of ill health for the widow, a trip to a physician and the dread pronouncement of tuberculosis. Not an uncommon affliction in those times, its diagnosis was generally followed by a recommendation for a move to the high and dry climates of Colorado and New Mexico.

Even in the face of the forced move from the homestead, Antrim demonstrated his desire to sink permanent roots in Kansas soil. It was likely deemed impractical for Mrs. McCarty to retain possession of the quarter section with the house and other improvements so on June 16, 1871, she sold the claim.[23] The next day Antrim filed on another unimproved claim directly northeast of the McCarty quarter and paid the usual price at the land office.[24] Possibly Antrim had hopes of returning to Kansas when the widow's health had improved. Although this was not to be, it is known that Antrim did retain possession of the latter claim for a long period of time.

In the land records extant at Wichita, there are still echoes of the mystery surrounding the Antrim-McCarty relationship and between the lines of various records and depositions made long after the widow and her consort had departed, one can perceive the questions which their relationship must have raised in the prairie village. In 1887 one purchaser of Antrim real estate deposed that in 1871, he had known William Antrim and that at the time, "said Antrim was an unmarried man."[25] In another deposition the same purchaser stated that he had known Catherine McCarty in 1871 and that "she was an unmarried woman" at the time.[26]

In 1892 the same purchaser was still having difficulty proving an unencumbered title to city lots acquired from Mrs. McCarty and he made a statement containing some doubtful information about the widow. Nevertheless it is of interest if for no other reason than to illustrate the mystery which even then surrounded the widow McCarty and her movements. Henry J. Cook's deposition was as follows:

> State of Kansas, Sedgwick county, ss:
> Personally appeared before me Henry J. Cook, who being by me first duly sworn, deposes and says that he is the identical H. J. Cook who purchased lots 48 and 50 on Chisholm street in the City of Wichita, Sedgwick county, Kansas on the 25th day of August, 1871 from one Catherine McCarty which deed of purchase is recorded

in Book C at page 33 of the Deed Records of Sedgwick county, Kansas. That said Catherine McCarty was on said 25th day of August, 1871 and on date of said deed of purchase an unmarried and single woman. That he gave the said Catherine McCarty a mortgage upon the said premises for the sum of $445 on said 25th day of August, 1871 which said mortgage is recorded in Book A at page 129 of the Mortgage Records of Sedgwick county, Kansas, that about six months after the giving of said mortgage, the affiant fully paid the same, that said Catherine McCarty then resided in the city of New Orleans, La. and said mortgage was not released of record, that soon thereafter, the said Catherine McCarty died, to wit: about the year of 1873, that at the time of her death, said Catherine McCarty was a single woman.

H. J. Cook

Sworn to and subscribed before me this 18th day of July, 1892

H. T. Dedrick, Notary Public.

My commission expires Jan. 8,1895

Filed for record August 5th, 1892 at 12 o'clock

S. L. Barrett, Register of Deeds[27]

If the deponent's statements could be entirely believed, one might assume that New Orleans was the next stopping-off place in the McCarty itinerary. Certainly Cook should have known the widow's whereabouts at the time he allegedly paid off the stated mortgage, but in the light of present day knowledge, his statement is rendered doubtful by his allegation that Catherine McCarty was a single woman at the time of her death. Today's historian cannot accept his statement as a basis for piecing out the legend of Billy the Kid and his boyhood, but yesterday's lawyer could—and did—accept it as an unchallenged basis for proving an unencumbered title to a valuable piece of real estate.

Henry Cook's deposition at least establishes the terminal date for the McCarty family's sojourn in Kansas and the date of August 25, 1871—or shortly thereafter—must stand as the most reliable one for the family's departure for Denver, New Orleans, or New Mexico. Wherever the family may have gone initially, the trail of the Antrim-McCarty liaison does not appear again in documentary form until the marriage at Santa Fe a year and a half later.

A better source, perhaps, for information about the immediate destination of Antrim and the McCartys upon their departure from Wichita

can be found in an interview a Denver reporter had with the Kid's supposed younger brother, Joseph Antrim, in 1928. Joe Antrim was then
an aged and penniless nonentity shuffling about the Denver streets,
but he recalled that in 1871, he had arrived in Denver "with his father,
a Wells-Fargo Express agent."[28] Joe Antrim volunteered nothing further
about his—or his older brother's—earlier life, but reminisced at length
about his own experiences as a faro dealer of long standing.

From all the evidence here presented, it can be seen that the Kid,
through the acts of his mother and stepfather-to-be, left numerous well
defined signs of his passing through Kansas. It is a source of continual
wonder to this writer that in all the backtracking done by those who
have trailed the legend of Billy the Kid, these signs had not been previously noticed. But of even more wonderment is the fact that Henry
McCarty's sojourn in Kansas was not more completely revealed in the
presses of the day or in the writing of Ash Upson. There were others
besides Upson who it would seem should have known about the Kid's
Kansas years, for many of those with whom he shared experiences and
confidences also shared with him a "formerly of Kansas" background.
Dave Rudabaugh, a close associate for a part of the Kid's New Mexican
depredations, had spent a part of his boyhood near Eureka, Kans.[29] In
some of the lonely nights on the "hoot owl" trail, Rudabaugh and the
Kid might have exchanged yarns about their respective boyhoods in
Kansas, but it is understandable that Rudabaugh did not pass them on
for publication.

Alexander A. McSween, one of the tragic figures in the Lincoln County
War, also spent some time at Eureka, where he was a Justice of the Peace
in 1873.[30] Mrs. McSween, the former Sue E. Homer, had been a resident of Atchison, Kans., before marrying McSween.[31] In the rapport
existing between the Kid and the McSweens it seems most unlikely that
some exchange of reminiscences about former days in Kansas would not
have taken place, but if such was the case Mrs. McSween never repeated
them later.

Strangest of all these unexplainable associations, however, appears
the likelihood that one Jessie Evans, another of the Kid's associates, also
had a Kansas boyhood. The background of Jessie Evans has been even
more nebulous than that of the Kid but some light may be shed on his
antecedents by Kansas newspaper accounts published in 1871 dealing
with the misdeeds of a youthful *Jesse* Evans who hailed from Elk City

Alexander Anderson McSween, ca. 1870. Author's Collection.

in Montgomery county, quite near the Coffeyville area of the Bonney family legend.

On June 26, 1871, one J. J. Allen and the Evans family (composed of father, mother and son Jesse) were arrested, along with others, on a charge of passing counterfeit money.[32] All were charged with being part of a ring which had been operating in the county for some time. They were taken to Independence for a preliminary hearing. The senior Evans

Susan McSween Barber, "the Cattle Queen of New Mexico," ca. 1920. Robert G. McCubbin Collection.

apparently were released without trial but Jesse's case was heard in Topeka, where a local newspaper told the final outcome.

In U.S. District Court, John J. Allen who had plead guilty of passing counterfeit money, and Jesse Evans, who had been convicted of the same offense, were called up and sentenced, the former to one year in the penitentiary. The latter, who is only a boy, was fined $500 and most kindly admonished by the court.[33]

After the court's admonition, the youthful Jesse Evans disappeared from the pages of Kansas records having left only this brief trace of his stay. If New Mexico's Jessie Evans shared a Kansas background with Billy the Kid, he spoke no more of it than did Dave Rudabaugh.

At Wichita, Jim Antrim could have added much that would have helped clear up the twisted story of Henry McCarty's early years. Unfortunately he displayed a reticence on the subject which matched that of his brother William and it is extremely doubtful that Jim Antrim was the authoritative source who passed on to editor Marsh Murdock the material that was published. Little information has been found, relating to Jim Antrim's life at Wichita, which would shed any light on the legend of Billy the Kid. Born in 1849 in the state of Indiana, he was living at Indianapolis with his parents in 1870.[34] Some records at Wichita indicate that Jim came to Kansas in the spring of 1871 and filed on a small parcel of land directly northwest of the McCarty claim.

On May 21, 1872, Jim Antrim was appointed second assistant marshal of Wichita[35] under Marshal Mike Meagher, and he was to follow the career of Wichita policeman in broken periods of service for many years. Although contemporary newspaper accounts indicate that he was always a popular policeman, his career was not marked by acts of special significance. His existence on the frontier police force has been overlooked in the misbegotten babel over the legendary exploits of one Wyatt Earp.

There is some reason to believe that Henry McCarty may have returned to Wichita for a brief period before his career as the Kid was fully launched, and one can only speculate that a visit to "Uncle Jim's" may have played a part in his alleged return to Kansas. That episode is, however, another story, one which lacks the documentation desired by this writer, and one which could only be filed with the rest of the apocrypha dealing with the Kid. Considering the plentitude of that type of Kid literature, the story is better left to rest in the archives until sufficient documentation can be produced to warrant its retrieval.

So for the time being, the trail of the Kid's Kansas legend—and the documentation behind that legend—must be summed up as the story of little Henry McCarty and his introduction to a fascinating frontier world on the Kansas prairie; the story of Catherine McCarty, "widow of Michael," and her procrastinating courtship with "a man named Antrim"; and the story of William Antrim's patient efforts to build a home for the widow and her family and the tragic disappointments which must have been his lot.

ACKNOWLEDGEMENTS

The writer wishes to acknowledge his indebtedness for the assistance rendered by the various staff members of the Kansas State Historical Society; the Indiana State Library; the Wichita City Library; the Social Science Division of the Indianapolis Public Library; and the Western History Department of the Denver Public Library. Also to Joseph W. Snell and Ed Bartholomew for their encouraging assistance and a special thanks to Phil K. Goodyear and R. M. Long, both of Wichita, for providing the single clue which pointed out the Kid's Kansas trail.

NOTES

1. William A. Keleher, *Violence in Lincoln County* (Albuquerque, University of New Mexico Press, 1957), p. 310.

2. Wichita (Kans.) *Weekly Eagle.*

3. Kansas City (Mo.) *Daily Journal,* July 27, 1881.

4. "Deed Records of Sedgwick County," Book A, p. 219.

5. *Ibid.,* Book A, p. 369.

6. *Ibid.,* Book B, p. 168.

7. Reproduction of panoramic sketch of Wichita, 1873, in author's private collection.

8. "Deed Records of Sedgwick County," Book A, p. 414.

9. "Application and Proof of Catharine McCarty," Bureau of Land Management, Department of the Interior. Certified copy in the collection of the author.

10. John L. Forkner and Byron H. Dyson, *Historical Sketches and Reminiscences of Madison County, Indiana* (n.p., 1897), p. 186. This source quotes the Anderson (Indiana) *Gazette* of April 8, 1853.

11. Records of the National Archives, Washington, D.C.

12. Indianapolis City Directories, 1865–1870.

13. *Logan's Annual Indianapolis Directory,* 1868.

14. Records of the National Archives, Bureau of Pensions questionnaire. Some corrections in Antrim's spelling have been supplied.

15. Philip J. Rasch and Robert N. Mullin, "New Light on the Legend of Billy the Kid," *New Mexico Folklore Record,* Vol. VII, 1952–53, pp. 1–5.

16. Records of the National Archives, Washington, D.C.

17. Rasch and Mullin, *op. cit.*, pp. 1–5, quoting the Silver City (N.M.) *Enterprise,* January 3, 1902.

18. Wichita *Vidette,* August 13, 1870.

19. "State of Kansas vs. George P. Murray," Case Records of the Sedgwick County District Court, Case No. 9.

20. Wichita *Vidette,* October 13, 1870.

21. Wichita *Vidette,* November 24, 1870.

22. El Dorado (Kans.) *Walnut Valley Times,* March 3, 1871.

23. "Deed Records of Sedgwick County," Book B, p. 165.

24. *Ibid.,* Book A, p. 478.

25. *Ibid.,* Book B, p. 168.

26. *Ibid.,* Book C, p. 33.

27. *Ibid.,* Book 127, p. 402.

28. Denver *Post,* April 1, 1928. p. 15.

29. F. Stanley, *Dave Rudabaugh, Border Ruffian* (Denver, World Press, Inc., 1961), p. 4; "Kansas State Census," 1875, Spring Creek township, Greenwood county, p. 6, line 15.

30. Wichita *Weekly Eagle,* June 12, 1873, in an item credited to the Eureka *Herald.*

31. Keleher, *op. cit.,* p. 54; Atchison (Kans.) *Daily Champion,* August 24, 1873.

32. Neodesha (Kans.) *Citizen,* June 30, 1871.

33. Topeka *Daily Commonwealth,* November 11, 1871.

34. "United States Census," 1870, Marion county, Indiana. The Antrim family was then living in Indianapolis' second ward.

35. "Miscellaneous Papers," Records of the City of Wichita.

CHAPTER TWELVE

The Boyhood of Billy the Kid

Robert N. Mullin

Robert Norville Mullin (1901–1982) was one of the most committed, and one of the most successful, of all the early amateur historians who set out to pursue the truth about Billy the Kid. His interest began when he was eleven years old in El Paso and Pat Garrett stopped by the Mullin family home for a front-porch chat with Bob's father. When Bob and some of his pals asked Garrett to tell them about Billy the Kid, Garrett shooed them away; but the incident fired Bob with an ambition to find out more—and that ambition stayed with him for the rest of his life. He made his first trip to the Kid's Lincoln, New Mexico (by an odd coincidence, he was born in Lincoln, Nebraska), in 1914 and every chance he got thereafter—first as a bookstore manager, then as manager of his own oil company, and finally as a senior marketing executive for Gulf Oil; he arranged his travels so as to include places in Texas, Arizona, and New Mexico where he could learn more. He was one of the very first to search the Lew Wallace Papers in Indianapolis and to talk to the family of Robert Widenmann in Ann Arbor, Michigan. He it was who, using his daughter Frances as an amanuensis, located the marriage record of Catherine McCarty and William H. Antrim in the Presbyterian church at Santa Fe, one of the most important discoveries ever in Billy the Kid research. In 1956 he made a major (and, typically, uncredited) contribution to Frazier Hunt's *The Tragic Days of Billy the Kid;* he also edited and published (assuming all the costs and taking none of either the glory or the money) *Maurice Garland Fulton's History of the Lincoln County War* (1968), still considered by many to be as definitive a work on the subject as anything yet published.

The excerpt from his monograph that follows, based upon his many years of research, is a perfect example of his gentlemanly, scholarly work, a pioneering attempt to document as authentically as was (then) possible the boyhood of Billy the Kid and his life in Silver City.

The boy who staggered up to the Heiskell Jones ranch house near Seven Rivers, New Mexico, before dawn one day about the first of October, 1877, told "Ma'am" Jones his name was William Bonney. He was starved, footsore and weary. Ma'am Jones afterward recalled that the first thing she noticed was that the young stranger's feet were bruised and bleeding; his boots had been discarded when the soles became entirely worn away by the sand and stones.

Later he told how, after briefly visiting Mesilla, he had joined company with Tom O'Keefe, a lad about his age, who was going to the Pecos valley in search of work. Together they rode through the Organ mountains and across the Tularosa basin, but instead of following the longer and safer route by way of the Tularosa, Ruidoso and Hondo valleys, the boys took a shortcut straight across the northern part of the Guadalupe mountains. Unfamiliar with conditions in the country, they did not realize that this was a section where intruders were all too frequently victims of roving bands of Apaches.

AN ENCOUNTER WITH THE INDIANS

On the second day of their journey they were climbing an old Indian trail along the side of a cliff when they spied a pool of water in the bed of the canyon below. Taking their empty canteen, Billy had made his way down to the water and was about to return when he heard the sound of gunfire. He took cover in the brush. After a time, seeking concealment behind the rocks, he climbed back up to a point from which he could view the place where he had left his companion. A cautious search of the vicinity failed to reveal any trace of O'Keefe or the horses. It seemed obvious that the Indians had killed or captured O'Keefe and made off with their mounts, along with bedrolls, guns and rations.

It was this story of his encounter with the Indians, free from heroics, that was later to be embellished by Ash Upson into a spectacular account of how Billy scorned concealment, pursued the Indian band and slew some as his pistol "belched forth a stream of death-laden fire."[1] Upson's account makes exciting reading; it is too bad that it isn't true.

The lad kept himself hidden until nightfall, he told his hosts, and then resumed his journey alone and on foot. He was unarmed and without a supply of food; the water in his canteen was gone long before he reached the arid foothills east of the mountains. After two days and three nights, remaining concealed during the daylight hours and traveling in the dark of night, he made his way through the mountains and down Rocky Arroyo until he came upon a ranch house, the Jones place.[2]

This was the boy who within a few months was to begin the construction of our number-one Western legend and lay the foundation for the contradictory views of his character which the American public has debated ever since. "The most thoroughly bad man of all the bad men ever known in the West,"[3] said the left wing; "the only white man who slew out of pure wantonness."[4] A modern Robin Hood, the right wing called him—a friend of the poor, a protector of innocence and virtue, a knight in boots and *chaparejos* slaying dragons on the plains of New Mexico. The late Maurice Garland Fulton gathered up and put together most of what can be known about Billy Bonney, and his notes and interviews, plus others accumulated since his death, show quite clearly that, at least during Billy's earlier years, he was no better and no worse than many another of that area and era—he was, in fact, a rather normal boy of the Southwestern frontier.

THE PARENTAGE OF WILLIAM BONNEY

Some aspects of his story, it must be admitted, are still mysterious and are likely to remain so. Why he chose the name William Bonney is one of them. Theories as to his parentage and birthplace are legion. "Billy the Kid's true name was William [Henry] McCarty. He was born in the state of New York (some have located his birthplace as New York City but this is doubtless a mistake) in the year 1859 or 1860." So wrote John Woodruff Lewis, under the pseudonym Don Jenardo, in the *Five Cent Wide Awake Library*, issue of August 29, 1881, less than three weeks after the Kid's death. There is almost no connection between the story told in this Nickel-Library account and the actual facts, but the statement about the New York birthplace was accepted and repeated by other writers, including Marshall Ashmun Upson, actual author of *The Authentic Life of Billy the Kid*, by Pat F. Garrett, first published at Santa Fe, NM., in 1882. In this book Upson, who claimed that he had known the family in Santa Fe and Silver City, said the boy was born in New York, November 23, 1859. Henry's stepfather understood that the lad's natural father had died in New York.[5]

The possibility has been advanced that Henry McCarty was indeed Patrick Henry McCarthy, who was born to Catherine Devine McCarthy and her husband, Patrick, in New York, September 17, 1859.[6] Those inclined to accept Indiana as the place of birth have suggested that Joseph and Henry may have been the sons of Joseph McCarty of Cass county, Indiana, listed in the census records as a farmer; others have named as the father Joseph McCarty, recorded in the 1880 census as a native of Indiana, a farmer in Greene Township, Grant County, not far from the communities of Indianapolis and Anderson. On the other hand, Henry McCarty may very well have been the son of Katherine McCarty Bonney of New York and her husband William, as one branch of the Bonney family has good reason to believe.[7] Regardless of which of these or other beliefs one accepts, it seems safe to surmise that in choosing the name Bonney, Henry McCarty was probably reverting to a parental family name.

BILLY'S PLACE OF BIRTH

Cincinnati, Ohio, Springfield, Illinois, and even Limerick, Ireland, are among the cities claimed by some as the place of Billy the Kid's birth; the states of Kansas, Missouri, New Mexico, Indiana and New York have been named, most frequently the last one. New Mexico Territorial Governor Lew Wallace, to whom the Kid was both an ally and a source of trouble, wrote that W. Bonney "was brought to Indiana when he was a small boy and reared in Indianapolis and Terre Haute."[8] Sheriff Harvey Whitehill, who had occasion to be acquainted with the family in Silver City, was quoted as saying: "His right name, you know, was Henry McCarty and he was born in Anderson, Indiana."[9] The young fellow himself, on hearing that Territorial Governor Axtell had been replaced by General Lew Wallace of Indiana, is said to have told Sam Corbett jokingly that he and the new governor "ought to get along real cozy" since both were from the same state.[10]

Whether Billy the Kid was born in New York or elsewhere, it is evident that Catherine McCarty and her two sons were living in Marion County, Indiana, at the close of the Civil War; it is equally evident that at that time she was acquainted with the man she was later to marry, William H. Antrim of the town of Huntsville, situated between the communities of Indianapolis and Anderson.[11] Antrim had been discharged as a private from Co. "I," 54th Regiment, Indiana Volunteer Infantry, September 26, 1862.[12] In later years he said he had "lived at Wichita, Kansas, first year after leaving Service."[13] Perhaps he did spend the first year after his discharge at what was later Camp Beecher and after 1870, officially the town of Wichita. In making this statement, however, Antrim's memory may have betrayed him as to dates. Six years previously he had said that he left Indianapolis for Wichita in 1869; he made no reference to a previous residence in Kansas.[14] Even in giving the date 1869 he may have been ahead a year, since his name does not appear on the rolls of Sedgwick County's U. S. Census taken in July, 1870.[15] In any event he was in Indianapolis at the close of the Civil War.[16] Parenthetically, it may be noted here that Ash Upson and other writers, in saying that the family migrated to Coffeyville, Kansas, in 1862, apparently confused the towns of Coffeyville and Wichita. The township site of Coffeyville was not plotted until 1871, at which time Antrim and the McCartys had for some time been living in Wichita.

MIGRATION OF THE FAMILY WESTWARD

Mrs. McCarty purchased a town lot in Wichita on September 14, 1870, and the following March filed on a quarter-section of public land near the town, upon which she had settled on August 10, 1870.[17] She operated a hand laundry in Wichita, while Antrim seems to have done some farming, while augmenting his income by work as a carpenter and a part-time bartender. Henry Cook, to whom the widow sold her town property in August, 1871, understood that about six months later the lady was in New Orleans.[18] If this is true, her stay must have been brief. In later life her elder son Joe Antrim recalled that he had gone to Denver with his "father" in 1871.[19]

Joe, called "Josie" as a child, has sometimes been referred to as younger than his brother Henry, but this is apparently in error. At Phoenix, Arizona, in January, 1952, the writer talked at length with Chauncey O. Truesdell, a schoolmate of the McCarty boys at Silver City in 1873 and 1874. He said that Henry was sometimes called by the name of his stepfather, Billy Antrim. When asked how he was sure that Joe was the elder, Mr. Truesdell recalled that while neither boy was big for his age, Joe was the larger and sat toward the rear of the schoolroom with the more advanced pupils, while Henry, or Billy, "sat near the front with us younger

ones." Others have confirmed Mr. Truesdell's statement. In a letter
to M. G. Fulton, dated April 29, 1932, another schoolmate, Anthony B.
Conner, wrote that "Joe was the older"; and in an interview published in
the *Silver City Enterprise* on January 3, 1902, Mrs. Robert C. Bell, daughter
of Sheriff Harvey Whitehill, recalled "Billy and his elder brother, Joe."
When Joe died in Denver, November 25, 1930, his death certificate
recorded his age as 76, thus indicating that he was born about 1854,
some five years before the reported year of Billy the Kid's birth.

On March 1, 1873, "Mr. William H. Antrim and Mrs. Catherine McCarty,
both of Santa Fe, New Mexico," were joined in matrimony by Rev. D. F.
McFarland of the First Presbyterian Church of Santa Fe. Henry and Josie
McCarty were recorded as witnesses.[20] Almost immediately thereafter the
family departed for Silver City.

W. H. ANTRIM: MINER IN NEW MEXICO

Like so many men who went west in the years following the Civil War
with the hope of striking it rich in gold or silver mines, William Antrim was
an inveterate prospector. His prospecting in Colorado had not proved
rewarding, but it seems highly probable that when he took his wife and
stepsons to Silver City, he was impelled by the reports of rich strikes in that
district. Until he moved to El Paso in October, 1912, he never ceased to
make prospecting trips between his periods of paid employment.

The move to Silver City, like the previous moves to Colorado and to
Santa Fe, may have been in search of a climate beneficial to Catherine,
who suffered from tuberculosis. According to those who knew her,
Catherine, throughout her illness, displayed fortitude and good cheer.
Lewis Abraham, a young neighbor at Silver City, remembered that "Mrs.
Bill Antrim was a jolly Irish lady, full of life and mischief."[21] To help support her family, Mrs. Antrim took in boarders at the "log cabin at the
end of the bridge over the Big Ditch" in Silver City, even after health
worsened, and until four months before her death. One wonders whether
some of the combination of tough fiber and lightheartedness which were
to characterize Billy the Kid were not a heritage from his mother.

Whatever the derelictions of Billy the Kid, and they were many,
Henry McCarty's boyhood in Silver City was the normal one of a boy
growing up in a frontier mining camp. He was no better and no worse
than the other boys of his age. It is true that in later years, after the

Former home of the Antrim family, Silver City, ca. 1884. The original log cabin was at the far end of the building. The Kid, who was known as Henry Antrim, lived here with his family until the death of his mother, Catherine Antrim, on September 16, 1874. Photograph by Alfred S. Addis. Courtesy Museum of New Mexico, negative no. 99054.

fame of the Kid as a desperado had become widespread, some of his elders who had known the youngster in Silver City began to look back in search of marks of delinquency. After thirty years a newspaper reporter ascribed to Sheriff Harvey W. Whitehill a story to the effect that Henry McCarty had once been accused of stealing some butter.[22] Garrett's *Authentic Life of Billy the Kid* tells in circumstantial detail how "a filthy loafer . . . made an insulting remark" about Billy's mother and how the boy, with his pocket knife, "its blade dripping with gore," slew the villain. A 1936 brochure, *Picturesque Southwest,* had a different version: "His gun notch number one was for Sam Jacobs, who made love to his sister Jeannie but wouldn't marry her." No legal record or newspaper mention of either such killing has been found. When Garrett's book appeared, there was a general denial among the citizens that the lad had ever killed anyone in Silver City. As for "sister Jeannie," those who have made a serious study of the Antrim family have found no evidence that Joe and Henry ever had a sister; in fact, Anthony Conner stated flatly in his letter of April 29, 1932, to M. G. Fulton that "Mrs. Antrim had only two children. Joe was the older."

BILLY'S NORMAL LIFE AT SILVER CITY

Legend to the contrary, Henry's life in Silver City was no more or less adventurous than those of other youngsters. In fact, it was tame compared to that of his chum Anthony B. Conner, young brother of Sarah Ann (Mrs. Richard S.) Knight at whose home Henry lived for a time after his mother's death. Still in his teens, Anthony regularly rode his pony carrying the mail over the dangerous forty-mile road between Silver City and Ralston until 1878 when his father, who was the U. S. Mail contractor, was ambushed and killed by Indians five miles from the Knight ranch.

It was Anthony Conner who, after Billy the Kid had been identified as the Henry McCarty who had spent his boyhood in Silver City, recalled that: "Billy was one of the best boys in town. The story of his killing a man here in Silver City is all foolishness. Billy was about 12 and I was 13. I know he was a better boy than I was. . . . I never remember Billy doing anything out of the way any more than the rest of us. We had our chores to do, like washing dishes and other duties around the house."[23] Billy was "full of fun and mischief," according to his schoolmate, Louis Abraham.[24] Sheriff Whitehill's son Harry wrote: "My sister and I went to school with Billy the Kid. He wasn't a bad fellow."[25] His teacher, Miss Mary Richards, in later years recalled that "Billy (they called him Henry then) was no more of a problem in school than any other boy," and that he was "always quite willing to help with the chores around the schoolhouse."[26] Even while still a schoolboy, he liked to sing and dance and performed as "end man" in the school minstrel show and in amateur theatricals at Morrill's Opera House.[27]

After his mother's death, September 16, 1874, Henry went to live with Mr. and Mrs. Del Truesdell, whose son Chauncey was a somewhat younger schoolmate of his. Henry worked for his board and room by waiting on tables and washing dishes at the Star Hotel operated by Mr. Truesdell. "Henry was the only kid who ever worked there who never stole anything. Other fellows used to steal the silverware—that kind of stuff was scarce in the camp," recalled Mr. Truesdell.[28] Later, when William Antrim secured employment at Richard Knight's butcher shop, Henry "helped out" around the shop. During this period Mr. Antrim and his stepsons boarded at the Knight home in Silver City and frequently visited Knight's ranch at the south end of the Burro mountains. When Mr. Antrim went to work at the mill near Georgetown, Henry remained in Silver City to continue in school. His sleeping place in Mrs. Brown's house was what he called "home" when, for the first time in his life, Henry McCarty found himself in trouble with the law—and in jail.

FIRST BRUSH WITH THE LAW

The trouble started with what R. Athon of Silver City referred to as merely a "kiddish prank." The story that Henry stole clothing from some chinamen has been repeated so generally that it has become accepted as fact. More than a quarter of a century after the event, Sheriff Whitehill's recollection was that the boy, "scarcely 15 years of age . . . had stolen $70.00 from a chinaman" at Georgetown.[29] The fact of the matter is that the theft occurred in Silver City, not Georgetown, that the loss involved laundry, not money, and that Henry McCarty did not commit the theft. The *Grant County Herald* of Sunday, September 26, 1875, recorded the circumstance:

"Henry McCarty, who was arrested on Thursday and committed to jail to await the action of the grand jury, upon the charge of stealing clothes from Charley Sun and Sam Chung, celestials sans cue, sans Joss sticks, escaped from prison yesterday through the chimney. It is believed that Henry was simply the tool of 'Sombrero Jack,' who done the actual stealing whilst Henry done the hiding. Jack has skipped out."

Playful George Shaffer, nicknamed "Sombrero Jack," may have thought that filching a bundle of washing was a good joke on the chinamen, and the two boys may have considered it a lark when the older man gave them the bundle to hide; but after two days locked up in jail, young Henry could hardly have seen anything humorous in the situation. It may be, as generally believed, that Sheriff Whitehill merely intended to frighten the boy and teach him a lesson. But Henry could not know this. Although he declined to name the boy who had joined him in hiding the bundle of laundry given them by George Shaffer, he must have dreaded having to face his stepfather, and he had no idea what fearful punishment the law might have in store for him. He squeezed his way up through the chimney to freedom and struck out for Arizona.

Now he was on his own.

NOTES

1. *The Authentic Life of Billy the Kid by Pat F. Garrett,* originally published at Santa Fe, N. M., 1882, and generally accepted as the work of newspaperman Marshall Ashmun Upson.

2. Account given the writer by Maurice Garland Fulton, ascribed to members of the Jones family and others. Later a detailed account of the Jones family's activities before, during and after the Lincoln County War was given to Mrs. Eve Ball of Ruidoso, N. M., by Mr. Sam Jones. For the account of Billy the Kid's arrival in Lincoln County, and for much other information in this article, the writer is indebted to Colonel Fulton, whose interviews with participants and others close to events in Lincoln County during the 1870's and 1880's, as well as his study of contemporary letters and documents, began in the early 1920's and continued over a period of thirty-three years.

3. Emerson Hough, "The True Story of Billy the Kid," *Everybody's Magazine,* September, 1901.

4. Arthur Chapman, "A Man All Bad," *Outing Magazine,* April, 1905.

5. William H. Antrim, U. S. Bureau of Pensions application executed April 2, 1915, at El Paso, Texas, then his home.

6. Certificate of Baptism, Church of St. Peter, New York. Copy supplied the writer by Mr. Wm. J. Carson. Spelling the name "McCarthy" may be in error, as Municipal Archives and Records Center of New York City records a son born Sept. 18, 1859, to "McCarty, Patrick, and Catha" in the Borough of Manhattan.

7. Various interviews by the writer in New York City, 1958–1960, with Miss Lois Telfer, descendant of Thomas Bonney, who came to America in 1634.

8. Interview with Gen. Lew Wallace, *Indianapolis Press,* June 23, 1900.

9. *Silver City Enterprise,* Jan. 1, 1902.

10. Sue E. McSween (Barber) to M. G. Fulton, White Oaks, N. M., summer, 1927.

11. Deposition of Wm. H. Antrim dated March 25, 1871, recorded in Book "A," Deed Records of Sedgwick County, Kansas. For further details and docu-

mentation of the Indiana-Kansas period of Antrim and the McCartys, see W. A. Koop's excellent article, "Billy the Kid, the Trail of a Kansas Legend" in the September, 1964, issue of *The Trail Guide,* Kansas City, Missouri.

12. William H. Antrim, Declaration for Pension signed January 13, 1913. National Archives.

13. Ibid.

14. Ibid.

15. Letter to the writer from W. E. Koop, July 6, 1966.

16. Koop, "Billy the Kid," *op. cit.*

17. Ibid.

18. Deposition of H. J. Cook, July 18, 1892, recorded in the Deed Records of Sedgwick County, Kan., brought to light by W. W. Koop, 1964.

19. Interview with Joe Antrim, *Denver Post,* April 1, 1928.

20. *Record Book, Marriages Performed by D. F. McFarland* (p. 161) and Santa Fe *County Book of Marriages* ("A" pp. 37–8) brought to light in April, 1953, by Mrs. Frances Daseler, daughter of this writer who, in collaboration with Phil J. Rasch, was searching for documentable facts in the life of Wm. Bonney. See *New Mexico Magazine,* May, 1953 (pp. 26, 40–1), and Roswell, NM., *Record,* April 26, 1953, as well as Associated Press dispatches in various newspapers, April, 1953.

21. Mrs. W. C. Totty of Silver City, NM., WPA File, New Mexico Historical Society, Santa Fe, N. M.

22. *Silver City Enterprise,* Jan. 3, 1902.

23. *Silver City Independent,* March 22, 1932.

24. Mrs. W. C. Totty, *op. cit.*

25. Mrs. Helen Wheaton, from papers of Mr. Gilbert Cureton of Silver City.

26. Letter to the writer from Mrs. Patience Glennon, daughter of Mary Richards, May 15, 1952.

27. Various sources, including statement of Henry Whitehill in the papers of Mr. Gilbert Cureton.

28. Chauncey O. Truesdell to the writer, Jan., 1952.

29. *Silver City Enterprise,* Jan. 3, 1902.

CHAPTER THIRTEEN

First Blood: Another Look at the Killing of "Windy" Cahill

Frederick Nolan

In 1956, Frederick Nolan, then twenty-five, became an "instant" Billy the Kid historian when he located in the archives of the British Foreign Office a substantial file of documents and original correspondence between the British and American governments relating to the death of John Tunstall and subsequent events, including letters written by many of the participants in the Lincoln County War. Soon after, he was given unconditional access to Tunstall's letters and diaries, and by 1959—although he had never set foot in the United States— he had completed a biography based upon them. Because of financial difficulties, the University of New Mexico Press did not publish the book until 1965, by which time Nolan was energetically pursuing a publishing career. He nevertheless maintained a regular correspondence with many of the leading authorities—among them Robert N. Mullin, William A. Keleher, Eugene Cunningham, Maurice Garland Fulton, and of course, Philip Rasch—but it was not until 1987 that he reappeared in print with a long biographical study of Alexander and Susan McSween. This had grown out of his intention to proceed with a book like no other ever written on the subject of the Lincoln County War, a mammoth work utilizing transcripts or citations from all the relevant documentation—letters, diaries, military reports, governmental documents—and graced with appended biographical studies of principal characters. Published in 1992, *The Lincoln County War: A Documentary History* was followed by *Bad Blood: The Life and Times of the Horrell Brothers* (1994), *The West of Billy the Kid* (1998), and an annotated edition of Pat Garrett's *The Authentic Life of Billy the Kid* (2000). He has also written many articles for historical and academic publications; the one that follows was written after a visit to Bonita and Fort Grant, Arizona, in 1999.

Built in 1873 at an initial cost of $18,000 (a further $25,000 was allocated a year later to furnish the post), Fort Grant, Arizona, was designed to accommodate three companies of cavalry and one of infantry. Situated at an altitude of 3,985 feet, in the towering shadow of 10,516-foot Mt. Graham, the 42,341-acre reservation was declared by an executive order dated April 17, 1876, published as General Order No. 17, Dept. of Arizona, 1876.

By that time, clinging to the southeastern border of the military reservation like a small child hanging on to its mother's skirt, a then-unnamed settlement (it did not become Bonita until 1887, but is referred to by that name for convenience) had sprung up. With perhaps at its peak a transient population of one thousand souls, it consisted of two buildings actually on the military reservation—a four-roomed adobe called the Hotel de Luna operated by notary public and justice of the peace Miles Leslie Wood, and the building that housed post sutlers Norton & Stewart—and, maybe half a mile to the south and west down one of the half dozen or so wagon trails emanating from the Fort, a further scatter of buildings that included Milton McDowell's store, an adobe *cantina* owned by George Atkins, Lou Elliott's dance hall and a blacksmith shop operated by ex-infantryman Frank Cahill. Four or five hundred yards away on the east side of Grant Creek and near the Tucson trail was a brothel run by George McKittrick; the soldiers who were its main clientele called it "The Hog Ranch," which speaks volumes about the pleasures to be found inside.

Today, apart from the Bonita Store (originally McDowell's), a huge barn of a place with fifteen-foot-high ceilings, every one of those buildings is gone: only a few scattered stones here, or a half-buried footing over there, indicate where they once stood. They, and every single one of the men and women who lived and worked in them would probably be completely forgotten today had it not been for one single event: the arrival there in the spring of 1876 of a teenage fugitive from Silver City who went by the name of "Kid" Antrim.

"[He] came to Bonita about April 19," wrote Miles Wood, who owned the Hotel de Luna. "[H]e worked for a few days for [me] but he got to running with a gang of rustlers [here;] this place was the headquarters of the gang." Although perhaps no more than sixteen years of age, the Kid was already a practicing, if not very successful, gambler, a probability underlined by the fact that soon after his arrival at Bonita, as noted by Miles Wood, he went into the horse-stealing business with a young ex-soldier known as Johnny Mackie.

Born John R. McAckey in Glasgow, Scotland, on July 21, 1849, Mackie (the name also appears on company registers as Mackay) had been a

14-year-old schoolboy when he enlisted as a musician in the 1st P.H.B. Maryland Volunteers [later part of the 13th Maryland Infantry]. Captured at Harper's Ferry on September 15, 1862, just a couple of months after his enlistment there, and paroled the same day, he was sent to Alexandria, Va., from which place he deserted in January 1863. Discharged at Baltimore May 29, 1865, he dropped out of sight for a few years before re-enlisting in Company G of the 6th Cavalry at Harrisburg, Pa. December 30, 1871, and being posted to Fort Richardson, Texas.

He had also seen service in Kansas and New Mexico before coming to Arizona and was still in uniform when on Sunday, September 19, 1874, in McDowell's saloon in Bonita, he shot and badly wounded one T. R. Knox in a dispute over cards. Arrested and confined in the military guard-house, Mackie stood trial on October 2, and was acquitted on grounds of self-defense. His military career ended shortly thereafter and he was discharged at Camp Grant, Arizona on January 4, 1876. Sharp as a tack and a smart talker, Johnny was dark-complected, with dark hair and hazel eyes; at 5"7' and 120 pounds he was about the same size as the Kid.

"Soldiers would come from Fort Grant to visit the saloons and dance Houses here," Miles Wood recorded. "Billy and his chum Macky would steal the saddles and saddle blankets from the horses and occasionally they would take the horses and hide them out until they got a chance to dispose of them. A Lt. [Lieutenant] and a doctor from the Fort came down they said they would see that no one took their horses so they had a long Pick[e]t rope they carried the end of the rope in their hands and went to the bar inside. Macky talked to the officers while Billy cut the ropes from the horses and run off with the horses leaving the officers holding the pieces of rope. The Q[uarter] M[aster, Capt. Gilbert Cole Smith] came to me and I issued warrants for the two of them, but they had gone to Globe, so I sent the warrants to Globe. The constable [at Globe] arrested Billy but he gave the slip to the constable and got away. He arrested Billy again and started down to Grant with him [but] when he arrived at Cedar Springs [at the southern end of Eagle Pass] Billy escaped again."

On November 17, 1876, although his commanding officer Major Charles Elmer Compton had promulgated an order placing the Hog Ranch off limits to soldiers, First Sergeant Louis C. Hartman, 6th Cavalry, decided to take a chance and sample its delights. When he came out, his horse, saddle, bridle and blanket—estimated worth $150—were gone. Knowing he would be held personally responsible for the loss, Hartman reported the theft to his C.O., who directed the sergeant to raise a detachment of four men and pursue the thief or thieves. They caught up with Kid Antrim riding the stolen horse near Globe City on November 25; lacking warrants, they could not arrest him, but they reclaimed the horse, and left the Kid afoot. If they hoped that would put an end to his thieving, however, they were sadly deceived.

On February 10, 1877, the Kid and Mackie stole three army horses at Cottonwood Springs; they belonged to Company F, Camp Thomas. That did it: six days later, First Sergeant Hartman appeared before justice of the peace Wood to swear a complaint against "Henry Antrim, alias Kid" for the theft of his horse and its accouterments the preceding November. "I issued warrants," Wood recalled. "I sent an old man, a constable down to arrest the boys. He came back and said he could not find them. I sent him down three times, but he always said he could not find them. I knew he did not want to find them."

Just a few days later, on March 25, Miles Wood was looking out of the window of his Hotel de Luna when he saw the Kid and Mackie coming his way. "I told the waiter I would wait on them myself," he said. "I had the breakfast for the two placed on a large waiter [tray] and I carried it in to them. I shoved the platter on the table in front of them and pulled a six gun from under it and told them to put up their hands and then to go straight out the door."

Two and three-quarter miles up the long, straight road leading to the Fort he marched the discomfited thieves at gunpoint; there, they were thrown into the guardhouse, a shaky-sounding 12-foot-high building made of overlapping boards standing upright in a foundation of stone and mud mortar with a dirt floor and a wood shingle roof. Just to be on the safe side, Wood arranged for the prisoners to be shackled by the local blacksmith, Frank Cahill, known to everyone locally as "Windy."

Just exactly who was "Windy" Cahill? He may have been the Francis Cahill, occupation "horseshoer," who enlisted in the 32nd Infantry in New York in 1868 at the age of 22, although there is some room for doubt, first, because he gave his birthplace as Dublin (on his deathbed he said it was Galway) and second, because his army records give his height only as 5" 4¾', which hardly makes him the "large man with a gruff voice and a blustering manner" one contemporary, cowhand Gus Gildea, recalled.

The year after his enlistment, Cahill's regiment was consolidated with the 21st Infantry; he appears to have served most of his three-year stint at Camp Crittenden, near Sonoita and the Mexican border. When, in accordance with General Orders 23 dated March 16, 1871, the Army was ordered to reduce its total complement to 30,000 men, all company commanders were required to recommend for discharge any "indifferent soldiers" in their commands. One of these was Cahill, which indicates that he should not be confused with the far from indifferent soldier John F. Cahill, also a blacksmith, who appears in John G. Bourke's *On the Border with Crook.*

Frank Cahill was discharged from the US Army on June, 30, 1871 and went to work as a blacksmith at old Camp Grant on Aravaipa Creek near its junction with the San Pedro River (scene of the infamous April 30, 1871 massacre). When the Army terminated Camp Crittenden in 1873 and moved its complement of troops to the "new" Fort Grant, Cahill seems to have transferred his blacksmithing activities to the civilian settlement there that later became Bonita. Which raises an interesting point: in that time and that place, "blacksmithing" was also a slang term for pimping. If, as at least one earlier chronicler of these events seems to have believed, Cahill was also running a saloon and brothel, he may well have been blacksmithing in both senses of the word, which would certainly add resonance to the exchange between him and the Kid in their final, fatal encounter.

"Windy"—they called him that, said cowboy Gus Gildea, "because he was always blowin' about first one thing and another"—started picking on the Kid soon after the boy first came to Bonita. "He would throw Billy to the floor, ruffle his hair, slap his face and humiliate him before the men in the saloon," Gildea recalled. If that was so, maybe Windy Cahill used the occasion of his shackling to humiliate Billy some more. If he did, it was not something the Kid would readily forget.

"That night," Wood continued, "my wife and myself were at a reception at the Colonel's house when the Sergeant of the guard came to the door and called the Colonel out. In a few minutes he came in and said the Kid was gone, shackles and all."

But not for long. Less than six months later, and in spite of the fact that he knew there were warrants outstanding against him, the Kid was back in Bonita.

Which raises another interesting, if probably unanswerable question: did he come back specifically to settle his grudge with Cahill? If not, why did he go there at all? Reflect: during that summer of 1877, the best

authorities suggest the Kid went to work at the hay camp of army contractor H. F. "Sorghum" Smith near Camp Thomas. "He hadn't worked
very long," said Smith, "until he wanted his money. I asked him if he was
going to quit. He said 'No, I want to buy some things.' I asked him how
much he wanted and tried to get him to take $10 . . . [but he] asked for
$40. I gave it to him. He went down to the post trader and bought him-
self a whole outfit: six shooter, belt, scabbard and cartridges."

Bearing in mind the fact that the Kid couldn't have earned much
more than the standard dollar a day laborer's wage in a hay camp, it
follows he would have had to work for Sorghum Smith for at least a
couple of months, and maybe longer, to have been good for a $40 advance.
Which begins to make it look suspiciously like the only reason he took
the job was so he could buy a gun. And that as soon as he got one, he
went back to Bonita.

On Friday, August 17, he turned up in George Atkins' *cantina* "dressed
like a country Jake," according to Gus Gildea, "with store pants on and
shoes instead of boots. He wore a six gun stuffed into his trousers." And
he may have been hunting trouble, because before too long he and
"Windy" Cahill got into an argument. In Cahill's own version of events,
he said he called the Kid a pimp and Billy called him a sonofabitch. It
would be interesting to know why. Perhaps, as another version suggests,
the argument was a carryover from the preceding night when Cahill had
kibitzed a card game in which the Kid was involved, loudly advising him
how to play his hand. Yet another infers trouble between the two men
over a woman, perhaps Cahill's.

Whatever the reason, they "got to wrestling to see who could throw
the other down," said Wood, who was an eyewitness. The wrestling esca-
lated into a scuffle that took them out of the building. "Cahill was larger
and stouter than the Kid and threw him down three times which made
the Kid mad," Wood said, "and he pulled his gun and stuck it in the
stomach and fired and killed Cahill."

As the gutshot blacksmith writhed on the floor—in fact he did not
die until the following day—the Kid ran to a nearby hitching rail and
fogged out on John Murphey's racing horse Cashaw, known to have the
fastest feet in the Sulphur Springs valley. There being no doctor in the
settlement, Cahill was carried two and a half miles to the post hospital
at Fort Grant where Assistant Surgeon Fred Crayton Ainsworth did what

The grave of Francis P. "Windy" Cahill (*nearest to camera*) near Fort Grant, Arizona. Cahill was a civilian blacksmith who is remembered for only one thing: he was the first man to be killed by Billy the Kid. Photograph by the late James A. Browning.

he could for him. When told he could not live, Cahill asked Miles Wood
to take down his last words:

> I, Frank P. Cahill, being convinced I am about to die, do make the
> following as my final statement:

> My name is Frank P Cahill. I was born in the county and town of
> Galway, Ireland; yesterday, August 17th, 1877, I had some trouble
> with Henry Antrim, otherwise known as Kid, during which he shot
> me. I had called him a pimp, and he called me a s— of a b——;
> we then took hold of each other; I did not hit him, I think; saw
> him go for his pistol, and tried to get hold of it, but could not and
> he shot me in the belly; I have a sister named Margaret Flannigan
> living at East Cambridge, Mass., and another named Kate Conden,
> living in San Francisco.

Shortly after making this statement, Cahill died. Miles Wood convened
an inquest at which the six jurymen James L. Hunt, Milton McDowell,
Bennett E. Norton, T. McCleary, Delos H. Smith and Chisum foreman
George Teague delivered a verdict that the shooting had been "criminal
and unjustifiable, and that Henry Antrim, alias Kid, is guilty thereof."

As all the world knows, the Kid rode East, into New Mexico Territory
and legend. Until now, however, no one has ever been able to write *finis*
to the story of Windy Cahill. But history left us one clue that perhaps
now makes that possible: the military roster of interments at the Fort
Grant cemetery, which records that on August 19, 1877, "a citizen" was
interred in Grave Number 12. Who else but Cahill could that civilian—
for that is what the word infers—have been?

The old Fort is today an Arizona State Prison, off limits to civilians, but
it is still possible—although not by any means easy—to access what was
once the post cemetery, which is now adjacent to a later, larger one. In
the former military section a row of stones extends about halfway across
the plot, equally spaced and periodically painted white by the local
community which uses the newer burial ground. These stones mark the
original graves, fourteen in all. Although one or two of the stones are
missing, the simple tablet over the twelfth grave is still there, and it does
not seem unreasonable to conclude it marks the last resting place of
Francis P. "Windy" Cahill, the first man—but not the last—to make the
fatal mistake of underestimating the vengeful nature of Billy the Kid.

CHAPTER FOURTEEN

The Kid

Lily Casey Klasner

Nearly all the extant descriptions of Billy the Kid (by people who actually knew him during his lifetime) were written by his friends—kids he went to school with, the Coe cousins, Paulita Maxwell, even Pat Garrett—and most of them were, if not affectionate, generally sympathetic. Here, however, is one that is not. Lily Casey knew the Kid very well. She didn't like him or any of the crowd he rode with. She didn't like his boss, "good honest innocent" Tunstall, and she didn't like his partner, "jackleg lawyer" McSween. And in the process of setting history—as she saw it—straight, Lily painted a rare portrait of the Kid and his contemporaries as seen from the hostile side of the fence.

Born in Mason County, Texas, in 1862, Lily had walked most of the way from there to New Mexico with her family in 1867. Her father, Robert Adam Casey, a tough ex-soldier who ran some cattle and a gristmill on the Rio Hondo about halfway between Lincoln and Roswell, was murdered when she was thirteen; his assassin was the first criminal to be judicially hanged in Lincoln County. Lily married Joe Klasner at Laredo, Texas, in 1893, and he came to live on the Casey ranch. (The marriage was dissolved in 1937.) In 1896, the Casey clan got into a water dispute with former Texas Ranger William H. "Buck" Guyse, which culminated in his being shot to death by Lily's brother Adam. It was alleged that when it happened, Lily was holding Guyse's arms so that he couldn't get at his pistol.

In the late 1920s, sure that she could emulate the bestselling success of Burns's *Saga of Billy the Kid,* Lily—now in her mid-sixties—determined to put into book form the account of her pioneer family's experiences that she had been writing down since her early teens. Failing to interest a publisher, she enlisted Maurice Garland Fulton as a collaborator; when that arrangement came to grief (as, nearly, did Fulton himself) in 1929, Lily teamed up with local schoolteacher Eric Bruce. He, too, gave up on the project, for much the same reasons as Fulton: neither could reconcile Lily's version of history with the record. In fact, when

Fulton took issue with her over her factual and chronological inaccuracies, Lily interpreted it as an insult to her veracity and came after him with a six-gun.

As a result of her intransigence, no book or manuscript had been completed at the time Lily died in 1946, and the trunk full of manuscript and historical documents she had collected during her lifetime was left rotting in an old adobe until 1968, when Ruidoso historian Eve Ball heard of its existence. When the trunk was located, Mrs. Ball found in it not only Lily's wedding dress, but also a welter of typescript, unclassified papers, and notebooks, many damaged by water and mice, others obviously having survived a fire. Among these were Fulton's original notes and several versions of the story he had begun and abandoned. Using his templates (and quite a lot of his work), Eve Ball eventually edited and in 1972 published Lily's story as *My Girlhood Among Outlaws*.

The hitherto unpublished document that follows is not an excerpt from that book, but one segment of the—very—raw material from which the finished book was fashioned. Although little more than a draft setting down what she remembered (and as often omitting what she chose to forget) about the Kid and the Lincoln County War, Lily's sixteen typed pages literally crackle with a venom—missing entirely from the book—that starkly illustrates how strong feelings were on both sides in 1877.

In creating my linking text, I have tried—sometimes adding information from one page to related material on another—to put Lily's disjointed narrative into rough chronological order. I have paraphrased as little as possible, and except when corrections have been unavoidable, I have left her spelling and grammar unaltered. Although her recollections are sometimes hard to follow and rarely match known historical data, they nevertheless paint an interestingly different picture of Billy the Kid to set beside the one of the *caballero muy simpatico* created in the Walter Noble Burns school of history.

[*The first time Lily ever saw the Kid was soon after he had been released from the cellar jail in Lincoln.*]

I remember how fair and white [he] looked for he had been down in that dungeon[.] Ten feet under ground and just a boy about fifteen past he said he was not sixteen yet[.]

[*The Kid had been*] right here in Lincoln dungeon jail [*for helping Jesse Evans and "the Boys" to steal horses, among them John Tunstall's buggy team.*] Some horses were stolen on the Rio Ruidoso among them was John H Tunstal's buggy Team he called The Daples Greys them being of a beautiful white tinged with pearly gray, very prettily built and well matched. [*Tunstall would of course have known the anonymous British nursery rhyme that begins "I had a little pony / His name was Dapple Grey."*]

[*Upon learning of the theft of his team,*] Tunstal[l] promptly under advice of Lawyer McLain [McSween] swore out a complaint and sent Major

Braidy High Sheriff down after them. He found them at the Old Beckwith Place, now Lakewood. . . . Just as innocent appearing Jessie Evans
Frank Baker Tom Hill and Billy the Kid as doves. . . . The sherif had to
bring Them all up and put them in the Lincoln County dungeon jail
ten feet under ground where They languished for some time. McLain and
Thunston [Tunstall] would let no one go their bail. These two gentlemen
had taken the reins in their own hands and were indeavouring to wrest
the power of being monarchs of the intire country from Murphy and
Nolan [Dolan] Co., who had been as the Czar of the upper part of the
county and now had extended their dominions by moving their cows
down in the Pecos country.

[*If correct, this places the Kid in Lincoln County early in September 1877.
Tunstall and McSween's horses were stolen September 18 and taken to Shedd's
ranch; Brewer, Scurlock, and Bowdre pursued the thieves but were unable to
recover the animals.*]

[*The Kid*] told my mother that his home and mother were at Silver City,
New Mexico. . . . At the time he was riding a stolen Chisum horse which he
wanted to trade to my mother for a beautiful little bright bay race mare my
brother had traded for on the Hondo just before we left. "My God, man,
don't you know that is a Chisum stolen horse you have?" [*Ellen Casey said.*]
"I could not have that horse in my outfit at all, I woulden't get started with
him until the owner would have me arrested and brought back a way up to
Lincoln County Seat over 200 miles and put me in jail and give me all
kinds of trouble and costs. Where did you get that horse?"

He answered "Some of the Pecos Party gave him to me to ride when
they turned us all out of jail, just the other day. I am a stranger in this
country I do not know many people nor their brands. I was there in jail
with the rest of the boys when the Pecos warriors came, turned us all
out, told us to get on those horses and strike a "B" line for the Lower
Pecos Valey in Texas beyond old Green Wilson's The Alcalde (Justice of
the Peace) at Lincoln's jurisdiction. . . .

[*At this juncture, the first chronological problem arises; this conversation is
supposedly taking place after the Kid was delivered from the Lincoln jail—in
other words, after November 16; but the Caseys left Lincoln County for Texas
with all their stock, including Tunstall's (or, as they saw it, their) cattle, around
October 20.*]

Mother then said You know that McSween and Tunstal have stolen
the biggest part of my cattle and jumped my Feliz ranch and I have

gathered what few I had left and I am trying to get to Texas with them and my boys so they won't get in trouble and get killed. You know I am a poor crippled widow woman with five little children to rear and I do not want any trouble with this gang of outlaws for there is nothing too low-down crooked or vile for the McSween Gang to do, I know them and there is nothing they will stop at nor the Murphy-nolan [Dolan] ring either. The only show I see to keep my boys from getting into trouble and killed or killing some body is to take them and what little I have left out of the country until this cattle stealing war is over and the law can prevail, as it is both parties are stoping at nothing where the other is concerned and we will have no peace until the leaders of both parties are killed off.

HOW McSWEEN & TUNSTALL JUMPED THE CASEY CLAIM

[*Lily claims that Robert Casey discovered the Feliz Valley in the fall of 1868, when he and a squad of cavalry led by Lieutenants Cushing and Yeaton from Fort Stanton were chasing Mescalero leader Jose de la Paz, who had stolen 325 head of Casey's cattle. Military records indicate that 115 Casey cattle were stolen November 14, 1869; the Cushing-Yeaton pursuit took place between November 18 and 23, and most of Casey's stock was recovered. A second sortie into the Guadalupe Mountains left Fort Stanton December 19 and returned January 6, 1870. Yeaton was wounded on this expedition.*]

Cushing and Yeaton . . . followed the trail going South East, the first water they struck about twenty five miles south was the Rio Feliz a beautiful, clear stream bubling up suddenly[,] running for some ten miles and then as suddenly sinking and completely disapearing. Father claimed it for his cow ranch as by discovery for he was the first white man out there except the United States soldiers.

My father took his cattle over there and built valuable Improvements, a farm, Irrigation dam and ditch, an adobe (sun dried brick) house, a corral or pen for his stock this at the head waters and then down about two miles he built a very good rock house and rock corral. This for stock cattle and he lived there peacefully during his life time no one ever thought of claiming or disputing his right. The original government survey had never been run so a squaters right fileings were all that could be made and he had Old man A J fountain as his lawyer make all these for him. . . . McSween was a "Jackleg" Lawyer and stooped to making trouble for every little petty case and he would take a fee on both sides of the case. There was no lawer in this big county but him. He was simply a villain and no disguise, said to be possessed of seven Devils. . . . This villian of a Jackleg lawer Mclain and Hunstal with their diabolical banditti stole most of the [Casey] cattle and jumped the Feliz ranch, Putting Billy the Kid there to hold the place. The country was for years so lawless and run by corrupt rings that they finally beat more poor old mother out of the place by might not right.

[*Lily's account willfully ignores the facts. Robert Casey had indeed squatted on land in the Feliz Valley and made a few "improvements," but neither he nor any member of his family had made any effort to file a claim. Under the terms of the Desert Land Act, Tunstall made proper filings at La Mesilla and—had he lived—would have obtained full title to it. To make matters worse, Mrs. Casey got into debt, and her cattle were attached by Sheriff William Brady and put up for sale; acting for Tunstall, McSween bought them at a bargain price. This encouraged the Caseys to perceive Tunstall as a moneyed usurper, McSween as his crooked lawyer, and themselves as victims.*]

The Kid then said the mare you have is a stolen animal. Mother cut him short saying How dare you say to me I have a stolen animal in my outfit? The Kid answered I guess I ought to know, for I stole her myself. I had to make my getaway between two suns. There was no other horse nor time I could get I had to leave presto changeo. [*NB: this is a Lily-ism, not a Kid-ism.*] She belongs at Las Cruces to Marriana Barrela's [*Mariano Barela, sheriff of Doña Ana County*] little girl; Barrela sent me word just the other day by Jesse Evans that if I did not bring the mare back he would come and kill me that the little girl was broken hearted and crying her eyes out for her pet mare.

Mother said "I came by this mare honest," I bought her from an honest man, my neighbor Frank McCullum who is responsible to me for her value. I have a legal bill of sale for her from him he warrents and guarantees her title to me. If any one can prove better title and take her by law, I can come back on McCullum for the value and damages and all costs. Mother said I was the innocent purchaser of this mare. I did not know she was stolen. But I do know the one you have is stolen for Mr. Chisum never sells his horse brand in this country. If I take the horse I would be complicated and an accessor[y] for stealing with you.

Manuel Barela, sheriff of Doña Ana County. Author's Collection.

When the Kid could not get the mare he made a long pitiful talk to [my] Brother William to get work and go with us on to Texas. Will was a very good hearted honest boy and wanted mother to let the Kid go but she feared it was only a ruse of his and when we got a way down on the Llano Stacado (Stake Plains) he would run a way and leaving us a foot come back stealing not only the mare but all of her horses. . . .

You are a very young boy [*Ellen Casey said to the Kid.*] How come you to start out so little and young to stealing? He said I dident like to go to school I was Idle around town and got in with some bad company and got in a lot of trouble, I knew Jesse Evans was down here and thought I would come over and stay with him awhile and maby get work, I knew this mare was a race mare and I had to hurry. We came through the country to Tularosa and from there to the Feliz and then over to the Hondo Stiad [stayed] with Frank McCullum and traded him this mare. My partner and I had ridden pretty fast and hard, she was not usto [used to] hard treatment and could not stand it. Besides, I knew that when I got to Jessie he would know the brand and make me trouble, so I got shut of her. You know Jesse has a stand in over there with some of those officers and you have got to let their stuff alone.

Mariano Burrela, then sheriff of DonAna County, was a particular friend of Jessie Evens; so when the Kid stole this mare from Barrela and did not bring her back, it caused hard feeling between Evens and Kid, But Eveans let the Kid stay with his crowd and the next star (?) of note.

It was in the night when we come down in to the Hondo [*the Kid continued*], We lay out in the hills and rested a while; we did not want to come down to show ourselves too much in the daytime. We were looking for a place to sleep and met your neighbor [McCullum]. He told us we could stay with him, me, Tom Okeiff [O'Keefe] that's my partner and we did. Next morning, the mare was stiff and sorefooted, wanted to go lame, about given out. McCullum offered to trade me a fresh horse and I was only too glad because I wanted to get on down the Pecos to catch up with Jessie.

[*The Kid hung around until evening and then went back to his camp, Lily records.*] Will almost cried said he was so young and innocent looking, we all beg for him to be allowed to go with us, he had just been turned out of the Old Lincoln County Dungen Jail with Jessie Evens, Frank Baker, Tom Hill and a mexican who did go to Texas with us by the name of

Jose Chavez [*Lucas Gallegos*] he was in for some minor offense. [*Actually, it was murder.*] The liberators [*i.e., the Pecos Warriors*] took him along to keep him from telling on them. At Seven Rivers where there were no Mexicans they were talking about rigging up some escuse to kill him to get him out of the way, saying dead men tell no tales. We all knew this old Mexican so when Will came and told us what they were talking about doing, Mother interceeded and offered to take him a way down in Texas where she was going to save his life and she did. I relate this to show how hardened this Banditi was and how little they regarded a humane life. Or even their own.

[*Not exactly as written, the following has been put into logical sequence.*]

[*The Kid went on down to the Seven Rivers country, Lily says, and stopped at the Murphy-Dolan cattle camp at what she calls Blake Springs—Black River, identified also as*] "Now the town of Artesia in Eddy County New Mexico" where Murphy Dolan and Company had bought the holdings from old man Blake [Black] and began to call it the Murphy Dolan Blake Springs. . . . One time brother Will [who] was present, told us how awfully bad Mortin [William Morton] abused the Kid telling him to leave, that he could not hang arround any of his cow camps any longer. The Kid Poor boy was a stranger in these parts of the country and alone and in trouble, and he had to take the "cussin out" but told brother Will "Never you mind It's a long lane has no turn, I'll just lay for that guy and you see if I don't get him in the end." And he did when his Banditti foully murdered Mortin Baker and McClusky at Blackwater in the Capitan mountains while on their knees to Pray.

This is what made the bitter animosity between Billy the Kid and Billy Mortin. [*Morton, who was*] cow boss of all of the Murphy Nolan Co cow camps had a girl, a beauty in every way; she was called the "Bell" of the Pecos valley. And the Kid got to meddling in [*and Morton,*] although a fine man in many ways, was very jealous hearted, he could not take good naturedly the Kid's trying to cut in on him. The Kid then was only considered a little outlaw tramp just hanging around any where he could get to stay. Billy Morton was from Richmond, Virginia, and of the blue-blooded [illegible] He had run a way from home at the age of fourteen to go West, grow up with the country, and make a fortune; as many did whether by fair or foul means, let me tell you Mortin was climing the ladder of fortune pretty fast for so young a man, thats what got him killed was to get him out of the way.

HOW THE KID WAS TRICKED BY McSWEEN & TUNSTALL

[*Later,*] McSween and Tunstall courted the Kids friendship, thinking him a young boy and they could get him to turn states evidence the next court and put a lot of the MurphyDolan party in the penatentiary or run them out of the country. The Kid being an outlaw and a regular thief anyway . . . saw the wisdom of coming around and he played traitor to his Jessie Evans gang and joined the McLain Hunstal party. Hunstal pretended he took a great liking to the Kid he being so young and a poor orphan boy in bad company[,] he Hunstal would give him work and a chance to reform and go straight and make a man out of himself. This was his talk, but the truth was he thought he would get on the good side of the Kid and get him to turn states evidence against not only the Jessie Eveans Gang but also Mortin and the Murphy Nolan Co. Gang. He could be a key witness and give lots of information where they could get damning proof of wholesale cattle rustling right there on the Pecos river. . . . This was why this good honest innocent Englishman took such a fancy to the Kid, to use him as a tool, and the Kid was smart enough and crooked enough to change crowdes, but he sure rued it in the end. The Kid had caught on a lot, but was afraid to tell even what he did know if he did he would not be safe even in Lincoln Dungeon ten feet under ground as he found out when a bunch of the Pecos Warriors came up and turned out all of the prisoners.

CHAIN GANGS: HOW THE RUSTLING RACKET WORKED

[*The Kid*] was now large enough to ride and belong in a way to the Jessie Evans Chain Gang. . . . By Chain Gang is meant that at first it Was Evans, Baker, Jimmy McDonald [McDaniels] and others[.] [*They*] would russel the stuff down in this part of the Pecos valley and take it up by the Penascos, [*through what is now Cloudcroft to*] La Luz, Tuleroso, and to The white Sands, and there [*at McDaniels's ranch in San Nicolas Canyon or Shedd's ranch*] they would be met by a gang from that country who would take the bunch and push them out in to Arizona and then an other one father out to Colorado.

These gangs were well oiled up and in good working order. The Murphy Nolan Co on the Pecos, The Jessie Evans [gang] between who turned them over to the McKinly [Kinney] gang of Las Cruces, who shoved on out to The Arizona [Clanton-McLaury] gang and so on, even as far as the Black Hills.

EVENTS LEADING TO THE KILLING OF TUNSTALL

Again our friend [*Lily is referring to Eugene Cunningham, author of* Trig-gernometry, *who also edited Sophie Poe's book* Buckboard Days; *Lily did not think highly of either*] you are some what wrong as to MurphyDolan murdering Tunstal. . . . Lawyer Mcsween collected insurance money for the Widdow Scholand and her two little orphans girls. He kept it she turned it over to the MurphyDolin Co., for collection. They brought suit in the District Court, got judgement and an attachment sent W. B. [J. B.] Mathews called (Billy) a duly appointed deptuty sheriff over to attach all of the stock over there Known as the McSween Tunstal property. Billy the Kid's Banditti was there as they had been ever since they had stole our cattle and ranch[.] Tunstal was there and he was spokesman saying the property was his and he refused service and resisted the officer[.] Mathews was no fighting man and he only had a man or two with him so he decided to go over to the Middle Penasco[.] Stay all night and come back so he said[.] But Dolan was over there . . . handy to see that the officer carried out this execution to his taste[.] Mathews the officer and Nolan held a council of war, decided to stay all night and early next morning early to come back with a larger force and attach this property by serving the papers on Hunstal who was there and in charge, leave a man to look out for things and come on back to report to the Mur-phynolan Ring. So far everything was done through the District Court and under the color of law, The Papers were under the proper proce-dure, regular, and the officer was properly appointed and qualified. These are matters of record and physical fact. The Murphynolan ring were in the right and The Billy the Kid McLain Hunstal gang were dead wrong and resisting the law. So they held a counsel of war saw where they were in a trap and decided to take a daylight start and come over to get advice from their Jackleg lawer McLain at Lincoln. Each took a lot of horses that the Officer had included in his attachment for it was a blanket attachment and called for all of this property on the entire ranch claiming it belonged to McLain. They took the law into their own hands saying "These horses are my saddle horses and my buggy team I am going to take them with me even if I do have to fight. When the officer Mathews got their next am [morning], with his big menacing party, he found only the cook there, who was more than amiable, saying he had no horses or he guessed he would have been gone, too.

He gave the officer all the necessary information as to all of the horses that had been taken, how many men who they were and where they went and as to how early they left. Presto change, Nolan [Dolan] councelled to send an officer and possie after them for removing attached Property, a violation of the law.

Very quickly Billy Mortin who happened to be there was called on to serve the law and his country as well as The MurphyNolan ring one [reason] being [he was] their main cattle boss most certainly help up hold the law and help to protect their stock and these were their attached horses. If these parties left the country with them they were gone and MurphyNolan would be the loser thus they reasoned.

Mortin and his possie started as full fledged officers of the law to overtake and bring these parties back with these levied on horses, Also hanging around and following closely behind were the Jessie Evans, Frank Baker, Tom Hill gang, who were only watching their chance to get even with McLain and Hunstal for having them arrested and kept in jail, with out bail, or even their mail. Both parties rode very hard but the sheriff's party kept gaining on the others and over took them in Bear Canon as they had come to an old trail cutting a cross to The old Dick Brewer Place [on the Ruidoso] now owned by Wilbur Coe.

Some of the main leaders of this party were R. W. [R. M.] (Dick) Brewer, main leader, Billy the Kid (Handy) man then and up until later (being only a lad in his early teens he said sixteen) John Middleton, Fred Wayth, Henry Brown, John H. Hunstal. The[y] were watching back all the time and as the[y] rode up on a hill they saw coming down the canon round a curve a possie of men who had gotten pretty close to them before they saw them. The leaders at once turned off the road in to the timber so as to have a better show to either get away or fight if the[y] had to. All of these men in the Hunstal party were western men and knew the tactics, but Hunstal, who seemed bewildered and did not run[.] John Middleton shouted at him several times come on, run.

[Lily's account of the Tunstall murder ended here. In another (badly damaged) memoir, "My Impression of John Tunstall," she said [italicized words are guesses

at what is missing,] Tunstall would not run. He was the only brave one of
[*his men*]. I just as soon believe he tried to run but being [*a poor rider*]
couldn't, the country being so rough and timbered and [*Tunstall was
cert*]ainly not used to this rough, rocky ground. . . . in my mind Tom Hill
[*killed Tunst*]all for when Hill was in jail in the underground dungeon at
Lincoln Tunstall fought and opposed his getting bond and wanted to
keep the Evens Hill gang in jail. This everybody knew Hill naturally had it
in for Tunstall.

LILY'S ASSESSMENT OF BILLY THE KID

The Kid had a great personality and could ingraciate himself in people's
good graces very quickly; he had a laughing blue eye always smiling and
laughing, quick and more than acomidating, very good hearted, had an
innocent timid look—all of this took with the girls at once[.] He even as
young as he was, had a girl in every town that he staid in any length of
time. This was his safety guard for they would find out everything that
was going on and be sure to let him know and keep him posted. Girls
Palls were a whole lot more to be trusted than men Palls. He was always
bringing them some little, though costly present in the way of jewelry:
what did he care what it cost, because he stole all his money anyway.

THE KID'S BACKGROUND

The Kid told many pittiful stories about his child hood life, hard ships
misfortunes and even more. That his mother was in Silver City a poor
widdow woman with a worthless husband, his stepfather, who abused
and misstreated him very badly. His mother ran a little restaurant to
make a living the husband would even steal her money to gamble on,
and even was cruel to his mother and abused her, that he [Billy] had
gotten up large enough to take up for his mother thus had trouble with
the old man and had to leave home or kill him. . . .

What we arrived at from all his talk and tales was that he was just a
trifling no acount street urchen and little bum arround the town had
never been made iether to go to school nor work, had picked up a lot
of bad raising and habits with the vicious element he run with, got in
bad [trouble and] was about to be caught and prosecuted so stole this
mare and came to the Lower Pecos.

Lillian Casey Klasner, ca. 1885. Robert G. McCubbin Collection.

Right here and now let us tell not only you, Mr. Eugene Cunningham, but the world that this [*job working for Tunstall*] was Billy the Kid's first association with cattle and it was [*as one of*] a bunch of cowthieves and not cowboys. All the cow boy[s] and cow men resent him being given the honorable name of cowboy when he was never associated with cattle except to steal them. . . . We claim as a positive fact and we know where of we speak with damniable proof that William H. Bonney, better known as Billy the Kid was never at no time nor place a Chisum Cowboy nor ever drove or worked in any way any of the long rial [long rail, Chisum's brand] as it was sometimes called. I have this from every one of the Chisums not one day in any way or maner did he work for them and the

only times he was ever there was while on the dodge with the McSween
outlaws and afterwards stealing these Chisum cattle but by then Chisum
had sold his intire brand to Hunter and Evens of Kansas. . . .

AND WHEN IT WAS ALL OVER . . .

The MurphyNolan crowd got back where they tried to claim some
respectability at least they got under Governer's Lew Wallace's Pardon,
and the Kid did not but was hunted and hounded as a vicious outlaw
until killed. At that time Pat Garret who was especially elected sherriff
of Lincoln County about all of the southesternPart of The Territory of
New Mexico to exterminate Billy the Kid and His Banditti was haled as a
savior of the country and applauded to the skies. Now over fifty years
hence the reaction of the public mind of Desperate criminals of Billy
the Kid type is something fearful to consider. Newsreels made shots of
the New York boy Desperado since his death of his dastardly deeds. And
the amazing thing about it was that the audience applauded! There can
be no doubt interest in Billy the Kid has been at a highpitch in the last
few years. But the thought that law-abiding citizens of the Country
should cheer an out-law who has demonstrated repeatedly that he hates
society and has no regard whatever for human life or property rights is
unthinkable. The Kid was a menace as long as he was at large and the
people of the United States should hang their heads in shame. On some
stolen fleetest horse two belts of cartridges and a forty five sixshooter on
his waist with the best of automatic rifles he was a ruthless outlaw, apparently without fear. but caught without arms he was a rat and it's time the
public realized that fact.

CHAPTER FIFTEEN

The Fight at Blazer's Mill, in New Mexico

Almer Blazer

There have been many, many accounts of the fight at Blazer's Mill on April 4, 1878. By and large, most of them have hewn pretty closely to the version first laid down by Emerson Hough in *The Story of the Outlaw* (1905), and which he deemed "perhaps the most remarkable combat of one man against odds ever known in the West."

Here, reprinted for the first time since 1939, when it appeared in Marvin Hunter's *Frontier Times*, is the only eyewitness account by a nonparticipant—and it offers a version of the story totally different from the accepted one.

Almer Blazer (1865–1949), who was thirteen at the time of the gunfight, reminds us that back then, unlike today, Blazer's Mill was a sizable community with stores and a blacksmith shop and other facilities scattered around it. He provides details of some of the other people who were there on that fateful April day. In addition to his little sister Emma and his friends Wellington (Wellie) Pitts and Si (as in Cyrus), one of the five children of Joseph and Martha Marshall, Almer mentions Dr. Blazer's son-in-law and daughter, Jabez and Ella Hedges; Clara Godfroy (not Godfrey) and her daughters Kate and Louisa; "Old Joe" Weaver the cook; sawyer Samuel "Captain" Miller; carpenter Richard Ewen; dry goods merchant George Maxwell and his wife, Carmen; and others now forgotten by history.

This version of events—which makes no attempt to hide the fact that the writer was at best only a partial witness—is fascinating for a number of reasons. For one, he names Billy the Kid and not Charlie Bowdre as the man who gave Roberts his fatal wound; for another, he makes no mention of Blazer foreman David Easton's part in these events, of John Middleton and George Coe's being wounded, or of the presence of Kate Godfroy's fiancé, Assistant Surgeon Daniel Appel, who was summoned urgently by telegraph from Fort Stanton to do what little he could for the mortally wounded Roberts. And note especially that even immediately after reading Burns's *Saga of Billy the Kid,* Almer Blazer still refrains from anywhere referring to Roberts as "Buckshot," a nickname one would have expected to be inextricably stuck inside the head of a thirteen-year-old. In sum, it demands that the reader reconsider the whole story of that bloody April day at Blazer's mill.

EDITOR'S NOTE: At times during the past twenty-five years the editor of the *News* has requested Mr. A. N. Blazer to write up reminiscences of this section of the country. At various times he has assisted with notes and statements in the preparation of historical articles. Recently he read the portion of the "Saga of Billy the Kid," now running serially in the New Mexico Tribune and whose author is Walter Noble Burns. The story of Billy the Kid was published in book form two years ago by Doubleday, Page & Co.

In the main the author quotes Frank Coe, of the McSween faction, as to the Blazer Mill fight. Mr. Coe states that himself and cousin, George Coe, are the only surviving eye-witnesses and that Roberts, the lone Murphy faction antagonist and deputy sheriff was shot by Charlie Bowdre. That Almer Blazer saw about as much of the fight as was practicable, goes without gainsaying. He gives a version that is slightly at variance with Mr. Coe's tale in other particulars and says that the single shot that hit Roberts came from the gun of Billy the Kid, and in this he quotes Billy, who came that way in charge of two deputies on the way from Mesilla to Lincoln after he had been convicted and sentenced [to death] for the murder of sheriff Brady of Lincoln county.

Mr. Blazer in justice to his family sets at rest the old legend that the deputy Roberts and the leader of the posse, Brewer, were dumped into one grave. This was positively not the case.

The situation at the time and which precipitated the uneven fight by thirteen expert riflemen against one lone deputy who could not raise a rifle to his shoulder are that the lone deputy was surprised. The fight occurred at a time when the Murphy and McSween factions seemed to be evenly matched in resources and numbers. The McSween bunch including Billy the Kid, George and Frank Coe, Charlie Bowdre and Brewer and a number of others, were scouting around after Murphy men, when they accidentally ran into a Murphy deputy at the Blazer premises. Mr. Blazer tells his interesting reminiscences as follows:

Almer Blazer, ca. 1920. He was the only nonpartisan eyewitness to the gun-fight at Blazer's Mill on April 4, 1878. Robert G. McCubbin Collection.

Mescalero, N. M., July 16, 1928

I have just been reading the account of the Roberts-Brewer fight here; which is an installment of the "Saga of Billy the Kid" running as a serial in the *New Mexico State Tribune*, and as I am referred to as "Emil Blazer" and have been asked several times if it was true that I saw the fracas, I feel like writing it up as I remember. I was only in my thirteenth year then but my recollection of the affair is very vivid and while I do not under take to challenge anyone's version I believe the following to be the facts:

All old timers will remember Captain Miller; he had been employed by my father for a few months at the time, and with Johnny Patton, Numa Strain, Dick Ewin, and a crew of laborers was engaged in repairing the saw mill.

Roberts and Miller had at some previous time been associated (I believe in Buffalo hunting on the plains east of the Pecos) and were quite chummy. A few days before the fight Roberts came to the mill and stayed with Miller in his headquarters where he was batching with the other boys on the job, and the morning before the shooting a Mexican from Tularosa told Miller that there was a bunch of "Tejanos" coming from town to kill Roberts.

When Roberts received the information he said he had only stopped to say good bye and that he would pull out and leave the country but had wanted to stay a few days longer hoping to get a letter he expected and told Miller where to send it if it came. He had a horse and a mule and packed the horse and. rode the mule out across the canyon to the south trail which passes down the creek through pinon and cedar thickets to the Nogal Canyon and over the mountains to La Luz.

Roberts had been gone an hour or two when Brewer and his men came riding up the road and said they wanted feed for their horses and their dinner. They didn't ask for it nor in any way intimate that any one would think of refusing them; this had been the custom of both parties in the Lincoln county war for some time, first one side would come along and feed and eat and go on, then a bunch of the others would come along in few days making threats, because their enemies had been entertained, and do the same thing, neither one of them ever offered to pay nor even say thank you.

Godfrey [Frederick C. Godfroy] was Indian Agent at the time and had father's house rented, except father's personal room and a room at the back used as a store. The posse just took possession of the place practically, and did as they pleased. We (my sister, Mrs. Hedges, her husband and baby, my younger sister and myself) lived in a frame house opposite the mill about two hundred yards west of the "big house" where the fight took place, and a boy friend, Wellie Pitts was staying with me. Joseph Maxwell and his family lived in a house between ours and the mill, and there were several Mexican families on the place.

Soon after Brewer and his men arrived, Wellie Pitts and Si Maxwell (we were all about the same age—around 13 or 14) went up the corral where they were feeding their horses and father was there. He immediately told me to go to the house and I started but about that time the men began going up to the house where old Joe Weaver, who was cooking for Godfrey was getting dinner for them under direction of Mrs. Godfrey; he caught sight of us boys and hailed us to get a bucket of water for him and the eloquence of his language on account of his extra work entertained us so well that we got no further. By the time we had delivered the water the men had gotten together at the front of the house and were discussing matters of sufficient interest to entertain us until dinner was announced and they went into the dining room.

We boys remained near the southeast corner of the house for a time where "Old Joe" continued to voice his opinion of having to prepare an extra meal for such a bunch as that, and I remember he was very pale and shaky, and said someone had threatened to "shoot him up if he didn't hurry the grub." Mrs. Godfrey and her girls were waiting on the table I think, for we saw nothing of them.

Our attention was diverted from this entertainment by something crossing the creek, where we had established a toy saw mill and as [live]stock had on a former occasion caused damage to our mill we left Joe without an audience and started to the rescue. It was a false alarm however, and when we got around the corner of the house, we saw it was Roberts on his mule without his pack horse. He stopped on the bank of the creek for a moment and looked at the toy [mill] which we had, in the excitement of the arrival of Brewer, left running at full speed and failed to stop later.

Roberts, during his stay with Miller, had been much interested in our mechanical activities and would sit on the bank of the creek and help us with suggestions and an occasional lift, but on this occasion did not wait for us to arrive but rode on across the road and threw his rope around an old stump that stood near the southwest corner of the house and tied his mule, and we made a move to meet him as he started toward the store.

I remember thinking that he didn't intend to stay long for both his belts were hanging on his saddle horn, and afterwards we found that his six shooter was in the scabbard on one of the belts, and his Winchester was in the scabbard on the saddle.

He had taken a few steps toward the store and we were just in front of the house when some one stepped out and shouted back "here is Roberts" and jumped back into the house. Roberts shouted to us "get out of here" and pulled his gun out of the scabbard and ran behind the southwest corner of the house; we lost no time getting around the other. Old Joe had gone back to the kitchen and we started in that direction but before we got to the door the shooting began on the other side of the house and three or four of the men ran out of the kitchen door and around the back of the house toward the excitement, and we changed our minds and ran east toward a log house some distance away, the shooting behind the house kept up and the log house seemed a long way off so I changed my course and ran across the creek and behind the corral where I thought the danger of stray bullets would be nil.

On my arrival there the shooting had stopped and I recovered my courage to the extent of peeping around the corner after a few minutes, where to my consternation I saw two men with Winchesters in their hands, running directly toward me; I didn't stop to think that they couldn't be after me but put another corner of the corral behind me in the least possible time before stopping to consider the matter, in fact I was near the next corner before stopping for breath.

It was only a minute or two after my arrival there until the men came around the second corner of the corral and I remember that I was thoroughly frightened at their appearance, but had presence of mind to remember that around the next corner my course of retreat would be directly toward the point of the original excitement, and accordingly lost no time getting down the hill to the lumber yard back of the mill; at this point I made a stop and another observation, which revealed the fact that the men were still moving in the general direction of my retreat which renewed my panic and I made another run into the mill itself, when I discovered from there that I still was in their line of advance I jumped into the tail race and waded down to the west end of the blacksmith shop, where I found quite an assemblage [*illegible:* of the men?] belonging to the place.

My arrival among them was so unexpected that they began to question me excitedly as to where I had come from, why and so forth. When I told them they were amused at my scare and began making fun of me, some of them had their lunches and were eating which reminded me that I was hungry and I crossed the road below the shop and went home keeping the house between me and the big house. After getting my dinner I returned to the blacksmith shop where most of the men still were, to find out if they knew where two shots had been fired from that we heard while I was at the house; they were not sure but thought one of them had been fired from the mill and the other from up on the hill somewhere, and none of them cared to investigate. Nor did I.

Soon after this father arrived by the same route I had before dinner. It appeared that he had still been in the barn when the shooting began and stayed there until some of Brewer's men had come for the horses and told him how things were, saying that Brewer and Boudre had gone down to the mill and that Boudre had taken a shot at the door where Roberts was and then came back but that Brewer was still down there somewhere and they had decided to go on as soon as he came.

Father had found Brewer dead in the mill when he arrived there, and told us that he was shot through the head and there was nothing could be done for him until it was safe to go and carry him out. It was only a little while after this that three of the posse, including the Kid, came to us, having made a circuit of the mill through the field south of the mill. They were looking for Brewer, and became excited when father told them what had happened to him. The Kid told father that he would have to go and put Roberts out of the house, to which father replied that he would not. Then the Kid said he would kill him if he didn't, and father said that Roberts would do the same thing if he tried to put him out and he didn't see it would make much difference so far as he was concerned.

The Kid then called him a damned old fool and said they would burn the house, to which father replied that he knew of no way to prevent them from that. Father went back with them to where the others were waiting and after some talk they left without doing further damage.

It was thought that Roberts was wounded, but no one knew how badly, and we thought that it was probable that he might take a shot at any one who went near him, so no one showed themselves where he could see them from the door until late in the evening when Johnny Ryan (who worked for [Dolan &] Riley as trader's clerk at the Agency) arrived from Tularosa.

He was a man of remarkable appearance, being small and very white, bald headed and smooth shaved, and had been familiar with Roberts, so it was thought safe for him to find out how Roberts was and he took off his hat, carrying it in his hand and a large white silk handkerchief in the other walked straight up the road to the foot of the hill from where he called until Roberts answered. Then he went up to the door and talked to Roberts telling him that his enemies had gone and that he wanted to come in and try to help him.

Several went at once when called and found Roberts on a mattress on the floor in front of the door to father's room, and lifted him onto the couch. When I first saw him he seemed to be in a faint. He did not move or speak, but I was told that he had remained conscious until Miller promised to stay with him until he died and keep them from coming back and killing him.

The following morning he asked to see us boys and when we went in he seemed almost himself but very weak and pale, and he and Miller told us all about what happened. After we saw him pass the corner of the house he got into the doorway of father's room and as they began coming around the corner shooting at him he shot at them as they came in sight, exposing himself as little as possible, and succeeded in keeping them back until the Kid slipped up along tile wall which he failed to see until he was so close that he pushed his Winchester against the Kid's belly and pulled the trigger just as he fired, but all the cartridges had been fired out of his gun and the Kid's shot passed through the facing of the door and then struck him about two inches to the left of the navel passing through his body and coming out just over the right hip. He then got the door open and inside of the room; he got father's gun and a belt of cartridges and pulling the mattress off the couch laid down on it before the door which he left ajar but could see no one to shoot at for some time. Then the shot came from the mill; it passed a couple of feet over him through the crack of the door and buried itself in the back wall. This attracted his attention to that point and after watching for a while saw a hat raise slowly over a log; he waited until he thought it high enough to have a head in and fired. This was the shot that killed Brewer.

When Roberts started away in the morning he had gone down the trail until he saw Brewer and his men coming up the road, and then turned back and kept in sight of them most of the way until a half mile or so below the mill where the trail runs through a dense cedar thicket. As he came into that the others were a considerable distance ahead of him, the going was rough, and he had to stop to adjust the pack on his horse, and did not hurry, so that by the time he came to the edge of the mesa where the cedars end, the posse had their horses in the corral and the men were at dinner in the house so that he saw no sign of them and concluded they had gone on. He had seen the mail buck board pass up ahead of them and he concluded to see if his letter had come, he tied his horse and left him at the edge of the cedar intending to go back and continue his journey, then rode over to the store where the post office was and met his death; a —— would be —— in believing that Robert 's time had come and the Kid still had work to do, which he certainly lived to do.

I did not know the members of the posse except the Kid, who being so notorious had naturally interested me on the occasions of a number of previous visits, and their names and history is better left to the recollection of their surviving companions; however, I would say that I do not remember hearing of them describe the occasion just as I remember it.

There are numerous minor discrepancies in all the accounts of the occasion that I have seen, as for instance it is generally stated that Roberts shot Brewer with a Sharp's Buffalo gun, when in fact he used my father's gun (which I still have which is an officer's pattern Springfield, fitted with globe sight and as nearly a perfect gun as there was at that time). It has been said that it must have been an accident[al]ly good shot. However with that gun an average good shot with a rest, as Roberts had, and at the distance he was firing (about two hundred yards) would make a poor shot not to hit anything he could see distinctly, and he was better than an ordinary good shot. Several persons seem to have claimed to have shot Roberts, but I see no reason to doubt his version of the incident and the powder burnt bullet hole through the door facing at least corroborated the story, and afterward when Ollinger and Bell had the Kid here on his way to Lincoln, after his conviction, he described the fight graphically on the spot without material difference from Robert's version, calling attention to the bullet hole. All kinds of stories are told of the burial of these men and I have never seen the facts in print. Brewer lay in the hot sun for several hours and when we finally got to Roberts, making it safe to go to where the body lay, it was in such a state that it was necessary to hurry the burial as much as possible, accordingly every one competent to help were put to making the coffin, digging the grave and other necessary preparations. He was buried that evening with every possible honor under the circumstances, in a home made coffin it is true, (there was no other kind for anyone) decently lined with white cloth and covered with black neatly tacked on the boards of which it was made, and as good as could be provided at the time and place.

Roberts died the following day a little before noon and as it was certain that he could not live long the preliminary work on his coffin had been done and it was ready by the middle of the afternoon and he was buried about four or five o'clock some twenty hours after Brewer so that it is impossible that they were buried in the same coffin, or the same grave, as some accounts have it.

It is stated in the publication previously referred to that Roberts went into the front room of the house and fired from a front window, which

could not have been the case, for the room he was in had no communication with the rest of the house and any one could have gone into the
front or back doors and reached any room in it without coming in
sight of him. I have never seen it stated that the Lincoln war was of any
advantages to any one. Nevertheless it appears to me to have been the
beginning of the "reign of law" in New Mexico. Prior to that time the
"bad men" seem to have been in the majority and had their own way,
judging from the stories I have heard, and were congregated on both
sides for this effort to control the country, with the result that a large
number of them were killed. In fact it appears that there were very few
done to death that did not need killing on general principles, while
the few of the better citizens who lost their lives did so in a good cause.

The conclusion of the Lincoln war proper did not end the destruction of the renegades. They got together from both parties to the number
of 40 or 50 to cooperate in cattle rustling and called themselves the
"rustlers." It was generally conceded that they were the cream of the outlaws and men with no sense of honesty or principle and while it is true
they committed a few murders they generally [——] in connection with
their stealings, which is not strange, but at least half of them were killed
in quarrels among themselves, and the rest of them driven out of the
country by their own associates, thus leaving the better element in control.
While it is true that at times subsequently there have been outbreaks of
lawlessness, the country has never been controlled by the "bad men."

CHAPTER SIXTEEN

The Mackyswins and the Marfes

Francisco Trujillo

Students of the Lincoln County War have frequently remarked upon, even lamented, the lack of any personal accounts of participation in those events by the many native New Mexicans who so strongly supported—and in some cases even died for—the McSween-Tunstall faction, or why they did so, or for that matter why they so notably did not support the other side.

However, there is one such account, made in 1937, when he was about eighty-five years old, by Francisco "Kiko" Trujillo of San Patricio, New Mexico. His story, transcribed by Edith Crawford of Carrizozo as part of the Franklin D. Roosevelt–era WPA Federal Writers' Project, is a remarkable document; despite its many inaccuracies, it vividly reveals the way men of his ethnic background and age perceived some of the events of the Lincoln County War. (In 1880 Trujillo, who was justice of the peace at San Patricio, was a thirty-two-year-old laborer, with a wife, Margarita, age thirty, and a son and daughter ages twelve and eight, respectively.)

In many ways the narrator is oddly selective: he is involved in events as early as November 1877, yet completely fails to mention the death of Tunstall (or, indeed, to make any reference to the Englishman at all), the fight at Blazer's Mill, the Dudley Court of Inquiry, or the murder of Huston Chapman. It may well be, of course, that the reason he failed to do so was that Mrs. Crawford didn't ask him.

Apart from one or two brief interpolations to straighten out his chronology, and the correction of names that either Trujillo misremembered or Mrs. Crawford (or her translator) rendered phonetically (you can almost *hear* Trujillo saying "Mac-eh-sween" and "Mar-fee" as he told his story), the document is reproduced exactly as he dictated it seventy years ago.

I arrived at San Patricio in the year 1877. During the first days of October Sheriff Brady appointed a committee [posse] to pursue some bandits whom we found at Harry Baker's [Hugh Beckwith's] ranch at Siete Rios [Seven Rivers]. There we arrested them and brought them to the jail at Lincoln. In November the people of Peñasco went to take the bandits out from jail. Among the people coming from Peñasco, was Billy the Kid.

[*The Brady posse left Lincoln on October 12, 1877, in pursuit of members of the Jesse Evans gang, a.k.a. "The Boys." Charged with stealing horses from John Tunstall and Dick Brewer, Evans, Tom Hill, George Davis, and Frank Baker were arrested on October 17 at Seven Rivers and incarcerated in the underground jail in Lincoln. On the night of November 16, a party of Seven Rivers men (and if Trujillo was right, one or two from the Peñasco area as well) led by Andy Boyle "delivered" the prisoners. Whether the Kid was one of the deliverers or one of those delivered is still a moot point.*]

At about the same time Francisco Trujillo, my brother, Juan Trujillo and I went to Pajarito [*in the mountains south of the Ruidoso*] to hunt deer. We were at the mouth of the Pajarito Canyon skinning a deer, when we saw two persons passing. One was Frank Baker, the other was Billy Mote [Morton]. One was a bandit and the other a body guard whom Marfe [Murphy] kept at the [Black River] ranch. The last one was a thief also. When they passed my brother said "Let us get away quickly, these are bad people." So, we got our horses, saddled them and left in the direction of San Patricio. On the way we met the bandits and the people who were coming from the jail at Lincoln.

The bandits surrounded Juan, my brother. I started to get away but Billy the Kid followed me telling me to stop. I then turned around and saw that he was pointing a rifle at me so I jumped from my horse and aimed my gun at him. He then went back to where the people were and aimed his gun at Juan saying "If Francisco does not surrender I am going to kill you." Lucas Gallegos [*who had been in the Lincoln jail awaiting trial for murder but was freed at the same time as the others*] then shouted "Surrender, friend, otherwise they will kill my *compadre* Juan." Billy then took my gun from where I had laid it and we returned to the place where the people were.

Billy then said to me "We have exchanged guns now let us exchange saddles." I said that suited me picking up the gun when another Texan said "Hand it over you don't need it." At this point Lucas Gallegos interposed saying to my brother "Let me have the pistol, *compadre*." Then my brother gave Lucas the pistol in its holster. Then and there we parted and left for San Patricio to recount our experiences.

In December Macky Swin [McSween] and Marfe went to court about a guardianship [*the settlement of the Emil Fritz will*] and a decision was rendered in favor of Macky Swin [*the probate court having turned down Murphy's claim against the Fritz estate for $76,000 on January 10, 1878*]. When Marfe saw that he had lost out he ordered his men to kill Macky Swin or some of his companions. Macky Swin hearing of the order that Marfe had given gathered his people in order to protect himself. Among those he rounded up was Billy the Kid, Charley Barber [Bowdre] and Macky Nane [Frank MacNab]. In addition to these three men, six more got together and Macky Swin made them the same promise, to the effect that a prize of $500 was to be awarded to each person who killed one of the Marfes.

It was then and there that Billy the Kid organized his people and went out in search of Frank Baker and Billy Mote whom he apprehended on the other side of the Pecos river and brought to Lincoln where it was planned to execute them. Later when they talked it over further with the rest, it was again decided to kill them but not to bring them to Lincoln. One of the gang named McLoska [McCloskey] said that he preferred to be shot himself rather than to have one of those men killed. No sooner had he said this, when he found himself shot behind the ear. After they killed McLoska, Frank Baker and Billy Mote were promptly executed. From there Billy's gang left for San Patricio where Billy asked for Francisco Trujillo in order to deliver back to him his gun. It was here that they hired a Mexican boy to go to Lincoln for provisions and to collect the reward that Macky Swin had promised for the Marfes whom they had just killed.

A few days later Macky Nane, Frank Coe and Alex Coe [Ab Saunders] were on their way to Picacho from Lincoln. [*Trujillo's chronology went adrift at this point: Morton and Baker were killed March 9, but the events he now describes took place on April 29, 1878.*] When they reached the Ojo [Fritz Spring] ranch they were confronted by the Marfes [*a "posse" of Seven Rivers men led by Robert Beckwith, who claimed to be a deputy sheriff*]. They made Frank Coe prisoner and shot Alex Coe on the leg, while the Indian, Juan Armijo [Manuel Segovia], ran after Macky Nane and killed him by order of Robert Baker [Beckwith]. Macky Nane had been the leader whom Macky Swin had had for a [body]guard. Within a few days a complaint was sworn against the Indian, Juan Armijo, and Sheriff Brady deputized Jose Chaves [y Chaves] to arrest him. [*Once again, Trujillo's chronology is off: these events*

took place in mid-May, and Sheriff William Brady was already dead; it was Sheriff
John Copeland who deputized Chaves and the others.]

Chaves then named seven men beside himself in order that they
should go with him to look for Armijo and he in turn deputized eight
Americans and eight Mexicans and altogether they left for Siete Rios
where they found Juan across the Pecos river, as well as two other Texans.
When Atanasio Martinez, John Scroggin[s], Billy the Kid and I arrived
at the door of the hut, Juan Armijo spoke up and said "How are you
Kiko?" "Come on out," I said to Juan. "You have killed Macky Nane" to
which he nodded in assent but adding that it was by order of Robert
Baker under threat of being prosecuted himself, should he fail to carry
out instructions. [*Segovia said*] I then made my way to Macky Nane who
had been hiding behind some tree trunks in an effort to defend himself
against those who were shooting at the house, and killed him.

When we left the hut, accompanied by Juan, he said to me "Don't let
them kill me Kiko!" Seeing a string of people coming from Siete Rios
we ran to [a] nearby hill and from there towards the plains and then
headed for Roswell, on the other side of the Pecos river, and came out
two miles below at Gurban [Good Bend Crossing?]. It was here that Billy
the Kid, Jose Chaves and Stock [Scurlock] proposed to kill the Indian,
Armijo. I said to Chaves "Is it not better to take him in and let the law
have its course?" Charley Bargar [Bowdre] then came up to me and said
"Come on Francisco, let us be running along."

As I came up to Charley, I turned and saw the Indian Armijo riding
between them very slowly. When Charley and I had gone about fifty yards
we noticed that the Indian had gotten away from his captors and was
riding away as fast as he could. Billy the Kid and Jose Chaves took out
after him and began to shoot at him until they got him. Several of us
congregated at the place where he fell. Billy the Kid then said to me
"Francisco, here are the saddle and trappings that I owe you." I then
commanded Esequio Sanchez to do me the favor of bringing me the
horse the Indian Armijo had been riding, in order that I might remove
the saddle which was covered with blood. Noting my disgust Doke [Doc,
i.e., Scurlock] said that he would take it and clean it and let me have his
in the meantime. And so, we exchanged. Our business finished we turned
homeward and crossed the river at a point called "Vado de los Indios"
[Indian Ford]. At this side of the Pecos river, we slept. In the morning
we arose and went to Aleman to have breakfast. There we found Macky

Swin at John Chisum's ranch. Breakfast being over Macky Swin told us
to go into the store and take anything that we wished.

[*The first known settlers on South Springs River in the 1860s were an old
German named Eisenstein and his wife. They lived in a dugout overlooking the
springs, which, according to Lily Klasner, were known for many years as El Ojo del
Aleman, literally "the German's Spring," but always called Dutchman's Spring.*]

At this point it was decided to leave Captain Stock to guard over Macky
Swin. [*Scurlock was "captain" of the party.*] Of the original eight Mexicans in
the party, four were left to join the Americans, not having admitted the
other four to do so. Macky Swin then asked us to meet him the following
Monday at Lincoln because said he "As soon as I arrive, Brady is going
to try and arrest me and you should not let him get away with it. If I am
arrested I shall surely be hung and I don't want to die, while if you kill
Brady you shall earn a reward." [*Trujillo's chronology is awry again. The
events he now describes would have to have taken place in the final days of
March 1878.*]

From [Chisum's] we left for Berrendo [a plazita on Berrendo Creek
northwest of Roswell] where we found a *fandango* in progress. We were
enjoying ourselves very thoroughly when Don Miguel came up to us
and said "Better be on your way boys because presently there will arrive
about fifty Marfes who are probably coming here to get you." Esteco
[Esequio], our leader, agreeing with Don Miguel, commanded us to
saddle our horses. We had not been gone half a mile when we heard
shouts and gun shots so we decided to wait for the gang and have it
out. Our efforts were of no avail, however, as the gang failed to show up.
We then pursued our course toward the Capitan mountains and arrived
at Agua Negra at day break and there we had our lunch. At this point
the party broke up, the Anglos going to Lincoln, the Mexicans to San
Patricio whence they arrived on Sunday afternoon. Billy the Kid then
said to Jose Chaves, "Let us draw [lots] to see who has to wait for Macky
Swin tomorrow at Lincoln." The lots fell to Charley Barber, John Milton
[Middleton] and Jim French White, whereupon the leader decided that
all nine Anglos should go.

Bill[y] thought that it was best for none of the Mexican boys to go
and when Chaves protested saying that the Anglos were no braver than
he, Bill[y] explained that Brady was married to a Mexican and that it
was a matter of policy, all Mexicans being sentimental about their own.
Chaves being appeased urged the rest to go on promising to render

assistance should a call come for help. A Texan name Doke said that since his family was Mexican too, he would remain with the others. Stock then gave orders to proceed. The horses were saddled and they left for Lincoln. Doke, Fernando Herrera, Jesus Sais and Candelario Hidalgo left for Ruidoso. The next morning Don Pancho Sanches left for Lincoln to make some purchases at the store.

Being in the store about eleven, the mail arrived and with it Macky Swin. There also arrived Brady and a Texan name George Hamilton [Hindman]. At this juncture Brady also arrived where he found Billy the Kid, Jim French, Charley Barber and John Melton. They were in the corral from whence two of the gang shot at one, and two others at the other, where they fell. Billy the Kid then jumped to snatch Brady's rifle and as he was leaning over someone shot at him from a house they used to call "El Chorro." Macky Swin then reached the house where the nine Macky Swins were congregated—the four who were in the corral and five who had been at the river. There they remained all day until nightfall and then proceeded to San Patricio.

The next morning they proposed going to the hills should there be a war and so that it could be waged at the edge of town in order not to endanger the lives of the families living there. The same day, toward evening, six Mexicans came to arrest Macky Swin. They did not arrive at the Plaza but camped a little further down between the *acequia* and the river at a place where there were thick brambles. Shortly after the Mexicans arrived Macky Swin came with his people to eat supper at the house of Juan Trujillo [in San Patricio]—that being their headquarters, that also being their mess hall having hired a negro [George Washington] to prepare the meals. After supper they scattered among the different houses, two or three in each house.

In one of these at the edge of town Macky Swin and an American boy whose name was Tome [O'Folliard] locked themselves in. Next day early in the morning the six Mexicans who had been looking for Macky Swin showed up. When they arrived at the house where Macky Swin was Tome came out and shot at the bunch of Mexicans and hit Julian Lopez in the arm, about forty Marfes came down to San Patricio killing horses and chickens. At this point there arrived two Marfes, an American and a Mexican. The American's name was Ale Cu [Lally Cooler, i.e., Charlie Crawford], and the Mexican's Lucio Montoya. When the Macky Swins became aware of them, they began to fire and killed all the horses. The

Josiah Gordon "Doc" Scurlock and family, ca. 1898. One of the "Regulators" who fought for the Tunstall-McSween faction, Scurlock "went straight" and lived a long and respectable life in Texas. *Front row, left to right:* Ethlinda (Linda); Dolores (Lola); Antonia Miguela (Herrera) with Josephine Gladys, born August 2, 1895; Presley Fernando; William Andrews; Josiah G. Scurlock; John Josiah. *Back row, standing at left:* Amy Antonia; Josiah Gordon, Jr. Courtesy Michael Stewart.

two Marfes ran away to San Patricio where the rest of the Marfes were tearing down a house and taking out of the store everything that they could get hold of. From there all the Marfes went to Lincoln and for about a month nothing of interest occurred.

I don't recall exactly when Macky Swin, who was being hounded down by the Marfes, was killed but I do remember that he gathered together all his friends and went back home to Lincoln accompanied by eight Mexicans and two Americans, also his wife. When the Marfes found out that he was in the house they surrounded him but seeing that they were unable to hurt him they caused to be brought over a company of soldiers and a cannon from the nearby Fort. Notwithstanding this Macky Swin instructed his people not to fire. For this reason the soldiers had to sit until it was dark. The Marfes then set fire to the house and the soldiers returned to the fort. When the first room burned down, Ginio

Salaza[r] and Ignacio Gonzales came out to the door but the Marfes knocked them down and left them there, dazed. When the flames reached the middle room, an American proposed to go out through the doors of the kitchen on the north side. No sooner did he jump than the Marfes knocked him down. Francisco Samora jumped also and he too was shot. Vincente Romero was next and there the three remained in a heap. It was then proposed by Billy the Kid and Jose Chaves y Chaves to take aim at the same time and shoot, first to one side then to the other. Chaves took Macky Swin by the arm and told him to go out to which Macky Swin answered by taking a chair and placing it in the corner stating that he would die right there. Billy and Jose Chaves then jumped to the middle door, one on one side, and the other on the other. Then Robert Bakers [Beckwith] and a Texan jumped and said "Here is Macky Swin." Drawing out his revolver he shot him three times in the breast. When the last shot was fired Billy the Kid said "Here is Robert" and thrust a revolver in his mouth while Jose Chaves shot at the Texan and hit him in the eye. Billy and Chaves then went along the river headed for San Patricio where they both remained for some time.

In October the Governor accompanied by seven soldiers and other persons came to San Patricio camping. Having heard about the exploits of Billy the Governor expressed a desire to meet him and sent a messenger to fetch him. The interview was in the nature of a heart to heart talk wherein the Governor advised Billy to give up his perilous career. At this point occurred the General Election and George Kimbrall was elected Sheriff of the county. Obeying the Governor's orders he called out the militia having commissioned Sr. [Juan B.] Patron as Captain and Billy the Kid as First Lieutenant. During that year—that of '79—things were comparatively quiet and Billy led a very uneventful life. [*Once again Trujillo's chronology goes wrong: George Kimbrell was appointed (not elected) sheriff on January 1, 1879; Wallace's first visit to Lincoln was in March. He and the Kid had their famous meeting on March 17; there is no record of the governor's ever having visited San Patricio. The "militia"—the Lincoln County Riflemen—was formed in the same month; Billy the Kid was never a member of the unit.*]

About the last part of October of the same year, the Governor issued an order that the militia should make an effort to round all bandits in Chaves [Lincoln] county, a task which the militia was not able to accomplish hence it disbanded. Billy the Kid received an honorable discharge and would probably have gone straight from then on had it not been that at this juncture the District Court met and the Marfes swore a complaint against him and ordered Sheriff Kimbrall to arrest him. Billy stubbornly refused to accompany the Sheriff and threatened to take away his life rather than to be apprehended.

Again nothing was heard for a time and then Pat Garrett offered to bring in the desperado for a reward. The Governor having been made aware of the situation himself offered a reward of $500. Immediately Pat Garrett accompanied by four other men got ready to go after Billy and found him and three other boys, whom they surrounded. One morning, during the siege, one of Billy's companions went out to fetch a pail of water whereupon Pat Garrett shot at him, as well as the others, hitting him in the neck and thereby causing him to drop the pail and to run into the house. With a piece of cloth, Billy was able to dress the wound of the injured man and at least stop the hemorrhage. He then advised the wounded man to go out and to pretend to give himself up, hiding his fire arm but using it at the first opportune moment to kill Pat. Charley did as we was told but when he went to take aim, dropped dead. Bill[y] and the other three companions were kept prisoners for three days but finally hunger and thirst drove them out and caused them to venture forth and to give themselves up. Billy was arrested there being no warrant for the others.

[*There were, of course, warrants for the three outlaws captured at Stinking Springs; what remains questionable is the killing of O'Folliard and Bowdre, for neither of whom Garrett had a warrant.*]

Then followed the trial [of the Kid,] which resulted in a sentence to hang within thirty days. News of the execution having spread about people began to come in for miles around to be present on the fatal day but Billy was not to afford them much pleasure having escaped three days before the hanging. A deputy and jailer had been commissioned to stand guard over him. On the day of the escape at noon the jailer told the deputy to go and eat his dinner and that he would then go himself and fetch the prisoners. It was while the jailer and Billy remained alone that the prisoner stepped to the window to fetch a paper. He had somehow gotten rid of his hand cuffs and only his shackles remained. With the paper in his hand he approached the officer and before the latter knew what his charge was up to, yanked his revolver away from him and the next instant he was dead. Billy lost no time in removing his keeper's cartridge belt as well as a rifle and a "44 W.C.F." [Whitney center-fire shotgun?] which were in the room.

When the deputy heard the shots he thought that the jailer must have shot Billy who was trying to escape and ran from the hotel to the jail on the steps of which he met Billy who said "hello" as he brushed past him, firing at him as he dashed by. Billy's next move was to rush to the hotel and to have Ben Esle [Ellis] remove his shackles. He also provided for him a horse and saddled it for Billy upon the promise that he was to leave it at San Patricio. True to his word Billy secured another horse at San Patricio from his friend Juan Trujillo promising in turn to return the same as soon as he could locate his own.

Billy now left San Patricio and headed for John Chisum's cattle ranch. Among the cow boys there was a friend of Billy Mote who had sworn to kill the Kid whenever he found him in order to avenge his friend. But Billy did not give him time to carry out his plan killing him on the spot. From there Billy left for Berrendo where he remained a few days. Here he found his own horse and immediate sent back Juan Trujillo's. From Berrendo Billy left for Puerto de Luna where he visited Juan Patron, his former captain. Patron did everything to make his and his companion's stay there as pleasant as possible. On the third evening of their stay there was to have been a dance and Billy sent his companion to make a report of what he saw and heard. While on his way there, and while he was passing in front of some abandoned shacks, Tome was fired upon by one of Pat Garrett's men and killed. No sooner had Billy heard the distressing news than he set out for the house of his friend Pedro Macky [Maxwell] at Bosque Grande [Fort Sumner] where he remained in hiding until a Texan named Charley Wilson [Joe Grant], and who was supposed to be after Billy, arrived.

The two exchanged greetings in a friendly fashion and then the stranger asked Billy to accompany him to the saloon, which invitation Billy accepted. There were six or seven persons in the saloon when the two entered. Drinks were imbibed and a general spirit of conviviality prevailed when some one suggested that the first one to commit a murder that day was to set the others up. "In that case the drinks are on me," said Charley who commanded all to drink to their heart's content. Billy then ordered another round of drinks and by this time Charley who was feeling quite reckless began to shoot at the glasses not missing a single one until he came to Billy's. This he pretended to miss, aiming his shot at Bill[y] instead. This gave Billy time to draw out his own revolver and before Charley could take aim again, Billy had shot the other in the breast twice. When he was breathing his last Billy said "Do not whisper you were to eager to buy those drinks." It was Billy's turn now to treat the company.

[*More chronology problems: The Kid killed Joe Grant on January 10, 1880. Tom O'Folliard was killed at Fort Sumner, not Puerto de Luna, on December 19, 1880. Both events occurred long before the Kid's escape in April 1881.*]

Quiet again reigned for a few days. In the meantime Pat Garrett was negotiating with Pedro Macky [Maxwell] for the deliverance of Billy. When all details were arranged for, Pat left for Bosque Grande [Fort Sumner] secretly. At the ranch house, Pedro hid Pat in a room close beside the one Billy was occupying. Becoming hungry during the night Billy got up and started to prepare a lunch. First he built a fire, then he took his hunting knife and was starting to cut off a hunk of meat from a large piece that hung from one of the *vigas* when he heard voices in the adjoining room. Stepping to the door he partially opened it and thrusting his head in asked Pedro who was with him. Pedro replied that it was only his wife and asked him to come in. Seeing no harm in this Billy decided to accept the invitation only to be shot in the pit of the stomach as he stood in the door. Staggering back to his own room it was not definitely known that the shot had been fatal until a cleaning woman stumbled over the dead body upon entering the room, the following morning.

CHAPTER SEVENTEEN

Five Days of Battle

Philip J. Rasch

The article that follows illustrates starkly how wide the gap is between oral recollections of the legendary Kid, such as that of Francisco Trujillo, and the carefully documented approach taken by Philip J. Rasch. It is possible here to see clearly how much wider Rasch's range and grasp of events had become in the few years since his first "paper" on the subject was published. It was groundbreaking then; even fifty years on, it is difficult to fault his account of the events of July 14–19, 1878, which culminated in the defeat of the McSween faction and the death of its leader in what Andy Boyle characterized as "the Big Killing." It should be noted, however, that—shaped by his early friendship with James Dolan's daughters—the author's sympathies were always largely with the House, and that he considered Tunstall a money-motivated, even greedy adventurer, and lawyer McSween "as crooked as a dog's hind leg." So here he skirts discussing Dudley's motives in bringing troops to Lincoln and dodges the question of whether—as the Kid himself later claimed—soldiers fired at some of the men making their escape from the burning house. He also avers that Assistant Surgeon Daniel Appel was the only soldier out of camp that night when there is absolutely no way he could have known that for certain.

Amazingly, in spite of the intensive research that has been done on the subject in the half-century since this article first appeared, there are still questions about these events that cannot be answered. Who was the Joseph Smith who wrote that cocky letter to his boss on the last day of the fighting—and what happened to him? Who was George Bowers, said to have perished in the fire? Was he the same man as the Thomas Cullins, a.k.a. Joe Rivers (an alias later used by a man named *Joe* Bowers), said to have been buried in the cellar of the McSween house—and if he was, why was no trace found of him during the extensive 1986–88 archaeological "digs" on the site? Who was the mystery man known only as "The Dummy," supposed to have been feigning dumbness so as to avoid answering questions? And when and whence is a new Philip Rasch going to come along with all the answers?

FOREWORD: During the years following the War Between the States, Lawrence G. Murphy and Emil Fritz, doing business as L. G. Murphy & Co., became virtual economic and political dictators of Lincoln County, New Mexico. After the death of Fritz, James J. Dolan and John H. Riley became the active partners in the concern. In 1877 Alexander A. McSween, a Lincoln lawyer; and John H. Tunstall, a wealthy young Englishman, backed by cattle baron John S. Chisum, opened a store and bank in Lincoln, directly challenging Dolan-Riley for the control of the County.

Chisum had already earned the enmity of the small ranch owners, (see Philip J. Rasch, "The Pecos War," *PanHandle-Plains Historical Review*) who now rallied around Dolan-Riley. On February 18, 1878, Tunstall was murdered by a sheriff's posse composed of Dolan-Riley sympathizers. Open warfare resulted. In quick succession Sheriff William Brady, George Hindman, William Morton, Frank Baker, William McCloskey, Richard Brewer, Bill Williams, alias Andrew L. Roberts, Frank McNab, James A. Saunders, and Tom Childron, alias Tom Hill, were shot down. Murphy fled to Santa Fe; Riley took refuge on the range. Dolan and the newly-appointed sheriff, George W. Peppin, continued to press the fight against McSween.

Affairs came to a climax in July, 1878, when a pitched battle between the two sides raged for five days in the plaza of Lincoln, the county seat. The fight resulted in a defeat for the McSween partisans, but financially ruined Dolan-Riley. Lincoln County was plunged into anarchy. Murder, rape, arson, and theft became the order of the day, leaving behind a legacy of bitterness which persists to some extent to this day.

The actions of Lieutenant Colonel N. A. M. Dudley, commanding Fort Stanton, were investigated by a Court of Inquiry, which finally exonerated him. The following account of the battle at Lincoln is based primarily on two sources: the weekly reports made by Dudley to his superior, Colonel Edward Hatch, Commanding the District of New Mexico, and the sworn testimony given by participants in the affair at the Court of Inquiry. Many of the details are admittedly controversial. The sworn testimony contains statements so directly contradictory that they can be accounted for only on the supposition that at times the truth was deliberately disregarded. Nevertheless, the writer believes that the story as here presented is correct in all essential points.

Lawrence G. Murphy and friends at Fort Sumner, ca. 1873. Soon after this photograph was taken, post trader (and *de facto* Indian agent) Murphy was ejected from the fort for dubious business practices; he moved ten miles down the road to Lincoln and carried on as if nothing had happened. *Left to right:* Capt. Charles Styer; Lt. Orsemus Boyd; Emil Fritz; Lt. Casper H. Conrad; Lt. Col. August V. Kautz; Capt. Chambers McKibbin; Mrs. Mary McKibbin (*seated*); Capt. William McCleave; Mrs. Frances A. Boyd (*seated*); Lawrence G. Murphy. Photo by N. Brown. Courtesy Museum of New Mexico, negative no. 101417.

By the middle of July, 1878, it had become evident that Alexander McSween's Regulators were in desperate straits. Harried on every side by the Dolan-Riley faction, they assembled at San Patricio for a council of war. Their decision was born of their desperation: they decided to stake every thing on one throw of the dice and to attempt to seize Lincoln by force. An alliance was affected with Martin Chavez, of Picacho, and his Mexican followers, and on the night of Sunday, July 14, the Regulators took up positions in the plaza. Chavez, Fernando Herrera, and seven other Mexicans manned the Montana house. McSween, Henry McCarty (alias William Antrim, alias Bill Bonney, alias Billy the Kid), Harvey Morris,[1] Jose Chavez y Chavez, Yginio Salazar, Florencio Chaves, Ignacio Gonzales, Vincente Romero, Francisco Zamora, Jim French, Tom O'Folliard, Jose Maria Sanchez, Joseph J. Smith, Thomas Cullins (alias Joe Rivers), and George Bowers defended the McSween house. Henry Brown, George Coe, and Sam Smith were barricaded in the warehouse behind the Tunstall building, in the back rooms of which were living Dr. and Mrs. Taylor F. Ealy, their two small daughters, and Miss Susan Gates. Charles Bowdre, Josiah G. "Doc" Scurlock, John Middleton, "Dirty Steve" Stevens, and others to the number of about a dozen garrisoned the Isaac Ellis home. A group of perhaps five men occupied the Patron house.

Sheriff George W. Peppin, taken completely by surprise, had only a small force under his immediate command. Deputy Sheriff Jack Long held the Torreon, a round tower which had originally been erected for defense against Indian raids, with Jacob Mathews, James B. Reese, Sam Perry, Jim McDaniels, George A. Rose (Roxie), and a man known as "The Dummy." Peppin, Pantaleon Gallegos, Lucien Montoya, Andrew Boyle, and one other man occupied the Wortley Hotel. With them was James J. Dolan, who was recuperating from a broken leg suffered in a fall from his horse. A Mexican was hastily dispatched for Deputy Sheriff William B. "Buck" Powell, who was in the vicinity of San Patricio, ordering him to bring his men to Lincoln at once. As they entered the plaza about six o'clock in the evening, they were fired on from the McSween house and a horse was killed. With reinforcements received the next day, the sheriff's force was brought up to twenty-six or twenty-eight men, including Joseph H. Nash, Robert M. Beckwith, Robert Olinger, Wallace Olinger, John Thornton, Jim Hurley, John Hurley, —— Prince, Benjamin "Buck" Waters, Deputy Sheriff Marion Turner, John Chambers, Charles Crawford (alias Lalacooler or Lally Cooler²), John Kinney, John Jones, Tom Jones, Jim Jones, Jessie J. Evans, —— Hart, —— Collins, John W. Irving, Jake Owen, Jose Chavez y Baca, Milo L. Pierce, William Johnson, R. L. Bryan, Thomas Cochran, and John Galvin, in addition to those previously named.

The sheriff held two warrants each for Antrim, Brown, Scurlock, and Bowdre on charges of murder, one for Jose Chavez for horse stealing, one for Coe for murder, and one for McSween, charged with assault to kill. The next morning Long made the gesture of attempting to serve the warrants, was greeted with gunfire, as he no doubt anticipated, and beat a hasty retreat.

The presence of Dolan-Riley partisans in the Torreon, which was on property owned by McSween, led to trouble between Saturnino Baca and the McSweens. Mrs. McSween had already accused Baca of having sent men to San Patricio to kill her husband and had warned that if he was harmed she would retaliate, come what might. Baca, although a Dolan-Riley supporter, occupied a house owned by McSween adjacent to the tower. McSween was furious when he learned that Baca had per-mitted Long and his men to enter the Torreon. He immediately sent his rentor a written notice to vacate within three days because "You have consented to the improper use of the property by murderers for the purpose of taking my life."[3]

When Assistant Surgeon D. M. Appel was sent to the plaza to attend Julian Lopez, a posseman who had been wounded in the fighting at San Patricio, the Bacas told him that they were in fear for their lives and begged for a guard. Appel visited McSween to discuss the situation. Livid with rage, McSween informed the doctor that the Bacas were on his ground and harboring his enemies, and that they would leave if he had to burn them out. He had been hiding in the hills long enough, he snapped; he had now returned to his home and no one would drive him away alive. Quieting down then, he gave the officer his written con-sent for soldiers to occupy the Torreon to protect the Baca family. Baca, however, decided to move and wrote Lieutenant Colonel Dudley, com-manding Fort Stanton, for the loan of wagons, pleading in justification for this aid his five years of service in the Union forces and the recent confinement of his wife.

Scurlock appeared before Justice Wilson and executed an affidavit denying that he had threatened to kill Colonel Dudley and Johnny Brady. Isaac Ellis and his son Benjamin signed affidavits to the effect that Crawford had threatened their lives and stolen their best horse. Appel returned to Fort Stanton with these papers to lay the matter before his commanding officer.

Things remained quiet the rest of the day, but about midnight Dan Huff, a citizen of Lincoln, died in agony, in spite of the administrations of Dr. Ealy. He had tried to remain neutral, but is supposed to have been poisoned by a relative who objected to the fact that he had been friendly with the McSweens. The next evening two of McSween's colored servants, George Washington and Sebrian Bates, dug a grave adjacent to that of Tunstall and were in the process of lowering the body into it when they were driven away by shots from the Torreon.

On the 16th Peppin wrote Dudley, requesting the loan of a howitzer. Until this time Dudley's weekly reports had been scrupulously fair in their attitude toward the two factions. His answer to Peppin, however, threw off all pretense and allied him firmly with the Dolan-Riley side:

. . . and in reply would state I fully realize your difficult situation. My sympathies and those of all my officers are most earnest and sincerely with you on the side of law and order . . . I do not hesitate to state now that . . . were I not so circumscribed by laws and orders, I would most gladly give you every man and material at my Post to sustain you in your present situation . . .[4]

To Hatch he reported that "The . . . Dolan-Riley faction . . . I fear will get the worst of it."[5]

Private Berry Robinson was sent to Lincoln with the letter for the sheriff. As he reached the outskirts of the plaza, several shots were fired at him. Peppin immediately capitalized on the incident by writing Dudley that

The McSween party fired on your Soldier when coming into town. My men on seeing him tried there best to cover him, but of no use. The soldier will explain the circumstances to you.[6]

The following morning Dudley appointed Captain G. A. Purington, Captain Thomas Blair, and Appel a Board of Officers to investigate the shooting. In spite of McSween's denials, they concluded that the shots had come from his house. While in Lincoln they learned that Peppin had sent Crawford, Montoya, and three other men up in the hills south of the town to drive the McSween riflemen off the roofs of the buildings held by them. Crawford had been shot by Herrera and was lying helpless on the hillside. Blair and Appel went to assist him, whereupon either they or the wounded man were fired at from the Montana house. However, Crawford was taken to the post hospital, where he died a week later.

The 17th was relatively quiet, although that night Ben Ellis was shot in the neck while in his corral feeding his mules, but this was the proverbial lull before the storm. Fighting was resumed on the morning of the 18th and continued almost incessantly.

During the day Thomas Cullins was killed and buried in the cellar of the McSween house. George Bowers was seriously wounded. In spite of these reverses the high morale of the Regulators is evident in a letter written by Joseph Smith the next morning:

I thought I would write you a few lines to let you know what the people are doing up here. We have taken the town. One was killed yesterday, and one wounded. Ben Ellis was shot through the neck by one of the guards. Everything is fair in war. Seen Jim Reese the other morning walking down the street. I heard Collins sing hunger the other morning. I heard Jim Reese cried because he was on the other side. He says he is in it and can't get out of it. All of them have taken an oath to stand by each other until death, so I guess we will get to kill a lot of them fore they get away. Capper, you must not think hard of a fellow for quitting you; but I wanted to go, so I went. The U.S. troops have stepped aside, and given us full swing. There is 45 of us citizens have turned out. I tell you it makes a fellow's hair stand up when bullets come whistling through the air; then I get cooled down, I don't mind it much. Best respects to Sam. Harvey Morris sends his respects to all. Had a little excitement yesterday evening. The Murphy's told some woman in town that they got a condemned cannon and was going to bombard the town. Tried to scare us out, but we didn't scare worth a darn.

Well, I must quit writing. Good luck to you. Tell Bill Nagle he can have them gloves.[7]

From the standpoint of the sheriff the situation was becoming desperate. Johnson and two other men had been wounded in the shooting and removed to the post hospital. Many of the possemen were discouraged and wanted to leave the fight. Dolan, Kinney, Perry, Roxie, and several others went to Fort Stanton to consult with Dudley. They told him frankly that there was no way of getting the McSween men out of the house without his assistance. The colonel was noncommital. He answered that he had had numerous appeals for help from non-combatants; that his howitzer was broken but that blacksmith Nelson would work on it all night and on the following day troops would go to Lincoln to protect women and children.

That evening he called a conference of his officers. At the suggestion of Captain Purington, those present signed their names to the following statement:

General N. A. M. Dudley Lieut Col 9th Cavalry having asked the undersigned Officers their Opinions and advice as to the advisability of placing Soldiers in the Town of Lincoln for the preservation of the lives of the women and Children, and in response to the numerous petitions received from persons in that town, do hereby place on record their concurrence in the measures adopted by General Dudley believing them to be in Course of right and humanity.

About ten o'clock on the morning of the 19th Dudley rode into the plaza, accompanied by five officers, thirty-five men, the howitzer, and a Gatling gun. Drawing rein in front of the Wortley Hotel, Dudley issued a grim warning:

Mr. Sheriff, I want you to understand that I have not come to Lincoln to assist you in any way. I have come solely to protect the women and children; the men can take care of themselves. I propose to go into camp within half a mile of the town. If my camp is attacked, or an officer or man killed or wounded from a shot fired by either party from any house, I shall demand the parties who did the firing be turned over to me, and in case of failure I shall request the women and children to leave the house, and I shall open fire on it with my howitzer, and arrest the parties in the house. I do not know what houses your party or McSween's occupy; I shall treat both parties exactly alike.[8]

The posse heard him out in silence. Plans had already been made to assault the McSween house. As the troops marched on, the possemen took up their assigned positions. Robert Olinger led a party into the Stanley house. John Hurley was sent to the Wilson jacal. Dolan moved into the Mills house. Peppin took position in the Torreon. Mathews, Gallegos, Jim Jones, and Perry entered the Schon residence.

Dudley went into camp about 300 yards east of the McSween house and about 30 yards from the Patron home, on property leased by Washington from Ellis. The men occupying Patron's house promptly abandoned it. The colonel ordered the howitzer trained on the door of the Montana building and sent Captain Blair to repeat his ultimatum to Chavez and to advise that the women and children should leave. Chavez soon led his men down to the Ellis home. Mrs. Montana then sent word to Dudley that she had prepared a room for him and his officers, but he replied that they would stay in camp. Dr. Appel was instructed to inform Ellis of the purpose of the troops. He soon returned to camp for some bandages for Ben Ellis, bringing Isaac with him so that the Colonel could talk with him personally.

Sergeant Andrew Keefe was ordered to tour the village and inform the people that the Army would give them protection if they would come to the camp. He found the plaza almost deserted; not more than a dozen families were still present.

Upon his return the Colonel sent him for Peppin. Dudley told the Sheriff that a number of the McSween supporters had congregated at Ellis', and suggested that they be headed off. After some delay Peppin, Jim Hurley, Robert Beckwith, John Jones, and Thornton ran down to the Ellis place. They found the defenders were riding off into the hills to the north of the town. Shots were exchanged and Jones was slightly wounded. While Peppin searched the house and store, Beckwith obtained a bucket of coal oil. As the men returned up the street, Dudley remarked disgustedly that they could have captured the men in the Montana house if they had come when he first sent for them.

About ten minutes after the troops went into Camp, McSween's seven-year-old niece brought the commanding officer a note:

> Would you have the kindness to let me know why soldiers sur-round my house. Before blowing up my property I would like to know the reason. The constable is here and has warrants for the arrest of Sheriff Peppin and posse for murder and larceny.[9]

To this Dudley ordered his adjutant, Lieutenant M. F. Goodwin, to reply that

> I am directed by the Commanding Officer to inform you that no soldiers have surrounded your house, and that he desires to hold no correspondence with you; if you desire to blow up your house, the commanding officer does not object providing it does not injure any U. S. soldiers.[10]

On receipt of this answer, Mrs. McSween decided to go to the camp and talk with Dudley personally.

"Colonel Dudley," she asked, "what is your object in bringing your troops to Lincoln?"

"Mrs. McSween, I am not aware that I have to report my movements to you. However, I am here simply to offer protection to women, children and non-combatants, and to prevent the wanton destruction of property."

"Then why do you not protect myself, my sister and her children?"

"I cannot protect them while they are in that house. Your sister or your husband or anyone else who comes to my camp will be given protection."

"Colonel Dudley, my husband and I hold you in high regard."

"I thank you, Madam, for the compliment," replied the officer lifting his hat.

"Will you not have the firing stopped so that I can remove my things from my house?"

"I am sorry, but I cannot interfere with the civil authorities. I understand that the sheriff has warrants for various parties, including your husband, and he must be the judge of the means to be used in serving them."

"I have been told that you are going to blow my house up."

"You have been misinformed. But that should not worry you much, since I have a letter from your husband stating that he is going to blow your house up himself."

"If you have received any such letter I do not believe that my husband wrote it."

"I will read it to you." The colonel stepped back into his tent, picked up the letter and read it aloud.

"I do not believe that my husband wrote that. Let me see the handwriting," exclaimed Mrs. McSween, reaching for the note.

"I will not trust you to handle it, because I believe you would tear it up if you had the chance," replied Dudley, stepping backward. "If your husband will surrender I will give you my word of honor as an officer that he will not be molested or hurt in any way. I will take him to the post and give him all the protection that I can."

"I must say one thing before I leave, Colonel," answered Mrs. McSween. "Your being in town with your troops looks a little too thin."

Dudley blinked. "Will you repeat that?"

"Your being in town with your troops today looks a little too thin."

"I do not understand such slang phrases, Mrs. McSween. The ladies with whom I am accustomed to associate do not use such language and I do not understand what you mean by 'too thin.' "

Mrs. McSween turned to leave, but paused to ask one more question. "Colonel, why do you have that cannon pointed at my house?"

"Madam, if you will look again you will see that it is pointed in the opposite direction."

"I believe you know more about guns than I do," Mrs. McSween laughed as she left the camp.[11]

Dudley sent for Justice of the Peace John B. Wilson and demanded that he issue a warrant for the arrest of McSween for the attempted murder of Private Robinson. Purington, Blair, and Appel accompanied the Justice back to his office to make the necessary affidavit, but Wilson returned to the camp and demurred that a writ for an offense involving

a soldier should he issued by a U. S. Commissioner. When the Colonel
became abusive and threatened to put him in irons if he did not issue
the paper promptly, Wilson went back to his office and prepared the
warrant. It was delivered to Sheriff Peppin, who appointed Bob Beckwith
a deputy sheriff and instructed him to serve it.

The sheriff then ordered the McSween's three colored servants,
Washington, Bates, and Joseph Dixon, to join the posse and carry lumber
to burn the McSween house. However, Washington, who had been captured at San Patricio, was exempted when Dudley objected that he was a
paroled prisoner. The combined Chavez-Ellis party now advanced over
a hill opposite the camp and started firing at the posse. The shots were
returned by a detachment of the posse led by Peppin, and the soldiers
turned the howitzer in their direction. When the attacking party saw
this, they ran back over the hill. They did not again appear on the scene,
although later on a group of six or seven men gathered opposite the
camp and fired promiscuously into the western end of town.

As the morning wore on, a group of about thirteen or fourteen men,
led by Deputy Sheriff Turner, made a dash to the front of the McSween
house, tried to pry the window sills off with their butcher knives, poked
their guns through the windows, and demanded that the defenders
surrender. Jim French replied that they had warrants in their guns for
all of the posse.

About half past one Long entered the besieged house and poured
the coal oil on the floor of the northeast kitchen (a part of the building
occupied by the Shield family) and the Dummy started a fire. This
burned out in about ten minutes. After leaving the house Long and the
Dummy came under heavy fire from the Tunstall store and were forced
to jump into the privy sink. Here they were shortly joined by Powell,
who had come under the defenders' sights while getting water. Boyle
was grazed along the neck by a bullet from the Tunstall marksmen, but
half an hour later piled a sack of shavings and chips and some kindling
thrown to him by Nash against the back door of the northwest kitchen
and succeeded in getting a fire started.

Gunfire became so heavy that Dudley and his men were forced to
seek refuge inside an unfinished adobe building just west of their camp.[12]
Dr. Ealy sent Miss Gates to ask Dudley for an escort of soldiers to remove
his personal property from his rooms in the Tunstall building, since he
had received word that it too would be burned. That ill-feeling may

have existed between the two men is suggested by the fact that she also brought a note to Appel, asking him to use his influence to obtain this favor. Appel, Blair, Goodwin, and three enlisted men went to the Ealy residence and removed a wagonload of goods. However, the soldiers reported to Dudley that Ealy had used "some threatening and impudent language"[13] to them, and he refused to permit them to return.* Around 5:30 that evening Dudley received letters from Mrs. Ealy (written on the advice of Appel) apologizing for her husband's conduct and asking for a guard to remove her family and Miss Gates from their home. A wagon was hitched up and Captain Blair and Dr. Appel, with five enlisted men, went up to the Tunstall building. Mrs. McSween requested the same protection from Blair, and with her sister, Mrs. Shield, and the latter's five children, the Ealy family and Miss Gates, was assigned quarters in the Patron house.

Appel then inquired of Washington, "George, can't you take me to some near place where we can see the fun?"[14, 15] Washington guided him to the Wilson jacal. Appel afterwards remarked feelingly, "I don't think I cared to get any nearer to the fight . . ."[15] Later claims were made that while attempting to escape from the burning house, members of the McSween party were fired upon by soldiers. In evaluating them it is important to remember that Appel was the only soldier out of the camp at the climax of the fight.

The fire burned down the west side, across the front and back up the east side of the McSween home. During the afternoon there was an explosion within the building and the fire began to gain rapidly. The house became a huge torch, lighting up the hills on both sides of the town. The occupants were driven into the sole remaining room, the northeast kitchen. Three choices were open to them: to burn, to make an attempt to escape, or to surrender. Bowers chose the first alternative. Unable to move, he preferred death in the burning building to surrender to the posse.

His fellows chose the second. About half an hour after dusk, the defenders burst from the house in two groups. The first group, including Antrim, Chavez y Chavez, French, O'Folliard, and Morris, dashed from the kitchen through the gate in the plank fence along the east side of the building, apparently bound for the Tunstall store. Morris was killed

*Editor's note: During the printing of this 1955 article, a number of errors were made in setting the footnotes. (The errors were reproduced in a 1997 anthology.) From note 13 on, the citations do not match the key numbers in the text.

just as he reached the gate. Three members of the posse suddenly appeared around the corner of the Tunstall building and fired almost point blank at the fleeing men. The fugitives turned toward the Rio Bonito and made their escape into the friendly darkness.

The second group, in which were McSween, Gonzales, Romero, Zamora, and Salazar, attempted to reach safety through the gate in the adobe fence on the north side of the house. Rifle fire from possemen concealed behind the wall was so heavy that they were driven back into the dark corner between the chicken house and the wood pile. About five minutes later they made a second attempt to reach the gate and were again repulsed. Two of the Mexicans sought shelter in the chicken house. The scene was set for what Boyle[16] later succinctly termed "the big killing."

After a pause of perhaps ten minutes, McSween called out, "Will you take us as prisoners?"

Beckwith answered, "I will. I came for that purpose but it seems necessary to kill you to take you."

"I shall surrender."

"I am deputy sheriff and I have a warrant for you." As Beckwith stepped forward, followed by Nash, John Jones, and The Dummy, McSween cried despairingly, "I shall never surrender!"[16, 17] Immediately a shot from the chicken house killed Beckwith. Retribution was so swift that McSween's body fell on top of Beckwith's. His men made another desperate attempt to escape, and this time some of them got through the gate and into the covering night. Nash and Boyle got a log, poked a hole into the chicken house, and demanded that the men in there surrender. They replied that they would not and had never intended to do so. Boyle then fired a few shots into the inside of the structure. It is not apparent from the evidence whether these men were Romero and Zamora, both of whom were killed at this stage of the fighting.

Salazar had been shot in two places and had fallen close to the adobe wall. Boyle gave him a couple of kicks and was about to add a finishing shot, but Pierce called to him, "Don't waste another shot on that damn greaser; he is already dead and we may need all our ammunition later on."[18] During the night Salazar crawled the thousand yards to the home of Jose Otero, where his sister-in-law, Nicolasita Pacheco, was staying.

About eight o'clock the firing died away. Beckwith's body was then taken up to the former Dolan-Riley store.[19] Dudley seems to have been much moved by his death. He wrote Hatch that Beckwith had been a gentleman well known in the country and recognized as one of the most upright, energetic, and industrious men of the community, who I believe lost his life in the conscientious discharge of loyal duty. He belonged to one of the best families in his section of the country, and his loss will be deplored by every good citizen, who had the good fortune to know him. I personally know that this slight tribute to his memory is equally appreciated by the Officers of my command and the citizens of this county.[20]

With his permission the body was interred at Fort Stanton with military honors, an action which the Judge Advocate of the Department of the Missouri later cited as a positive demonstration of partisanship.[21]

The following morning Justice Wilson convened a coroner's jury. The jury found that McSween, Morris, Zamora, and Romero "came to their deaths by rifle shots from the hands of the Sheriffs posse, while they the above named persons were resisting the Sheriffs posse with force and arms," and that Beckwith "came to his death by two rifle shots from the hands of the above named persons . . . in the discharge of his duty."[22] Peppin prepared to bury McSween, but Mrs. McSween hysterically forbade him to touch her husband's body. Dudley himself chased off the fowl who were pecking at the dead man's eyes and ordered the corpse covered with a quilt.

Kinney and three of his men noticed the blood stains Salazar had left on the ground and trailed him to the Otero house. They threatened to kill the wounded man, but left when Dr. Appel, who had answered a plea from Nicolasita, warned that if they harmed his patient he would personally see to it that all four were hanged. Justice Wilson was called and Salazar[23] executed an affidavit giving a brief account of the fight. This was supplemented by an "On Honor" statement prepared by Appel,[24] which contained additional information given by Salazar, including confirmation of the fact that Beckwith was killed only after McSween had agreed to surrender.

David M. Easton, the local business manager for Catron, had some Mexicans carry the bodies of McSween and Morris up to the Tunstall store. They were wrapped in blankets, placed in boxes, and buried near Tunstall and Huff without ceremony of any kind. On his arrival at the store Easton found that the door had been broken in and the merchandise was being carried off. Jessie Evans and Kinney were trying on new suits. Jake Owens was putting on hats. Boyle and others were looking for items which suited their fancy.

Easton sent for Sam Corbet, who was nominally in charge of the store, and Sheriff Peppin. The sheriff stated that he was almost powerless to stop the looting, but would assign a guard of two men to assist Corbet. Corbet, however, refused to remain at the store. Dudley and Appel came in and looked around. Appel told Corbet that he would have the looters arrested if he would swear out warrants, but Corbet said he was afraid that he would be killed if he did so. Easton and Corbet then nailed up the store and left.

About four o'clock that afternoon Dudley took his troops, with the exception of a small guard left for the protection of the Bacas and others who might care to avail themselves of it, back to Fort Stanton. With them went the Ealys and the Shield family. Dudley's undisguised contempt for Ealy made it impossible for them to stay at the Fort for any length of time, and about a week later these refugees left for Las Vegas.[25]

The five days of fighting had resulted in a decisive victory for the Dolan-Pepin forces, but Dudley took a somber view of the prospects for the future:

> One thing is sure, both parties are still determined, the fearful sacrafice of McSween's clique on the 19th inst does not seem to satisfy either side. A deep revenge will be sought by the sheriffs posse for the loss of their pet leader *Beckwith,* and if possible a still stronger spirit exists on the part of the McSween men to retaliate for the death of their headman, McSween. . . . Men who have the reckless courage to attack a building in bright mid-day, its walls forming a perfect protection, against any modern musketry to its inmates, pierced as this castle of McSween's was, with scores of loop holes for rifles on every side and angle, to say nothing of the flat roof, protected by a perfect wall of defence, and for hours hugging the walls, exposed to the fire of not only from the loop holes, but from the roof and adjacent buildings held by McSween men, charging this position across a space perfectly exposed to the fire of McSween's men for a distance of nearly three hundred yards, are not of a character to be easily induced to abandon a course they believe is only half completed. A similar remark can

be made of the party holding this structure, who held the same fortification for five days, the last nine hours gradually retreating from one room to another, as the heat compelled them to do what no amount of leaden missles from the rifles of the attacking party could do, and for an hour finally, all huddled in one room, nearly surrounded by the flames, some as it is claimed, preferred to being burnt rather than surrender to the Sheriffs posse. More desperate action than was exhibited on this unfortunate day by both sides is rarely witnessed.[26]

On the morning of the 21st Easton and Edgar Walz found a mob of Mexicans pillaging the Tunstall store. They claimed that they had been told by Mrs. McSween to take what they wanted. When Easton[27] asked Mrs. McSween about this, she replied, "I would rather have the Mexicans living on the creek have the goods than any of Peppin's gang of murderers."

"You can do as you please," Easton answered. "If you have any interest in having the goods saved I will aid you, but if the goods are to be allowed to be stolen by anyone I will go home."

"If you think the store will not be burned down and that the goods can be saved, I would be glad to have you help put the goods back," she replied.

Easton and Walz were able to recover some of the property and once more nailed up the doors and windows. That afternoon the store was again broken open. Corbet refused to come down, so Easton had Bates and Dixon nail it up again. Apparently it was not disturbed thereafter.

The question of why the Regulators, possessing the twin advantages of surprise and superiority in numbers, were so decisively defeated is an interesting one. The advantage of surprise was lost when they took up defensive positions instead of mounting an attack against the Sheriff's force before it could obtain reinforcements. The advantage of superiority in numbers was dissipated by the placement of the men in houses too widely dispersed to permit communications, co-operation and mutual support. . . .

That Long, Boyle, and The Dummy were able to enter the McSween house, set a fire and leave without interference and that Turner and his men were able to reach the very walls of the house and fire through the windows without the loss of a man indicates that the defense was not properly organized. The thirteen men still effective, aided by an enfilading fire from the Tunstall warehouse, should have been able to put up a better defense than they did.

The men at the Ellis house should certainly have been able to hold it against the Sheriff and his handful of possemen. Having abandoned this strongpoint, their failure to press home a determined assault to relieve their beleaguered companions permitted the moment of decision to pass to the posse. Even at the very climax of the battle, a diversionary attack from across the Rio Bonito could have driven Boyle and his party away from the adobe wall north of the McSween house and provided the defenders with an opportunity for a successful escape.

The arrival of Dudley and his troops tremendously increased the psychological pressure on the Regulators, but can hardly have been the decisive factor. The key to the problem is the fact that the comparatively large number of men originally posted in the homes of Montana, Patron, and Ellis took practically no part whatever in the fighting. Seizure of a large part of the village without any sort of a strategic plan for exploiting this move and the complete absence of tactical control over the various units into which the aggressive force was divided spell only one thing: a lack of competent leadership.

In spite of the partisan actions of Dudley, the rout of the McSween force appears to have resulted primarily from the fact that Dolan, Peppin, and his deputies provided more determined and effective leadership than was available to their opponents. McSween, like Tunstall, was ill equipped by nature and training for the role he aspired to play among the desperate men of Lincoln County. Their failure to recognize that the society of Lincoln County was one that would respond to the symbols of legal chicanery with gunfire[28] resulted in their own destruction and that of many of their followers. The end had been foreshadowed by the previous failure of the Regulators to win even a single victory in their clashes with the sheriff's posse.

NOTES

1. According to R. N. Mullin, Morris was a tubercular patient who was reading law with McSween.

2. According to the Tombstone *Prospector*, January 17, 1892, a lally cooler was three diamonds and a pair of clubs. It composed the highest hand in the deck, but could be played only once an evening.

3. A. A. McSween to Capt. Saturnino Baca, July 15, 1878.

4. N. A. M. Dudley to G. W. Peppin, July 16, 1878.

5. N. A. M. Dudley to Acting Assistant Adjutant General, District of New Mexico, July 16, 1878.

6. George W. Peppin to N. A. M. Dudley, July 16, 1878.

7. Joseph J. Smith to Howard Capper, July 19, 1878.

8. N. A. M. Dudley to Acting Assistant Adjutant General, District of New Mexico, July 20, 1878.

9. A. A. McSween to Gen. Dudley, July 19, 1878.

10. From testimony of Lieut. M. F. Goodwin at the Dudley Court of Inquiry, June 24, 1879.

11. This conversation is a composite from the testimony at the Dudley Court of Inquiry and is not to be understood as being verbatim.

12. R. N. Mullin believes that this building was being erected as a Presbyterian Church and school for the Rev. Dr. Ealy.

13. D. M. Appel "on Honor" statement, July 20, 1878; Mrs. T. F. Ealy to Dr. Appel, undated.

14. Testimony of George Washington at the Dudley Court of Inquiry, May 26, 1879.

15. Testimony of D. M. Appel at the Dudley Court of Inquiry, June 25, 1879.

16. Testimony of Andrew Boyle at the Dudley Court of Inquiry, June 17, 1879.

17. Testimony of Joseph Nash at the Dudley Court of Inquiry, June 18, 1879.

18. Miguel Antonio Otero, *The Real Billy the Kid*, New York: Rufus Rockwell Wilson, Inc., 1936, p. 126.

19. On January 19, 1878, U. S. District Attorney Thomas B. Catron, President of the First National Bank at Santa Fe, had accepted a mortgage on the store, its stock, 40 acres of land adjoining Lincoln on the west and 1500 cattle on Black River (near present day Carlsbad) to secure him for endorsing a Dolan-Riley note. When the partnership was dissolved by mutual consent on May 1, 1878, he sent his brother-in-law, Edgar A. Walz, to take over the store. Riley went out on Catron's cattle range near Seven Rivers and took no part in the fighting in Lincoln. Catron later sold the merchandise to J. C. Delaney who operated the store until the building was sold to Lincoln County in 1880. See Edgar A. Walz, *Retrospection*, Santa Fe: Privately printed, 1931, and J. W. Hendron, "The Old Lincoln Courthouse," *El Palacio*, XLVI: 1–18, January, 1939. Robert W. Beckwith, son of H. M. Beckwith and Refugia Pino Beckwith, was born October 10, 1850.

20. N. A. M. Dudley to Acting Assistant Adjutant General, District of New Mexico, July 20, 1878.

21. D. G. Swain to Assistant Adjutant General, Department of the Missouri, September 23, 1879.

22. Proceedings of Coroners Jury, July 20, 1878.

23. Affidavit of Hino Salacar [Yginio Salazar], July 20, 1878.

24. N. A. M. Dudley to Acting Assistant Adjutant General, District of New Mexico, July 23, 1878.

25. For subsequent events in the life of the Ealy family, see Ruth R. Ealy, "Medical Missionary II," *New Mexico Magazine*, 32:22 *et seq.*, April, 1954. Miss Gates married J. Y. Perea at Zuñi on December 25, 1878.

26. Testimony of David M. Easton at Dudley Court of Inquiry, May 21, 1879.

27. S. I. Hayakawa, *Language in Thought and Action*. New York: Harcourt, Brace and Company, 1949, pp. 196–197.

CHAPTER EIGHTEEN

In His Own Words (1)

Hard on the heels of his March 7, 1879, suspension (at the behest of Governor Lew Wallace) from command at Fort Stanton, Lt. Col. Nathan A. M. Dudley demanded a court of inquiry to clear his name with respect to accusations made against him in connection with his intervention—in defiance of the June 18, 1878, act of Congress that debarred the military from involvement in civil disturbances—in the street battle that ended with the July 19 firing of the McSween house and the death of McSween and five others. His request reached Washington coincident with a series of charges and specifications set forth by Susan McSween's lawyer, Ira E. Leonard, which included the murder of McSween, the burning of his home, the plundering of the Tunstall store, and the earlier slandering of Mrs. McSween.

Dudley's request was speedily granted, and the court of inquiry—not a court-martial but merely an examination of the charges leveled against him to establish whether they warranted a full military tribunal—was mounted. Proceedings opened on May 9, 1879 (the first witness to appear was Governor Wallace), and continued for most of that month; well over a hundred witnesses were summoned to appear. To clarify matters: the recorder (Capt. Henry H. Humphreys) was in effect the prosecutor, assisted by Lew Wallace's friend and amanuensis Ira E. Leonard. The "defense" was conducted by Santa Fe attorney (and paid-up member of the Santa Fe Ring) Henry L. Waldo, and the presiding officer or "judge" was Col. Galusha Pennypacker (who just happened to be a personal friend of the "defendant," Col. Dudley). Waldo and Humphreys presented their closing arguments on July 9, and on July 18, "after careful consideration and mature deliberation," the court found that Dudley was not guilty of the charges but that his actions had been prompted by "the most humane and worthy motives and by good military judgment." It was a whitewash, a perfect paradigm of the old saying that military justice is to justice as military music is to music.

William H. Bonney (acknowledging his nickname "the Kid" but not "*Billy* the Kid") appeared as a witness on the afternoon of May 28 and in the morning of the following day. Although his testimony, confined by the court to the events of July 19, is pretty bloodless, it is one of the rare documents that actually give us some indication of the Kid's personality and how he spoke. What a shame they didn't have video recorders in those days!

Court of Inquiry Rooms Fort Stanton, N.M.

May 28, 1879

18th day

10 AM Court met pursuant to adjournment:

Present:

Col. G. Pennypacker, 16th Infantry. Major N. W. Osborne, 15th Infantry. Captain H. R. Brinkerhoff, 15th Infantry. Captain H. H. Humphreys, 15th Infantry, Recorder.

WILLIAM BONNEY, a witness being duly sworn, testified as follows.

Q. BY RECORDER: What is your name and place of residence?

ANSWER: My name is William Bonney. I reside in Lincoln.

Q. BY RECORDER: Are you known [as] or called Billy Kidd, also Antrim?

ANSWER: Yes Sir.

Q. BY RECORDER: Where were you on the 19th day of July last and what, if anything, did you see of the movements and actions of the troops in that city, state fully?

ANSWER: was in the McSween house in Lincoln, and I saw soldiers come from the post with [the] sheriff's party, that is the sheriff's posse joined them a short distance below there, the McSween house. Soldiers passed on by and the men dropped off and surrounded the house, the sheriff's party. Shortly after the soldiers came back with Peppin, passed the house twice afterwards. Three soldiers came and stood in front of the house, in front of the windows. Mr. McSween wrote a note to the officer in charge asking what the soldiers were placed there for. He replied saying that they had business there, that if a shot was fired over his camp, or at Peppin, or at any of his men, that he had no objection to blowing up, if he wanted, his own house. I read the note myself, he handed it to me to read. I read the note myself. I saw nothing further of the soldiers until night. I was in the back part of the house. When I escaped from the house three soldiers fired at me from the Tunstall store, outside corner of the store. That's all I know in regards to it.

Q. BY RECORDER: Did the soldiers that stood in front of the windows have guns with them while there?

ANSWER: Yes Sir.

Q. BY RECORDER: Who escaped from the house with you and who was killed at the time, if you know, while attempting to make their escape?

ANSWER: Jose Chavez escaped with me, Vincente Romero, Francisco Zamora and McSween.

Q. BY RECORDER: How many persons were killed in that fight that day, if you know, and who killed them, if you know?

ANSWER: I seen five killed, I could not swear to who killed them, I seen some of them that fired.

Q. BY RECORDER: Who did you see that fired?

ANSWER: Robert Beckwith, John Hurley, John Jones, those three soldiers, I don't know their names.

Q. BY RECORDER: Did you see any persons setting fire to the McSween house that day, if so, state who it was, if you know?

ANSWER: I did, Jack Long, and there was another man I did not recognize.

Recorder stated he had finished with the witness.

Cross examination:

Q. BY COL. DUDLEY: What were you, and the others there with you, doing in McSween's house that day?

ANSWER: We came here with Mr. McSween.

Q. BY COL. DUDLEY: Did you know, or had you not heard, that the sheriff was endeavoring to arrest yourself and others there with you at the time?

ANSWER: Yes Sir. I heard so, I did not know.

Q. BY COL. DUDLEY: Then were you not engaged in resisting the Sheriff at the time you were in the house?

ANSWER: *Objected to by Recorder.* The Court has already ruled that nothing extraneous from the actual occurrence that took place, and Col. Dudley's actions in connection therewith, should be further inquired into and nothing has been called out to the witness to authorize this mode of cross examination, it cannot be a matter of defense to Col. Dudley or justify his actions however much the parties may have been resisting the sheriff or civil authorities.

Col. Dudley, by his Counsel, states he does not deem it necessary to make a reply to the objection. Objection sustained.

Q. BY COL. DUDLEY: Were you in the habit of stopping and visiting at the house of McSween before that time?

ANSWER: Yes Sir.

Q. BY COL. DUDLEY: In addition to the names you have given, are you also known as the "Kid"?

ANSWER: I have already answered that question, Yes Sir, I am, but not "Billy Kid" that I know of.

Q. BY COL. DUDLEY: Were you not and were not the parties with you in the McSween house on the 19th day of July last and the immediately preceding, engaged in firing at the sheriff's posse?

ANSWER: *Court objects to the question.* Lt. Col. Dudley, by his Counsel, ask[s], does the Court intend to rule here, that after [having] gone into this matter of firing into the McSween house by testimony of this witness, it is not permissible to show all circumstances under which this firing took place, as a part of the *res gestae* [the events relating to the case], and to leave it so far as this witness is concerned [it is] as though the firing into the house was without cause or excuse. It is asked for information in order to guide us in the further examination of this witness.

Court cleared and closed.

Court opened and its decision announced. Col. Dudley and his Counsel and Mr. Ira E. Leonard and witness being present.

The Court directs the case to proceed, calling attention to its previous rulings which were deemed sufficiently explicit.

Q. BY COL. DUDLEY: What time of day was it when you escaped from the house?

ANSWER: About dusk.

Q. BY COL. DUDLEY: Whose name was signed to the note received by McSween in reply to the one previously sent by him to Col. Dudley?

ANSWER: Signed N.A.M. Dudley, did not say what rank, he received two notes, one had no name signed to it.

Q. BY COL. DUDLEY: Are you as certain of everything else you have sworn to as you are to what you have sworn to in answer to the last proceeding question?

Ira E. Leonard, Governor Lew Wallace's "right-hand man" in Lincoln. In 1881, he was Billy the Kid's defense counsel in the first of his two trials at La Mesilla. Courtesy Sidney Leonard Gardner.

ANSWER: Yes Sir.

Q. BY COL. DUDLEY: From which direction did Peppin come the first time the soldiers passed with him?

ANSWER: Passed up from direction of where the soldiers camped [i.e., east to west], the first time I saw him.

Q. BY COL. DUDLEY: What direction did he come from the second time?

ANSWER: From the direction of the hotel from the McSween house.

Q. BY COL. DUDLEY: In what direction did you go upon your escape from the McSween house?

ANSWER: Ran towards the Tunstall store, was fired at, and there turned towards the river.

Q. BY COL. DUDLEY: From what part of the McSween house did you make your escape?

ANSWER: The Northeast corner of the house.

Q. BY COL. DUDLEY: How many soldiers fired at you?

ANSWER: Three.

Q. BY COL. DUDLEY: How many soldiers were with Peppin when he passed the McSween house each time that day, as you say?

ANSWER: Three.

Q. BY COL. DUDLEY: The soldiers appeared to go in company of threes that day, did they not?

ANSWER: All that I ever saw appeared to be three in a crowd at a time after they passed the first time.

Q. BY COL. DUDLEY: Who was killed first that day, Bob Beckwith or McSween men?

ANSWER: Harvey Morris, McSween man, was killed first.

Q. BY COL. DUDLEY: How far is the Tunstall building from the McSween house?

ANSWER: I could not say how far, I never measured the distance. I should judge it to be 40 yards, between 30 and 40 yards.

Q. BY COL. DUDLEY: How many shots did those soldiers fire, that you say shot from the Tunstall building?

ANSWER: I could not swear to that on account of firing on all sides, I could not hear. I seen them fire one volley.

Q. BY COL. DUDLEY: What did they fire at?

ANSWER: Myself and Jose Chavez.

Q. BY COL. DUDLEY: Did you not just now state in answer to the question who killed Zamora, Romero, Morris, and McSween that you did not know who killed them, but you saw Beckwith, John Jones, and three soldiers fire at them?

ANSWER: Yes Sir. I did.

Q. BY COL. DUDLEY: Were these men, the McSween men, there with you when the volley was fired at you and Chavez by the soldiers?

ANSWER: Just a short ways behind us.

Q. BY COL. DUDLEY: Were you looking back at them?

ANSWER: No Sir.

Q. BY COL. DUDLEY: How then do you know they were just behind you then, or that they were in range of the volley?

ANSWER: Because there was a high fence behind, and a good many guns to keep them there. I could hear them speak.

Q. BY COL. DUDLEY: How far were you from the soldiers when you saw them?

ANSWER: I could not swear exactly, between 30 and 40 yards.

Q. BY COL. DUDLEY: Did you know either of the soldiers that were in front of the window of McSween's house that day. If so, give it?

ANSWER: No Sir, I am not acquainted with them.

Redirect:

Q. BY RECORDER: Explain whether all the men that were in the McSween house came out at the same time when McSween and the others were killed and the firing came from the soldiers and others?

ANSWER: Yes Sir, all came out at the same time. The firing was done by the soldiers until some had escaped.

Recorder stated he had finished with the witness.

Q. BY COL. DUDLEY: How do you know, if you were making your escape at the time and the men Zamora, Morris and McSween were behind you, that they were killed at that time, is it not true that you did not know of their death or the death of either of them until afterwards?

ANSWER: I knew of the death of some of them, I did not know of the death of one of them. I saw him lying down there.

Q. BY COL. DUDLEY: Did you see any of the men last mentioned killed?

ANSWER: Yes Sir, I did, I seen Harvey Morris killed first, he was out in front of me.

Q. BY COL. DUDLEY: Did you not then a moment ago swear that he was among those who were behind you and Jose Chavez when you saw the soldiers deliver the volley?

ANSWER: No Sir, I don't think I did. I misunderstood the question if I
   did. I said that he was among them that was killed and not behind me.
Witness then withdrew.

*The Court adjourned at 4.10 p.m., to meet again on Thursday, May 29, 1879
at 10 a.m.*

CHAPTER NINETEEN

The Capture of Billy the Kid

James H. East

In 1920, down on his luck and hoping to make some extra money, Charles A. Siringo put together yet another version of the story of Billy the Kid. Little more than a rehash of stories he had told earlier in *A Texas Cow Boy* and *A Lone Star Cowboy*, his short, privately printed *History of "Billy the Kid"* was beefed up a little by a some new—and probably invented—tales based on their "intimate acquaintance." It is much more notable for containing a vivid firsthand account of the deaths of Tom O'Folliard and Charlie Bowdre and the capture of the Kid— events Siringo regretted having missed throughout his life—written by Jim East, one of the six men who had been with Pat Garrett's posse in December 1880.

Born in Kaskaskia, Illinois, James Henry East (1853–1930) was fifteen when he went to Texas and became a cowboy. In 1880 he went to work for Bates and Beal on the LX Ranch below Tascosa, and was one of the men sent by their fore-man ,W. C. "Outlaw Bill" Moore, to help Garrett capture the Kid. He makes it quite clear that such an assignment was all in a day's work. "Some writers," he said many years later, "have had a good deal to say about us Texans 'bringing law to the Pecos.' After these long years I don't believe Garrett's posse from Tascosa thought much about establishing the law. We were just an ordinary bunch of cowpunchers—not professional 'gunmen'—working for $30 per mo. and told to go down to the Pecos and try to recover cattle strayed or stolen and incidentally to get any rustlers that came in the way. Didn't get many cattle but some of the rustlers."

In November 1882, East succeeded Cape Willingham as sheriff of Oldham County and sixteen other attached Texas counties, a high-risk job he held for four years, which included involvement in the infamous moonlit midnight gun battle that exploded in Tascosa on March 21, 1886. East also killed gambler Tom Clark in another shooting at that place in 1890. He later opened a detective agency in

Amarillo, and then moved to Douglas, Arizona, where he became chief of police for two years and also served as a city judge. His memoir is all the more valuable because shortly before his death, East burned all the letters and other documents he had saved throughout his life with a view to writing his autobiography.

In order to get a true record of the capture of "Billy the Kid" and gang, the author wrote to James H. East, of Douglas, Arizona, for the facts. Jim East is the only known living participant in that tragic event. His reputation for honesty and truthfulness is above par wherever he is known. He served eight years as sheriff of Oldham County, Texas, at Tascosa, and was city marshal for several years in Douglas, Arizona.

Herewith his letter to the writer is printed in full:

Douglas, Arizona
May 1st, 1920

Dear Charlie

Yours of the 29th received, and contents noted. I will try to answer your questions, but you know after a lapse of forty years, one's memory may slip a cog. First: We were quartered in the old Government Hospital building in Ft. Sumner, the night of the first fight. Lon Chambers was on guard. Our horses were in Pete Maxwell's stable. Sheriff Pat Garrett, Tom Emory, Bob Williams, and Barney Mason were playing poker on a blanket on the floor. I had just laid down on my blanket in the corner, when Chambers ran in and told us that the "Kid" and his gang were coming. It was about eleven o'clock at night. We all grabbed our guns and stepped out in the yard.

Just then the "Kid's" men came around the corner of the old hospital building, in front of the room occupied by Charlie Bowdre's woman and her mother. Tom O'Phalliard was riding in the lead. Garrett yelled out: "Throw up your hands!" But O'Phalliard jerked his pistol. Then the shooting commenced. It being dark, the shooting was at random.

Tom O'Phalliard was shot through the body, near the heart, and lost control of his horse. "Kid" and the rest of his men whirled their horses and ran up the road.

O'Phalliard's horse came up near us, and Tom said: "Don't shoot any more, I am dying." We helped him off his horse and took him in, and laid him down on my blanket. Pat and the other boys then went back to playing poker.

James Henry East about the time he wrote his account of the capture of the Kid. Courtesy Hazel M. White.

I got Tom some water. He then cussed Garrett and died, in about thirty minutes after being shot.

The horse that Dave Rudabaugh was riding was shot, but not killed instantly. We found the dead horse the next day on the trail, about one mile or so east of Ft. Sumner.

After Dave's horse fell down from loss of blood, he got up behind Billy Wilson, and they all went to Wilcox's ranch that night.

The next morning a big snow storm set in and put out their trail, so we laid over in Sumner and buried Tom O'Phalliard.

The next night, after the fight, it cleared off and about midnight, Mr. Wilcox rode in and reported to us that the "Kid," Dave Rudabaugh, Billy Wilson, Tom Pickett, and Charlie Bowdre had eaten supper at his ranch about dark, then pulled out for the little rock house at Stinking Spring. So we saddled up and started about one o'clock in the morning.

We got to the rock house just before daylight. Our horses were left with Frank Stewart and some of the other boys under guard, while Garrett took Lee Hall, Tom Emory and myself with him. We crawled up the arroyo to within about thirty feet of the door, where we lay down in the snow. There was no window in this house, and only one door, which we would cover with our guns.

The "Kid" had taken his race mare into the house, but the other three horses were standing near the door, hitched by ropes to the vega poles.

Just as day began to show, Charlie Bowdre came out to feed his horse, I suppose, for he had a moral* in one hand. Garrett told him to throw up his hands, but he grabbed at his six-shooter. Then Garrett and Lee Hall both shot him in the breast. Emory and I didn't shoot, for there was no use to waste ammunition then.

Charlie turned and went into the house, and we heard the "Kid" say to him: "Charlie, you are done for. Go out and see if you can't get one of the s—of-b——'s before you die."

Charlie then walked out with his hand on his pistol, but was unable to shoot. We didn't shoot, for we could see he was about dead. He stumbled and fell on Lee Hall. He started to speak, but the words died with him.

Now Garrett, Lee, Tom and I, fired several shots at the ropes which held the horses, and cut them loose—all but one horse which was half way in the door. Garrett shot him down, and that blocked the door, so the "Kid" could not make a wolf dart on his mare.

---

*Editor's note: morral, Sp.: a nosebag.

We then held a medicine talk with the Kid, but of course couldn't see him. Garrett asked him to give up, Billy answered: "Go to h—l, you long-legged s— of a b——!"

Garrett then told Tom Emory and I to go around to the other side of the house, as we could hear them trying to pick out a port-hole. Then we took it, time about, guarding the house all that day. When nearly sundown, we saw a white handkerchief on a stick, poked out of the chimney. Some of us crawled up the arroyo near enough to talk to "Billy." He said they had no show to get away, and wanted to surrender, if we would give our word not to fire into them, when they came out. We gave the promise, and they came out with their hands up, but that traitor, Barney Mason, raised his gun to shoot the "Kid," when Lee Hall and I covered Barney and told him to drop his gun, which he did.

Now we took the prisoners and the body of Charlie Bowdre to the Wilcox ranch, where we stayed until next day. Then to Ft. Sumner, where we delivered the body of Bowdre to his wife. Garrett asked Louis Bousman and I to take Bowdre in the house to his wife. As we started in with him, she struck me over the head with a branding iron, and I had to drop Charlie at her feet. The poor woman was crazy with grief. I always regretted the death of Charlie Bowdre, for he was a brave man, and true to his friends to the last.

Before we left Ft. Sumner with the prisoners for Santa Fe, the "Kid" asked Garrett to let Tom Emory and I go along as guards, which, as you know, we did.

The Kid made me a present of his Winchester rifle, but old Beaver Smith made such a roar about an account he said "Billy" owed him, that at the request of "Billy," I gave old Beaver the gun. I wish now I had kept it.

On the road to Santa Fe, the "Kid" told Garrett this: That those who live by the sword, die by the sword. Part of that prophecy has come true. Pat Garrett got his, but I am still alive.

I must close. You may use any quotations from my letters, for they are true. Good luck to you. Mrs. East joins me in best wishes.

Sincerely yours,

JAS. H. EAST

The author had previously written to Jim East about "Billy the Kid's" sweetheart, Miss Dulcinea del Toboso. Here is a quotation from his answer, of April 26, 1920:

"Your recollection of Dulcinea del Toboso, about tallies with the way I remember her. She was rather stout, built like her mother, but not so dark.

The Santa Fe, New Mexico, County Jail, on Water Street, ca. 1880. The Kid, along with Dave Rudabaugh, Billy Wilson, and others, was incarcerated in this dump from December 27, 1880, through March 28, 1881, the last month in solitary confinement. The site is now a parking lot. Courtesy Museum of New Mexico, negative no. 10276.

"After we captured 'Billy the Kid' at Arroyo Tivan, we took him, Dave Rudabaugh, Billy Wilson, and Tom Pickett—also the dead body of Charlie Bowdre—to Fort Sumner.

"After dinner Mrs. Toboso sent over an old Navajo woman to ask Pat Garrett to let 'Billy' come over to the house and see them before taking him to Santa Fe. So Garrett told Lee Hall and I to guard 'Billy' and Dave Rudebough over to Toboso's, Dave and 'Billy' being shackled together. As we went over the lock on Dave's leg came loose, and 'Billy' being very superstitious, said: 'That is a bad sign. I will die, and Dave will go free,' which, as you know, proved true.

"When we went in the house only Mrs. Toboso, Dulcinea, and the old Navajo woman were there. Mrs. Toboso asked Hall and I to let 'Billy' and Dulcinea go into another room and talk awhile, but we did not do so, for it was only a stall of 'Billy's' to make a run for liberty, and the old lady and the girl were willing to further the scheme. The lovers embraced, and she gave 'Billy' one of those soul kisses the novelists tell us about, till it being time to hit the trail for Vegas, we had to pull them apart, much against our wishes, for you know all the world loves a lover. It was December 23rd, 1880, when the 'Kid' and gang, Dave Rudebaugh, Tom Pickett and Billy Wilson—were captured, and Charlie Bowdre killed.

"The prisoners were taken to the nearest railroad, at Las Vegas, where a mob tried to take them away from the posse, to string them up. They were placed in the County jail at Santa Fe, the capital of the Territory of New Mexico, as the penitentiary was not yet completed. Dave Rudebaugh was tried and sentenced to death for the killing of the jailer in Las Vegas. Later he made his escape and has never been heard of since."

CHAPTER TWENTY

In His Own Words (2)

By far the most complete word picture we have of the Kid by an eyewitness—and one only a year or two older than he—was written by Lucius M. "Lute" Wilcox, city editor for the *Las Vegas Gazette,* who interviewed Billy outside that city's jail on Monday, December 27, 1880. The Kid, Dave Rudabaugh, and Billy Wilson had been brought into Las Vegas under heavy guard the preceding day by Pat Garrett and his deputies—Barney Mason, Jim East, Tom Emory, Frank Stewart, Louis Bousman, et al.—and were about to be taken to the depot, where a train was waiting to take them to Santa Fe. While making no apologies in his behalf, the two-part interview (Wilcox talked to Billy again just before the train pulled out for Santa Fe) is one of the very few sympathetic hearings the Kid seems ever to have had, and contrasts violently with the word pictures of him painted by writers who never actually saw him or spoke to him.

It is all the more surprising, then, that six months later, on June 2, 1881, Wilcox (clearly cashing in on having actually talked to the now-notorious Kid) was telling the *Kansas City Evening Star* a much more sensational tale. The Kid, he claimed, had been a New York bootblack who killed his first man in Ohio, and had boasted of having dispatched a total of thirty-six in all. He was a "tin can artist" who could "throw a can into the air and keep it there with shots while he fired twelve bullets at it," who "never uses the double action revolver . . . a peculiarity I never could explain." Wilcox obviously felt qualified to add that Billy "seems to court newspaper notoriety and enjoys reading the account of his atrocious work. He is a slender young fellow, lantern jawed, rather shabby in his appearance from long sojourn on the plains, has clear blue eyes. No one would ever imagine murder lurked behind them."

Born in western Pennsylvania in 1858, Lucius Merle Wilcox had printer's ink in his veins. He began his education at age twelve as a printer's devil in the office of the *Elle County Democrat* in Ridgeway, Pennsylvania, and other local papers. He was a reporter for the *Cleveland (Ohio) Leader* from ca. 1875 until 1878 and for the

Denver Tribune from 1878 to 1879; editor of the *Trinidad (Colo.) Daily News* from 1879 to 1880; and then city editor for the *Las Vegas (N.Mex.) Daily Gazette* from 1880 to 1885, when he relocated to Denver and established the magazine *Field and Farm* with Capt. L. W. Cutler. On June 18, 1890, Wilcox married Henrietta Stiles of Washington, Indiana; after losing his sight that same year, he became president of the United Workers for the Blind of Colorado, a post he held for ten years. He continued to publish *Field & Farm* until 1920 and was also the author of a number of books, among them *Irrigation Farming* (1895) and *Frontier Sketches* (1902). He died in 1925.

THE KID: INTERVIEW WITH BILLY BONNEY—
THE BEST KNOWN MAN IN NEW MEXICO

With its accustomed enterprise the GAZETTE was the first paper to give the story of the capture of Billy Bonney, who has risen to notoriety under the sobriquet of "the Kid," Billy Wilson, Dave Rudabaugh, and Tom Pickett. Just at this time everything of interest about the men is especially interesting and after damning the party in general and "the Kid" in particular, through the columns of this paper we considered it the correct thing to give them a show.

Through the kindness of Sheriff Romero, a representative of the GAZETTE was admitted to the jail yesterday morning.

Mike Cosgrove, the obliging mail contractor, who has often met the boys while on business down the Pecos, had just gone in with four large bundles. The doors at the entrance stood open and a large crowd strained their necks to get a glimpse of the prisoners, who stood in the passageway like children waiting for a Christmas tree distribution. One by one the bundles were unpacked disclosing a good suit of clothes for each man. Mr. Cosgrove remarked that he wanted "to see the boys go away in style."

"Billy, the Kid" and Billy Wilson who were shackled together stood patiently up while a blacksmith took off their shackles and bracelets to allow them an opportunity to make a change of clothing. Both prisoners watched the operation which was to set them free for a short while, but Wilson scarcely raised his eyes and spoke but once or twice to his compadre. Bonney, on the other hand, was light and chipper and was very communicative, laughing, joking and chatting with the bystanders.

"You appear to take it easy," the reporter said.

"Yes! What's the use of looking on the gloomy side of everything. The laugh's on me this time," he said. Then looking about the placita, he asked "is the jail at Santa Fe any better than this?"

Las Vegas, New Mexico, ca. 1884. Tunstall, the McSweens, and John Chisum were visitors to Wagner's Hotel (*left*). J. Evetts Haley Collection, Haley History Center, Midland, Texas.

This seemed to trouble him considerably, for, as he explained, "this is a terrible place to put a fellow in." He put the same question to every one who came near him and when he learned that there was nothing better in store for him, he shrugged his shoulders and said something about putting up with what he had to.

He was the attraction of the show, and as he stood there, lightly kicking the toes of his boots on the stone pavement to keep his feet warm, one would scarcely mistrust that he was the hero of the "Forty Thieves" romance which this paper has been running in serial form for six weeks or more.

"There was a big crowd gazing at me wasn't there," he exclaimed, and then smilingly continued, "Well, perhaps some of them will think me half man now; everyone seems to think I was some kind of an animal."

He did look human, indeed, but there was nothing very mannish about him in appearance, for he looked and acted a mere boy. He is about five feet eight or nine inches tall, slightly built and lithe, weighing about 140; a frank open countenance, looking like a school boy, with the traditional silky fuzz on his upper lip; clear blue eyes, with a roguish snap about them; light hair and complexion. He is, in all, quite a handsome looking fellow, the only imperfection being two prominent front teeth slightly protruding like squirrel's teeth, and he has agreeable and winning ways.

A cloud came over his face when he made some allusions to his being made the hero of fabulous yarns, and something like indignation was expressed when he said that our Extra misrepresented him in saying that he called his associates cowards. "I never said any such a thing," he pouted. "I know they ain't cowards."

Billy Wilson was glum and sober, but from underneath his broad-brimmed hat, we saw a face that had a by no means bad look. He is light complexioned, light haired, bluish-gray eyes, is a little stouter than Bonney, and far quieter. He appeared ashamed and not in very good spirits.

A final stroke of the hammer sent the last rivet on the bracelets and they clanked on the pavement as they fell.

Bonney straightened up and then rubbing his wrists, where the sharp edged irons had chafed him, said: "I don't suppose you fellows would believe it but this is the first time I ever had bracelets on. But many another better fellow has had them on too."

With Wilson he walked towards the little hole in the wall to the place, which is no "sell" on a place of confinement. Just before entering he turned and looked back and exclaimed: "They say, 'a fool for luck and a poor man for children'—Garrett takes them all in."

We saw him again at the depot when the crowd presented a really warlike appearance. Standing by the car, out of one of the windows of which he was leaning, he talked freely with us of the whole affair.

"I don't blame you for writing of me as you have. You had to believe others' stories; but then I don't know as any one would believe anything good of me anyway," he said. "I wasn't the leader of any gang—I was for Billy all the time. About that Portales business, I owned the ranch with Charlie Bowdre. I took it up and was holding it because I knew that sometime a stage line would run by there and I wanted to keep it for a station. But, I found that there were certain men who wouldn't let me live in the country and so I was going to leave. We had all our grub in the house when they took us in, and we were going to a place about six miles away in the morning to cook it and then 'light' out. I haven't stolen any stock. I made my living by gambling but that was the only way I could live. They wouldn't let me settle down; if they had I wouldn't be here today." And he held up his right arm on which was the bracelet. "Chisum got me into all this trouble and then wouldn't help me out. I went up to Lincoln to stand my trial on the warrant that was out for me, but the territory took a change of venue to Dona Ana, and I knew that I had no show, and I skinned out. When I went up to White Oaks the last time, I went there to consult with a lawyer, who had sent for me to come up. But I knew I couldn't stay there either."

The conversation then drifted to the question of the final round-up of the party. Billy's story is the same as that given in our Extra, issued at midnight on Sunday.

"If it hadn't been for the dead horse in the doorway I wouldn't be here. I would have ridden out on my bay mare and taken my chances of escaping," said he. "But I couldn't ride out over that, for she would have jumped back, and I would have got it in the head. We could have staid in the house but there wouldn't have been anything gained by that for they would have starved us out. I thought it was better to come out and get a good square meal—don't you?"

The prospects of a fight exhilarated him, and he bitterly bemoaned being chained. "If I only had my Winchester, I'd lick the whole crowd," was his confident comment on the strength of the attacking party. He sighed and sighed again for a chance to take a hand in the fight and the burden of his desire was to be set free to fight on the side of his captors as soon as he should smell powder.

As the train rolled out, he lifted his hat and invited us to call and see him in Santa Fe, calling out adios.

CHAPTER TWENTY-ONE

The Kid's Escape!

On Thursday, April 28, 1881, Billy the Kid escaped from confinement in the Lincoln County courthouse (formerly the Murphy-Dolan store), killing the two deputies—James W. Bell and Robert Olinger—who had been assigned to guard him. Almost instantly he became the subject of headline news all across America. The immediacy of his sudden celebrity was, for the time and place, astonishing: within eighteen days of the story's appearance in the *Santa Fe Daily New Mexican*, the (surprisingly accurate) details of the escape appeared in the *National Police Gazette* of New York under the headline "BILLY THE KID'S EXPLOIT," and in other newspapers all over the country.

Here, however, are the first "eyewitness" accounts of the events of that bloody day to have appeared in print, from which, by and large, all subsequent accounts have been derived. The first news appears to have arrived in the territorial capital by telegram from Socorro on April 30, just two days after the escape; the next segment is the *New Mexican*'s editorial overview of events. However, it is the last two letters in the final paragraphs headlined "Gone Again" that contain the meat and potatoes. Note how specific the report from Lincoln is about the time of day these events took place, and the fact that the Kid fired both barrels of Olinger's shotgun simultaneously, while the version arriving only shortly thereafter is already beginning to alter small details. Terse, concise, and dramatic, these few hundred words from unknown hands swiftly became an inseparable part of the legend of Billy the Kid. What is amazing is how long it took for them to be incorporated into the historical record.

THE KID'S ESCAPE!

—

Full Details Of His Escape
From Jail At Lincoln

—

The Shooting of His Guards
With Their Own
Weapons

——

Desperation Unto Death, with
The Coolness of a Turpin.

——

His Threats of Revenge Upon
Sheriff Garrett and
Others

——

General Alarm Throughout
The Country

——

Mingled With Sorrow for
The Dead Guards

——

THE PARTICULARS OF THE KID'S ESCAPE

Special Correspondence of the New Mexican

FORT STANTON, N. M.,
April 30, 1881

EDITOR NEW MEXICAN:

The particulars of the escape of the notorious "Billy the Kid," are about as follows: Robert Ollinger and J. M. Bell were the two guards. The former had just gone to his supper, and Bell was sitting down on the floor, when "Kid" approached him, talking in his pleasant way. Quick as lightning he jumped and struck Bell with his handcuffs, fracturing the skull. He immediately snatched Bell's revolver and shot him through the breast. Ollinger, hearing the shot, ran from the house where he was eating supper (about seventy-five yards away) and just as he entered a small gate at the end of the house where "Kid" was confined, the latter, being in an upper story window, said, "Look out Bob," and immediately after fired a charge of buckshot into him, killing him instantly. "Kid" then went and made a man, who was in the corral of the house, saddle a horse for him; which being done, he jumped on and rode away, saying, "Adios, boys!" He has repeatedly threatened different men's lives since his arrest, and every person believes that he will put his threats into effect. The day before he escaped he said: "People thought me bad before; but if ever I should get free, I'll let them know what bad means."

A DESPERADO AT LARGE

It is doubtful if any event could excite a keener public interest in this Territory than that which was reported by a meagre telegram from Socorro, Saturday evening—the escape of William Bonny, better known as the "Kid," from the jail where he was incarcerated awaiting the day of his execution, set for May 13th. The surprise and alarm were heightened by the sad intelligence that he had killed two of his guards, who were both well known throughout the Territory as brave men and intrepid officers, to whose special keeping he had been entrusted. The circumstances of the escape as they have now come to hand exhibit a subtle calculation on the part of the prisoner, and a coolness and steadiness of nerve in executing his plan of escape, that the highly wrought story of Dick Turpin can hardly furnish a counterpart to.

A mere boy—he is but 22 years of age and almost diminutive in size—he has made a record which the oldest criminal in the country can scarce equal, not alone for the number of his offenses against the law, but for the heinousness of the crimes he has committed. For months he was a terror to Lincoln county, his name on every tongue, and his adventures the theme of general conversation; and when he was finally captured by Sheriff Garrett, it afforded a sense of relief to every citizen of the county—and of the Territory as well.

The number of crimes for which he might be tried was really an embarrassment to the court, in determining which should take precedence. When it was decided, the trial occupied but a brief time, the verdict of guilty was promptly rendered and the sentence pronounced. He was taken under strong guard to Lincoln, and it was determined to protect him from lynch law of which there was some apprehension, at all hazards. He was safely delivered there and was treated with more than due consideration by the men whom he did not hesitate to kill to effect his escape.

The threatened revenge which he has made from time to time against sheriff Garrett and others who were specially offensive to him naturally occasions no small share of uneasiness now that he is at large and at liberty to execute his threats if he shall so incline.

GONE AGAIN

The New Mexican's extras proclaimed yesterday the particulars of the escape of Billy, the "Kid" from the Lincoln county jail on Friday evening, the announcement of which was made in Sunday morning's issue. The account was read eagerly by everybody, and particularly by the hundreds of friends of the men who fell victims to the daring outlaw, and created a feeling which was a mixture of astonishment at the absolute recklessness of the deed, and earnest sorrow for the fate of Ollinger and Bell. The details of the distressing affair are given in a letter written from Lincoln, which reads as follows:

Last evening between 5 and 6 o'clock deputy sheriff J. W. Bell was left to guard the "Kid" while the rest went to supper. Kid was kept under guard in one of the upper rooms of the Murphy building. He had shackles on his ankles, and a pair of handcuffs locked (both) on one wrist, leaving one free. Those who went to supper were eating in the coffee-house, nearly opposite and about seventy-five yards distant. A single report of fire-arms upstairs at the house where "Kid" and Bell were left, alarmed the party. Bob Olinger seized his hat and ran over. As he entered the side gate— at [the eastern] end of, and a little in front of the building, a voice from above attracted his attention. He looked up halting as he did so, and Kid fired both barrels of a double-barrelled shotgun (Bob's own gun). The weapon was heavily charged with buck shot, which fell into Bob's heart. He fell forward dead. Kid then broke the gun over the sill and threw the fragments at Bob's dead body, saying as he did so: "You damned son of a bitch, you won't corral me with that again."

Bell lay dead in the back yard with one bullet through him and two gashes on his head, apparently cut by a blow from the handcuffs. It is supposed that Kid caught him off his guard, stunned him by a blow from his handcuffs, seized his revolver and shot him. Bell then ran down stairs and fell in the yard, dying instantly. The "Kid" then kicked open an adjoining door, where the arms were locked up, took six rifles

Ameredith Robert Olinger with James J. Dolan, ca. 1879. A fighter for the Murphy-Dolan faction during the Lincoln County troubles, Olinger—who loathed the Kid as much as the Kid loathed him—died like a dog when the Kid cut him down during his jailbreak at Lincoln on April 28, 1880. Robert G. McCubbin Collection.

into the front porch (above); compelled some one to throw him a hammer or hatchet, broke his shackles, ordered a horse brought to the door, and rode off, taking with him four revolvers and a Winchester rifle. Sheriff Pat Garrett was at White Oaks. Through the courtesy of the commanding officer at Fort Stanton a coffin and the post ambulance was sent for Bob's remains, and they will be buried in the cemetery there to-morrow.

This is terrible and the Kid is free with his threats of murder thick in the air. He said, I understand, that he wanted to live long enough to kill Governor Wallace, or as he put it, "that damned old son of a bitch Wallace." He cannot be too vigilantly on his guard. Kid has also threatened Garrett and if he can effect his death Lincoln county will be remanded to the worst reign of terror it has yet had.

Republicans complain of the Democratic posse comitatus act. Will they give us anything better? I am too nervous to write more. I feel terribly over Bob's death. He was my friend, the friend of law and order and the peace of the commonwealth.

The following letters to the NEW MEXICAN also contain some further particulars in regard to the affair.

WHITE OAKS, New Mexico, April 30, 1881

EDITOR NEW MEXICAN:——Two United States deputies were killed at Lincoln with their own weapons, on the evening of the 28th by Billy the Kid who succeeded in making his escape by snatching a six shooter from the scabbard of J. W. Bell, United States deputy in charge. Getting the drop on Bell he ordered him to surrender. Bell refused and was shot dead. Goss a man in rear of building in which the Kid was confined hearing the shots ran out to the side of the building, meeting Bob Olinger another United States deputy. Bob had been at supper and was about to enter the building. Goss said "Kid has killed Bell." The words had no more than passed his lips when a shot was heard and Olinger threw up his hands, and fell dead with the remark: "Yes and he has killed me too." It proved too true; Olinger fell dead. The Kid then coming down into the street ordered Mr. Goss to saddle up Billie Burt's horse, which was standing in the court house yard, which Goss did. Kid mounted the horse, but the horse bucked, throwing the Kid. The Kid who seemed to have charge of the town ordered his horse caught which was done. He remounted making a success this time, with a pleasant farewell to the bewildered by-standers the Kid rode towards Fort Stanton. He expressed himself as being sorry for

killing Bell but said he had to do it to make his point. There is great excitement in this camp over the Kid's escape. Sheriff Pat Garrett is here, he leaves
to-night to hunt Kid's trail. After Kid had killed Olinger with his (Olinger's)
double barreled shot gun he broke the gun in two pieces throwing the pieces at
Olinger. The Kid had fired upon him from the porch remarking as he did so
"there you son of a b—— you will never follow me again."

WHITE OAKS, N. M., April 30, 1881

EDITOR NEW MEXICAN,——Dear Sir: There is no further news in regard
to the "Kid's' escape. All former reports are confirmed. Pat Garrett, with Mr.
[William] Goodlett, a former deputy in Colfax county leave to-day to strike
"Kid's" trail. He says he will follow him to the end. J. W. Bell's body will be
brought here for burial. Bob Ollinger will be buried at Ft. Stanton.

The above is the record of as bold a deed as those versed in the
annals of crime can recall. It surpasses anything which the Kid has ever
been guilty of so far that his past offenses lose much of their heinousness in comparison with it, and it effectually settled the question as to
whether the Kid is a cowardly cut throat or a thoroughly reckless and
fearless man. Never before has he faced death boldly or run any great
risk in the perpetration of his bloody deeds. Bob Ollinger used to say
that he was a cur and that every man he had killed had been murdered
in cold blood and without the slightest chance of defending himself.
The Kid displayed no disposition to correct this idea until this last act
of his, when he taught Ollinger by a bitter experience that his theory
was anything but correct. When the Kid left Mesilla for Lincoln he was
accompanied by a very strong guard including some of the most reliable men in the Territory, and every precaution was taken to render
him absolutely secure. Bob Ollinger was called aside by a gentleman
from Santa Fe and privately warned of the danger which the custody of
the Kid placed him in. "You think yourself" said the man alluded to, "an
old hand in the business, capable of guarding successfully any prisoner.
You are brave, ready with your weapons, and able to cope with any man
almost with or without firearms. You have guarded many prisoners, and
faced danger many a time in apprehending them, and you think that
you are invincible and can get away with anything. But I tell you, as
good a man as you are, that if that man is shown the slightest chance on

earth, if he is allowed the use of one hand, or if he is not watched every moment from now until the moment he is executed, he will effect some plan by which he will murder the whole of you before you have time to even suspect that he has any such intention."

This earnest caution produced only a smile upon the face of the self-reliant guard, who answered that there was no more chance for the "Kid's" escape than there was for his going to heaven. He would be closely guarded all the time, and had men about who were brave and determined. Bob's warning was almost prophetic. If the supposition in regard to the manner in which the prisoner got the best of Bell is correct, the deed was almost a fulfilment of the prediction. The fact that both handcuffs were locked on one wrist, indicates that the guards had allowed the prisoner that freedom of the hand which Ollinger was warned would prove fatal.

It is said in regard to the career of Bonny, that he was first led to adopt the life of an outlaw by reading dime novels. He is only twenty-two years old now, and when he first "turned out" was a mere boy thirsting for notoriety as a desperado. He has been very successful in achieving this, and stands at the top of the ladder of fame, a fit subject for a novel himself. There is no information in regard to the course pursued by the authorities of Lincoln county, nor of any steps taken to re-capture the prisoner, and nothing which would indicate in what direction he has gone has been received here. It is supposed that he will make his way into old Mexico if possible, as it will be remembered he and Rudabaugh were endeavoring to do when they and their comrades were captured at Stinking Springs.

CHAPTER TWENTY-TWO

Facts Regarding the Escape of Billy the Kid

Leslie Traylor

Other than that he was a keen supporter of J. Marvin Hunter's magazine *Frontier Times,* and an amateur historian much like Robert N. Mullin who covered a lot of the same ground, nothing much is known about Leslie Traylor. This article appears to have been his only contribution to the Kid literature. Bearing in mind the relative obscurity of the magazine in which it was published, however, it was a surprisingly influential one. While there are many demonstrably incorrect statements—"Goss" didn't hack off the Kid's leg shackles with an ax; Yginio Salazar died in 1936, not 1935; Olinger and Bell, whose first name (rather than his job) Traylor seems to think was Guard, were not buried behind the old courthouse, nor were their remains disinterred and taken to Seven Rivers; Charlie Foor wasn't in Fort Sumner in 1881; Garrett didn't kill Billy with a .44 Winchester; and so on—some of the "facts" that Traylor harvested from his 1933 and 1935 interviews with Yginio Salazar, Ramon Maes, and Francisco Salazar in Lincoln, and Vicente Otero, Francisco Lovato, Jesus Silva, and Charlie Foor in Fort Sumner were destined to become inextricably entangled in the (then) post-Burns burgeoning of the legend of Billy the Kid.

Naively accepting at face value everything he had been told—things in some cases quite possible, and in others simply out of the question—Traylor presented his findings as "proof" that Garrett's account of the Kid's escape and how James Bell died was badly flawed; that the Kid was planning to kill himself if he was unable to escape; that Sam Corbet had appeared as a witness for the prosecution at the Kid's trial; that Billy had two children who both died of diphtheria; that he was warned by both Vicente Otero and Juan Patron that Garrett was nearby during the day he was killed; that Poe and McKinney were "hidden" so as not to frighten Billy off; that Garrett killed the Kid with a .44 Winchester; and so on.

Traylor also offered for the first time—officially, as it were—the wishful suggestion that someone other than the Kid had been killed in Pete Maxwell's room that July night in 1881. (Of course, in 1936, when this piece appeared, it was entirely possible that, if indeed he had not been killed in 1881, the Kid might still be alive.) Most of this was soon forgotten, but three of Traylor's propositions—that the Kid killed Bell and Olinger at midday and not late in the afternoon; that Sam Corbet concealed a pistol in the outside privy behind the old courthouse to facilitate the Kid's escape; and, most seductive of all, that perhaps he hadn't been killed at all—had a powerful and lasting effect upon the legend that persists to the present day.

While on a trip through the west during the summers of 1933 and 1935, I decided I would visit Lincoln, New Mexico, county seat of Lincoln county, the scene of the Lincoln county war, and also Fort Sumner, New Mexico, which is about seven miles up the Pecos river from old Fort Sumner, as I had read several books on the exploits and death of Billy the Kid. So it was my pleasure to visit the quaint little city of Lincoln, nestling in the Rio Bonito valley on the Rio Bonito river, some 5,700 feet above sea level, sixty miles west of Roswell, New Mexico, there to visit the scene of the three day's battle at Lincoln, and to converse with the people who knew something about its history, as well as the true facts regarding the escape of W. H. Bonney, commonly known as Billy the Kid.

At Fort Sumner, New Mexico, where I also visited, still live a number of the people who knew Billy the Kid, and with some of them I conversed in both Spanish and English about the notorious desperado. Many versions have been written about how the Kid killed his guards, how he secured the pistol that sent a bullet through Guard Bell's heart, as to where Bell died, whether at the foot of the stairs in the Lincoln county court house, or in the corral back of the court house, whether the guards were killed during the noon hour, or as to whether they were killed late in the afternoon, as to what route Billy took on leaving Lincoln for his final farewell. I believe I have gathered some data, that will throw some light on many doubtful incidents, and I shall recite the different stories as to how Billy escaped, also quote a dispatch sent out of New Mexico, as well as stories told by Billy and his friends.

One of the first dispatches sent out of Santa Fe, New Mexico about Billy's dramatic escape is as follows:

From Galveston, (Texas) News, May 11, 1881:

Chicago, May 3rd:—A telegram from Santa Fe, New Mexico says:—
Full particulars of the escape of Wm. Bonney, alias "Billy the Kid,"

on April 30th last, from the jail in Lincoln county have reached here. The Kid was in charge of Bob Alinger [*sic*] and J. W. Bell, deputy sheriffs, cool and brave men. It seems, however, that by docile behavior, the prisoner put them off guard. On the evening of the day in question, Alinger had gone to supper, leaving Bell to watch the prisoner. Bell was sitting on the floor talking when the Kid, who was heavily shackled and handcuffed, approached him pleasantly and suddenly jumped at him with the swiftness of a wild cat, hitting him on the head and fracturing his skull. He then snatched Bell's pistol and shot him in the breast. Bell ran down the steps and fell at the foot a corpse—the Kid kicked open the door, procured a hatchet and knocked off his shackles. He also broke open the door of the armory and took possession of several guns and pistols. Bob Alinger, hearing the shot, left his supper and ran toward the jail. When entering a gate leading through the jail fence, the Kid, who was upstairs, shot him with a gun loaded with buck shot, killing him instantly. The town of Lincoln seemed terror stricken, and nobody thought of opposing the Kid. He stole a horse and rode off armed with four revolvers and a Winchester rifle. He has expressed a determination to kill Governor Lew Wallace, who failed to pardon him, and who, by a curious coincidence, signed the Kid 's death warrant at Santa Fe on the same day that he escaped at Lincoln. [*end quote*]

In 1933, I talked with Higinio Salazar, now deceased, and who participated in the three day's battle at Lincoln in 1878, and who was a bosom friend of Billy, on leaving the McSween home at night during the fight, was shot down in front of the door with four others. However, later during the night Salazar crawled away to safety, recovering from his wounds and lived until some time in 1935.

When I interviewed him in 1933 he was living two or three miles above Lincoln on the Rio Bonito and he told me a similar story told in "The Saga of Billy the Kid," as to how Billy secured the gun while playing cards with Guard Bell, and later shooting Bell as he ran down the steps. Salazar talked with Billy the Kid the night of the day Billy made his escape, Billy telling about his escape, having slept in the woods near Higinio Salazar's residence, Higinio furnishing him a blanket for the night. Another story that Billy told about his escape was to Mr. Francisco Lovato of Fort Sumner, New Mexico, and who is living at the present time at the age of 75 years, and with whom I conversed during the summers of 1933 and 1935. Billy told his friend that while he and Bell were coming up the stairs in the Lincoln county court house that as he reached the top of the stairs, he had one hand free from the handcuffs and that he turned around just as Bell reached the top of the stairs and struck Bell on the head with the handcuffs, stunning him and taking his gun away from him; that he asked Bell to surrender but Bell would not do so; that he shot Bell, who fell dead at the foot of the stairs. Mr. C. W. Foor, a veteran frontiersman of Fort Sumner, N.M. who is still living at the age of 86 years, told me that he once asked Pete Maxwell what Billy had to say about the killing of Guard Bell, and he replied that Billy asked Bell to loosen the handcuffs, as they were hurting him, that Billy held his hands as high as his face, that when Bell took out the key to loosen them a little, and as Bell was turning to walk away he slipped his right hand out of the handcuffs, grabbed Bell's gun as quick as lightning and shot him on the spot without saying a word. Billy told Pete Maxwell that he hated to kill Bell, but it was a case of Bell dying or him dying.

I will now discuss Pat Garrett's theory as to how Billy the Kid secured his gun, killing Guard Bell and Bob Ollinger. During the summer of 1935 I left Roswell, N.M. for Lincoln, N.M., in company with Mr. Ogle Underwood of Roswell, who works for the Bus Company running in and out of Roswell, and on our way to Lincoln I told him in my opinion it was almost impossible for Bell to have been shot as Pat Garrett stated in his book, "The Authentic Life of Billy the Kid." If Mr. Garrett made any mistakes as to how Bell was killed we can account for them more or less by him being excited on his return to Lincoln after his two deputies had been killed, and he and his posse taking the trail of Billy immediately, and for the fact that he was undergoing a terrible mental strain, also he was probably being misinformed by someone. My friend and I parked the car in front of the old Lincoln county court house, then crossed to the opposite side of the street to the La Paloma Bar, owned by Ramon Maes, who has the keys to the old abandoned court house. Maes knows the present inhabitants of Lincoln as well as being acquainted with the names of the old inhabitants who helped to make history in Lincoln county, and it was from him that I was enabled to learn many facts in regard to the Lincoln county war.

Mr. Underwood and I looked through the old court house, then we sat down and read Mr. Garrett's theory as to how Billy secured the gun and killed Guard Bell. The securing of the gun seems reasonable, but as to what part of the body Bell was shot in, and as to how, did not seem reasonable. In advancing his theory Mr. Garrett says: "At the Kid's request Bell accompanied him downstairs and into the back corral where was the jail latrine. As they returned, Bell, who was inclined to be rather easy going in his guarding of the Kid, allowed the latter to get considerably in advance. As the Kid turned on the landing of the stairs he was concealed from Bell, and being very light and active, he bounded up the stairs, turned to the right, pushed open with his shoulder the door of the room used as an armory, which, though locked, was easily opened by a firm push, entered the room, seized a six-shooter, and returned to the head of the stairs just as Bell faced him on the landing of the stairway, and some twelve steps beneath. The Kid fired and Bell, turning, ran out into the corral in the direction of the little gate, but fell dead before reaching it."

In another part of the story Mr. Garrett says: "It was found that Bell was hit under the right arm, the ball passing through the body and going out under the left arm. On examination it was evident that the Kid had made what was for him a very poor shot, and that his hitting Bell at all was a lucky accident. The ball had hit the wall on Bell's right, then caromed, and passed through his body, and buried itself in the adobe wall on his left." Bell and Ollinger were buried near the court house before Mr. Garrett arrived at Lincoln, and later the remains were disinterred and taken to Seven Rivers, N.M., so evidently Mr. Garrett received his information as to what part of the body Bell received the fatal wound from some one in Lincoln. The populace of Lincoln, as well as many old timers will tell you that Bell was shot through the heart, the bullet passing through the breast and shoulder. The hole where the bullet was imbedded in the adobe wall is at the foot of the stairway, and on the far side from the top of the stairs, also it is above the shoulders of the height of an average man. We found no signs of where a bullet had caromed. If Bell, on entering to go up the stairway had been shot as he faced Billy the Kid, whether the Kid was at the top of the stairs or near the bottom, Bell would have been shot through and through, from front to back, and the bullet hole would have been a foot or more lower than it was. If Billy had shot Bell from the top of the stairs, and Bell had been about three steps from the top, then Bell's breast, or any person of average height would have been in line with

Billy, and the bullet hole, in the adobe wall which is at the foot of the stairway, and on the far side in the center. So we reached the conclusion that if Bell had been shot while on the stairway, he was almost at the top of the stairs when he was killed.

The people of Lincoln all agree that Ollinger was shot from a window on the east side of Billy's room, upstairs, just after Ollinger entered the gate of the court house yard, as he was coming to the court house to see what had happened. Some say the Kid shot him with both barrels at once, with Ollinger's shot gun, others say the Kid later went out on a balcony and shot him with the other shell left in the gun. After investigating Mr. Garrett's theory as to how the Kid secured the pistol, and as to how he killed Bell, we went to see Ramon Maes again for information. He advised us to see Francisco Salazar, who came to live in Lincoln after Billy escaped, and before visiting him we saw a few of the old historic houses, one of them the Juan Patron saloon and store, which is vacant, and is in charge of a man who lives just across the street, who was a child when Billy the Kid made his dramatic escape, but he does not remember the Kid. However, he will gladly show any one where Billy carved the letters "KID" on the right side of the door as you enter the old Patron building. There are the initials of two other persons underneath, but the caretaker does not know what they stand for. The old McSween store is still standing today, and back of the store between the outside of the wall of the corral and the river bank are buried the bodies of McSween, Chapman, Tunstall, and Morris, who helped make history for Lincoln county, New Mexico. We visited Francisco Salazar and were courteously received. There we ascertained that he had married one of the daughters of Captain Satur[n]ino Baca, one of the first settlers of Lincoln county. Captain Baca was sitting on his porch when Sheriff Brady passed by and saluted him. Only a few moments later Sheriff Brady lay dead in the streets of Lincoln, a victim of the bullets of Billy the Kid and his crowd.

We asked Salazar how Billy secured the gun that killed Guard Bell, and we were told his brother-in-law, Bonifacio Baca, told him that Sam Corbett left the gun in the jail latrine for the Kid, that when the Kid and Bell went to the jail latrine during mid-day, when Ollinger had the other prisoners across the street for their mid-day meal, the noted desperado secured the gun and concealed it on his person, and in returning to the guard room the Kid was naturally in the lead, and as he ascended

William Brady, ca. 1870. Sheriff of Lincoln County, partisan supporter of the Murphy-Dolan party, he was assassinated by six or seven of the "Regulators" (one of whom was the Kid) in Lincoln on April 1, 1878. It was for this murder that the Kid was sentenced to be hanged. Author's Collection.

the stairway, that on reaching the top he quickly turned around and shot Bell through the heart, who was near the top of the stairway. Bell tumbled down the stairs and lay at the base, and when found there by the people of Lincoln he was a corpse. It can easily be understood now why the Kid told different versions about getting the gun that killed Bell. He did not want to make trouble for the man who was instrumental in him securing the gun that kept him from being hung, therefore he was obligated to protect the man who helped him escape. Sam Corbett was at one time the postmaster of Lincoln, N.M., and having married one of the daughters of Captain Satur[n]ino Baca, was a brother-in-law of Bonifacio Baca. He left Lincoln more than thirty years ago, and has never been heard from since. Bonifacio Baca and Sam Corbett were witnesses for the Territory of New Mexico against Billy the Kid when he was tried for the murder of Sheriff Brady. Francisco Salazar said that Bonifacio Baca kept a diary and had a great deal of data in it pertaining to Lincoln county, and that he no doubt had an account of the escape of Billy the Kid, and as to how he secured the gun that killed Bell. A man once came to Lincoln that was interested in Lincoln county and its history; he met Bonifacio Baca who showed him the diary, and on gaining the confidence of Baca, took his book that contained the diary, and it was understood that a book was to be written; that Bonifacio and the writer would share the profits equally, but it was not long until the man wrote Mr. Baca that his diary had been destroyed by fire. If this valuable diary has not been destroyed, then whoever has it should surrender it to the Baca family. Billy the Kid was placed in the Lincoln county court house under guard on April 21, 1881, making his dramatic escape on April 28, 1881, after having killed his guards during the noon hour. Some people say the Kid escaped at supper time, or late in the afternoon, but the people of Lincoln, as well as many old timers, say the guards were killed during the mid-day meal. Such men as Higinio Salazar, deceased, George Coe, author of "A Frontier Fighter," Francisco Salazar, at present living in Lincoln, and brother-in-law of Bonifacio Baca and Francisco Gomez, who lives on the outskirts of Lincoln, [and claims he] saw Billy the Kid about 2 p.m. at his father-in-law's house the day Billy made his dramatic escape. As to whether Bell died at the foot of the stairs or in the corral, I was told by Higinio Salazar that Billy the Kid said Bell died at the foot of the stairs; also Francisco Gomez and Francisco Salazar of Lincoln corroborate what [Yginio] Salazar told me.

Before making his escape Billy commanded a man by the name of Goss, who worked around the court house at Lincoln, to cut the chain that connected the shackles on his legs. He placed the chain over a piece of wood and Mr. Goss cut it with an axe while Billy sat down with a pistol in his hand to see that it was well done. After cutting the chain Mr. Goss was commanded to saddle a horse from the stable belonging to Billy Burt, deputy clerk of the probate court. The horse was named Collie and was a horse that always bucked a little when mounted by a rider, and when Billy mounted him he was thrown to the ground.

Billy hadn't had the natural use of his legs for four months, as his legs had been shackled, so when he mounted the horse he was naturally awkward and fell off. Some writers say that the Kid rode several miles up the Rio Bonito Canyon before he left the canyon for a farewell view of Lincoln; but it is a mistake. When leaving Lincoln he went up the river on the left hand side about one-fourth of a mile, riding through the wheat field of Ataviano [Octaviano] Salas, to his house. Francisco Gomez, the son-in-law of Ataviano Salas, is living today in Lincoln and he says that when Billy rode up to his father-in-law's place, he, Gomez, was living on his father-in-law's place at that time, and Billy was asked, "Why are you riding through my wheat field?" Billy then answered, "Wait a minute, give me a drink of water or a cup of coffee." He was given a cup of coffee with goat's milk in it. Then Billy said, "I have just killed two birds down in town." Then Francisco Gomez said, "What have you done?" "I have killed my guards," answered Billy. Gomez says it was about 2 p. m. when Billy came to his father-in-law's house. From there Billy crossed the canyon to the right hand side and went through Spring Canyon, formerly called Baca Canyon, which is about half a mile above Lincoln. Stopping there a short while at the home of Jesus Padilla, he went to the home of Jose Cordova, where Cordova and Sepio [Scipio] Salazar removed the shackles from his legs. Then Billy went to the home of his old friend Higinio Salazar, who lived in Las Tablas, where he was furnished bed clothing by Salazar to sleep nearby in the woods, and in about two days Billy made his way in the direction of old Fort Sumner where he remained nearby on different ranches for a time.

History records that Wm. H. Bonney was killed on July 14, 1881, at 11:30 p. m. at old Fort Sumner, N.M. in the room of Pete Maxwell by Pat Garrett, sheriff of Lincoln county, New Mexico. Ever since then, from time to time, and up to the present, there have been rumors that

Billy the Kid was not killed, and today there are old frontiersmen who maintain that Billy is still living. If he is still living, then it is only a question of time until the controversy will be settled.

The coroner's jury at Fort Sumner pronounced the Kid dead on July 15, 1881. People who have visited Lincoln to satisfy their curiosity should also visit Fort Sumner, New Mexico, as they will find people there who knew Billy the Kid well, and will tell you true stories about him that have never appeared in a book and probably never will. A number of old time residents in Fort Sumner that I met and talked to, and heard their stories from their own lips, amazed me. One of the most interesting characters that I met was Don Vicente Otero, who was born in Valencia, N.M., and who died at the age of 95 years during February, 1935. Otero told me he was a good friend of Billy the Kid, and I told him in Spanish what my mission was, and he gladly told me that he would be pleased to talk with me about his old friend Billy.

Otero stated that he was working on a ranch for Pete Maxwell, south of old Fort Sumner, when one day as he was riding into Fort Sumner, he saw Pat Garrett and some other men near Fort Sumner; that he recognized Garrett, but they did not speak to one another. Garrett, he said, was looking through a telescope and he naturally thought of the predicament that his friend Billy was in as he rode into Fort Sumner.

He met Billy the Kid on the street and told him that Pat Garrett was nearby, but Billy seemed to be unconcerned and did not take his advice seriously. Otero also told me that Juan Patron of Lincoln, N.M., had advised the Kid of Garrett's arrival nearby. On Otero's return to the ranch he saw Garrett again and he thought of returning to advise the Kid again, but was in fear that Garrett might think he was returning to advise the Kid, so he continued on to the ranch. This statement by the old veteran was made in the presence of his stepson, Francisco Lovato, who is still living at the age of 75 years, and Pete Lovato, the son of Francisco Lovato.

This true story has been handed down from generation to generation. Francisco Lovato and his son will tell you that Pat Garrett and Billy the Kid had been good friends, that before Pat Garrett married Billy skinned cattle and sold the hides in order to help pay for the wedding of his friend Garrett. Billy, after killing his two guards in Lincoln, visited a ranch near Lake La Title [Little Tule?], about 30 miles east of old Fort Sumner. While on the ranch he told his friend that while he was a prisoner at Lincoln waiting to he hung, he was determined that they should never hang him, that he did not care much about death, but he only wanted a chance to get a gun and fight it out with his guards, and his chance finally came when he took the gun away from Bell and shot him through the heart. Billy said he was prepared to die with strychnine, as he had a bottle of it concealed on his person, that he did not wish to give his enemy, Robert Ollinger, the pleasure of seeing him hung.

Another interesting old character living at Fort Sumner today is Jesus Silva, who was a servant at the Maxwell home, and was present during the night of the tragedy; he is eighty-five years old and is now almost blind, but is able to walk around his home, and when I saw him last in the summer of 1935 he was in his yard feeding his chickens. He told me his story of the tragedy as he knew it, stating that the night Billy the Kid was killed that he and Billy had been together, and had been drinking beer, that they did not know any one was near enough to hear them talking. Billy told him he was hungry, so Silva said he told the Kid that a calf had been killed that day, and that the meat was hanging on the porch, that he could go and get some of it. Billy decided to go and get some of the meat, going in a circuitous route to Pete Maxwell's room. Pat Garrett and his men were not over fifteen feet away he says, when the conversation took place, and he stated that Garrett told him the next day that he could have killed the Kid then, but was afraid of getting the wrong man, and as he knew that the Kid was going to Maxwell's room, he, Garrett, took a direct route to Maxwell's room and got ahead of the Kid, telling Pete Maxwell to keep quiet and not to say anything, as the Kid would be there shortly to get permission to get some meat. When the Kid came to the door and was entering, Garrett was sitting on Pete Maxwell's bed, and he shot the Kid with a forty-four Winchester killing him instantly. Silva said that he was at home when he heard the shot, and they sent for him, that when he arrived they were afraid to go into the room, and as he knew the Kid well and was not afraid, he went in with a light and found him dead, lying face downward with a pistol in one hand and a butcher knife in the other. Silva says he prepared the body for burial, and he told me Billy did not bleed much until he was preparing his body for burial. I asked him where Garrett's deputies were when Billy came to Maxwell's room and he replied that they were instructed to conceal themselves so they would not frighten the Kid when he came to Maxwell's room.

Mr. C. W. Foor, who is living at the present time in Fort Sumner, came to old Fort Sumner to live about September, 1881. He and a number of

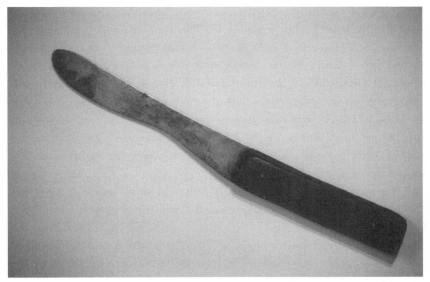

The butcher knife the Kid was carrying the night he was killed. Robert G. McCubbin Collection. Photograph by the author.

other citizens erected a suitable granite monument to Billy and his two pals, Thomas O'Folliard and Charles Bowdre, the monument being in the old Fort Sumner burial ground about one-third of a mile east of the old fort.

When Mr. Foor and I visited the old cemetery in 1933, the vandals had begun to chip off pieces of the monument as souvenirs and I suggested to Mr. Foor that the monument should be protected in some way. He told me on my last visit to Fort Sumner that he had taken up the matter with some of the officials at Fort Sumner, but that nothing had been done about it.

Mr. Foor will tell you, as far as he was able to ascertain, that Billy the Kid was the father of two little girls, one of them is incidentally referred to in "The Saga of Billy the Kid," by Walter Noble Burns. This child was born about the fall of 1879, the other child having been born in the early part of 1882. Mr. Foor says both of the little girls died about 1887 with diphtheria, within forty-eight hours of one another, and were buried in the old cemetery near old Fort Sumner, which cemetery is now usually referred to as Hell's Half Acre. During the summer of 1935 I visited the old cemetery accompanied by Francisco Lovato, his son

Pete, and a friend of theirs who was accommodating enough to furnish us transportation in his automobile. The old cemetery was originally surrounded by an adobe wall, but now it is surrounded by a wire fence, the entrance being on the north side as before. Lucian [Lucien] B. Maxwell, the cattle king and father of Pete Maxwell, is buried in the old cemetery, but the exact site of his grave is unknown. His son Pete died in 1898 and there is a monument erected to his memory, supposedly near where his father is buried. The monument to Billy the Kid and his pals is badly defaced where Billy's name appears; the vandals are still chipping off pieces of stone.

I was told by Pete Lovato that his father helped Vicente Otero bury the remains of Thomas O'Folliard and Chas. Bowdre, who were killed in December, 1880, by Pat Garrett and his men, and that his father said that O'Folliard and Bowdre were not buried by the monument erected to the three pals, but were buried to the left of the entrance to the cemetery by the side of the old adobe wall, and now where the fence is. After viewing the monument to Billy and his pals, I asked Francisco Lovato where O'Folliard and Bowdre were buried and he said, "Come with me and I will show you." We walked back to the entrance and he pointed out what appeared to be a dim outline of two graves alongside of the fence and an equal distance from it. He said, "Somewhere by the side of this fence they were buried." Regardless of where the three pals were buried the monument serves its purpose just the same.

In reference to certain incidents pertaining to the escape and death of Billy the Kid, the writer has tried to weigh all obtainable evidence, and has come to the conclusion that Billy the Kid did not take the gun away from his guard that caused the death of his two guards but obtained a pistol from a friend who concealed it in the jail latrine; that on reaching the top of the stairs in the Lincoln county court house, he shot Guard Bell through the heart, who was near the top of the stairs; that his two guards were killed during the mid-day lunch hour; that after leaving Lincoln, he left Rio Bonito Canyon through Spring Canyon, about one-half a mile above Lincoln; that his two friends, O'Folliard and Bowdre, were not buried where the monument to the three pals is, but buried about forty feet or more away from the monument; that Billy the Kid was notified of the close proximity of Pat Garrett and his two deputies by his friends, Vicente Otero and Juan Patron; that Garrett's two deputies were not on the front porch of the Maxwell home when the tragedy occurred, but were concealed nearby as instructed by their chief; and that there are reasons to doubt that W. H. Bonney was the person killed in Pete Maxwell's room on the night of July 14th, 1881.

CHAPTER TWENTY-THREE

The Killing of Billy the Kid

John W. Poe

John William Poe (1851–1923) was born in Kentucky. He left home when he was seventeen and by 1871 was working on a construction crew for the Atchison, Topeka & Santa Fe Railroad. By the time he was twenty, he was hunting buffalo on the plains of west Texas, and later—without a single killing—he was an effective and admired town marshal at Fort Griffin, no small achievement in so tough a frontier settlement. In 1879 he was appointed a deputy U.S. marshal, stationed at Fort Elliott in the Texas Panhandle. He ran for sheriff when Wheeler County was organized, but lost the election to Henry Fleming by one vote. Cattle theft was rampant, but Poe so successfully reduced it that when the Panhandle Stockmen's Association was formed, he was appointed to look after their interests. It was while employed in this work that he was sent to New Mexico with "practically unlimited authority to act for and represent them," to use his own words, "with the view of suppressing and putting an end to the wholesale raiding and stealing of cattle, which had been and was then carried on by Billy the Kid and his gang of desperadoes."

He reached Lincoln County in March 1881 and headed straight for White Oaks, a new and booming mining town. There he met Pat Garrett, who told him the Kid was safe in jail (albeit not in Lincoln, as Poe has it), and who, after Poe had explained his business, swore him in as a deputy and sent him to Tombstone to trace some Panhandle cattle that had been driven there. Poe got back to White Oaks on the same April day the news reached there that the Kid had escaped from jail in Lincoln, killing his guards. He and Thomas C. "Kip" McKinney were Garrett's backup deputies at Fort Sumner the night the Kid was killed.

The following year, Poe and Garrett had a falling-out over a land transaction that terminated their friendship, if such it ever was. In the election that same year, Garrett was a candidate for the Territorial Council, and Poe for sheriff of Lincoln County. Poe was elected but Garrett was not, and the defeat did nothing to heal the breach between them. Poe served very successfully for two years before turning his energy to ranching. In 1883 he married Sophie Alberding; there were no children. The rift between Poe and Garrett widened further in 1890; when Garrett decided to run for sheriff of newly created Chaves County, Poe opposed his candidacy, and Garrett was rejected by the electorate. That same year, Poe became co-founder and president of the Bank of Roswell, New Mexico, and in 1900 he was named president of the Citizens Bank of Roswell. Beset by financial difficulties, Poe died while undergoing treatment at a Battle Creek, Michigan, sanatorium in July 1923, possibly a suicide.

The letter that follows was, as far as can be ascertained, his first attempt to write down his recollections of the part he had played in the death of Billy the Kid. He later expanded it at the request of historian Earl A. Brininstool, who published it privately as a booklet. It is that version which was eventually published in book form—with a long introduction and afterword by Maurice Garland Fulton—as *The Death of Billy the Kid* in 1933. This version, however, has never before appeared in print.

Mr. Charles Goodnight
Goodnight P.C., Texas

Dear Mr. Goodnight:

I have in the odd moments I could spare from my business pieced together a sort of history of the part I played in the killing of "Billy the Kid" and the final breaking up of his outlaw gang. If you remember, I made my report to the Canadian River Cattlemen, of which organization you were a leader, on my return from New Mexico late in 1881. However, I am glad to comply with your request to write you more fully of the matter.

There is no need, I think, to remind you of the manner of my employment, as you recommended me to the organization as a man who could do the job of rounding-up the stolen cattle, and, if I could, end the stealing.

When I was employed I went directly to White Oaks, a lawless and rough mining camp in Lincoln County, N.M., which place I reasoned would most likely be headquarters of the outlaws. The Kid had many followers, both from the fact that men of his character actually followed him and took part in his raids, and because many were terrorized into supporting him. Soon after I arrived in White Oaks Pat Garrett, the sheriff of Lincoln County, came to the place and I immediately looked him up and made my business known to him. Garrett quickly offered his cooperation, and explained to me at quite some length the situation in Lincoln County and all of New Mexico, as far as

John William Poe and his wife,
Sophie Alberding, in 1883. Poe, a
former Texas lawman, was acting as
Pat Garrett's deputy the night the
Kid was killed. Robert G. McCubbin
Collection.

that is concerned. He said that the Kid was safely in jail in Lincoln, but that
his gang was still running loose.

Garrett told me that the Panhandle cattle and many New Mexico cattle had
been driven to Arizona and that the outlaws had brought back stolen cattle and
horses from Arizona. He said that if I would go on to Arizona, in the Tombstone country and do what I could to recover the cattle, he would do all he
could to protect my interests in New Mexico. I readily agreed, but, as I
reported, I recovered very few cattle in Arizona.

Late in April I returned from Arizona and met Garrett again in White
Oaks. While we were there working out a plan to round up the outlaws, we
learned that the Kid had shot his way out of the Lincoln jail. He had become
friendly with the jailer and at the first opportunity struck him over the head
with the chain used as hand-cuffs, and, procuring the keys, armed himself. His

two guards, deputies Ollinger and Bell, he shot down as they returned to the jail from supper.

Garrett immediately left for Lincoln, asking me to remain in White Oaks for the time being and keep a lookout for the Kid, as Garrett thought the outlaw might make for the hide-out of some of his gang there. In Lincoln Garrett organized several posses and started them out in several directions, not knowing where the Kid might go. However, none of the posses found any trace of the Kid and Garrett finally decided that he had gone into old Mexico. I continued my watch at White Oaks until early in July, when I received information which led me to believe that the Kid was in hiding at Fort Sumner, N. M. While keeping my watch for the Kid at White Oaks I had scoured the surrounding country and recovered many stolen cattle and hides belonging to the Canadian River cattlemen, as I reported long ago.

In the early part of July following the Kid's escape in April, I was approached by a man in White Oaks whom I had known in Texas, and, though addicted to alcohol, he was a man of good principles. He had previously shown a desire to help me. This man told me, in strict confidence, as he felt his life depended on me keeping his secret, that he had been sleeping in a livery stable owned by friends of Billy the Kid, and that a short time previous he had over-heard a conversation which convinced him that the Kid was living at Fort Sumner. This man further said that at two different times since he had escaped, Billy the Kid had been in the vicinity of White Oaks and had conversed with the two men whose conversation he overheard.

I doubted the possibility of this information being correct, as I did not think that the Kid could stay in Eastern New Mexico without his presence there being known. However, due to the Kid's wide acquaintance, and the following he had, I came to the conclusion that there was possible truth in the statements, and I at once communicated the information to Garrett, riding to Lincoln and laying the matter before him personally. Skeptical as I had been, Garrett doubted the statement more. He said, however, that if I thought we ought to search out the clue, he and I would ride to Roswell and get one of his trusted deputies named McKinney, and the three of us would go to Fort Sumner with the determination of unearthing the Kid if he was there. This was agreed upon and the following day we went to Roswell and found McKinney, who also disbelieved the story, but said he was willing to go with us to Fort Sumner.

After a few hours spent in Roswell arranging for the trip we left after sundown, starting out in a different direction from that which we intended to take. When we were well out of the town we circled back and headed for Fort

Sumner. We stopped at midnight, picketed our horses, and slept on our saddle blankets until daylight. Again in the saddle, we rode to within five or six miles of Fort Sumner and again picketing our horses, slept until morning.

As I was not known in Fort Sumner, it was here decided that I should ride into the place and reconnoiter and get such information as was possible, while the other two men were to remain out of sight in the sand hills for the day, and, in case of my failing to return before night, meet me at a designated point about four miles from Fort Sumner. I then left my companions and rode into the town, arriving sometime before noon. Fort Sumner at that time had a population of about four hundred, nearly all of them Mexicans, there being perhaps not more than two or three dozen Americans in the place, and a majority of these were "tough" or undesirable citizens. But all of them were in sympathy with the Kid.

As soon as I got into the town I noticed that I was being closely watched on every hand, and soon after I stopped my horse at a hitching post in front of a store with a saloon annex, a number of men gathered around and asked where I was from and where I was going. I answered with as plausible a story as I could on the spur of the moment, telling them I had been mining in White Oaks and was on my way to the Panhandle, where I lived. This story served the purpose to some extent, and I was invited to have a drink at the saloon, and I thought I had better do so, though I took only a small quantity of liquor. I had several short drinks around, as was the custom, and then went to a restaurant to eat.

After I had finished a square meal, the first I had had for several days, I loafed about the village for some hours, talking casually with the people I met in the hope of learning something definite as to whether or not the Kid was there or had been there, but was unable to learn anything further than that the people with whom I talked were still suspicious of me. It was plain to me that many of them were on the alert expecting something to happen. We learned later that the situation in Fort Sumner was very tense that day as the people knew the Kid was in hiding near there. I believe that if my mission had become known I would have stood no chance whatever for my life.

It had been understood when I left my companions in the morning that in case of my being unable to secure definite information in Fort Sumner concerning the Kid, I was to go to the ranch of a Mr. Rudolph, a friend of Garrett's, whose ranch was located seven miles north of Fort Sumner at a place called Sunnyside, with the purpose of securing from him, if possible, some information of the whereabouts of the man we were after.

Accordingly, I started from Fort Sumner about the middle of the afternoon for Rudolph's ranch, arriving there sometime before night. I found Mr.

Rudolph at home and presented the letter of introduction which Garrett had given me, telling him that I wished to stop overnight with him. After reading the letter, Rudolph said that Garrett was a good friend of his and that he would be glad to accommodate me.

After we had eaten supper, I engaged him in conversation, discussing conditions of the country generally for some little time and gradually led up to the subject of Billy the Kid's escape, and remarked that I had heard reported the Kid was near Fort Sumner. Upon my making this statement Rudolph showed plainly that he was agitated and remarked that he had heard the report but did not believe it. He said the Kid was too shrewd to stay in a country infested with officers on the watch for him and knowing that a price was on his head. We talked on about other things but every time I mentioned the Kid the same signs of agitation showed in the old man's actions and talk.

I told him, after a time, the object of our errand, and that I had come to him with the express purpose of learning, if he knew, the exact location of the Kid's hideout. Rudolph then became more nervous than before and reiterated his belief that the Kid had left the country and that he was positive he was not around Fort Sumner. We learned afterward that Rudolph was well aware of the Kid's presence at Fort Sumner, but, like many other men, he was afraid to say so.

As darkness came on, I told Rudolph that my horse was rested enough that I believed I would push on and meet my companions. This I did, much to Rudolph's relief, as I thought at the time. I rode directly to the point agreed on as our meeting place, and, strange to say, as I rode up from one direction I saw them coming to the place from another. We held a consultation on what I had learned from Rudolph and the attitude of people in Fort Sumner, which was nothing definite, but at the same time I was convinced in my own mind that the Kid was in the vicinity of Fort Sumner.

Garrett had little confidence in my conclusions but said he knew of a certain woman's house in Fort Sumner that he thought the Kid most likely to visit if he was there. He said if the Kid was there we would likely see him enter or leave the house during the night, and proposed that we hide in a grove of trees near the house and watch. This course we agreed upon and we entered a peach orchard near the house at about nine o'clock that night, stationing ourselves in the gloom or shadow of the trees, as the moon was shining very brightly.

We watched here without seeing anything until after eleven o'clock when Garrett again said he believed we were on a cold trail and proposed that we leave the town without letting the people know we had been there in search of the Kid. I proposed that, before leaving, we go to the residence of Peter

Maxwell, a man I did not know, but who was reputed to be respectable and well-fixed, and who should, according to my reasoning, be willing to assist in the arrest of the Kid.

Garrett agreed to this and led us from the orchard by circuitous by-paths to Maxwell's house, a building formerly used by the officers at the Fort.

When we arrived at the residence, a long low structure of adobe and standing end to and flush with the street, with a porch on the south side which was the direction from which we approached, the premises all being enclosed by a paling fence, one side of which ran parallel to and along the edge of the street, up and across the end of the porch to the corner of the building, Garrett said to me, "This is Maxwell's room in the corner; you fellows wait here while I go in and talk to him." Garrett then stepped on the porch and entered Maxwell's room through the open door, left open on account of the extremely warm weather, while McKinney and I stopped on the outside, McKinney squatting on the outside of the paling fence and I sitting on the edge of the porch in the small, open gateway leading from the street.

As I had never seen either the Kid or Maxwell I was placed at a great disadvantage in the events which quickly followed. It was probably not more than thirty seconds after Garrett had entered Maxwell's room when my attention was attracted from where I sat in the little gateway to a man approaching me from the street outside of and along the fence some forty feet away. I noticed that he was only partially dressed and was both bareheaded and barefooted, or rather had nothing on his feet but socks, and, as it seemed to me, was fastening his trousers as he hurried along.

Maxwell's was the only place in Fort Sumner that I had not thought of looking for the Kid, and I was entirely off my guard, and the thought that came into my mind was that the man hurrying along was either Maxwell or some guest who had had occasion to go to the rear of the house during the night. He came on until he was almost within arm's reach of where I sat in the gate before he saw me, as I was partly concealed by the gatepost. When he did see me he covered me as quick as lightning, sprang on the porch and called out in Spanish "Quien es (Who is it?)." He backed away from me toward the door through which Garrett had passed only half a minute before still repeating his query "Who is it?" in Spanish. At this I stood up from where I had been seated, stepped onto the porch and told him not to be alarmed[,] that he should not be hurt, still without suspicion that he was the man we were looking for.

As I moved toward him trying to reassure him he backed up into the doorway of Maxwell's room where he halted for a moment, his body concealed by the thick adobe doorway, put his head out and asked for the fourth or fifth time, in Spanish, who I was. I was in a few feet of him when he disappeared into the room. From then until after the shooting I was unable to see what took place on the inside on account of the darkness but plainly heard what was said on the inside. An instant after this man left the door I heard a voice inside inquire in a sharp tone, "Pete, who are those fellows on the outside?" An instant later a shot was fired in the room followed immediately by what seemed to be two other shots. However, there were only two shots fired, the third report, as we learned afterward, being made by the rebound of the second bullet which had struck the adobe wall and rebounded against the headboard of the bed.

I heard a groan and a gasp or two as of someone dying in the room. A moment or two later Garrett came out, brushing against me as he passed, stood by me close to the wall, at the side of the door and said, "That was the Kid that came in there and I think I got him." I said, "Pat, the Kid would not come to this place, you have shot the wrong man." When I said this Garrett seemed for a moment to be in doubt himself as to whom he had shot but soon spoke up and said, "I know his voice too well to be mistaken; I am sure it was the Kid."

Soon after Garrett had come out, Pete Maxwell rushed squarely into me in a frantic effort to get out of the room and I certainly would have shot him but for Garrett striking my gun down and saying "Don't shoot Maxwell." By this time I had begun to realize that we were in a place which was not above suspicion, such as I had thought this house to be. As Garrett was positive the Kid was inside I came to the conclusion that we were up against a case of kill or be killed, as we had from the beginning realized it would be when we came face to face with the Kid. I have always been grateful that I did not shoot Maxwell, for I learned afterward that he was a well-meaning man but was utterly terrorized by the Kid and his gang.

Maxwell went in search of a light, which he sat in a window, as he did not dare go into the room, and we looked in. There was a man dead on the floor who was quickly identified by Garrett and Maxwell as the Kid.

I do not believe more than thirty seconds elapsed between the time I first saw the Kid coming up the fence and the time he was killed. Garrett said that as he had entered Maxwell's room he leaned his Winchester against the door facing and went over and sat on the head of Maxwell's bed. He had no sooner seated himself than he heard the Kid asking me who I was and that he recognized the voice. The Kid then entered the room and asked, "Pete, who are those fellows outside?" Garrett then made a move toward his six-shooter, but the Kid saw him, for the first time, and covered him. Garrett fired without

The Maxwell house at Fort Sumner. The Kid was killed in the corner room nearest the camera. Robert G. McCubbin Collection.

rising from his seat at the head of the bed. The Kid fell, his own pistol shot going wild. This was shortly after midnight July 14, 1881. Later that day, after the coroner had rendered a verdict of justifiable homicide, the Kid was buried in the old military cemetery at Fort Sumner.

With the Kid gone the other outlaws were soon killed, captured, or driven out of the country and the Lincoln County troubles cleared up. The Kid's passing had a good effect all over the Southwest, as no other similar band of outlaws ever tried to overpower the officers of the law.

I believe that this covers the part I played and answers your questions and I think that it is the truth of the matter. While it has never been properly written, it has not been allowed to die in my memory as I have recounted it to the curious many times.

Hoping that this finds you as well as you were the last time I saw you, I am,

Sincerely yours
John W. Poe (signed)

CHAPTER TWENTY-FOUR

Death and Burial of Billy the Kid

Col. Jack Potter

Texas-born Jack Potter (1864–1950) was the real thing, a "fightin' parson's boy" who grew up to be a cowboy. He first came up the trail from Texas in 1882, and between 1884 and 1893 he worked at Fort Sumner, where his employers, the New England Cattle Company, had purchased all the buildings and improvements from the heirs of Lucien Maxwell. Later he served in the New Mexico legislature and for many years was justice of the peace in Union County. After he won second prize in a writing contest, he began submitting stories to the local newspaper, the *Union County Leader;* and these and others that he wrote for pulp magazines such as *Ranch Romances* were collected in a book in 1932, privately printed at Clayton, New Mexico. Later, Potter submitted articles to *New Mexico Magazine,* whose editor, George Fitzpatrick, persuaded the governor of New Mexico to bestow upon him in 1935 the "honorary Colonelship" that he was so proud of. "Colonel Jack" made no bones about the tallness of his tales about trail drives and cowboying, and minded not at all when someone called him "the most cheerful liar in the state." As he himself said, "it would kill a cowboy plumb dead to tell his experiences without handling the truth in a hazardous way."

Eugene Cunningham used to tell a story about a hard-bitten cowhand he had once known who had been in Fort Sumner the night the Kid was killed, and saw his body laid out on a table before his funeral. After a long, thoughtful moment, the cowboy said, "Kid, I never seen you lookin' so good." While there is no doubt that was how a lot of people felt about the Kid's death back in 1881, "Lead Steer" Potter's account of the Kid's funeral is a little less hostile and, in the absence of any other, has an endearing authenticity. It's easy to picture Garrett commandeering planks from an abandoned house to make a coffin, the procession to the cemetery led by Vicente's wood wagon followed by everyone in the town—even the bartender, who we may assume was Beaver Smith—and most of all, the presence and performance of the Sanctified Texan, Hugh

Leeper (possibly one of the ten children of James and Ruthe Leeper of Hawkins County, Tennessee), who had been the subject of another Potter "tale." His history, Potter said, was "cloudy, and the only thing definitely known of his past was a rumor that he was a fugitive from a southern state. . . . But no matter how shady his past may have been, it was generally conceded that he was fairly well educated and was an accomplished scholar of the Bible." It's just a shame that Col. Potter didn't see fit to tell us more.

Coroner's Verdict
Territory of New Mexico
Precinct No. 27
County of San Miguel

To the attorney of the First Judicial District of the Territory of New Mexico:

GREETINGS:

This, the fifteenth of July, A.D. 1881, I, the undersigned Justice of the Peace of the precinct above named, received information that there has been a death in Fort Sumner in said precinct, and immediately upon receiving information, proceeded to the said place and named M. Rudolph, Jose Silva, Antonio Savedra, Pedro Antonio Lucero, Lorenzo Jaramillo, and Sabel Guitierrez as a jury to investigate the matter and the meeting in the house of Lucien B. Maxwell. The said jury proceeded to a room in said house where they found the body of William Bonney, alias "Billy the Kid" with a bullet wound in his chest on the left side, and having examined the body, they examined the evidence of Pedro Maxwell which is as follows:

> While Pat Garrett was sitting on the corner of my bed talking to me, Billy the Kid came to the door with pistol in hand and asked me, 'Quien es (Who is it?) Quienes son los hombres afuera? (Who are the men outside?)' And when Pat Garrett fired two shots at him the said William Bonney fell on one side of my fireplace. Then I left the room. When I returned several minutes later the said Bonney was dead.

The jury has found the following verdict: We of the jury unanimously find that William Bonney was killed by a shot in his left breast in the region of the heart, fired from a pistol in the hands of Pat Garrett. And our verdict is that the act of said Garrett was justifiable homicide. And we are unanimous in the opinion that the gratitude of the whole community is due to said Garrett for the act, and that he deserves to be rewarded.

M. Rudolph, President
Antonio Savedra
Pedro Antonio Lucero
Jose Silva
Sabel Guitierrez
Lorenzo Jaramillo
Alejandro Seguro, Justice of Peace, San Miguel Co.

This is the way Jack Potter told the exciting story of the Kid:

Billy had been dead three years when I came to Fort Sumner in 1884, but folks there were still talking about him and the way Garrett shot him in the dark. The people of the Fort, home of Billy's staunch friends and his ladylove as well, were awakened just past midnight as news of the killing spread by excited messengers to each adobe dwelling. There was much wailing and weeping among the women: "El pobre Beely, pobre Beely (poor Billy)." Both factions of the male citizens, those who mourned his passing and those who agreed that Garrett should be rewarded, were excited and confused over the death.

The Sheriff instructed several Mexican ranch hands to remove the dirt roof of an abandoned adobe building and pull out enough ceiling planks to make a coffin, as time was too short to have new lumber shipped from Las Vegas.

Late in the afternoon, the corpse was loaded into Old Vicente's wood-hauling wagon which proceeded to the government cemetery followed by every person in Fort Sumner, even the saloon keeper who rarely closed down his business. The Sanctified Texan, who believed in predestination, preached the funeral and said that Billy's time had certainly come at last.

They told me he made remarks about Billy, "our beloved young citizen," and read from the 14th chapter of Job—"A man that is born of woman is of few days and is full of trouble—he fleeth like a shadow and continueth not." In closing he said, "Billy cannot come back to us, but we can go to him and will see him again up yonder, Amen."

The day after the funeral Pete Maxwell had his man pull a wooden picket from the parade-ground fence, saw off a foot or so, and nail it in a crossbar to the longer piece. Then he printed in crude letters "BILLY THE KID, JULY 14, 1881."

Later this marker was stolen by relic seekers and the second one, which replaced it, was also stolen. Now a granite stone marks the lonely grave, but it too has been chipped and scratched. Back in 1930 when I began to write down my memories, I had a letter from John Roark, a stagecoach driver, who swore he saw the uprooted grave marker strapped to a feller's luggage as he boarded a train back East.

I was riding along with Pete Maxwell and I asked him how he felt when he realized that he was trapped in bed between Sheriff Garrett and Billy the Kid. He drew up his reins, thought a minute and said: "I wish you had not asked me that question as I have tried to forget it all. I realized that I had three chances at being killed on the spot in the next instant. First by being between the two men; next, when the Kid fell forward, the butcher knife he had used to cut meat plunged close to my chest; and last, as I got out of bed to escape, I was stopped at the door by Deputy John Poe with his .45 in my stomach. The Deputy thought I was the Kid. I had a lot of explaining to do, pronto!"

So this was the final chapter in the life of one of the most colorful characters of the entire West. Billy was what you might call a gentleman desperado and a large number of people counted him a friend. As time goes on, future readers of Billy the Kid history will wonder whether the stories are true or just plain fiction. But to some of us old timers who lived through those days, *Billicito* still rides the country around and beyond the Pecos.

CHAPTER TWENTY-FIVE

Billy the Kid: A Case Study in Epic Origins

Alfred Adler

Apart from the fact that he was most emphatically not the famous psychologist of the same name, no one seems to know anything at all about the Alfred Adler who wrote the following article. A little-known and quite remarkable piece that appeared in a highly respected journal, it is a scholarly study of the processes by which the Kid became a legend, which concludes that there is a commonality between the origins of his status as a folk hero and those of many other folk heroes of the past. For all its erudition and earnestness, however, modern-day readers may be forgiven for wondering half a century later if it was not some kind of literary joke (that final footnote, for example) and find themselves—as perhaps the Kid might have done had he been able to read it—struggling not to laugh, not so much at the validity of Mr. Adler's conclusions as at the wondrous pretentiousness of his prose.

That having been said, there is no question that he is correct in observing that when the times need a legend, the people create one. As the British historian Eric Hobsbawm has observed in a chapter headed "The Noble Robber" in his book *Bandits* (rev. ed., New York: New Press, 2000), this phenomenon also "to some extent expresses the wish that the people's champion cannot be defeated, the same sort of wish that produces the perennial myths of the good king—and the good bandit—who has not really died, but will come back some day to restore justice. Refusal to believe in a robber's death is a certain criterion of his 'nobility.' . . . For the bandit's defeat and death is the defeat of his people; and what is worse, of hope. Men can live without justice, and generally must, but they cannot live without hope."

How perfectly that final sentence illuminates the life of Billy the Kid.

The Iliad, the Mahabharata, the Nibelungenlied, and other extant epic poems are widely assumed to be the work of individuals, poets and redactors.[1] But there is still the passionately debated question of "origins." Did the subject matter originate from events in history, ascertainable by means of historical research, or did the epic develop around a nucleus of folklore, radically unhistorical in its nature and structure?

In general terms, the historians in the field may be said to proceed from the assumptions that "time dims the memory," that an epic is in the main the inaccurate and embellished account of happenings which could have been reported more accurately by more literate people. Perhaps most important of all, the historians do not seem to suspect that epics similar to each other could have arisen from different circumstances, at different times, in different places. Folklorists, on the other hand, often tend to look for themes older than recorded history, and basically unaffected by the various historical situations within which they have sprung into being.

History? Folklore? There is no easy decision as to which is the more significant for the birth of an epic. Conceivable, yet hardly explored, is a constellation other than an Either-Or: a folkloric pattern, older than any defined, historical date, resurging at a certain time and place, concurrent with certain historical events of that time, yet significant—socially significant—not because of such concurrences and coincidences, but mainly because of its very nature—folklore.

I propose to explore this possibility in the case of Billy the Kid.[2] An historical personage, connected with New Mexico's Lincoln County War of 1878, the Kid is a folk hero endowed with features told about folk heroes, thousands of years before the Lincoln County War. In his case, there was no slow transformation of history into legend. Two years before his attested death in 1881, Mrs. Wallace, in a letter to her husband, then territorial governor of New Mexico, refers to the legendary boast that the Kid has killed a man for every year of his life.[3] It was too soon for time to have dimmed the memory! In his actual life, the Kid was "a nuisance, not to say an appreciable menace."[4] As a folk hero, he has become a factor in the social history of New Mexico. If justified, my treatment of the case of the Kid may shed some light upon a fascinating area of New Mexican culture, and it may encourage the pursuit of similar approaches to other epic labyrinths.

To begin with, in what sense is the Kid a folk hero? Does his "heroism" meet the standards set up for folk heroes by modern cultural anthropologists' standards such as Lord Raglan has supplied?[5] Paradoxical as some of them may seem, they are commended as conclusions arrived at on the basis of a comprehensive, comparative study of mythology and folklore. No concession to gratuitous assumptions about "heroes," they emphasize certain traits found in "heroes" over a wide range of distribution, traits more indicative perhaps as they are less conspicuously "heroic." Lord Raglan's useful, though perhaps not definitive criteria, are herein applied, with some modifications[6] to the heroic *Gestalt* of the Kid.

Like Oedipus, Theseus, Romulus, Moses, Elijah, Nyikang, Arthur, and Robin Hood, the Kid has no certain burial place, but "holy sepulchres." According to the historical accounts, the Kid is buried in the old military burying ground at Fort Sumner, New Mexico, where his grave is shown. Contrary to history, however, there is the tradition that his remains are in Las Cruces, New Mexico,[7] and there is the persistent insinuation that he did not die at all on July 14, 1881, but has been seen much later in different places.[8] In spite of this uncertainty, in the folk mind, as to his burial place, he has "holy sepulchres." In the museum at some distance from the grave at Fort Sumner, "relics" are shown: the table on which they laid him after he had been shot; the linen cloth bearing traces of his blood; and, on the table, a trace of his blood "still touched by spellbound visitors."[9] The "finger" of the Kid hardly has been located, but there were "pilgrims" to see this "relic," and they paid admission for "a peek."[10] Near Las Cruces, New Mexico, in La Mesilla, we see a chest alleged to contain his personal belongings. On August 29, 1950, a "sacrilege" was perpetrated: "some varmint removed the marker from his grave."[11] In Escondido, New Mexico, he came close to being "Saint Billy the Kid."[12]

Like Heracles, Bellerophon, Dionysos, Sigurd, and Llew Llawgyffes, the Kid met with a mysterious death. As for the hill, or any steep place— where these legendary heroes often were killed—Maxwell's residence was at a fort. Regarding the circumstances of the attested death, J. W. Poe, a crown witness, calls it "a mystery."[13] Indeed, it was. Though reasonably coherent, the accounts of Garrett (who shot the Kid) and Poe (Garrett's deputy sheriff) are not entirely beyond the realm of doubt. Did the Kid carry a butcher's knife the night of his death, or knife and six-shooter? Poe and Garrett insist on the six-shooter,[14] but they were especially interested in describing the situation as one of "kill or be killed." Otero,[15] on the testimony of Jesus Silva and Deluvina Maxwell, insists that the Kid carried no pistol. If Otero is correct, the coroner's jury accepted an inaccurate statement of Pete Maxwell that the Kid had "*una pistola* (no knife mentioned!) *en la mano.*[16] Furthermore, much earlier, in his fight with Apaches, the Kid is said to have dashed to a camp, "a pistol in one hand, and a small dagger in the other."[17] These could have been a transfer of images.

The report of the coroner's jury is doubtful in more than one respect. It was signed by Mr. Rudolph, an educated man,[18] but the other, less reliable signatories, were *nativos.*[19] However, Mr. Rudolph was precisely the man suspected by Poe of withholding information on the Kid's whereabouts.[20] Mr. Rudolph and the *nativos* cannot be dissociated from those other inhabitants of Fort Sumner who, according to Poe,[21] were "on the alert," eager to hide the Kid. Once Garrett had decided that the man whom he had shot in the dark room was the Kid, what a wonderful opportunity for the coroner's jury (Rudolph and *nativos*!) to save their idol by making his death official! Garrett has found severe critics;[22] his veracity cannot be deemed beyond the shadow of a doubt. As a recorder of the Kid's death, Garrett cannot be considered impartial. He had personal interests invested; if not primarily to claim the reward, certainly to compensate for the humiliation inflicted on him by the Kid's famous escape from Garrett's custody in the Lincoln jail.[23] As for Poe and McKinney, Garrett's deputies present at the crucial time, did they or did they not know what happened? There is no evidence that McKinney knew. Poe writes that he himself had never seen the Kid up to the moment when the latter entered Maxwell's room,[24] and tells the happenings in the room "from Garrett's statement."[25] Furthermore, according to Fulton, the coroner's report "shows a feature making it unique, the codicil: '*estamos unánimes en opinion pue la gratitud de toda la comunidad es devida á dicho Garrett por su hecho y que es digno de ser recompensado.*'"[26] Does this bit of gratuity really seem "to echo the sigh both of strong relief and ineffable satisfaction"?[27] Or were the signatories officious so as to make their intentions seem especially trustworthy? With very different motives, Garrett as well as the jury might have been eager to declare the Kid officially dead. Although these remarks are no proof that the Kid did not die on July 14, 1881, they should indicate that even the *history* of the "hero's" death is "a mystery."[28]

Mysterious *history,* more mysterious tradition! Tradition said "treachery!" "They had to sneak up on him in the dead of night to murder him.[29] Such death by treachery was also the fate of Achilles, Siegfried, Arthur, Tristan, Roland, Samson, Krishna, Chang Fei. Raiko, Liongo, Tahaki,

Kwasina, Davy Crockett, Jesse James, and others. Now "the god (or hero) may die . . . but he dies of his own volition."[30] In the tradition, the Kid somehow was free to decide how he would "consent" to die, fighting like a man, not shot like a dog unarmed,[31] shot but not hanged.[32] Poe himself, as a sober, elderly business man, speaks of the crucial night as "fore-ordained."[33] Chained to the floor in the Lincoln jail, the Kid said to Sister Blandina: "I'll get out of this, you will see, Sister," and she *marveled* "at the assurance of the chained youth."[34] As he rode away from the burning McSween home, "more than fifty shots were fired at him," but "not a shot struck him."[35]

In the case of Billy the Kid, death and burial have been studied here as separate units, and on the basis of Raglan's criteria. For the "heroic" chronology from birth to death, Raglan's list, still the outline, will have to be implemented and modified by more recent findings. This is the outline: the hero's mother is a royal virgin, his father is a king, and often a near relative of his mother, but the circumstances of his conception are unusual, and he is also reputed to be the son of a god (and represented by certain animals); at birth (or in early childhood) an attempt is made, usually by his father or maternal grandfather, to kill him, but he is spirited away, and reared by foster parents in a far country; we are told nothing (little) of his childhood; on reaching manhood he returns or goes to his future kingdom; after a victory over the king (and/or a giant, dragon, or wild beast), he marries a princess, then the daughter (wife) of his predecessor, and becomes king; for a time he reigns uneventfully, and prescribes laws, but later he loses favor with the gods (and/or his subjects), is driven from the throne and city, (dies and is "buried").

The Kid's mother has become a part of the legend. She was "a genuine lady" with "soft golden hair,"[36] she "liked to dress better than the common run . . . stepping gingerly, and holdin' up her skirts to keep them out of the dust."[37]

She is said to have been of *rather distinguished* French background.[38] Additional clues are provided by these exotic and exalting undertones: "her grandfather born in Haiti . . . her family had gone to the island after the fall of Napoleon."[39] Billy's father "never married her."[40] The famous "insults" she suffered, and the Kid's urge to avenge them, are further hints of illegitimacy.

Son of "a god"? There are the Kid's "supernatural powers"; there is the belief that he was "immortal."[41] The totemic "animal" shape? There are his nicknames: "Billy the Kid," "Billy the Goat," "Billy Goat," "Billy the Scape Goat," "El Chivato."[42]

A tradition about a phase of his later boyhood, but with the earmarks of a childhood story, may be offered as an instance of how "an attempt is made to kill him, but he is spirited away. . . ." Mrs. Barber (widow of Alexander A. McSween) told Otero:[43] Soldiers working for Murphy (Murphy, an image of the hero's "hostile" father) were on the trail of the Kid who slept in the house of a Mexican couple, the couple sleeping on one mattress, the Kid on another one in the same room. Hearing the soldiers, the Kid *crept* to his friends, *whispering*. They covered him with their own mattress and lay down on top of it. The Kid was *almost smothered*. We have here the "foster parents," "the far away country" (the Mexican setting), we have "the spiriting away" in an atmosphere like a nursery (hiding, creeping, whispering, sleeping with "parents").

Instead of the "hostile father or grandfather on the mother's side," the Kid had a hostile stepfather (a "mother's relative"), and there are many images of fatherly, yet antagonistic older men: the blacksmith, the man who insulted his mother, Murphy, Chisum, Governor Wallace, Pete Maxwell (who "gave him away") and, in a recent motion picture, "The Kid from Texas," even Mr. McSween.

Quite persistent is the tradition of the Kid's rather effeminate appearance: delicate, slender frame, soft voice, small hands and feet, very different from those of rough cow punchers. These traits and the equally popular closeness to his mother and tenderness toward women in general, the inference that he could not do hard work, and, to cope with his environment, had to develop his marksmanship, classify him with a somewhat special group of "heroes," the mythico-literary Handsome Cowards.[44] In his early years, the Coward lives in a world of women (mother, foster mother, fairy), and fails to acquire manliness. Eventually, he turns into a Handsome Reckless. Many Arthurian heroes start as Cowards, as also do Achilles (in women's clothes) and Ulysses. The Handsome Coward finally outwits the Ugly Reckless. Now, one of the Kid's worst enemies was Bob Ollinger, who, though historical, has been described as an Ugly Reckless, "a huge tree trunk, with a regular Gorilla-like chest, heavy bull neck," but brave, "the most able deputy of Pat Garrett's posse."[45] "Big Bob called Billy the Kid an insignificant little runt,"[46] and, mockingly, declared that the Kid (in jail) is "just as tame as a *conejo*."[47] In the end, the Handsome "Coward" killed the Ugly "Reckless."[48]

Furthermore, the kid's delicacy puts him in the category of the Unpromising Hero, along with Perceval, David, Joseph, Dhruva Karna, Wang Shub, Franklin, Lincoln, Edison, and others.[49] His smallness of frame and hands equips him for Clever Roles: crawling out of the jail chimney, shaking off his handcuffs, masterly card playing and, like the small Hermes (also a cattle thief!), outwitting a big antagonist.[50]

Like Raglan's heroes, the Kid was motivated to leave his home and he "returned to (or arrived in) his future kingdom." Indeed, he "returned to (or arrived in)" Lincoln County,[51] there to occupy a position of sovereign significance. His transformation, in the shameful cart, from La Mesilla (where he was convicted) to the Lincoln jail was also a "return," an "unpromising return," followed by a decisive "victory" (the escape). As for "victories over the (father image of a hostile) king, giant, or dragon," the Kid caused much anxiety to Murphy, and to this other "cattle king" Chisum, killed the "giant" Ollinger, after having triumphed over Indians, animals, "not human beings," in his estimation.

The specific structure of heroic victories has been classified by Klapp under five headings: Feat, Contest, Test, Quest, and Clever Roles.[52] Feats, performances exceeding human capacities, are the Kid's "hypnotizing" escape from Governor Wallace's custody,[53] or the ride from a ranch north of La Mesilla to San Elizario and back, in a fabulously short time.[54] The Ollinger incident, a public defeat of a formidable rival, is a Contest. The escape from the Lincoln jail (April 28, 1881) is an historical event, but it has been acknowledged as a Test, as the completion of a superhuman task to prove heroic status, by the Santa Fe *New Mexican* (May 4, 1881).[55] That the hero became "king" after his "victory" (the escape) still is quite clear to any visitor in Lincoln, New Mexico.[56]

He did not exactly "marry a princess, often the daughter (or wife) of his predecessor," but there were several "princesses" in Lincoln who not only liked him as a dancer, but were encouraged by their elders to dance with him, the youth of *"buena gente, muy buena gente."*[57] If Pete Maxwell was a "hostile king," there is the rumor of the Kid's love for Pete's daughter.[58] In the motion picture, "The Kid from Texas," the Kid is in love with Irene, wife of McSween, a "hostile predecessor."

Mrs. McSween is said to have sung and played the piano, inspiring the Kid's gang the night when the McSween home burned down.[59] Was she one of the many Besieged Ladies (some of them Sirens) well known to the student of folklore in the British Isles?[60] The song (note 59) is about

350 LEGEND INTO HISTORY

a Scottish theme.[61] The role of a Besieged Lady is ambiguous at times. In need of a heroic rescuer, she also acts as an enchantress provoking a contest between her husband (or oppressor) and the rescuer. Now in "The Kid from Texas," the Lady plays, not while her house burns, but while causing a conflict between her husband and the Kid. The Lady's husband (father, oppressor) often appears to the hero as a deceptively Hospitable Host.[62] Is not Pete Maxwell such an Hospitable Host?

After his "inthronization," the hero "reigns uneventfully." After the burning of the McSween home, the night when the Kid had emerged to real fame,[63] he was "very wise in that phase of life,"[64] and "everything was moving along smoothly."[65] After his famous escape, "Garrett . . . failing to find any trace . . . gave up the hunt,"[66] another instance of "uneventful ruling." Did he "prescribe laws"? The Services and Benefactions ascribed to some folk heroes[67] are related with reference to various phases of the Kid's life. Eventually, however, the hero "loses favor with the gods (and/or his subjects), is driven from the throne and city." Now, "rumors were circulated that warrants were out for The Kid's arrest,"[68] and "a man . . . told [Poe] . . . that The Kid was yet in the country."[69] The Kid was hounded from "throne and city," "and the strain was beginning to tell on him."[70]

This brief, incomplete survey covers all and more than all the traits listed by Raglan.[71] In several instances *history* and *lore* seem to coincide. Put together, however, the traits represent a constellation of symptoms indicative for heroes of the widest distribution. Changing or omitting the historical names, we find that the coincidences with history are not history, but certain aspects of a folkloric *Gestalt* which might be seen and actually have been seen in history. As one compact whole, the body of traits is of the stuff folk tales are made of in many places at different times.

Asking why the historical Billy the Kid was made a folk hero, we feel that one of Professor Fulton's oral statements may well contain the nucleus of an answer: "The Kid was an unusual youth at an unusual time in an unusual place." Certainly, about 1880 New Mexico lived through "unusual times," charged with conflicting attitudes toward "right and wrong," "law and order." Socially, economically, and with regard to the cultural outlook in general, there was little agreement as to basic premises. For a while at least, the capacity to survive under such circumstances must have been questioned.[72] Now there appeared a youth who seemed to harmonize so many contradictions, and, at the same time, to represent a challenge to those who "contradicted." An insuperable performance, played with charming elegance, "as if there were nothing to it!" Where life seemed impossible, he certainly seemed to know how to live a full, impossible life. This sprightly acrobat must have been a reassuring sight for many, a formula for social cohesion. They were mistaken, but they were profoundly aroused. The image fair conjured before their marveling eyes could not be allowed to vanish. How could they "keep" it? All the rowdiness notwithstanding, they were Americans, Victorians, basically quite convinced of right and wrong as phrased by Victorians. There was no justification for the Kid in terms of right and wrong. Relentlessly reiterated assertions that Billy "was not so bad," "that he had not killed so many men," these never-conclusive expressions of personal opinions only show that a conclusive vindication in habitual terms was impossible. Never at home with Billy in a world of moral standards, his friends, and these were many, put him in a world to which moral standards do not quite apply, in a no-man's-land of moral standards. Reverting to, reactivating the deeper, never dormant layers of human expression on which there is myth and ritual, they made Billy a folk hero. Myths (mythoi) are "words" to explain certain "deeds," actions, rites (dramata):—rites celebrating the birth of a hero, his coming of age, his initiation (through Feats, Contests, Tests, and Quests), his consecration, "inthronization," his mysterious death and burial. Pre-Christian, Christianized, in some form or another, many of these rites are practically ubiquitous, forms of expression older than recorded history, and, when the occasion arises, ready to resurge.[73] Their content is not quite in harmony with the moral concepts of modern man, yet it is so old, so very much the very own of man, that he need not "justify" it in modern terms. Is it not natural that the image of a human being, loved but not justified on moral grounds, would have been "kept" in a place where it was possible to "keep" it, in an Avalon beyond good and evil? Whatever the historical substratum may have been, in "Avalon" all that is left is in accordance with "Avalon."

Indeed, the New Mexican folk hero has been "kept" in this place, there to remain, serenely undisturbed by the unceasing denial of, or apologies for, his historical existence. As a folk hero, he has become a witness for social cohesion. Is he not the work of people who did not seem able to live together? Why, they must have been able to live together, they were even able to create together—a folk hero.

To summarize and to conclude, my purpose has been to study the origins of an epic subject matter. Related to an historical situation, its pattern has not been found determined by the actual events. As a narrative pattern, it could have arisen out of a different set of events. However, it is a common human denominator, a nucleus of basic, extramoral agreement among people who did not seem to agree on anything; it is a piece of evidence that they were able to agree on very important things, where, in the windy regions of social strife literal agreements seemed impossible, they united to descend to the springs of folklore. The relatively well-known history of the time makes the case especially challenging for a distinction between actual historicity and historical (social) significance. The case of Billy the Kid leads us to formulate an hypothesis: created at a certain time, a legend is not a reflection of that time, but an indication that the time needed a legend. Will it seem worth while to test the hypothesis in other case studies of epic origins?

NOTES

1. Uniqueness of authorship *vs.* folk background of subject matter has been stressed by one of the most recent critics, J. Körner, in *Einfuhrung in die Poetik* (Frankfurt am Main, 1949), p. 42.

2. Research materials on Billy the Kid are listed in *A "Billy the Kid" Bibliographic Check List* prepared as an appendix to the reprint of *The True Life of Billy the Kid* (repr. R. F. Cummings, Fisherville, Mass. 1945). The *Check List* is based on the collections of L. P. Merrill, Fort Worth, Texas, and J. C. Dykes, College Park, Maryland, and has been revised in 1949. As Mr. Dykes kindly informed me, a more complete *Bibliography* is ready to he published by the University of New Mexico Press. Among the items on the *Check List* relevant for a study of the history of Billy the Kid are: Pat F. Garrett, *An Authentic Life of Billy The Kid, the Noted Desperado of The Southwest* (Santa Fe, New Mexico, 1882); *Pat F. Garrett's Authentic Life of Billy the Kid*, ed. M. G. Fulton (New York, 1927); M. G. Fulton and J. W. Poe, *The Death of Billy the Kid* (Boston and New York, 1933); M. A. Otero, *The Real Billy the Kid* (New York, 1936); M. G. Fulton and P. Horgan, *New Mexico's Own Chronicle* (Dallas, 1937); J. McKee, *"Ben-Hur" Wallace* (Berkeley and Los Angeles, 1947), especially pp. 149–162; E. Fergusson, *Murder and Mystery in New Mexico* (Albuquerque, 1948), pp. 49–71; J. H.[W.] Hendron, *The Story of Billy the Kid* (Santa Fe, New Mexico, 1948); M. H. Brothers, *Billy the Kid* (Farmington, New Mexico, 1949); Ch. A. Siringo, *A Texas Cowboy* (repr. W. Sloane Associates, New York, 1950), pp. 124–140, 160–177. Unpublished material is in the process of being sifted by the distinguished specialist on the Lincoln County War, Professor Maurice Garland Fulton, superintendent of the Courthouse Museum, Lincoln, New Mexico.

3. *Lew Wallace, An Autobiography* (New York and London, 1906), II, 920–921.

4. Fulton and Poe, *op. cit.*, p. 60.

5. Lord Raglan, *The Hero: A Study in Tradition, Myth, and Drama* (New York, 1937), pp. 178–199.

6. Especially, Orrin E. Klapp, *The Hero as a Social Type* (Ph.D. diss., University of Chicago, 1948), and "The Folk Hero," *JAF,* LXII (1949), 17–25; E. Brugger, "Der Schöne Feigling in der Arthurischen Literatur," *2RP,* LXI (1941), 1–44; LXIII (1943), 123–173, 275–328; LXV (1949), 121–162, 162–186, 186–192, 289–307, 308–337, 337–380, 381–408, 409–424, 425–432. For methods in general, see Stith Thompson, *The Folktale* (New York, 1946).

7. See the article on Billy the Kid in *World* (June 8, 1902), shown in enlarged form in the Old Courthouse, Lincoln County, New Mexico; the article on "Billy the Kid," by E. Hough ([*Everybody's*] *Magazine,* 1902), a photostatic copy of which was shown to the Writer by Professor M. G. Fulton.

8. J. F. Dobie, *A Vaquero of the Brush Country* (Boston, 1929), p. 167 (note 2); *This is New Mexico,* ed. G. Fitzpatrick (Santa Fe, 1948), pp. 49ff. (article by E. Cunningham, "The Kid Still Rides"). In the Western movie, "The Son of Billy the Kid," the Kid appears as a balding, middle-aged banker!

9. As the writer was told by the custodian on August 30, 1950.

10. See the article in *World,* June 8, 1902 (note 7); Ph. Le Noir, *Rhymes of the Wild and Wooly,* Santa Fe, New Mexico, 1920, containing "The Finger of Billy the Kid"; Fulton and Poe, *op. cit.,* 45–46.

11. Albuquerque *Journal,* August 30, 1950, p. 12.

12. F. G. Applegate, "New Mexican Legends," *Southwest Review,* XVII (1931–1932), pp. 199–208.

13. Fulton and Poe, *op cit.,* pp. 45–46.

14. *Ibid.,* pp. 34, 44.

15. [Otero], *op. cit.,* pp. 111, 190.

16. Fulton and Poe, *op. cit.,* p. 55.

17. Otero, *op. cit.,* p. 17.

18. Fulton and Poe, *op. cit.,* p. 53.

19. *Ibid.*

20. *Ibid.,* p. 24.

21. *Ibid.,* pp. 20–21.

22. Otero, *op. cit.,* pp. 93, 118, 128, 144, and a letter written by Geiss (whom the Kid forced to help him escape from Lincoln jail), shown to me, in the form of a typewritten copy, by Professor Fulton.

23. Brothers, *op. cit.,* p. 46.

24. Fulton and Poe, *op. cit.,* p. 31.

25. *Ibid.,* p. 42.

26. *Ibid.,* pp. 55–56.

27. *Ibid.,* p. 59.

28. See also H. Howard (Jack) Thorp, *Pardner of the Wind* (Caldwell, Idaho, 1945), p. 189. The circumstance that some of the Kid's friends later confirmed the Poe-Garrett version of the Kids death is no certain proof. Missing a conclusive,

consistent report, one may even ask if the reiterated insistence on the correctness of this version has not been an implicit refutation of rumors against it. If the Kid was "on the loose" after July 14, 1881, his friends, who knew, were interested in endorsing the version for a long time to come. Years later, when earlier associations with the Kid seemed much more objectionable in public opinion, wary survivors had an added motive for sticking to the version. About some of those who, later, did not care to remember their former closeness, see Fergusson, *op. cit.*, p. 61.

29. Otero, *op. cit.*, p. 179.

30. Raglan, *op. cit.*, p. 203.

31. From a letter of the Kid to Governor Wallace (photostatic copy in the Old Lincoln County Courthouse).

32. Hendron, *op. cit.*, p. 3.

33. Fulton and Poe, *op. cit.*, p. 50.

34. Sister Blandina Segale, *At the End of the Santa Fe Trail* (Milwaukee, 1948), p. 73.

35. Otero, *op. cit.*, p. 73. In the oldest "legendary" account, I. Constellano (Don Jernado), *The True Life of Billy the Kid* [New York, 1881], reprinted R. F. Cummings (Fisherville, Massachusetts, 1945), 15, we read: "the more superstitious regarded him as immortal . . . stories . . . as to his vanishing into air . . . sabres [driven] through his body without injuring him . . . belief that he could not be killed by a bullet of lead, that some . . . [had] bullets of silver to shoot him."

36. Otero, *op. cit.*, p. 3.

37. Brothers, *op. cit.*, p. 11.

38. Hendron, *op. cit.*, p. 5.

39. *Ibid.*

40. *Ibid.*

41. See note 35.

42. Dobie, *op. cit.*, p. 162; Fergusson, *op. cit.*, p. 49; Applegate, *loc. cit.*, p. 206; Siringo, *op. cit.*, p. 171.

43. Otero, *op. cit.*, pp. 114–115.

44. The type in its medieval literary affiliation has been studied by E. Brugger (see note 6).

45. Brothers, *op. cit.*, p. 52.

46. *Ibid.*, p. 39.

47. Hendron, *op. cit.*, p. 26.

48. The Kid shot Ollinger with the latter's own famous shotgun. So do various heroes (Perceval) slay the adversary (Klingsor) with the latter's own weapon (the sacred lance).

49. Klapp, *loc. cit.*, p. 18 (see note 6).

50. Constellano, *op. cit.* (repr. Cummings), p. 4; the article in *World,* June 8, 1902 (note 7); Otero, *op. cit.*, p. 2. About Hermes, cf. N. Brown, *Hermes the Thief* (Madison, Wisconsin, 1947).

51. Otero, *op. cit.*, pp. 26, 41.

52. Klapp, *loc. cit.,* pp. 19–20.

53. For the "hypnotizing" features of this escape, see *World,* June 8, 1902 (note 7). The history of kid's meeting with Wallace can now be read in J. McKee, *op. cit.,* pp. 149–162.

54. Otero, *op. cit.,* pp. 19–22.

55. The Quest is a prolonged endeavor toward a high goal which, at times, is not conclusively attained. The Kid's early developed tendency to treat women in a chivalrous manner and ruthlessly to avenge brutal "aggressors" (potential threats to womanhood) may be called a Quest.

56. The meeting with Wallace somehow gives the Kid "princely" status. In the end, Wallace turns into a "hostile father" (see note 53).

57. Fergusson, *op. cit.,* p. 60.

58. Brothers, *op. cit.,* p. 26; Fulton and Poe, *op. cit.,* p. xvi.

59. Constellano (repr. Cummings), *op. cit.,* pp. 9–10.

60. H. Newstead, "The Besieged Ladies in Arthurian Romance," *PMLA,* LXIII (1948), pp. 803–830.

61. The Kid's mother was said to have Irish connections. Otero, *op. cit.,* p. 3.

62. About Hospitable Hosts, see R. S. Loomis, *Arthurian Tradition and Chrétien de Troyes* (New York, 1949), pp. 278–286.

63. Brothers, *op. cit.,* p. 24.

64. *Ibid.,* p. 26.

65. Otero, *op. cit.,* p. 79

66. Fulton and Poe, *op. cit.,* p. 10.

67. Klapp, *loc. cit.,* pp. 21–22.

68. Otero, *op. cit.,* p. 79.

69. Fulton and Poe, *op. cit.,* pp. 12–14.

70. Hendron, *op. cit.,* p. 29.

71. One trait has been omitted: "His children, if any, do not succeed him." Now there is the "nester's" daughter. Fate prevented their marriage, and "the child that should have carried his name bore that of another man, who later married the girl" (Brothers, *op. cit.,* p. 26). Was there or was there not a child? The very inconclusiveness of the tradition hears out Raglan's point! In the Western, "The Son of Billy the Kid." the protagonist is almost negligible.

72. See the recent appraisal of Fergusson, *op. cit.,* p. 50.

73. The concept of the myth as "words" to explain a "deed," the rite, has been developed by J. E. Harrison in *Prolegomena to Greek Religion* (Cambridge, 1921). Miss Harrison's theory has been retained by Lord Raglan in his most recent *Origins of Religion* (London, 1949). On the reactivation of "ritualistic" attitudes, see L. Lévy-Bruhl, *Mythologie Primitive* (Paris, 1935), and his other books on *mentalité primitive.* Jung's analytic psychology of the "collective unconscious" is relevant, too. So are the *"Eranos" Jahrbücher* (published in Zürich).

CHAPTER TWENTY-SIX

Dreamscape Desperado

Paul Andew Hutton

Distinguished Professor of History at the University of New Mexico, the executive director of the Western History Association 1990–2006, a past president of the Western Writers of America and a multiple winner of its Spur and Stirrup awards, Paul Andrew Hutton (1949–) was associate editor of the *Western Historical Quarterly* from 1977 to 1984, and editor of the *New Mexico Historical Review* from 1985 to 1991. A four-time winner of the National Cowboy and Western Heritage Museum's Western Heritage Award, he is also the author of the prize-winning *Phil Sheridan and His Army* (1985), *The Custer Reader* (1992), and the forthcoming *Sunrise in His Pocket: The Life, Legend and Legacy of Davy Crockett*, not to mention a truly staggering catalog of dissertations and articles, both scholarly and popular, plus an equally awesome credit list of television productions and appearances as producer, scriptwriter, consultant, or presenter. There does not seem to be any aspect of western frontier history—from Quantrill's raiders to Pretty Boy Floyd, from the Earp brothers to the Alamo to the battle of the Little Big Horn—with which he is not intimately acquainted, nor any that he cannot eloquently, authoritatively, and with great panache write or speak about. He is presently mounting a major exhibition on the life and times of Billy the Kid, which will be unveiled at the Albuquerque Museum in 2007. Only slightly overtaken by time, and with an *envoi* that Scott Fitzgerald would have admired, his summing-up of how the Billy the Kid "history" became an "industry" remains as valid—and as readable—today as it was more than a decade and a half ago.

The last two years [1989–90] have witnessed Kid mania of unparalleled dimensions. Two Pulitzer Prize–winning authors have tackled Billy: first Larry McMurtry in 1988 with *Anything for Billy* and then N. Scott Momaday with last year's *The Ancient Child*. Nor were the historians silent. In 1989 Robert M. Utley penned as definitive a biography of Billy as we are likely to see in *Billy the Kid: A Short and Violent Life.* At the same time the Lincoln County Heritage Trust initiated a photo-analysis project to identify alleged Billy photographs and to settle the long-standing controversy concerning the claim of Brushy Bill Roberts of Hico, Texas, that he was the Kid. Utley chairs a panel that includes famed forensic pathologist Clyde Snow of Oklahoma and computer-analysis expert Thomas Kyle of Los Alamos. Their work has been widely reported in the national media, including articles in *Newsweek* and *Science* magazines.

Hollywood joined in with *Young Guns* in 1988. Billy galloped across the celluloid landscape in the person of teen heart-throb Emilio Estevez, piling up corpses and box office receipts at an equally astonishing rate. Film commentators credited the film with bringing back the long-dormant Western. A sequel [*Young Guns II*] just finished lensing near Santa Fe and is due out this summer. Television naturally responded. In 1989 NBC's "Unsolved Mysteries" series dealt sympathetically with the Brushy Bill tale, while the TNT cable network unleashed Val Kilmer as *Gore Vidal's Billy the Kid.* ABC commented on all this in a March 1990 segment of "Prime Time Live" with Sam Donaldson.

Such interest was great news for those manning the cash registers in Fort Sumner and Lincoln, communities that still exist in some measure because Billy the Kid once walked their streets, and also for the Billy the Kid Outlaw Gang Inc. of Taiban, a history-buff outfit that has grown to more than 1,100 members.

Billy rides across the popular imagination with a power shared by few other figures. He is a figure of international renown and, for better or worse, undoubtedly stands as the best-known New Mexican in history. Not bad for an itinerant gunman and sometime outlaw who perished in his 21st year. How Billy got to be so famous is well worth exploring. The place to begin is with the man who killed him.

In 1904 Pat Garrett took noted Western writer Emerson Hough to the old post cemetery at Fort Sumner to visit the Kid's grave. It took some searching, for the headboard was long gone and the plot overgrown with greasewood. Garrett identified the grave by its close proximity to those of Billy's pals, Charlie Bowdre and Tom O'Folliard. The aging lawman, who had but four years to live before his own violent death, lifted his canteen and toasted those who had made him famous. "Well," he said quietly, "here's to the boys, anyway. If there is any other life, I hope they'll make better use of it than they did of the one I put them out of."

For Billy at least, there would be another life—the mystical existence of a colossal American legend. Ironically, it was Garrett himself who was instrumental in creating that legend. Even before the Kid's death on July 14, 1881, the Territorial press had built him into the bold chief of a band of brigands, "a terror and disgrace of New Mexico," who was "urged by a spirit as hideous as hell." Such rhetorical overkill built the pressure that forced Garrett's relentless manhunt of the Kid. At the same time the Eastern press picked up the story of the Kid's escape from Lincoln, with the sensational New York *National Police Gazette* running several Kid stories. At least eight New York newspapers published stories on his death and even *The Times* of London ran an obituary on the slain outlaw. Within a year eight pulp novels, selling from a nickel to a quarter, appeared on Billy the Kid's short career of crime.

In response Pat Garrett decided to set the record straight, as well as cash in on his killing of the Kid, by penning his own version of the story. Working with an old friend, postmaster Ash Upson, Garrett had his *Authentic Life of Billy the Kid, the Noted Desperado of the Southwest, Whose Deeds of Daring and Blood have Made His Name a Terror in New Mexico, Arizona and Northern Mexico* on sale by the spring of 1882. Published by the *Santa Fe Daily New Mexican*, it was a commercial flop. Although few copies were sold it nevertheless, more than any other single source, created the legend of Billy the Kid. It became the major text for generations of historians, novelists, poets and filmmakers to follow.

"The Kid had a lurking devil in him," wrote Garrett, "it was a good-humored, jovial imp, or a cruel and bloodthirsty fiend, as circumstances prompted. Circumstances favored the worser angel, and the Kid fell." It was this image of the charming killer, not altogether untrue, that persisted. But to build himself up as the Kid's killer, Garrett credited Billy with far more killings than the record justified. Many of the daring rides, deadly encounters with Indians and Mexicans, and bold rescues of inno-cent settlers and trapped friends in the book's early chapters are stock episodes from the very dime novels Garrett was supposedly correcting.

Garrett did not invent the myth of 21 killings—one for each year of Billy's life—only crediting him with "white Americans." Several Indians and Mexicans are also victims of his cruelty in the book, although there is absolutely no evidence of such killings. It was Garrett's friend Emerson Hough who invented the 21 victims tale in 1901, and it stuck. Actually,

Patrick Floyd Garrett in 1881, shortly after he killed the Kid. Courtesy Craig Fouts.

Billy shot and killed four men and participated in the slayings of six others. That is an infamous enough record.

Charles A. Siringo, the famed cowboy detective who had joined Garrett on one of his hunts for the Kid, incorporated sections of the *Authentic Life* into his *A Texas Cowboy* in 1885. While Garrett's book failed miserably in the marketplace, Siringo's was a wild success with perhaps a million copies printed. It was constantly in print for 40 years, often in paper editions hawked on trains for a quarter, and firmly cemented the Kid's place of honor in Southwestern lore.

Through Siringo the Garrett saga finally reached a wide reading public. But Siringo was no plagiarist, and he added his own nimble touches to Billy's tragic story. His Billy is even more charming than Garrett's and his crimes far more justifiable by hard circumstances. It was Siringo who first told the Robin Hood-like tale of Billy, despite his own peril, ministering to a sick stranger. This little episode was co-opted by that master story-teller Eugene Manlove Rhodes for a 1926 *Saturday Evening Post* story, "Paso por Aqui," which in turn was used as the basis for the 1948 film *Four Faces West* with Charles Bickford as Garrett and Joel McCrea as the renamed Kid character. Such is the genealogy of legendry.

Despite the commercial success of Siringo's book, Billy pretty much vanished into regional obscurity by the turn of the century. A few dime novels featured him as a satanic foil to stalwart heroes like Buffalo Bill Cody, a 1903 play by Walter Woods attempted to rehabilitate him as a Robin Hood figure and O. Henry used him as the model for his Cisco Kid in the 1904 ironic short story "The Caballero's Way." But interest in the Kid nevertheless waned. Even the fabulously successful Cisco Kid evolved into a character totally unrecognizable as Billy the Kid. By 1925, when Harvey Fergusson wrote nostalgically of Billy in *The American Mercury*, he could ask, "Who remembers Billy the Kid?"

Newspaperman Walter Noble Burns remembered. His 1926 fictional biography *The Saga of Billy the Kid* became a main selection of the fledgling Book-of-the-Month Club and a runaway bestseller. Revitalizing the Kid's legend, it set the tone of Kid literature for the next 50 years. "A Robin Hood of the Mesas, a Don Juan of New Mexico whose youthful daring has never been equalled . . . ," ran the breathless dust jacket copy. Burns' Billy, the charming champion of the oppressed Hispanics, is outlawed by his attempt to avenge the murder of his friend John Tunstall. As in all classic outlaw sagas, betrayal becomes a central theme with Pat Garrett a Judas who sells out to the Santa Fe Ring and hunts down his old friend.

Inspired by the book, the Rev. Andrew Jenkins composed "The Ballad of Billy the Kid," which has become something of a minor classic recorded over the years by, among others, Woody Guthrie, Tex Ritter, Marty Robbins and Ry Cooder.

> I'll sing you a true song of Billy the Kid,
> I'll sing of the desperate deeds that he did,
> Way out in New Mexico, long ago
> When a man's only chance was his own fo'ty-fo.

Purchased by MGM, the book was brought to the screen in 1930 by King Vidor with football All-American Johnny Mack Brown in the title role of *Billy the Kid*. Garrett's image was softened to accommodate the affable screen persona of Wallace Beery. Filmed near Gallup, the film is equally renowned for its realistic settings, epic scope and Brown's horrible acting. Preview audiences reacted so negatively to Billy's death that the ending was reshot to allow the outlaw and his lady to escape while Garrett marks an empty grave. Only European audiences, evidently more accustomed to tragedy, got to see Billy die.

With the exception of silent films in 1911 and 1916, Billy had been ignored by Hollywood until Vidor's epic. That now changed with a vengeance, so that by 1990 there had been at least 48 films featuring Billy the Kid, more than for any other character from Western history.

Roy Rogers was a singing Billy in Republic's 1938 film *Billy the Kid Returns*. The success of that film led Producers Releasing Corporation (PRC) to produce a series of 17 Billy the Kid budget Westerns starring first Bob Steele and later Buster Crabbe. While these films had little to do with the historical Billy they nevertheless helped cement his position as a major American hero. Complaints from censorship groups about glorifying outlaws led PRC to change the name of Crabbe's character to Billy Carson after 1943.

At the same time that the Saturday matinee crowd was being rescued from Billy's bad example, their parents were getting a steady diet of the Kid's more mature adventures. Highbrows could debate the nuances of Eugene Loring's 1938 ballet *Billy the Kid*, with its magnificent Aaron

Copland score. The less sophisticated could follow the well-publicized race between MGM and Howard Hughes to get their Kid films into distribution first. Hughes won the race but his attempt to explore the erotic potential of the Kid's story with starlet Jane Russell so offended the Hays production code office that it delayed the film's release until 1943. This allowed MGM's glossy Technicolor remake of *Billy the Kid* starring Robert Taylor to strike first at the box office in 1941.

Taylor's depiction inspired cartoonist Geoff Campion to create *Billy the Kid*, a durable British comic book series that began in 1952. Campion's Billy, who looked exactly like Taylor, was a Lone Ranger clone battling evil land barons on behalf of widows and orphans from behind a black mask and shouting "Yip! Yip! Yip! Hi-Yo!" as he rode to adventure. French and Italian comic books also featured Billy, but usually in historical strips aimed at an adult audience. In the United States Billy was depicted in several comic book series from 1950 on, with the most successful published by Charlton from 1957 well into the 1980s. Despite the success of the comic book Billy, the outlaw youth never emerged as a figure in either juvenile fiction or nonfiction.

But if the kids could not find Billy in their local library they had no trouble viewing the boy who not only disobeyed adults, but shot them, at the local bijou. They sat enraptured before the flickering image of Lash LaRue in *Son of Billy the Kid* (1949), Audie Murphy as *The Kid from Texas* (1949), Don "Red" Barry in *I Shot Billy the Kid* (1950), Scott Brady in *The Law vs. Billy the Kid* (1954), Nick Adams in *Strange Lady in Town* (1955) and Gaston Sands in *A Bullet for Billy the Kid* (1963). Variations on the same theme were endless as Billy battled for religion in *The Parson and the Outlaw* (1957), against the Three Stooges in *The Outlaws is Coming* (1964) and with the forces of darkness in *Billy the Kid vs. Dracula* (1965).

Those who could not afford a movie ticket might stay at home and enjoy Clu Gulager as Billy on NBC's "The Tall Man" series. For two seasons, 1960–1962, rascally Billy would get himself into trouble only to be rescued and properly chastised by fatherly Barry Sullivan as Pat Garrett. Fortunately, low ratings did in Billy before Garrett did. But the Kid popped up elsewhere on the small screen in the person of Paul Newman on "Philco Playhouse," Robert Blake on "Death Valley Days," Ray Strickland on "Cheyenne," Joel Grey on "Maverick," Robert Conrad on "Colt .45," Robert Vaughn on "Tales of Wells Fargo" and Dennis Hopper on "Sugarfoot."

Billy proved an incredibly resilient hero, a sort of outlaw for all seasons, and this trait gave his legend a durability denied to other Western heroes. In 1957 the Kid's story was adapted to conform to the rebellious teen-ager obsession then sweeping the nation. Leslie Stevens' screenplay for *The Left Handed Gun,* based on a teleplay by Gore Vidal, was solidly in the tradition of *The Wild Ones* and *Rebel Without a Cause.* James Dean, the very symbol of teen alienation, was to play Billy before his untimely death gave the role to Paul Newman. In Arthur Penn's film, Billy, uncertain of new passions and old moralities, searches for both vengeance and personal identity after the murder of his surrogate father Tunstall (in reality Tunstall was only 24 when killed). His search for revenge alienates some friends and destroys others until Pat Garrett is forced to kill him. He falls sprawled in the dirt as if crucified, a victim of both his own limitations and society's indifference.

It seemed impossible to out-brood Newman's Billy, but Marlon Brando easily accomplished the chore in *One-Eyed Jacks* (1961). The locale shifted from New Mexico to southern California, and now the theme was betrayal. The film, directed by Brando, is awash with masochistic violence, as Karl Malden's sheriff whips the Kid and crushes his gun hand, as well as oedipal complications as the Kid romances the sheriff's winsome daughter, kills the sheriff and finally rides off into the California sunset with the girl. The movie is so overblown that it is good.

If Billy was a tormented adolescent in the 1950s and 1960s, he was everyman for the 1970s. In three dramatically different films the Kid reflected the divisions that then tore at the fabric of American society. Billy opened the decade in a traditional John Wayne Western, *Chisum* (1970). Turning history upside down, Wayne's Chisum, the ultimate benevolent capitalist, wipes out the bad guys in the Lincoln County War with the help of his reckless ally Billy. All is peaceful at film's end, although the Duke wrinkles his brow and frets over Billy's tendency toward nonconformist behavior. Two years later Stan Dragoti's *Dirty Little Billy* debunked the Kid's heroic image just as other films of that cynical period pilloried Jesse James, Wyatt Earp and Gen. Custer. Michael J. Pollard's Billy—lazy, degenerate and cowardly—lived in a world of filth and corruption, and fit right in. But Pollard's depiction of Billy as a sniveling punk held no appeal to the youthful audiences of 1972 and the film failed miserably at the box office. More attuned to the times was Sam Peckinpah's *Pat Garrett & Billy the Kid,* released the same year.

Kris Kristofferson's Billy was a charming anarchist and violent anachronism with no place in the corrupt new order that has come to power in the West. James Coburn's Pat Garrett must abandon obsolete conceptions of loyalty and sell out his old friend Billy. But Garrett's law, arbitrary and illegitimate, exists only to protect the rich. He finally realizes that he has committed spiritual suicide by killing Billy. As he rides out of Fort Sumner, a young boy follows and throws stones—a parody of the ending of *Shane*.

Peckinpah's film was one of the last successful Westerns before they vanished from movie screens for nearly 15 years. It was 20th Century Fox's "Brat Pack" hit *Young Guns* that gave a new lease on life to the dormant genre in the summer of 1988. Although it seemed to some an effort to transplant the Los Angeles Crips street gang into 19th-century New Mexico, the film's serious tone, authentic look, quick violence and personable young stars won over audiences. Although truer to history in innumerable details than previous films, the young guns nevertheless win their generation-gap range war, killing the chief villains in a finish as wildly inaccurate as the one in Wayne's *Chisum*. But, after all, this is Hollywood and not a history lesson.

Hollywood has found Billy the Kid to be a delightfully pliable subject—from Robin Hood to tormented adolescent, from quiet avenger to degenerate punk and from martyred symbol of freedom to hip gang leader he has been manipulated to satisfy new audiences. Each generation of moviemaker has reinterpreted a familiar story to fit a new vision, one shaped by the peculiar social milieu of a changing America.

Novelists have also been drawn to the Kid. Authors of mass market Westerns such as Zane Grey, Dane Coolidge, Nelson Nye, Tom Cutter and Matt Braun have all written of the Kid. Some Kid novels have even become minor classics, most notably Edwin Corle's *Billy the Kid* (1953), Charles Neider's *The Authentic Death of Hendry Jones* (1956), upon which *One-Eyed Jacks* was based, and Oakley Hall's *Apaches* (1986).

Great anticipation preceded the release of Larry McMurtry's *Anything for Billy* in 1988, his first Western since winning the Pulitzer Prize for *Lonesome Dove*. Although the book lingered more than four months on the *New York Times* bestseller list, many readers were disappointed, for McMurtry's farcical tale bore little resemblance to *Lonesome Dove*. The author has no use for Billy, who he depicts as tiny in stature, ugly to behold, constantly filthy, doltish and always murderous, with a conscience like "a blank domino." McMurtry, of course, is a Texan.

N. Scott Momaday, on the other hand, benefitted from an education at the University of New Mexico, which might help explain his lyrical, softly romantic version of the Kid in *The Ancient Child*. Momaday's novel, his first since winning the Pulitzer Prize for *House Made of Dawn*, was also eagerly awaited. His Billy is handsome, daring, articulate, always ready to laugh—truth seen through a poet's eye. "It has something to do with legend," Momaday writes, "and with the way we must think of ourselves, we cowboys and Indians, we roughriders of the world. We are lovers of violence, aren't we?" The reviewer for the *New York Times* was not amused. He criticized Momaday for not penning a diatribe against environmental spoliation, condemned him for daring to make a hero of Billy the Kid, who he sanctimoniously intoned, "began his career by helping to rob and murder three Indians." That old tale is pure fiction from Garrett's *Authentic Life,* and with it the reviewer made clear that his ignorance of history was equal to his insensitivity to Momaday's poetic literature. A similar viewpoint was expressed at the October 1989 Western History Association conference when a frustrated academic publicly complained that despite all the fine serious scholarship represented at the meeting the only book receiving any media attention was Bob Utley's *Billy the Kid*. It is frustrating for the academics when their own work goes unnoticed while the Kid, just as he challenged the establishment a hundred years ago, mocks them by his hold on the public's imagination. They take their potshots, but always miss.

Billy the Kid just keeps riding across the dreamscape of our minds—silhouetted against a starlit Western sky, handsome, laughing, deadly. Shrewd as the coyote. Free as the hawk. The outlaw of our dreams—forever free, forever young, forever riding.

Sources

Original publication information for the selections is as follows:

1. *The True Life of Billy the Kid,* by Don Jenardo (New York: F. Tousey, 1881).

2. "A True Sketch of 'Billy the Kid's' Life," by Charles A Siringo. Reprinted from Charles A. Siringo, *A Texas Cow Boy; or, Fifteen Years on the Hurricane Deck of a Spanish Pony, Taken from Real Life by Charles A. Siringo, an Old Stove Up "Cow Puncher" Who Has Spent Nearly Twenty Years on the Great Western Cattle Ranches* (Chicago: M. Umbdenstock & Co., 1885).

3. "Billy the Kid: The True Story of a Western 'Bad Man,'" by Emerson Hough. Reprinted from *Everybody's Magazine,* September 1901, 302–10.

4. "Billy the Kid: A Man All 'Bad,'" by Arthur Chapman. Reprinted from *Outing Magazine* 46, no. 1 (April 1905): 73–77.

5. "Billy the Kid," by Harvey Fergusson. Reprinted from *The American Mercury* 5, no. 18 (June 1925): 224–31. Used by permission of the Enoch Pratt Free Library, Baltimore, Maryland, in accordance with the terms of the bequest of H. L. Mencken.

6. "A Belle of Old Fort Sumner," by Walter Noble Burns. Reprinted from Walter Noble Burns, *The Saga of Billy the Kid,* 180–81, 183–86. © 1926 by Doubleday, a division of Random House, Inc. Used by permission of Doubleday, a division of Random House, Inc.

7. "Billy ('The Kid') Bonney," by N. Howard (Jack) Thorp as told to Neil McCullough Clark. Reprinted from N. Howard Thorp, *Pardner of the Wind* (Caldwell, Idaho: The Caxton Printers, 1945), 168–93. Used by permission of Caxton Press, Caldwell, Idaho.

8. "The True Trail of Billy the Kid," by Alvin Rucker. Reprinted from *The Daily Oklahoman* 37, no. 172 (June 30, 1929); no. 179 (July 7, 1929); no. 186 (July 14, 1929); and no. 193 (July 21, 1929).

9. "The Individual Song: 'Billy the Kid,'" by D. K. Wilgus. Reprinted from *Western Folklore* 30, no. 3 (1971): 226–34. © 1971 Western States Folklore Society.

10. "New Light on the Legend of Billy the Kid," by Philip J. Rasch and R. N. Mullin. Reprinted from *New Mexico Folklore Record* 7 (1952–53): 1–5. Used by permission of Virginia Rasch, Ojai, California, and Marjorie Jackson, Ann Arbor, Michigan.

11. "Billy the Kid: The Trail of a Kansas Legend," by Waldo E. Koop. Reprinted from *The Trail Guide* 9, no. 3 (September 1965): 1–16. Used by permission of Kansas City Posse of the Westerners, Kansas City, Missouri.

12. "The Boyhood of Billy the Kid," by Robert N. Mullin. Excerpt reprinted from Robert N. Mullin, *The Boyhood of Billy the Kid* (El Paso: Texas Western Press, 1967), 5–13. Used by permission of Marjorie Jackson, Ann Arbor, Michigan.

13. "First Blood: Another Look at the Killing of 'Windy' Cahill," by Frederick Nolan. Reprinted from *Outlaw Gazette* 13 (November 2000): 2–4. Used by permission of the author.

14. "The Kid," by Lily Casey Klasner. Used by permission of Tom Perry Special Collections, Harold B. Lee Library, Brigham Young University, Provo, Utah.

15. "The Fight at Blazer's Mill, in New Mexico," by Almer Blazer. Reprinted from the *Alamogordo (New Mexico) Times,* July 16, 1928.

16. "The Mackyswins and the Marfes," by Francisco Trujillo. Interview conducted by Edith L. Crawford at San Patricio, New Mexico, on May 10, 1937, as part of the Federal Writers' Project, 1936–40. Translated by A. L. White. WPA Federal Writers' Project, File 47, Drawer 1, Manuscript Division, Library of Congress.

17. "Five Days of Battle," by Philip J. Rasch. Reprinted from *Denver Westerners Brand Book, 1955,* 294–323. Used by permission of Virginia Rasch, Ojai, California.

18. "In His Own Words" (1). Judge Advocate General's Office, Records Relating to the Dudley Court of Inquiry, Record Group 153, CQ 1284, National Archives and Records Administration, Washington, D.C.

19. "The Capture of Billy the Kid," by James H. East. Reprinted from Charles A. Siringo, *History of "Billy the Kid"* (Santa Fe: Privately printed, 1920), 97–108.

20. "In His Own Words" (2). Reprinted from the *Las Vegas Gazette,* December 28, 1880.

21. "The Kid's Escape." Reprinted from the *Santa Fe Daily New Mexican,* May 3, 1881.

22. "Facts Regarding the Escape of Billy the Kid," by Leslie Traylor. Reprinted from *Frontier Times Magazine* 13, no. 10 (July 1936): 506–13, www.frontiertimesmagazine.com. Used by permission.

23. "The Killing of Billy the Kid," by John W. Poe. Earl Vandale Collection (2H 475), Center for American History, University of Texas, Austin, Texas. Used by permission.

24. "Death and Burial of Billy the Kid," by Col. Jack Potter. Reprinted from Jean M. Burroughs, *On The Trail: The Life and Tales of "Lead Steer" Potter* (Santa Fe: Museum of New Mexico Press, 1980), 137–39. Used by permission.

25. "Billy the Kid: A Case Study in Epic Origins," by Alfred Adler. Reprinted from *Western Folklore* 10, no. 2 (1951): 143–52. © 1951 Western States Folklore Society.

26. "Dreamscape Desperado," by Paul Andrew Hutton. Reprinted from *New Mexico Magazine,* June 1990, 44–57. Used by permission of the author.

Index